1-2-3
Made Easy

1-2-3
Made Easy

MARY CAMPBELL

Osborne **McGraw-Hill**
Berkeley, California

Osborne/McGraw-Hill
2600 Tenth Street
Berkeley, California 94710
U.S.A.

For information on translations and book distributors outside of the U.S.A., write to **Osborne/McGraw-Hill** at the above address.

A complete list of trademarks appears on page 513.

1-2-3® Made Easy

By the author of the bestselling *1-2-3®: The Complete Reference.*

1234567890 DODO 8987

ISBN 0-07 881293-3

PREFACE

1-2-3 is one of the best selling microcomputer software packages because it provides a powerful business tool to users from a variety of disciplines. Even if you are new to computing, you can master the features of 1-2-3 that have made it such a popular choice with business professionals. Whether you have Release 1A or the more sophisticated Release 2 introduced in the fall of 1986, you have the tools you need to create financial models and other calculations quickly.

Uses of This Book

1-2-3 Made Easy is designed to meet the needs of the new 1-2-3 user. If you have 1-2-3 already installed on your computer system, start in Chapter 1 and proceed sequentially through the chapters.

Make sure that you cover at least the first six chapters in this fashion since they provide all the building blocks — from data entry to saving your data and printing. After the first six chapters, a sequential progress is still the preferred course of action but you can read ahead if there is a particular topic of interest.

Users who do not have an installed copy of 1-2-3 to work with should begin with Appendix A. This provides the step-by-step instructions you need to install the program to run on your computer system.

Users of 1-2-3 who have learned the basics of the package on a trial-and-error basis can either start at the beginning to master the package through a logical progression or use the table of contents to focus on topics such as built-in functions and data management.

In addition to the coverage of 1-2-3 this book provides a quick overview of the Hal add-on. Through the examples in Chapter 13 you can get a glimpse of some of the time-saving features of Hal.

Organization of This Book

This book is divided into 13 chapters. In most cases, each chapter contains just the right number of new features to cover in a single session. The first few chapters provide the building blocks for your first model. After you have mastered these you will probably want to progress through the remaining chapters sequentially as they lead you to more advanced topics. If there is a particular topic you want to review immediately, the models in the later chapters are self-contained and do not require you to use examples from earlier chapters. An outline of the chapters follows:

Chapter 1 will get you started with the package. It explains the important features of 1-2-3's display. It also introduces you to the entry of numbers and labels on the worksheet.

Chapter 2 provides an introduction to the use of formulas on the 1-2-3 worksheet. You will learn how formulas add power to the worksheet through what-if capabilities.

Chapter 3 provides information to tailor the format of your entries to meet your needs. You will learn how to select currency, percent, fixed, scientific notation, date, or other formats for cells on the worksheet.

Chapter 4 shows you how to protect your investment in model building through the use of files which can be stored on your disk permanently. You will learn how easy it is to store or retrieve this data on your disk.

Chapter 5 covers everything you need to copy entries you have already made on the worksheet to other locations. In this chapter you will also learn techniques for rearranging the data on your worksheet so that 1-2-3 can share the work required to create or change models.

Chapter 6 provides explanations and examples of 1-2-3's print features. You will learn how to do everything from printing a draft of your worksheet to adding headers and other sophisticated options.

Chapter 7 introduces you to 1-2-3's built-in functions. These are formulas that are prerecorded and stored within the package for ready access. You will learn about the different catagories of functions which 1-2-3 offers and can select those that are of interest based on your particular needs.

Chpater 8 introduces 1-2-3's graphic features so you will have a tool for presenting numeric information in an understandable fashion. You will learn how to create pie charts, line graphs, and bar graphs.

Chapter 9 covers the data management features of the package. You can use these to create a simple database. You will also find examples that show you how to sort the information in the database and selectively copy information to another area of your worksheet to create a quick report.

Chapter 10 focuses on advanced built-in functions — more sophisticated than the ones in Chapter 7. They can add the power of logic and sophisticated business calculations to your models with minimal work.

Chapter 11 expands upon the basic file features and teaches you how to combine the data in several files into the current worksheet. You can use the features in this chapter to create consolidations for your business.

Chapter 12 examines the basics of 1-2-3 macros. With these macro features you will learn how to record keystrokes for execution at a later time.

Chapter 13 provides a look at some of the features of the

popular 1-2-3 add-on, Hal. This package allows you to bypass the 1-2-3 menus to accomplish tasks like formatting, sorting, database querying, and graphing. It also offers a host of other features that are not part of 1-2-3 itself. Even if you do not have a copy of Hal you will want to take a look at this revolutionary way of working with 1-2-3.

Appendix A provides step-by-step directions for installing 1-2-3 on your system. This will be your starting place if 1-2-3 is not already installed for you.

Appendix B provides a glossary of terms that are used frequently in the spreadsheet environment.

Appendix C provides a comprehensive list of the built-in functions which 1-2-3 provides. You can use this to explore functions which parallel the ones covered in Chapter 7 and Chapter 10.

Conventions Used in This Book

Several conventions have been used throughout this book to expedite your mastery of 1-2-3 and to make the process as easy as possible. These are:

Entries that you must make to duplicate examples within the book are shown in boldface within numbered steps.

The word **enter** is used to precede entries that you must make from 1-2-3's menus.

The word **type** is used to indicate other information that you must type in from the keyboard.

Uppercase letters are used when filenames are entered, although either upper or lower case will produce the same results.

Throughout the book, Release 2 is used as a reference to Release 2.0 and Release 2.01 of the 1-2-3 product to simplify the instructions.

I dedicate this book to my husband, Dave.

CONTENTS

Acknowledgements

I wish to thank the following individuals for their contributions to this book:

Jeff Pepper, acquisitions editor, Osborne/McGraw-Hill, who coordinated the resources needed to complete this project. Marty Matthews, technical reviewer, whose attention to detail and helpful suggestions improved the quality of each chapter. Liz Fisher, production editor, Osborne/McGraw-Hill, who coordinated the production phase and remained patient and resourceful as we attempted new ways to improve the quality and clarity of the screens in the book.

WORKSHEET BASICS

You are about to enter the world of 1-2-3. This journey will give you a new way of working with everyday business problems — a way that is both efficient and flexible. Traditionally, business problems are worked out on green-bar columnar pads, commonly used by accountants and business managers to evaluate financial decisions. 1-2-3 replaces the paper versions of these worksheets by turning your computer into a large electronic version of this columnar pad.

You will learn to use 1-2-3's worksheet features to handle the same types of problems previously solved on columnar pads. Applications such as budgeting, financial planning, project cost projections, breakeven analysis, and cost planning are some of the applications you might consider. You also will learn to pattern calculations after real-life situations and lay out models representing the problem to be solved on the electronic worksheet.

The electronic sheet of paper that 1-2-3 places into your computer's memory has a structure organized to help you construct these models. The electronic worksheet is arranged into rows and columns, allowing you to enter numbers, labels, and formulas. Making these entries on 1-2-3's worksheet offers significant advantages over making them on paper. For example, once you have entered a calculation on paper, it is difficult to make a change. However, 1-2-3 provides a number of features that facilitate change. On a paper worksheet, you must update calculations every time you change a number; however, because 1-2-3 can remember calculations, it recalculates the worksheet automatically when you update a number.

In this chapter you will look at spreadsheet organization, entering numbers and labels on the worksheet, correcting data entry

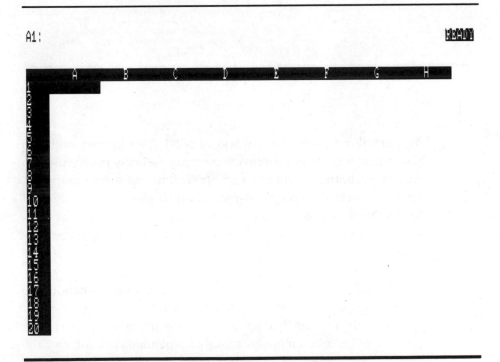

FIGURE 1.1 Left corner of worksheet visible on the screen

errors, and accessing 1-2-3's HELP features. Since the material in this chapter covers some of the basic building blocks of worksheet-model construction, you will want to master it completely before progressing to more advanced topics.

Although you probably are eager to start using 1-2-3's features right away, you may have to complete some preliminary work first in order to get maximum knowledge from this chapter. Before you begin, assess your current knowledge of the PC and whether your copy of 1-2-3 is ready to use. If you are a new PC user, read Appendix A before proceeding. If 1-2-3 has not yet been installed on your system, complete this step from the instructions in Appendix A before proceeding. Then, once you have filled in the gaps, continue reading and working with this chapter.

SPREADSHEET ORGANIZATION

When you load 1-2-3 into the memory of your computer, you will see only the upper left corner of your worksheet. Your display should match the one shown in Figure 1.1 (unless someone has changed the default column width). This initial display lets you glimpse the eight leftmost columns and the first 20 rows of the worksheet. The worksheet is much larger than it first appears. There are 256 columns in the worksheet, named A to IV. Single alphabetic letters are used first; then AA to AZ, BA to BZ, and so on. Rows are named with numbers rather than letters. Release 1A of the package has 2048 rows; Release 2 has 8192 rows. Figure 1.2 shows the entire worksheet, compared with the small portion that is visible when you first load the package.

The Cell Pointer

Each location on the worksheet is referred to as a *cell*. Each cell is uniquely identified by its column and row location. The column is always specified first to create cell locations such as A1, C10,

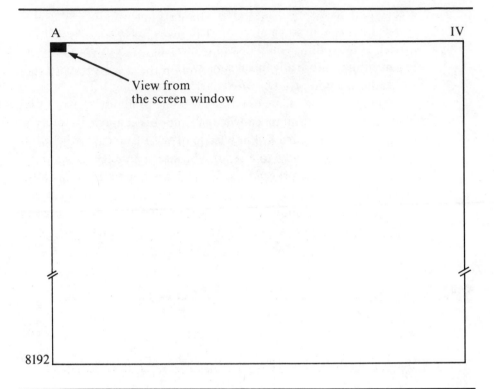

A   IV

View from
the screen window

8192

FIGURE 1.2 Entire worksheet with the small screen window highlighted

Z1025, and IJ850. A *cell pointer* always marks the current location
with a small highlighted bar. In a new worksheet, such as the one in
Figure 1.1, the cell pointer is located in cell A1. The location of the
cell pointer is extremely important: It marks the location of the
active cell, the only cell into which you can make an entry without
first moving the cell pointer.

Other Important Indicators

The top three lines of the screen are called the *control panel*. You
can see this panel in Figure 1.1; it is used to monitor most of your
1-2-3 activities. As you make entries on the worksheet, these entries

will appear in the control panel. The panel also monitors 1-2-3's activities and tells you when 1-2-3 is ready to proceed with new activities. In addition, the control panel functions as a place keeper, letting you know your current location on the worksheet and specifics about that location.

THE TOP LINE   The top line of the control panel always displays the location of the cell pointer in the left corner. This location is referred to as the *cell address*; it always matches the location of the cell pointer in the lower portion of the worksheet. As you begin to make worksheet entries, you will find that this location also displays the contents of the cell, as well as any width or formatting changes that you have applied. Figure 1.3 shows a 1-2-3 screen with $5 in cell C6. Here, the control panel tells you that the cursor is in

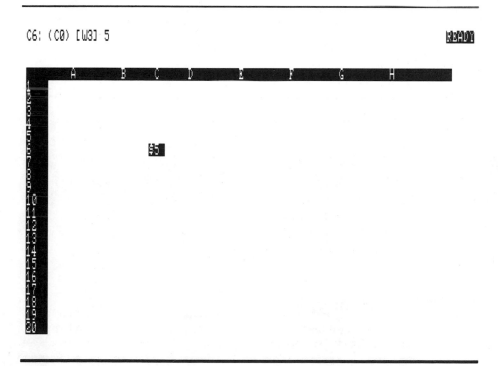

FIGURE 1.3   Control panel entries for cell format, width and contents

C6, that a format of currency with zero decimal places is used for the format (C0), and that the column has been assigned a width of three [W3]. The last piece of information is the contents of the cell, which is represented by the 5. All these special entries will be discussed in detail in later chapters.

EDIT	The cell entry is being edited. EDIT can be generated by 1-2-3 when your cell entry contains an error. It can also be generated by pressing F2 (EDIT) to change a cell entry.
ERROR	1-2-3 has encountered an error. The problem will be noted in the lower left corner of the screen. Press ESC to clear the ERROR MESSAGE, and correct the problem specified in the ERROR MESSAGE at the bottom of the screen.
FILES	1-2-3 wants you to select a filename to proceed. This message is also shown when you request a list of the files on your disk.
FIND	The /Data Query command is active.
HELP	A HELP display is active.
LABEL	1-2-3 has decided that you are making a label entry.
MENU	1-2-3 is waiting for you to make a selection from the menu.
NAMES	1-2-3 is displaying a menu of range or graph names.
POINT	1-2-3 is waiting for you to point to a cell or a range. As soon as you begin to type, the POINT mode will change to the EDIT mode.
READY	1-2-3 is currently idle and is waiting for you to make a new request.
STAT	Worksheet status information is being displayed.
VALUE	1-2-3 has decided that you are making a value entry.
WAIT	1-2-3 is processing your last command and cannot begin a new task until the flashing WAIT indicator changes to READY.

TABLE 1.1   Mode indicators

THE MODE INDICATOR The right corner of the top line of the control panel contains a *mode indicator.* When you first load 1-2-3 this indicator will display READY, indicating that 1-2-3 is ready to respond to whatever you enter. The mode indicator can tell you both that 1-2-3 is busy with your previous request or that it is ready to do something new. It can also tell you to correct an error, point to a worksheet location, or select a menu choice. Once 1-2-3's mode indicator changes from READY to another setting, you must either follow along with its plans or find a way to change the indicator. Many new users become frustrated at this point, but you can avoid frustration by watching the mode indicator and staying in sync with its current setting. Table 1.1 lists all the mode indicators you can encounter, along with their meanings. They will also be pointed out in later chapters, as new activities cause 1-2-3 mode changes.

OTHER CONTROL PANEL LINES Lines two and three of the control panel will take on special significance as you begin to alter cell entries and begin to use 1-2-3's features. When you use 1-2-3 commands, line two lists all your options at any point. Line three gives an explanation of each choice. The use of these lines to alter cell entries will be covered later in this chapter, and displaying options in this area is discussed in Chapter 3.

THE BOTTOM LINE OF THE SCREEN The bottom line of the display can also provide a variety of information, as shown in Figure 1.4. In Release 2, the left corner displays the date and time, which are updated constantly. This area is blank in Release 1A. If an error occurs in either release, it is temporarily replaced with an error message, such as Disk Full, Printer Error, or Disk Drive Not Ready. Whenever an error message displays in the left corner, the mode indicator displays ERROR in the upper right corner. This ERROR indicator will blink and your computer will sound a warning beep. You will not be able to proceed until you press the ESC (ESCAPE) key to acknowledge the error.

The area to the right of the date and time (or of the ERROR MESSAGE display) is used to inform you when certain keys have

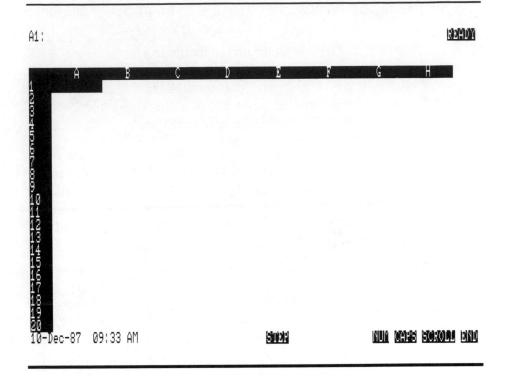

FIGURE 1.4 Indicators in the bottom line of the display

been pressed. It also tells you that 1-2-3 has encountered a special situation. Five of these indicators are designed to inform you that a certain key or key sequence has been depressed. These indicators are:

CAPS   This indicator lights up at the bottom of the screen when the CAPS LOCK key is depressed. Depressing this key causes the alphabetic keys to produce capital letters.

END   This indicates that the END key has been pressed. The END key is used to move the cursor to the end of entries in a given direction or to the end of a group of blank cells in a given direction. After using the END key, you must use an arrow key to indicate the direction. The END indicator reminds you to press an arrow key.

NUM   This indicates that the NUM LOCK key has been pressed and that you can enter numbers from the keyboard's numeric keypad. This provides an alternative to using the top row of keys to the right of ESC.

SCROLL   This indicates that the SCROLL LOCK has been pressed. It affects the way in which information scrolls off the screen. Without SCROLL LOCK, information scrolls off your screen one row or column at a time. With SCROLL LOCK, the entire window shifts each time you press the UP ARROW or DOWN ARROW.

OVR   OVR indicates that the INS (INSERT) key has been pressed. When editing cell entries, you will sometimes want to use the *overtype*. This lets you enter characters that replace the characters in the original entry, rather than adding them to the original entry.

There are also five other indicators that monitor advanced features and have broader meanings. These will be covered as they occur later on in this book.

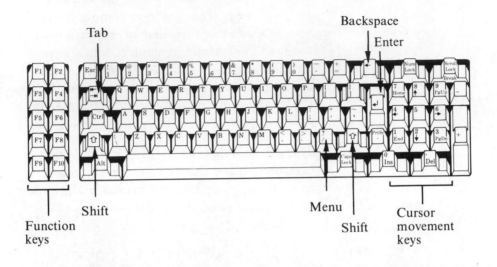

FIGURE 1.5   The PC keyboard

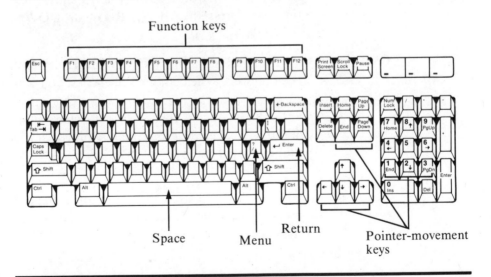

FIGURE 1.6   IBM's enhanced keyboard

MOVING AROUND ON THE WORKSHEET

Now you are ready to learn to navigate your way around 1-2-3's worksheet in preparation for constructing models with entries in worksheet cells. You will look at the basic features as well as at the more advanced options that let you to travel long distances quickly.

Basic Options

1-2-3's basic pointer movements are accomplished with the *arrow keys*. These may be located directly on the numeric keypad keys or they may reside on separate keys, depending on the age and model of your computer system. Figures 1.5 and 1.6 show two popular keyboard configurations, with the arrow keys highlighted. Even if your keyboard is slightly different, you should find it relatively easy to locate the keys with the arrows on them. If the arrow keys on your keyboard also house other functions, be careful that the keys are set for the arrow key function. For example, on keyboards where the arrow keys reside on the numeric keypad keys, if you depress NUM LOCK these keys will enter numbers rather than move the cell pointer. You can tell that NUM LOCK has been depressed by the NUM indicator in the bottom line of the display panel; in that case, press NUM LOCK a second time to remove the indicator from the screen before using the arrow keys to move the cell pointer.

MOVING WITH THE ARROW KEYS   Each of the arrow keys moves the cursor one cell in the direction indicated by the arrow. Your computer's keyboard is buffered and will record multiple presses. So if you hold down the arrow key, be careful to press it only once and to remove your finger, if you want to move the cursor only one cell at a time. Try the following exercise with these keys to become expert in their use.

1. With your cursor in the starting A1 location, press the RIGHT ARROW key once:
    Your cursor should now be in B1, as follows:

2. Press the RIGHT ARROW key a second time to move your cursor to C1.

3. Press the DOWN ARROW key twice to move your cursor to C3.

4. Press the DOWN ARROW key a few more times until your cursor reaches C20, as follows:

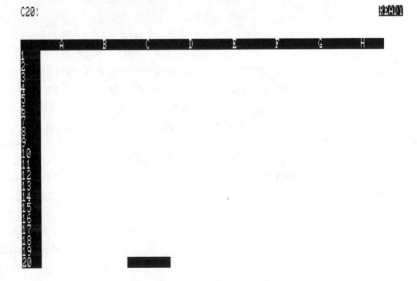

If you hold the DOWN ARROW key down and move too far down the screen, row 1 will scroll off the screen. You can move your cursor back up to line 20, but line 1 will not reappear until you move your cursor all the way back up to the top.

5. Press the RIGHT ARROW until your cursor is in H20;

then press it again to scroll a column off the screen as you move to I20. Your screen will look like this:

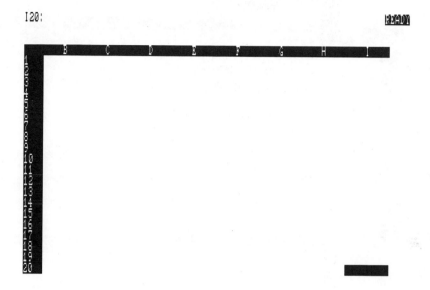

6. Press the UP ARROW until your cursor is in I1; then press the LEFT ARROW until the cursor returns to A1.

7. Press the LEFT ARROW key again.
   1-2-3 will beep, informing you that the cell pointer cannot be moved. You may want to practice with these keys a little more to ensure that you are comfortable with their use. You can use them to move to any worksheet location. Clearly, however, some shortcuts will be required. The arrow key method would take too long to move you to cell IV200, for example, and return to A1.

Quick Steps

There are a variety of methods for moving the cursor more quickly. Some use special keys to make the move to a new location; others use a combination of keys. The HOME key is the quickest way to

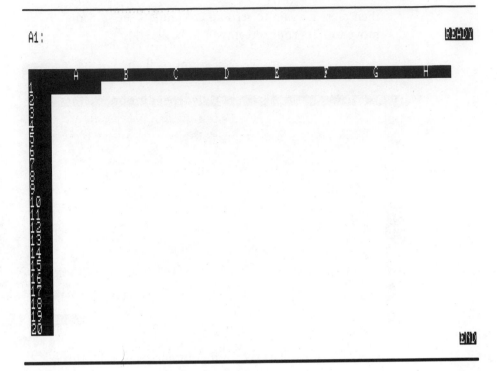

FIGURE 1.7   END indicator displayed in lower right corner

return to A1, the home position or beginning location on a work-sheet. As soon as you press this key, the cell pointer moves from its current location to A1.

PGUP AND PGDN   PGUP moves the cursor up 20 rows without moving it from its current column. Of course, this key works effectively only when the cursor is in row 21 or greater. If the cursor is in B1 and you press PGUP, 1-2-3 will beep at you and will not move the cursor at all, since the cursor is already at the top of the worksheet. If the cursor is in B5, PGUP will move it to B1; if the cursor is in B26, PGUP will move it up 20 rows to B6. *PGDN* does the exact opposite: It moves the cursor down by 20 rows. However, if you are fewer than 20 rows from the bottom edge of the sheet, then it will take you to the bottom.

THE END KEY   The END key can be used in combination with the arrow keys to move you to the end of the worksheet in the direction specified. When a worksheet contains data, END functions differently and moves you to the last blank cell, or to the last cell containing data in the direction you specify. END will stop at the last cell with an entry or the last blank cell, depending on whether it was resting on a blank cell or a cell containing data when you pressed it.

To use the end key and arrow combination, follow these steps:

1. Move the cell pointer to A1 then press the END key. Verify that the END indicator has appeared in the lower right corner of the worksheet, as shown in Figure 1.7. Next you will press the arrow key that specifies the direction in which you wish to move.

2. Press the RIGHT ARROW key. The cell pointer will move to the last cell on the right, IV1.

3. Press END followed by the DOWN ARROW key. The cell pointer is now in IV2048 or IV8192, depending on whether you are using Release 1A or Release 2 of 1-2-3.

Once you have placed entries on the worksheet, the END key can take on a different function. It will move the cell pointer to the last entry in the direction you indicate. Figure 1.8 shows a worksheet containing data with the cell pointer originally located in A2.

In the example shown in Figure 1.8, if you press the END key and then the DOWN ARROW key, the cell pointer will be relocated to A10, the last cell in column A that contains data. If you press the END key again and then the RIGHT ARROW key, the cell pointer will be relocated to E10, the last cell in row 10 that contains data.

THE CTRL KEY   The CTRL key can be used with the arrow keys to move a width of the screen to the right or left. Unlike the END key, CTRL is not pressed before the arrow key, but simultaneously with it. To move the cell pointer from A1 to G1, press CTRL and hold it down while pressing the RIGHT ARROW key. To move the cell pointer back to A1 again, press CTRL with the LEFT ARROW key.

THE GOTO KEY   Your last option for moving the cursor quickly is the GOTO option provided by the F5 key. To use this direct cell pointer movement, follow these steps:

1. Press F5.

2. Type **Z10** and press RETURN.
   1-2-3 immediately positions your cell pointer in Z10, regardless of the pointer's beginning location.

USING ALL THE BASIC CELL POINTER OPTIONS   The following comprehensive example uses a variety of the quick pointer movement features. It should help to reinforce your understanding of the various options. First press HOME to position your cursor in A1.

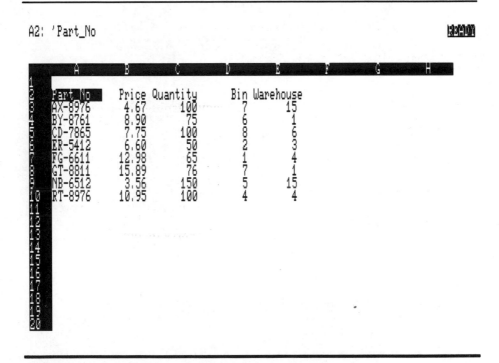

FIGURE 1.8   Worksheet containing data for use with END key

Then follow this sequence of entries.

1. Press PGDN twice to position the cursor in A41.

2. Press END, followed by the RIGHT ARROW key, to position your cell pointer in IV41.

3. Press CTRL-LEFT ARROW twice to move two screens to the left and position your cell pointer in HY41.

4. Press END, followed by the LEFT ARROW key, to position the cell pointer in A41.

5. Press END, followed by the UP ARROW key, to position your cursor in A1.

6. Press F5, enter **S2**, and press RETURN to place your cell pointer in S2.

7. Press HOME to return your cursor to A1.

CORRECTING ERRORS

You may wonder why you are already learning about error correction when you have not even made any cell entries yet. The reason is that everyone makes at least a few mistakes, and it is impossible to predict when you will make your first one. Therefore, it is best to be prepared before you begin to explore cell entries. There are several error-correction methods. Which one you use depends on whether you are still entering the entry you want to correct, or whether you have already finalized the entry by pressing RETURN or by moving the cell pointer to a new location.

Fixing an Entry Before It Is Finalized

To make a correction while making an entry into a cell, you can press the BACKSPACE key to delete the last character you entered. Suppose that you intend to enter "SALES" but that you leave out the E. To correct this, try this option with these steps:

1. Move your cursor to A1.
2. Type **SALS**, then press the BACKSPACE key to delete the last S.
3. Type **ES**. Do not press any additional keys. You will use this partially completed entry in the next example.

The ESC key is a more dramatic way to eliminate characters. It eliminates all the characters you have typed in a cell as long as you have not finalized the entry. Try this method with this step:

1. Press the ESC key. The entire entry, SALES, will disappear and 1-2-3 will be ready to accept a new entry.

There is one more error-correction method that allows you to edit an entry while you are making it. Since it functions the same whether or not the cell entry has been finalized, it will be discussed in the next section on finalized entry-correction methods.

Fixing a Finalized Entry

You can finalize and display entries in the cells in which you want to enter them by pressing RETURN or by moving the cell pointer to a new location. Once the entry is finalized in this way, you must use other methods for correcting mistakes.

RETYPING ENTRIES   One way to change a cell entry that has been finalized is to retype it. Follow these steps to create and correct finalized entries:

1. Enter **SALS** in A1 and press RETURN.
   This time you will find that neither BACKSPACE nor ESC will affect the entry. One method of changing the contents of A1 is to retype your entry.

2. With the cell pointer in A1, type SALES and press RETURN to make the correction.

This method gets the job done but requires a considerable amount of unnecessary typing.

EDITING A FINALIZED ENTRY A better method, especially for longer entries, is to edit the entry and change only the mistakes. You must be in the *EDIT* mode to make this type of change. To place yourself in EDIT mode, press F2 (EDIT). Later you will find that 1-2-3 will sometimes place you in EDIT mode when it is not happy with the cell entry you are trying to finalize. Regardless of how you get there, once you are in EDIT mode, the entry in the cell will be placed in the second line of the control panel, just as it was when you originally entered it.

Within the EDIT mode, the special keys that you used to move the cell pointer function around on the worksheet will function differently. Now the RIGHT and LEFT ARROW keys move you a character to the right or left each time you press them. This allows you to position your small flashing cursor on a letter that you want to delete, or to move it where you want to make an insertion.

The HOME key also takes on a new function within the EDIT mode: It moves you to the front of the entry. If the correction you need to make occurs at the beginning of the entry, HOME moves you to that location quickly. The END key moves in the opposite direction. It places the flashing cursor at the end of the entry.

Within the entry, two different keys can be used to eliminate characters. You can press the BACKSPACE key to delete the character to the left of the flashing cursor, and you can press the DEL key to delete the character above this cursor.

If you type a character from the keyboard it will be added to the right of this cursor location unless you first press the INS key to start the *overtype* setting (overtype replaces characters already in the entry). Let's try an example using each of these keys.

1. Type the characters **SELRS** in B2, as follows:

2. With the cell pointer still in B2, press F2 (EDIT).
   1-2-3 will display the entry in the cell in the second line of
   the control panel with a small blinking cursor at the end,
   like this:

3. Press the BACKSPACE key to move the cursor one position to the left to delete the S. Then type **Y**.

4. Press the LEFT ARROW key again to position the cursor
   under the R; then type **A**. Since 1-2-3 was in its default
   INSERT mode, the A was added to the left of the R.

5. Move the cursor until it is under the E and press the INS
   key once to go into overtype mode. Then type **A**. It will
   replace the E and look like this:

6. Press the RETURN key.

The entry will be finalized in the cell and will disappear from the edit line of the control panel. You can press the INS key again to toggle back to INSERT, as the opposite feature is activated each time you press it.

TYPES OF WORKSHEET ENTRIES

1-2-3 has two basic types of entries for worksheet cells: *labels* and *values*. Labels are text characters that can be used to describe numeric data you plan to place on the worksheet or to store character information. Label data can never be used in arithmetic calculations even if it contains numbers. Value data, on the other hand, consists of either numbers or formulas. Formulas result in numbers but are entered as a series of calculations to be performed. The numeric digits, cell addresses, and a limited set of special symbols are the only entries that can be made in those cells categorized as value entries. 1-2-3 attempts to distinguish label entries from value entries by the first character you enter into a worksheet cell. As long as this first character is not one of the numeric digits or characters that 1-2-3 considers as numeric, it will be treated as a label. 1-2-3 will generate a default label indicator for any entry it considers to be numeric. If you were to enter **Sales** in a cell, 1-2-3 would treat the entry as a label since the first character in the entry is an alphabetic character. Since 1-2-3 always makes its determination from the first character, entering **15 Johnson St.** causes 1-2-3 to reject your entry when you attempt to finalize it, since the first character is numeric and 1-2-3 attempts to treat the entire entry as a value. 1-2-3 is also very stubborn once it determines the type of entry it thinks you planned for a cell. The only way you can change its mind is by editing the cell contents or pressing ESC to start over. After a little practice with the label entries in your first few models, however, you will know all the tricks to put you in command of how your entries are interpreted.

Entering Labels

Label entries in 1-2-3 cells must all begin with one of the three acceptable label indicators. These are a single quotation mark ('), a double quotation mark ("), or a caret (^). Each of these three symbols causes 1-2-3 to align the contents of the cell differently. Beginning with a ' is the default option and causes the entry to be left aligned. 1-2-3 will even generate this label indicator for you if your entry begins with an alphabetic character or a special symbol that is not considered part of the value entry options. Using the " causes the entry to be right aligned in the cell, and using the ^ symbol causes the entry to be centered. If you choose right or center justification, begin your label entry with the special symbol and follow it immediately with the text that you wish the cell to contain. If you choose to begin a label entry with a character that 1-2-3 considers to be a value, you may start your entry with one of the three label indicators to trick the package into treating it like a label. Before starting an actual model, try each of these exercises, as follows.

1. Move your cell pointer to A1 with the arrow keys, type **AT**, and press RETURN.
   AT appears in the display of the worksheet. However, when you observe the entry in the control panel you will notice that it reads 'AT. The reason is that 1-2-3 generated the label indicator for you. Because of this indicator, your entry should also appear as left aligned within cell A1 and will match this:

2. Use the DOWN ARROW key and move the cursor to A2. Type **"AT** and press RETURN.
   Your entry should be right aligned in the cell display.

3. Use the DOWN ARROW key to move to A3. Enter ^**AT** and press RETURN. The entry should be centered in the cell, as follows:

A3: ^AT   READY

4. Use the DOWN ARROW key and move to A4. Type **3AT** and press RETURN. Notice that 1-2-3 beeps at you, will not accept this entry, and places you in EDIT mode.

5. Press the HOME key and add the single quotation mark at the front of the entry. Then press RETURN again. This time 1-2-3 accepts the entry. This is because you have asked it to treat the entry as a label, even though the first character is a number, by placing a label indicator at the front of the entry. Your worksheet should now appear like this:

A4: '3AT   READY

6. To have a blank screen displayed, enter **/Worksheet Erase Yes** by typing the slash (/) and the first letter of each word. This was just a practice exercise, so you can clear everything you have entered. You will find the commands required to erase an entire worksheet on 1-2-3's menus. For now you need to take the required key sequence on faith, but you will learn all the details in a later chapter.

Now you will put your newly acquired label entry techniques to work to build the model shown in Figure 1.9. This model compares

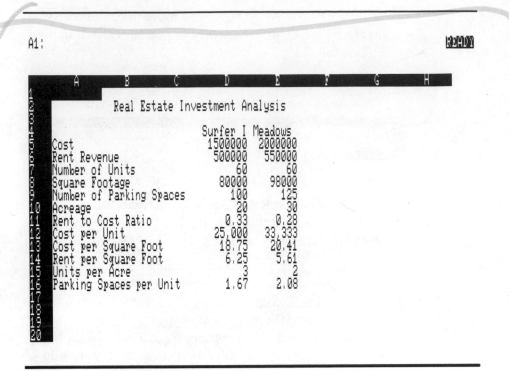

A1:   READY

```
              A         B         C         D         E         F         G         H
                        Real Estate Investment Analysis

                                     Surfer I Meadows
      Cost                            1500000  2000000
      Rent Revenue                     500000   550000
      Number of Units                      60       60
      Square Footage                    80000    98000
      Number of Parking Spaces           100      125
      Acreage                             20       30
      Rent to Cost Ratio                0.33     0.28
      Cost per Unit                   25,000   33,333
      Cost per Square Foot             18.75    20.41
      Rent per Square Foot              6.25     5.61
      Units per Acre                       3        2
      Parking Spaces per Unit           1.67     2.08
```

FIGURE 1.9   Real estate investment model

two investment properties. You could easily modify the model to compare two potential stock or bond investments or two departments or two sales managers. All you need is information pertinent to the subjects being compared. All the entries you make in this section of the chapter will be entered as labels. These labels can be used to describe the data the model will contain and the calculations the model will perform, as well as to provide an overall description of the model's purpose so you can see the versatility of label entries. You will continue to build this model by adding numeric entries in the next section of this chapter; and you will complete it in Chapter 2 by adding formulas.

Follow these steps to create the model shell shown in Figure 1.10:

1. Move the cell pointer to A5 with the arrow keys, and type **Cost**.

   This first step places the entries for the label that describes the detail entries in column A. You may wonder why you are not entering the title or heading line first. Often it is easier to choose an appropriate location *after* you have positioned the detail below it. A few rows are skipped to allow for the eventual addition of a heading and entries, which begin in row 5.

2. Press the DOWN ARROW key to move to A6 and finalize your entry.

   There are two methods for finalizing cell entries. You can use the arrow keys to move to a new location, or you can press the RETURN key. The DOWN ARROW key is a better method: You need to position your cursor for the next entry anyway, and this approach lets you both finalize and position with a single keystroke.

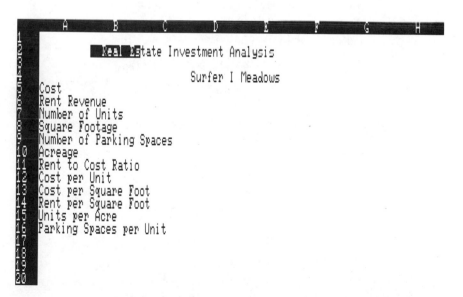

FIGURE 1.10 Label entries that build the shell

3. With your cursor in A6, type **Rent Revenue** and press
   RETURN. This time you are using the RETURN key
   rather than the DOWN ARROW key so you can examine the label entry in the cell in which you entered it.
   Notice the label indicator that is automatically generated
   for you at the front of the entry; this was also added at
   the front of your last entry. This label entry is different
   from the last one: It is longer than the default cell width
   of nine characters, which means that it is too long to fit in
   cell A6. However, 1-2-3 borrows display space from cell
   B6 rather than truncating the label entry to fit in A6. Had
   B6 contained data, its space would not have been available; 1-2-3 then would have truncated the display to fit
   within the nine-character width for column A. But even
   though the label entry may be truncated when displayed,
   1-2-3 will always retain the complete entry in memory.
   This approach means that complete label entries are
   always available for display in the event the cell width is
   increased or the cell to the right no longer contains an
   entry. Remember that these long label entries are always
   stored in the original cell where you entered them. If you
   choose to go back and edit the entry, you must edit this
   cell regardless of where the entry is displayed.

4. Move to A7 with the DOWN ARROW key. Type
   Number of Units and press the DOWN ARROW key
   again.

5. Complete the remainder of these vertical label entries
   by making sure that your cell pointer is in the cell specified, and make the entry shown.

A8	**Square Footage**
A9	**Number of Parking Spaces**
A10	**Acreage**
A11	**Rent to Cost Ratio**
A12	**Cost per Unit**
A13	**Cost per Square Foot**
A14	**Rent per Square Foot**
A15	**Units per Acre**
A16	**Parking Spaces per Unit**

6. Press F5, type **D4**, and press RETURN. Type **Surfer I** and finalize by pressing the RIGHT ARROW key. This step added the column headings, which represent the name of the first apartment house you are evaluating. The F5 (GOTO) key, the quickest way to position the cell pointer, was used for this entry.

7. Type **MEADOWS** and press RETURN.

8. Use the UP ARROW key and the LEFT ARROW key to move to B2.

9. Type **Real Estate Investment Analysis** and press RETURN. The heading is a little too far to the left. Using C1 for the entry would not work, since it would be too far to the right. A useful method is to add a few spaces at the front of the entry to position it exactly as you wish.

10. With your cursor in B2, press F2 (EDIT). Then press the HOME key to move to the front of the entry.

11. Press the RIGHT ARROW key once to move the cursor to the right of the label indicator. Press the SPACE BAR twice to add two spaces at the front. Then press RETURN. These extra spaces make your model look better by moving the heading toward the center.

The entry of the title should complete the label entries and lay the groundwork for the numeric data, which you will add in the next step.

Entering Numbers

Numbers are one of the two types of value entries that 1-2-3 permits. As value entries they follow much more rigid rules than label entries. Like labels, numbers are constant at a given point in time; they do not change as the result of arithmetic calculations. They are placed in a cell and will remain as you enter them unless you take some direct action to change them.

Numbers can contain any of the numeric digits from 0 through

9. The other characters that are allowable in numeric entries are ^ . + @ $ ( ). A percent sign can be used at the end of a numeric entry to indicate a percentage, but it is not allowed in other positions within the entry. Spaces, commas, and other characters cannot be added to numeric entries except by using the formatting options, which will be covered in Chapter 3. The only exception to this rule is the use of the letter E (either E or e), which can be used to represent numbers in powers of 10 (referred to as *scientific notation*). For example 3.86E-5 is .0000386. This number can also be represented as (3.86*10^-5) or 3.86E-5. The caret symbol represents exponentiation or the power of 10 that this number is raised to.

You will only enter the numbers for the constant numeric data on the worksheet. Even though numeric entries are considered constants, there is nothing to prevent you from updating any of these numbers, once they are entered by typing a new number or editing the existing entry. For this model, the numbers you will enter are the first six entries in the column. The other entries will be the result of formulas added in the next chapter; these cells will remain blank, initially. As you enter the first numeric digit in each cell, you will notice that the READY mode indicator is replaced by VALUE. The first character is all that 1-2-3 needs to determine the type of cell entry. Here are the steps to follow:

1. Move the cell pointer to D5 with the arrow keys. Type **1500000** and press RETURN.
   Notice that you did not enter any commas or other characters. You can have 1-2-3 add them at a later time as a formatting option, if you wish. Also, notice that 1-2-3 did not add a label indicator in front of this number since it considers it a value.

2. Move the cell pointer to D6 with the DOWN ARROW key. Type **500000**, then press the DOWN ARROW key.

3. Type **60**, then press the DOWN ARROW key.

4. Type **80000**, then press the DOWN ARROW key.

5. Type **100**, then press the DOWN ARROW key.

6. Type **20**, then use the UP ARROW key and the RIGHT ARROW key to move to E5.

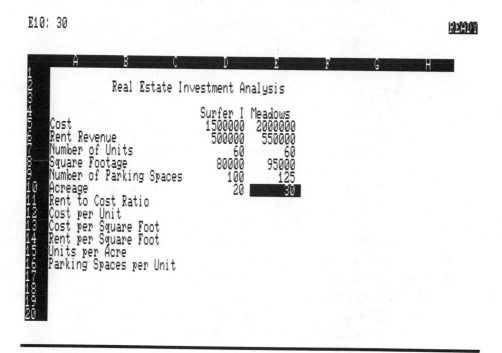

FIGURE 1.11 Adding numbers to the shell

7. Complete these same entries for the MEADOWS building with the following entries:

E5	2000000
E6	550000
E7	60
E8	95000
E9	125
E10	30

The result of entering each of the numbers is shown in Figure 1.11.

Remember that it is easy to change any of the entries. You can type a new number or edit the cell. Try a few changes, following these steps:

1. Move to E8 and press F2 (EDIT).

2. Press the LEFT ARROW key to move your cursor under the 5.

3. Press the DEL key to remove it.

4. Type **8**.

5. Finalize your entry by pressing RETURN.
   You also could have finalized with the UP or DOWN ARROW key. However, the RIGHT and LEFT ARROW keys are not options for finalizing while you are editing, since they take on the new function of moving within the cell entry.

Since this is the last entry that you will make in the model, save a copy of the model to disk. The commands that handle saving files are covered in Chapter 4 in detail. For now, all you need to know is that you need a menu command in order to save a file. You must enter **/File Save** followed by the name of the file you wish to save. If the file is already stored on the disk, you must confirm your desire to save by entering REPLACE. You can enter each of these commands by typing the first letter of the command, but you must enter the filename in full. Enter **/File Save REALEST** and press RETURN.

GETTING HELP

Navigating your way around the worksheet and entering numbers and labels in worksheet cells probably has seemed quite simple. That is because you have taken everything a step at a time. As you begin to add more skills to your toolkit of 1-2-3 options, you may find that you need a quick refresher of an earlier topic. Although you can always look back to the particular chapter or to your 1-2-3 reference manual, 1-2-3's onscreen help facility will often provide just the hints you need to complete your planned task. Accessing these help features is as easy as pressing F1 (HELP). You can do this even if you are in the middle of a task, such as entering a label in a cell. 1-2-3 will not disrupt the in-progress task; instead, it will set it aside temporarily to let you review help information on the screen.

If you press F1 (HELP) before starting a task, 1-2-3 will display a help screen relating the READY mode for your selection. Assuming that you are in READY mode, try this right now and press F1. If you are using Release 2, your screen should match the one in Figure 1.12. (The Release 1A HELP screens are similar but not always exactly the same, since some of the features of Release 1A are different.) To select information on any topic, just place your highlighted bar on the desired topic and press RETURN. If you choose Formulas or Numbers, additional information will be presented, such as the display in Figure 1.13. There may be additional levels of help that you can select in the same manner, depending on the topic. When you are through, leave HELP by pressing ESC. This returns you to the 1-2-3 task where you left off.

If you request help with F1 after beginning a task, 1-2-3 pro-

---

A1:   HELP

READY Mode

The mode indicator, READY, in the upper right corner of the screen means you can select a command or type a cell entry. The first key you press determines your action:

Formula or Number: Type a digit (0..9) or one of the characters
                     +, -, ., (, @, #, or $.
Label: Type any character except those that begin a
                     formula or number. Start with a label-prefix character to
                     create a label of a particular type: ' for left-aligned,
                     " for right-aligned, ^ for centered, or \ for repeating.
Command: Type /.
Special Function: Press a special key.

To learn more about this Help facility, press [END], then [RETURN].

Cell Entries   Mode Indicators
Help Index   How to Use Help

FIGURE 1.12 Help screen presented from READY mode

```
A1:                                                              HELP


VALUE Mode

You can enter either a number or a formula. These keys have special meanings:

[ESCAPE]        Cancels entry and returns to READY mode.
[BACKSPACE]     Erases character preceding cursor.
[DELETE]        Erases character at cursor.
[RETURN]        Completes the entry. 1-2-3 stores the number or formula
                in the current cell, recalculates all formulas (if the
                Recalculation setting is Automatic), and returns to READY mode.
[EDIT]          Switches to EDIT mode. Pressing it again returns you to VALUE mode.
[ABS]           Switches an address among Absolute, Mixed, and Relative.  Use only
                when highlighting to a cell or range while writing a formula.
[CALC]          Converts a formula to its current value.
Pointer-Movement Keys     Complete the entry and move the pointer.

Erasing Entries          Pointing to Ranges
Formulas                 Help Index
```

FIGURE 1.13 Requesting additional help for entering numbers

vides context-sensitive help. This is 1-2-3's best guess as to the type of help you need based on the entries you have made so far. Assuming that you were entering a label and wanted additional information on 1-2-3's label-entering rules, you could press F1 before finalizing. Try this by entering the label **Salaries** in a worksheet cell and pressing F1 before finalizing your entry. The HELP screen that is presented is shown in Figure 1.14 for Release 2. You still have the option of selecting help on less specific topics by choosing the HELP index at the bottom of the screen. This index provides a whole list of topics like the ones shown in Figure 1.15.

When you are finished using the HELP feature, you can press ESC again to return to the worksheet. Everything will be exactly as you left it. 1-2-3 effectively places a marker in your current location and records your actions up to that point before displaying the HELP screen so it can put things back exactly as you left them. Even the partially completed label entry will be waiting for you to finalize it. Since you do not wish to actually make another entry at this time you can press ESC again to eliminate it.

    1-2-3 can assist you when you encounter an error message. Just press F1 (HELP), select the HELP index, and choose ERROR MESSAGE to see an explanation of each, as well as actions that you can take to correct the error.

QUITTING A 1-2-3 SESSION

To end a 1-2-3 session you will need to enter **/Quit** then **Yes** to confirm that you are through. 1-2-3 assumes that you have saved the model in memory before quitting. It does not take any action to save your data for you.

    Entering this command removes 1-2-3 from memory and places you back at the system prompt. At this point, you can execute any new program that you wish.

```
A1:
'Salaries                                                           HELP


LABEL Mode

In LABEL mode, you can enter any type of label -- left-aligned, right-aligned,
centered, or repeating.  These keys have special meanings:

[ESCAPE]         Cancels entry and returns to READY mode.
[BACKSPACE]      Erases character preceding cursor.
[DELETE]         Erases character at cursor.
[RETURN]         Completes the entry. 1-2-3 stores the label in the current cell,
                 and returns to READY mode.
[EDIT]           Switches to EDIT mode. Pressing it again returns you to LABEL
                 mode.

Pointer-Movement Keys     Complete the entry and move the cell pointer.


Erasing Entries          Edit mode
Long Labels              Help Index
```

FIGURE 1.14 Requesting help while entering a label

SUMMARY

You have established a firm foundation in this chapter. You have learned how to control your location on 1-2-3's large worksheet. You have also mastered the basic entries that 1-2-3 allows, by adding labels and numbers to the worksheet. You also now have command of 1-2-3's help facility, and should feel free to use it without its affecting the task you are attempting to complete. As you move to Chapter 2, you will learn the ins and outs of entering formulas. These are the most powerful type of entry that 1-2-3 offers, since formulas allow you to use worksheets for what-if analysis and other planning tasks.

A1:   HELP

Help Index   Select one of these topics for additional Help.

Using The Help Facility   How to Start Over
Errors and Messages   How to End a 1-2-3 Session
Error Message Index
                                 Moving the Cell Pointer
Special Keys   Cell Entries
Control Panel   Erasing Cell Entries
Modes and Indicators
                                 1-2-3 Commands
                                 Command Menus
Formulas
@Functions   Column Widths
Cell Formats -- Number vs. Label
                                 Macros
Operators   Function Keys

Ranges   Menus for File, Range, and Graph Names
Pointing to Ranges   File Names
Reenterng Ranges

FIGURE 1.15   Looking at the help index

2

DEFINING
YOUR
CALCULATIONS

Calculations are an important part of many of the business tasks that you perform. Some calculations are simple. If you get a 10 percent discount when you purchase from a given vendor, it takes no great effort to calculate your savings. And it is simple to calculate the total number of employees in your group if the headcount increases by five. In fact, these calculations are so easy that you can compute them without even writing them down.

However, not all computations are this simple. For example, if you want to determine the most economic quantity to order for each item in your inventory, you will need to perform a much more complex calculation, one that is difficult to compute without writing it down. Even when you do write complex computations down on paper, mistakes are easy to make. And if conditions change slightly, the numbers in your computations are likely to change as well, requiring you to redo the calculations. Evaluating a series of conditions could cause you to spend a considerable amount of time redoing calculations.

1-2-3 provides an easy-to-use solution, one that eliminates the need for you to perform calculations yourself. You simply define to 1-2-3 the calculations you wish to perform, and it handles the computations. To do this you must determine each step in the computational process and record these instructions in a cell on 1-2-3's worksheet. These recorded instructions for handling calculations are known as *formulas*. Once these formulas are entered, 1-2-3 will handle all the work required for computing your results.

The process of entering these formulas is really quite simple and not too different from the way you entered numbers and labels in Chapter 1. These formulas will tell 1-2-3 what data to operate on and which of the operators will be used. A sample formula for profit might be Sales-Cost of Goods Sold; a sample formula for net payable on an invoice would be the Amount-(Amount*Purchase Discount).

This chapter will show you how to enter any of these formulas, using references to the worksheet cells that contain your data. This feature is very powerful; it allows you to reuse applications even when significant changes occur. This flexibility makes formulas a valuable addition to your worksheet models.

In this chapter, you will look at all the features provided by 1-2-3 to handle your calculations. You will find that they have wide applicability: The same methods are used to calculate interest expense, budget projections, salary increases, and any other calculation. In addition to the basics, you will also explore 1-2-3's full set of features for building more complex formulas, including the string formulas (these manipulate text data rather than numeric values).

FORMULA BASICS

Formulas, like the numbers you entered in Chapter 1, are value entries. Unlike numbers, however, they produce results that vary, depending on the entries they reference. This variability makes formulas the backbone of spreadsheet features: It allows you to make what-if projections based on changing entries on your worksheet. You can update the formula results without changing the formula itself. They only thing required is new entries for the variaables referenced by the formula.

The Basic Rules of Entry

To enter a formula in a cell, you must define to 1-2-3 the location of the variables involved and the operations you wish performed on them. 1-2-3 has three types of formulas it supports: arithmetic formulas, logical formulas, and in Release 2 text or string formulas. There are a few general rules that apply to all formulas and some special conventions that will be observed for the special types of formulas. The special rules will be discussed when each type of formula is discussed; but the general guidelines will be given at this time.

The first and perhaps most important rule is that the first character in a formula entry must always come from the following list of numeric characters: + – (@ # $. 0 1 2 3 4 5 6 7 8 9. The second rule is that formulas cannot contain extraneous spaces except within names or text. As you type the examples presented, be especially careful not to separate the formula components with spaces. The third and last rule pertains to the length limitation for a formula: As with other cell entries, it cannot exceed 240 characters. Unless you are building some really complex calculations, this last rule is not likely to impose a restriction.

ARITHMETIC FORMULAS

Arithmetic formulas are nothing more than instructions for certain operations: addition (+); subtraction (-); multiplication (*); division (/); and exponentiation (^), which represents raising a number to a specific power, such as 3 cubed or 2 squared. These are the same types of operations you can compute by hand or with a calculator. When you record these formulas on the worksheet, you can build the formula with the arithmetic operators and references to the numbers contained in other worksheet cells. The result of the calculation will be determined by the current value of the worksheet cell referenced. You can see the advantage of recording these formulas on a worksheet more clearly when you wish to change one of the numbers. All you need to do is change the number in the referenced cell. Since the formula has already been entered and tested, it will be available on a permanent basis. Anytime you wish the same set of calculations to be performed, you can enter the numbers involved without having to reenter the formula; the sequence of required calculations will be stored on the worksheet in the cell that contains the formula.

Entering Simple Arithmetic Formulas

1-2-3's formulas can be entered with numeric constants, as in 4*5 or 3+2. However, numeric constants within formulas are limiting: You would have to change formulas as conditions change. A better method is to store these constants in a worksheet cell. When you wish to use this value in a formula, you can use its cell address within the formula. Then, if the value changes, you need only enter a new number where it is stored; the formula will use it automatically. Using cell addresses in formulas requires one additional rule: Since cell addresses begin with non-numeric characters, an entry's initial alphabetic character (for example, A2+B3) will cause it to be treated as a label entry.

This means that an entry like this would appear in the worksheet cell just as you typed it, rather than performing any calculations. Try this with the following entries:

1. Move the cell pointer to A2, type **3**, and press RETURN.

2. Move the cell pointer to B3, type **2**, and press RETURN.

3. Move the cell pointer to D2, type **A2*B3**, and press RETURN.

No calculation is performed for you. 1-2-3 decided that the cell entry was a label, since its first character was alphabetic. This approach produces the following display, which does not perform any calculations:

D2: 'A2+B3

Several of the numeric characters can be used to begin a formula. The + is a logical choice as a character to add to the front of the formula: It requires only one keystroke and will not affect the contents of A2. Try this new entry to see the results.

1. Type **+A2+B3** in D2.

This time, 1-2-3 interpreted your entry as a formula and computed the result of adding the current contents of A2 to the current contents of B3. Since A2 contains a 3 and B2 contains a 2, after the formula is entered D2 displays a 5, as follows:

D2: +A2+B3

When you point to D2 you still see the formula you entered in the control panel. If, later on, you decided to change A2 to 10, the result displayed in D2 would change to a 12 as evidence that the formula was still doing its assigned task.

When you enter formulas using their cell address, 1-2-3 is not fussy and will accept either upper or lower case. The formula +A2*AB3 is equivalent to +a2*ab3 or +a2*Ab3 and computes the same results.

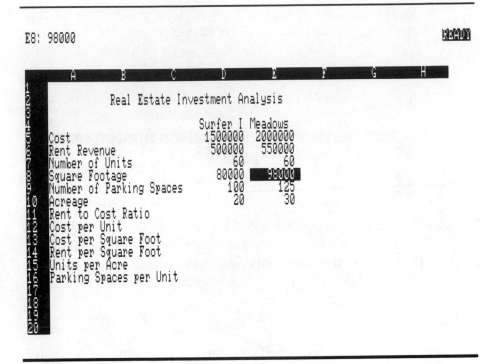

E8: 98000   READY

```
        A         B         C         D         E      F       G       H
1
2                    Real Estate Investment Analysis
3
4                                      Surfer I Meadows
5  Cost                                 1500000 2000000
6  Rent Revenue                          500000  550000
7  Number of Units                           60      60
8  Square Footage                         80000   98000
9  Number of Parking Spaces                 100     125
10 Acreage                                   20      30
11 Rent to Cost Ratio
12 Cost per Unit
13 Cost per Square Foot
14 Rent per Square Foot
15 Units per Acre
16 Parking Spaces per Unit
17
18
19
20
```

FIGURE 2.1   Investment model without formulas

Adding Formulas to the Real Estate Model

You will use your new formula techniques to add the formulas to
the real estate investment model that you started in Chapter 1. If
the model is still in the memory of your computer, you are ready to
begin. If you have just started a new 1-2-3 session and wish to recall
your copy of the model from your disk, type **/FRREALEST** and
press RETURN. The model shown in Figure 2.1 should be displayed on your screen in preparation for adding the formulas.

The first formula you need to enter is the rent-to-cost ratio.
You compute this ratio by dividing the rent by the cost. Each
investment will be evaluated separately; you will enter the computations for Surfer I first. Follow these instructions to add the
formulas:

1. Move the cell pointer to D11. This is an appropriate location for the first Surfer I calculation.

2. Type **+D6/D5** and press RETURN.
   Since the rent revenue for this property is stored in D6 and the cost is in D5, the formula will calculate the ratio you need. Your result should appear like the one in Figure 2.2, with the formula you entered displayed in the control panel and the result of the calculation shown in the cell. The next computation is cost per unit. This calculation splits the total cost evenly across all units to give you an estimate of what one unit cost.

3. Move the cell pointer to D12 with the DOWN ARROW key. Type **+D5/D7**.
   This formula divides the cost by the number of units. The next formula will allocate the cost on a square-footage basis.

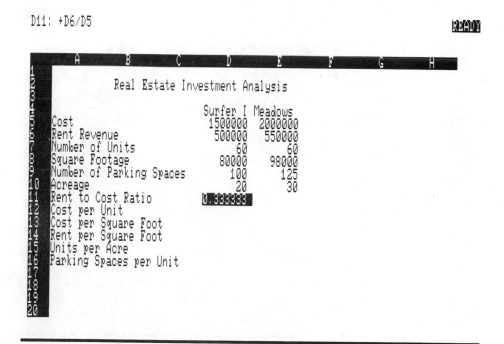

FIGURE 2.2   Formula entered in D11

4. Move the cell pointer to D13 and with the DOWN ARROW key. Then type **+D5/D8** and press the DOWN ARROW key.

The remaining three formulas for Surfer I follow the same pattern.

5. Type **+D6/D8** and press the DOWN ARROW key.

6. Type **+D7/D10** and press the DOWN ARROW key.

7. Type **+D9/D7** and press RETURN.

This completes the entries for Surfer I and produces the results shown in Figure 2.3.

Later, you will learn techniques for copying formulas like these to other locations rather than reentering a set of similar formulas for the Meadows property. For now you need practice with formula

---

D16: +D9/D7   READY

```
        A         B         C         D         E         F         G         H
 1
 2                    Real Estate Investment Analysis
 3
 4                                   Surfer I  Meadows
 5   Cost                             1500000   2000000
 6   Rent Revenue                      500000    550000
 7   Number of Units                       60        60
 8   Square Footage                     80000     98000
 9   Number of Parking Spaces             100       125
10   Acreage                               20        30
11   Rent to Cost Ratio              0.333333
12   Cost per Unit                      25000
13   Cost per Square Foot               18.75
14   Rent per Square Foot                6.25
15   Units per Acre                         3
16   Parking Spaces per Unit         1.666666
17
18
19
20
```

FIGURE 2.3 Analysis of the Surfer I property completed

entry, and the second set of formulas lets you look at another formula-entry method.

Entering Arithmetic Formulas With the Point Method

The formulas in the last section were all built by typing both the arithmetic operators and the cell addresses they referenced. This method works fine if you are an average typist and if all the referenced cells are within view on the worksheet. However, if neither of these conditions is true, typing the formulas may lead to a higher error rate than necessary. 1-2-3 provides a second method of formula entry, which can reduce the error rate. With this method, you type only the arithmetic operators, and you select the cell references by using the arrow keys to position the cell pointer on the cell you wish to reference. 1-2-3 adds the cell address to the formula being built in the control panel and changes the mode indicator from VALUE to POINT. This method provides visual verification that you are selecting the correct cell and eliminates the problems of typing mistakes. Follow these steps to add the first formula for the Meadows property, using the pointing method of formula entry:

1. Move your cell pointer to E11, then type **+.**
    You can use the + on the key next to the pointer movement keys or the one over the =.

2. Next move your cell pointer to E6. This will cause the cell address to appear in your control panel like this:

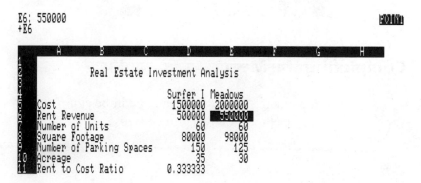

Note that the indicator in the upper right corner of the screen has changed to POINT.

3. Type /. Notice that the cell pointer returns to the cell where the formula is being recorded.

4. Move your cell pointer to E5. Your control panel will now contain the complete formula, as follows:

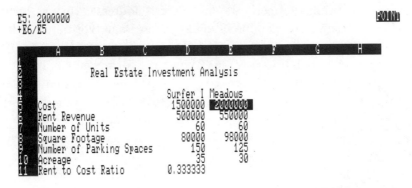

5. Press RETURN to finalize the formula. The following result will appear:

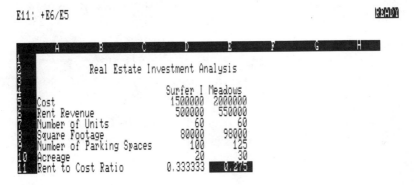

Completing the Meadows Formulas

The remaining Meadows formulas can be completed by using the pointing method, following these steps:

1. Move your cell pointer to E12 and type **+**. Then point to E5 with the UP ARROW key and type **/**. Next point to E7 and press RETURN.

2. Move your cell pointer to E13 and type **+**. Point to E5 with the UP ARROW key and type **/**. Point to E8 and press RETURN.

3. To enter the formula for rent per square foot, begin by moving the cell pointer to E14 and typing **+**. Use the UP ARROW key to move to E6. Then type **/**, move to E8, and press RETURN.

E16: +E9/E7

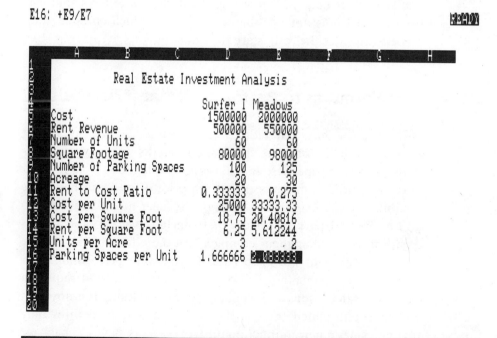

	A	B	C	D	E	F	G	H
			Real Estate Investment Analysis					
					Surfer I	Meadows		
5	Cost				1500000	2000000		
6	Rent Revenue				500000	550000		
7	Number of Units				60	60		
8	Square Footage				80000	98000		
9	Number of Parking Spaces				100	125		
10	Acreage				20	30		
11	Rent to Cost Ratio				0.333333	0.275		
12	Cost per Unit				25000	33333.33		
13	Cost per Square Foot				18.75	20.40816		
14	Rent per Square Foot				6.25	5.612244		
15	Units per Acre				3	2		
16	Parking Spaces per Unit				1.666666	2.083333		

FIGURE 2.4   Investment model with all the formulas entered

4. Move the cell pointer to E15 and type +. Use the UP ARROW key to move to E7. Type /, then move to E10 and press RETURN.

5. Move the cell pointer to E16 and type +. Use the UP ARROW key to point to the number of parking spaces in E9. Then type /, move to the number of units in E7, and press RETURN. The completed model is shown in Figure 2.4.

You will notice that RETURN was used to finalize each of the formulas. If you had attempted to finalize by pressing an ARROW key, the last reference in the cell would have been changed by this movement of the cell pointer. With the pointing method of formula construction, RETURN will always be your only way of finalizing a formula. Other than the differences in the entry method, these two sets of formulas will perform identically. Once a formula has been entered it is not possible to determine which entry method was chosen since the results are the same.

Using Your Formulas to Perform a What-if Analysis

Now that you have entered the basic formulas, your investment analysis model is complete. This kind of model will help you compare the two properties; in addition, it can assist you in your negotiations. You might feel that the price of one unit has more flexibility than the other; or perhaps the seller might be willing to add additional parking spaces or to include vacant land that is adjacent to the apartment complex. All these factors can change your evaluation of the properties. If you were performing your computations manually, each of the possibilities would require a new set of calculations and would be time consuming. But now that you have automated the calculations, each option requires only that you enter a new number on the worksheet to have the package perform a new comparison immediately.

Let's look at how easy it is to evaluate each change in conditions. Suppose that you were able to negotiate a new price of $1,600,000 for the Meadows building. To add the updated data to your model, follow these steps:

1. Move the cell pointer to E5.
2. Press F2 (EDIT) to enter edit mode.
3. Press the HOME key to move to the beginning of the entry.
4. Delete the first two digits by pressing the DEL key twice.
5. Type **16** to replace the digits you just eliminated.
6. Press RETURN to finalize your entry.

After entering these new entries, you will find that the results of formula calculations have been updated. They indicate that the rent-to-cost ratio and the cost per unit for the two properties are much closer than you might have thought.

Use the same process to add the updates for the Surfer I building. If you feel that the owners will agree to add 50 more parking spaces and include another 15 acres of land at the same purchase price, you will want to make the following changes:

1. Move the cell pointer to D9.
2. Type **150** and press RETURN.
3. Move the cell pointer to D10.
4. Type **35** and press RETURN.

Rather than editing the original entries, this time, the new figures were retyped. You will have to evaluate each situation to see which is the quickest method. For very short entries like these last two it is often just as easy to type the new entries.

As these last entries show, what-if analysis is quite simple once you have the formulas entered. The result of the most recent changes are shown in Figure 2.5. You could easily use these tech-

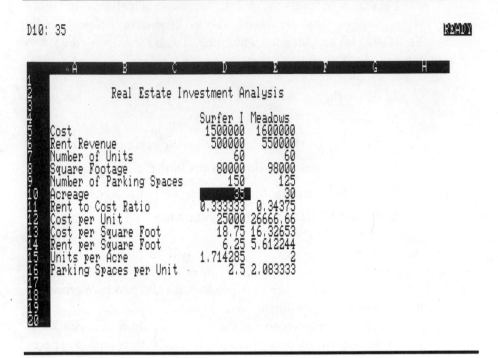

D10: 35   READY

```
      A          B         C         D         E        F        G        H
1
2                    Real Estate Investment Analysis
3
4                                   Surfer I  Meadows
5     Cost                          1500000  1600000
6     Rent Revenue                   500000   550000
7     Number of Units                    60       60
8     Square Footage                  80000    98000
9     Number of Parking Spaces          150      125
10    Acreage                            35       30
11    Rent to Cost Ratio           0.333333  0.34375
12    Cost per Unit                   25000 26666.66
13    Cost per Square Foot            18.75 16.32653
14    Rent per Square Foot             6.25 5.612244
15    Units per Acre               1.714285        2
16    Parking Spaces per Unit           2.5 2.083333
17
18
19
20
```

FIGURE 2.5   The result of a what-if analysis

niques to evaluate potential changes in purchase price or other options with only a minimal investment of time.

Now that you have updated your model with formulas and the results of what-if analysis, you will want to save the updated copy on disk to reflect the current status of the worksheet. Enter **/FS** and press RETURN. You did not have to type the file name this time, since it was saved previously. To ensure that the copy on disk is replaced with the current copy in memory, take one additional step: When 1-2-3's prompt message asks if you wish to Cancel the request or Replace the copy on disk, respond by entering an **R**.

Using Some of the Other Arithmetic Operations

The model you just completed used only the division operation in all of the formulas. Now let's look at another calculation that uses other operators to perform the computations. Erase the real estate calculations — you have saved them to your disk. Use the following entry:

1. Enter /**WEY**.

Now you will use the blank worksheet to lay out a model that computes an employee's gross pay, given an hourly rate of pay and regular and overtime hours worked. 1-2-3 does not assign the same priority to each of the arithmetic operators. You can use this to your advantage in constructing this formula. 1-2-3 evaluates formulas from left to right but it completes all the multiplication and division operations before coming back through the formula to perform addition and subtraction. Use a multiplication process to calculate regular pay, and then use another multiplication process to calculate overtime pay before adding the results of the two operations together. 1-2-3 will automatically do the two operations in this sequence, due to their priorities. Priorities will be covered in greater detail later in this chapter, along with a solution for altering the normal priority sequence. Keep this model simple for now: Enter just the basic information for one employee, following these steps:

1. With the cell pointer in A1, type **Employee** and press the RIGHT ARROW key.

2. Type "**Hours** and press the RIGHT ARROW key.

3. Type "**Rate** and press the RIGHT ARROW key.

4. Type "**O. Hrs** and press the RIGHT ARROW key.
   Notice that the " symbol was used at the beginning of the first three label entries. As you recall from Chapter 1, the " symbol causes 1-2-3 to right align the label entry in the worksheet cell. This means that the column labels will line up with the first value in the column.

5. Type **Gross Pay** and press RETURN.

6. Move the cell pointer to A2 with the **HOME** and DOWN ARROW keys and type **J. Smith**, then press the RIGHT ARROW key.

7. Type **40** and press the RIGHT ARROW key.

8. Type **3.75** and press the RIGHT ARROW key.

9. Type **10** and press the RIGHT ARROW key.
   Your entries should appear like this:

The next formula must calculate gross pay by multiplying regular hours by the rate of pay then multiplying overtime hours times 1.5 times the rate of pay. The result of these two multiplication operators will be added to obtain the gross pay. This sounds complicated but can be represented succinctly in the formula.

10. Type **+B2*C2+D2*1.5*C2** and press RETURN to have 1-2-3 compute these results:

You could add still more employees to this model, but for now, save it by entering **/FSPAY** and pressing RETURN. You can always retrieve it again after you have learned how to duplicate formulas in Chapter 5. For the time being, continue to look at other types of formulas. Clear the entries from your worksheet by entering **/WEY**.

USING LOGICAL FORMULAS

Logical formulas are used to compare two or more worksheet values. They use the logical operators = for equal, <> for not equal, > for greater than, >= for greater than or equal to, < for less than, and <= for less than or equal to. Logical formulas can be entered with the same methods used for arithmetic formulas; but unlike arithmetic formulas, they do not calculate numeric results. Instead, they produce a result of either a zero or a one, depending on whether the condition that was evaluated is true or false. If the condition is true, 1 will be returned; if the condition is false, 0 will be returned. For example, if D4 contains a 5, the logical expression +D4<3 will return 0, since the condition is false. This capability can be used to evaluate a series of complex decisions or to influence results in other parts of the worksheet.

If an expression contains both logical operators and arithmetic operators, the expression containing the arithmetic operators will be evaluated first. For example, the logical expression +D4*2>50 will be evaluated by first multiplying the current value in D4 by 2 and then performing the comparison.

Creating a Model to Calculate Commissions

One application of logical operators in a spreadsheet might be the calculation of a commission bonus. In your example, sales personnel are paid a quarterly bonus, which includes a regular sales commission and a bonus paid for meeting sales quotas. The regular commission is computed as 10 percent of total sales. The bonus is calculated by product. A bonus of $1000 is paid for each product for which the sales quota is met. A salesperson could thus gain $3000 by meeting quotas for three products.

Look at the steps required to build the commission model shown in Figure 2.6. First, follow these directions to add the labels that are required:

1. Move the cell pointer to B1, type **Commission Calculation**, and press RETURN.

2. Move the cell pointer to A4 and type **Employee:** and press the DOWN ARROW key.

3. Type **Sales Product 1:** and press the DOWN ARROW key.

D14: +C10+C11

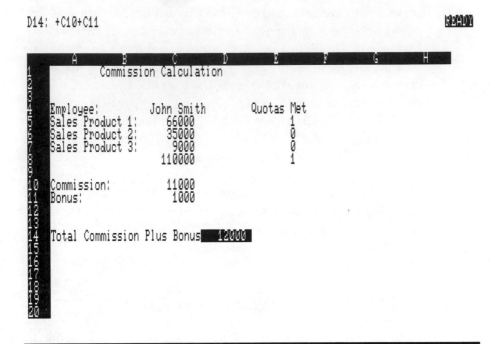

FIGURE 2.6   Completed commission model

4. Type **Sales Product 2:** and press the DOWN ARROW key.

5. Type **Sales Product 3:** and press the DOWN ARROW key three times to place the cell pointer in A10.

6. Type **Commission:** and press the DOWN ARROW key.

7. Type **Bonus:** and press the DOWN ARROW key three times to place the cell pointer in A14.

8. Type **Total Commission Plus Bonus** and press RETURN. Notice that a : has not been added at the end. This is for convenience since we do not wish this entry to display beyond column C. It means you do not have to widen the column to show more than the default of nine characters per column.

9. Use F5 (GOTO), type **C4** and press RETURN. Type

John Smith and press the DOWN ARROW key to enter the name of the employee for which you will be calculating commissions.

10. Type **66000** and press the DOWN ARROW key. Type **35000** and press the DOWN ARROW key. Type **9000** and press the DOWN ARROW key.

11. Position the cell pointer in E4 and type **Quotas Met**, then press the DOWN ARROW key.

Adding Formulas to the Commission Model

The number and label entries for this model are now complete. Your model should match the one shown in Figure 2.7. At this point it is time to add the formulas for calculating the regular and

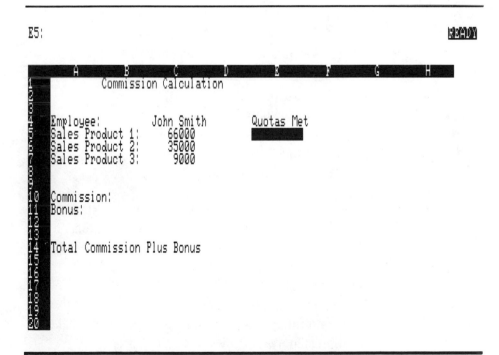

FIGURE 2.7 Building the model by entering numbers and labels

bonus commission. For the purpose of computing the bonus, assume that the quota is $50,000 per product. Use the following steps to enter the logical formulas for determining whether the sales quota in each category was met:

1. Type **+C5>50000** and press the DOWN ARROW key.
   This formula will produce a 1 if the product 1 quota is met and a 0 if it is not.

2. Type **+C6>50000** and press the DOWN ARROW key.

3. Type **+C7>50000** and press the DOWN ARROW key.

4. Total the number of quotas met by adding the result of each of the logical formulas — type **+E5+E6+E7** and press RETURN.
   In Chapter 7 you will learn a shortcut method for summing entries, but for now you will use simple addition.

5. Total the sales of all three products in the same fashion move the cell pointer to C8, type **+C5+C6+C7**, and press the DOWN ARROW key two times.

6. Enter the formula for commission in C10 by typing **+C8*.1** and pressing the DOWN ARROW key.

7. Type **+E8*1000** and press RETURN.
   This lets you calculate the bonus commission by multiplying the number of quotas met by 1000.

8. Position the cell pointer in D14, type **+C10+C11**, and press RETURN.

Your completed model should now match the one shown at the beginning of this section, Figure 2.6. The logical formulas it contains will respond to changes in the model's data. Let's try one:

1. Move the cell pointer to C7.

2. Type **73000** and press RETURN.
   You will find that a new commission of $19,400 is calculated immediately, as shown in Figure 2.8.

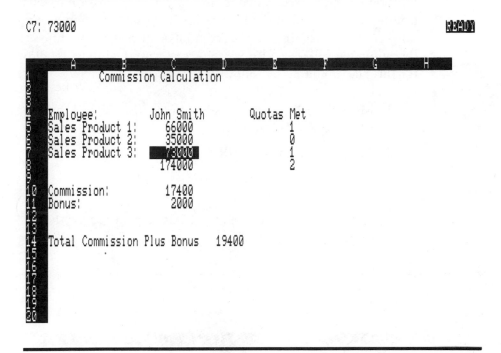

FIGURE 2.8 Changing the sales figures

Using Compound Operators

1-2-3 also has three compound operators that can be used with logical formulas. These operators are either used to negate an expression or to join two different expressions. The negation operator #NOT# has priority over the two compound operators, #AND# and #OR#. When the compound operator #AND# is used to join two logical expressions, both expressions must be true for the compound formula to return a *true*. If the two expressions are joined by #OR#, either one can be true for the condition to return a *true value*.

You can add a second condition to your commission calculation by using the compound operators. Let's say that bonus commissions require a minimum of six months of service in addition to the minimum sales level for a product. Revise the model to allow for this new condition by following these steps:

1. Move the cell pointer to A9 and type **Months in Job:** and press the RIGHT ARROW key twice.

2. Type **4** and press RETURN.

3. Press F2 (EDIT), type **#AND#C9>6** and then press the DOWN ARROW key.

4. Use the same procedure outlined in step 4 to revise the formulas in E6 and E7.

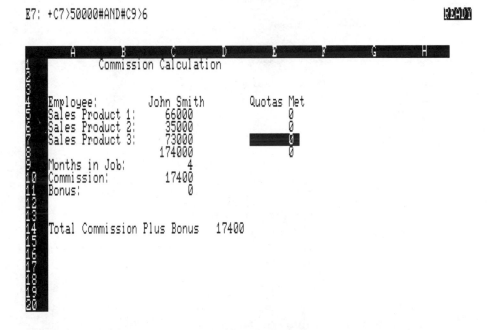

FIGURE 2.9   Adding compound conditions

You will find that the bonus commission in Figure 2.9 is now zero, since the employee has been on the job fewer than six months.

5. Move the cell pointer to C9 and type **8**, then press RETURN to see the bonus commission calculated again.

6. Enter **/FSCOMM** and press RETURN to save this worksheet to disk.

7. Enter **/WEY** to erase memory.

USING STRING FORMULAS

String formulas were added to 1-2-3 with the introduction of Release 2. Although they do not perform formula calculations as arithmetic formulas do, they enable character strings to be joined together to create headings or other data elements for the worksheet. String formulas use only one operator, the ampersand (&). This operator can be used to join variables containing character strings or string constants. For example, "John"&"Smith" will result in JohnSmith, "John"&" "&"Smith" will result in John Smith, and A1&A2&A3 will result in abc if A1 contains an a, A2 contains a b, and A3 contains a c. As with the other types of formulas, with string formulas you can either type the complete formula or point to the cell addresses referenced and have 1-2-3 place them in the formula for you.

Use the string formula feature to build a part number. In this model, separate data elements provide all the different components of All Parts, Inc. part number structure. The warehouse location, bin number, product type, and vendor are all combined to create a part number. Follow these steps to enter the data for the model:

1. Enter the worksheet heading by moving the cell pointer to B3, then typing **All Parts, Inc. Inventory Listing** and pressing RETURN.

2. Move the cell pointer to A5, type **Location**, and press the RIGHT ARROW key.

3. Type **Bin** and press the RIGHT ARROW key.

4. Type **Type** and press the RIGHT ARROW key.

5. Type **Vendor** and press the RIGHT ARROW key.

6. Type **Part No** and press RETURN.

7. Move the cell pointer to A6 and type **'5** and press the RIGHT ARROW Key. The single quotation mark is required since labels will not join values. Using the single quote ensures that the 5 is stored as a label.

8. Type **'12** and press the RIGHT ARROW key.

9. Type **AX** and press the RIGHT ARROW key.

10. Type **CN** and press the RIGHT ARROW key.

11. Verify that the cell pointer is in E6, type **+C6&" "&D6&A6&B6**, and press RETURN.

The part number for the first item will appear as shown in the following list:

For practice, you may wish to enter the data and the required string formula to build the several additional part numbers. Like the other formula types, changing the values for any of the variables will immediately change the results produced by the string formula.

The advantage of the part number display in the last example would occur if the model contained information on additional parts as well as fields to the right that were also important to view.

Using the string formula to build the part number, you could move the cell pointer to the right and view the other data without losing track of the part number, as follows:

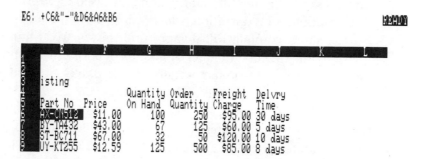

```
E6:  +C6&"-"&D6&A6&B6                                              READY
```

The full power of 1-2-3's string formulas will be realized when you learn to combine the string concatenation features with special string functions, which can extract a portion of a string entry. These special string functions can be used for complex combinations and are an excellent tool for correcting data-entry errors. Special string functions will be covered in Chapter 10.

PERFORMING MORE COMPLEX CALCULATIONS

When 1-2-3 encounters more than one operator in a formula, it does not use a left-to-right order to compute the result. Instead, it evaluates the formula based upon a set priority order for each of the operators. As you begin to build more complex formulas, you will see how important it is to understand 1-2-3's priorities in order to achieve the desired rules.

Table 2.1 shows the order of priority for each of the operators. You will notice that the parentheses are at the top of the list. This indicates that any expression enclosed within them will be evaluated first. The other operators that may cause confusion are the + and symbols shown in level 6 and level 4. The first set represent the positive or negative sign of a value. For instance, -5*3 indicates that the five is a negative number that should be multiplied by a positive three. On the other hand, in the expression 5-4*2 the minus symbol represents subtraction and has a lower priority than the multiplication operation, which will be carried out first.

A short example will demonstrate this clearly. Suppose you wish to add the total number of pounds of books in a shipment by combining the 10 pound weight of the books ordered with 3 pounds of stationery items and then multiplying the total weight by the per-pound shipping rate of 25 cents. You would not get the correct result if you entered 10+3*.25, since 1-2-3 would perform the multiplication first and calculate 10 plus 0.75, totalling 10.75 rather than the 3.25 you expected. To make 1-2-3 perform the

When more than one operator is used in a formula, it is important to know which operation 1-2-3 will perform first. This table shows the priority order for each operation that 1-2-3 can perform. If more than one operator has the same priority, they will be evaluated from left to right.

Priority	Operator	Operation Performed
8	(	Parentheses for grouping
7	ˆ	Exponentiation
6	+−	Positive and negative indicators
5	/*	Division and multiplication
4	+−	Addition and subtraction
3	=<> < > <= >=	Logical operators
2	#NOT#	Complex not indicator
1	#AND# #OR# &	Complex and, complex or, and the string operator

TABLE 2.1 Operation priorities

calculation your way, you need to enter the data as (10+3)*.25.
1-2-3 will evaluate the expression within the parentheses first and
carry out the multiplication second, resulting in the desired answer
of 3.25.

Let's look at another salary model to demonstrate the importance of the priority of operations and how you can control it with
parentheses. This model will project a single employee's salary
based upon his or her current salary, the increase percent you
choose to give the employee, and the month of the increase. Since a
lengthy formula is required, you will perform only the computation
for one employee. However, you will want to save it and add
additional employees once you have learned how to copy entries
from one cell to another.

To enter the data for the salary computation model, follow
these steps:

1. Type the following entries in the worksheet cells specified:

A2:	**Name**
B1:	**'1987**
B2:	**Salary**
C1:	**Increase**
C2:	**Month**
D1:	**Increase**
D2:	**Percent**
E1:	**'1988**
E2:	**Salary**

This completes the entry of the column labels and produces
these results:

```
E2: 'Salary                                                    READY

        A         B         C         D         E         F         G         H
1                 1987      Increase  Increase  1988
2       Name      Salary    Month     Percent   Salary
3
```

2. Type **J. Brown** in A3 and press RETURN.

3. Move the cell pointer to B3 and type **35900**.
   To look at the effect of giving the increase in month 5, you would need to enter a new number in C3. Try this now:

4. Type **5** in C3 and press RETURN.

5. Type **.06** in D3 and press RETURN. This latest entry represents the amount of the increase.

The last step is the most complicated: The formula must compute the current monthly salary and multiply it by the number of months that the individual will continue to receive this salary. The result of this first computation must then be added to the figure computed for the amount paid at the new salary level. The total dollars paid at the new salary level are computed by multiplying the current monthly salary by 100 percent plus the increase percentage by the number of months that the individual will receive the increased salary amount. Predictably, after such a lengthy explanation, the formula is quite long when it is recorded in the worksheet cell. This formula follows, along with an explanation of each of the component parts beneath it.

E3: ((B3/12)*(C3-1))+((B3/12)*(1+D3)*(12-(C3-1)))

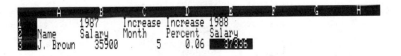

(B3/12)	Represents the annual salary divided by 12 to compute the monthly salary.
(C3–1)	The month of the increase minus one or the number of months the employee receives his or her current salary.
(1+D3)	Indicates that the employee will receive 100 percent of his or her existing salary, plus an increase represented by a decimal fraction in D3.

12–(C3–1)   The number of months that the employee receives the increased salary amount.

6. Combining all these, enter the following formula in E3: ((B3/12)*(C3-1))+((B3/12)*(1+D3)*(12-(C3-1)))

A few extra parentheses have been added to the formula expression to make it more readable. For example, the result would be the same if the parentheses were omitted from around (B3/12) since multiplication and division have the same priority. Using an extra pair of parentheses does not change the value of the expression as long as they do not change the order of operations. Feel free to add parentheses in this manner whenever they improve the readability of the formula without altering it. In this example, you have entered the data for only one employee, but this model could be expanded easily. After learning how to copy formulas, you can use it to add additional employees; but for now, save a copy of it to disk by entering /FSSALARY and pressing RETURN.

SUMMARY

In this chapter you have learned to add the power of formulas to your models. Whether you choose arithmetic, logic, or string formulas, they can let you change your mind about assumptions and other entries and still update your worksheets easily.

In Chapter 3 you will be introduced to 1-2-3's menu structure and learn techniques for customizing how your data is displayed. You can use these formatting features to add a professional appearance to your worksheet without altering the stored values for any of your worksheet entries.

3

CHANGING
THE WORKSHEET
APPEARANCE

Up until this point, you have accepted 1-2-3's choices for how to present your entries. You have used the package's default for the format in which the data has been displayed. It is great to have this default available; it lets you build a model that produces completely accurate results without having to concern yourself with how your entries should be displayed. But it is also great to know that 1-2-3 provides a set of powerful formatting options and other commands that let you change the default settings affecting the display of your entries. There are commands that let you select a new display format for all the values on the worksheet, or change the format for the value entries in a small section of the worksheet. Other 1-2-3 commands allow you to affect the alignment of labels, either before or after you enter them. Still other commands let you change the number of characters that can be displayed in a column, or hide certain columns from view. In this chapter, you will look at examples using each of these techniques. You will find that each of these 1-2-3 commands are easy to use and provide significant improvements in the appearance of your worksheet models. First, let's address how you access these commands, since they can be accessed only when 1-2-3's menu is on the screen.

1-2-3's MENU

1-2-3's menu system is designed to make 1-2-3's commands easy to access and remember. Only one keystroke is needed to access the menu system, and Lotus has chosen words that represent their function in building the menu. Each menu also includes an on-screen description for each menu choice. This HELP facility will make it easier for you to select the correct command as you are learning the package.

Activating the Menu

1-2-3's menu is activated by pressing the slash key (/) from READY mode. This key is located on the lower right side of your keyboard near the shift key. If the mode indicator currently reads WAIT, POINT, ERROR, or something other than READY, it means that 1-2-3 will not be ready to accept your request. If you type a slash when 1-2-3 is not ready to respond, the menu will not appear onscreen. Instead, 1-2-3 will make a beeping noise to let you know that it cannot process your request to view the main menu selections. You must take an action to return the indicator to READY before entering the slash (/). This action may be completing the entry you have already started, waiting for 1-2-3 to finish its current task, or pressing ESC to acknowledge that you saw an error message.

The Menu Structure

You will want to examine the menu structure that 1-2-3 presents. Type / to activate the menu and produce this display:

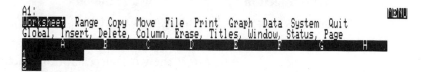

Notice that the mode indicator also changes to MENU (it will remain this way as long as one of 1-2-3's menus is displayed on the screen). The second and third lines in the control panel are devoted to the menu display. The topmost line shows the various menu choices; the line beneath it provides an explanation of the types of tasks performable by the currently highlighted selection in the top row. Currently, 1-2-3's main menu is on the screen. It is called the *main menu* because all selections must start at this point. By selecting one of the options in this display, you often are shown a submenu of choices. These allow you to refine your choice. Most of the main menu entries provide many options. You may be given as many as six levels of menus to select from before you get to your final choice. You need not be concerned with the complexity of the menus, however. The options are organized logically; it is easy to decide which path to select at any point.

The third line of the control panel describes each of the menu choices onscreen. Its purpose is to help guide you in making a selection. And if you make an inappropriate choice, there is an easy way to retreat and to start fresh down the path to the exact command you are seeking. Again, do not be discouraged by the complexity; you will not need to learn all the menu commands. You can accomplish 90 percent of your work using only a small percentage of the total menu. The other commands are there to provide sophisticated options for 1-2-3's power users.

Before you examine any one particular menu choice in further detail, take a quick look at each of the main menu selections to get an overview of the types of features each of them provides. Each main menu choice and the category of tasks it performs is listed below:

Menu Selection	Type of Task Handled
WORKSHEET	Think of the Worksheet menu anytime you wish to make a change that will affect the worksheet. Options include globally setting the format of value entries in the worksheet cells, inserting and deleting worksheet rows or columns, and erasing the entire worksheet.
RANGE	Think of the Range menu when the changes you wish to make are less extensive and will affect only a section of the worksheet. Options in the Range section include formatting a section of the worksheet, assigning a name to a group of worksheet cells, and erasing a section of the worksheet.
COPY	Use the Copy selection whenever you wish to duplicate the information in one group of worksheet cells into another group of cells. With this menu choice you do not have to select from additional submenus. You need only specify which cells you need to copy and where you want them copied to.
MOVE	Move is similar to Copy but it relocates data rather than copying it. Choose Move whenever this is the task you wish to perform. As with Copy, Move requires you to respond to its prompts rather than to select from additional submenus.

FILE

Consider selecting File whenever you wish to perform tasks that relate to saving or retrieving data stored on the disk. Options include saving a file, retrieving a file, and listing the directory of the current disk drive.

PRINT

Use the Print selection whenever you wish to obtain a hard copy of the worksheet that is currently in memory.

GRAPH

Graph is the option to select when you wish to create a graphic representation of data stored on the worksheet. Some of the options include defining the type of graph you wish to create, defining the data to be shown on the graph, and viewing the graph that is currently defined.

DATA

The Data commands are a special category that provide data-management features along with some special arithmetic features. The two most frequently used options under Data are the Sort option, which allows you to resequence your data, and the Query option, which allows you to locate and extract specific information from your model.

SYSTEM

The System option was added to Release 2 to give users access to the basic DOS commands without having to exit to 1-2-3.

QUIT

Quit exits 1-2-3 without saving the worksheet currently in memory. Use this selection only when you have completed your 1-2-3 session and have already saved your work.

Each of these main menu selections will be discussed in more detail as you proceed through this book. Next, you will look at how you can select the options from 1-2-3's menus.

Making Selections

You can select an option in any menu that is displayed by typing the first letter of the menu selection, using either upper or lower case. In other words, to select the first option, Worksheet, you can type a w or a W. If you type a letter that is not used on the menu, 1-2-3 will beep at you and will not respond until you enter a valid menu selection. A second way to make your selection is to use the RIGHT or LEFT ARROW key and move the highlighted bar (cursor) to the menu item you want and then press RETURN. This latter approach is preferred while you are learning the menu, since it causes 1-2-3 to display a description of the command you are about to choose in the third line of the control panel. If after reading this description, you decide it is not the correct selection, you can continue to move to new selections until the desired description is displayed. No action will be taken until you activate a menu choice by pressing RETURN.

Sometimes just pointing to a menu selection will cause you to change your mind. In that case, move the cursor to the Quit selection. The description will tell you to use it to end your current 1-2-3 session. Since you do not want to end the current session, reading this description should convince you not to select Quit.

Try a few selections so you can see how the process works.

1. Type / to activate the menu.

2. Select Worksheet by typing a **W** or by pressing RETURN, since the cursor is already positioned on that selection.

This is the menu that will appear:

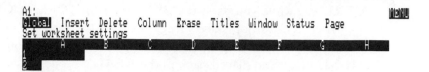

This menu shows all the options you have for affecting the work-sheet. Press RETURN to select Global from the submenu that is presented. When you select Global, a third-level menu is presented, which should match the following:

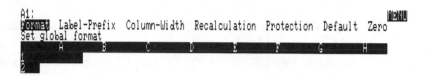

Since you are just examining the menu structure, do not make any additional selections at this time. Instead, examine the methods for backing out of menu selections to return to the previous menu and eventually to the READY mode. This is useful when you accidentally make an incorrect menu selection and want to back out of it to make a new choice.

The ESC key is used to back out of one level of menu selection. Try this key to see how it works.

1. Press ESC once. The menu of worksheet selections returns to the screen.

2. Press ESC again. The main menu appears with this second press.

3. Press ESC a third time.

The READY mode indicator appears. If you had made four menu selections you would have had to press ESC four times to return to READY mode. An easier way to return to READY mode is to press the CTRL-BREAK key combination. That is, hold down the

CTRL key while you press the BREAK or SCROLL LOCK key, and then release both keys. Regardless of the number of menu selections you have made, you will immediately be taken out of the MENU mode and placed back in the READY mode.

CHANGING THE FORMAT OF VALUE ENTRIES

The default format that 1-2-3 uses for all value entries is called the *general format*. It is somewhat unusual in that it does not provide consistent formats for all entries. The display it provides is affected by the size of the number that is entered in the cell. Some numbers display as they are entered, while others are altered to have a leading zero added or so they can be rounded to a number of decimal digits which will fit in the cell width you have selected. The general format also suppresses trailing zeros after the decimal point; if you enter them they will not appear in the display. Very large and very small numbers are displayed in *scientific format*, which means that exponential notation will be used. *Exponential notation* is a method of representing a number in abbreviated form by including the power of 10 that the number should be raised to. If 100550000 is entered in a cell when the general format is in effect, 1-2-3 will use scientific notation to display it as 1.0E+8. General format handles a wide variety of formats but often results in a display whose results have varying numbers of decimal places. This makes it less than desirable for many business models because of the inconsistencies in the display of decimal numbers. You encountered the inconsistencies in its decimal display with the investment model in Chapter 2. However, this inconsistency does not mean that this format is useless. It provides an ideal format in many situations. General format is useful when you want to minimize the space used to display very large or very small numbers. Scientific notation ensures that these numbers will be shown in a minimum of space and that the conversion will be handled for you automatically if required. It simply is not the display to use when you need to control the number of decimal places shown.

Formatting Options

There are many alternatives to the general display format. 1-2-3
provides a wide range of formatting options that allow you to
display your data with everything from dollar signs and commas to
percent symbols. You can even specify the number of decimal places
for most of the formats. The specific formats supported by 1-2-3 and
their effect on worksheet entries are shown in Table 3.1. You will
apply some of these formats to models you have already created.

Format	Cell Entry	Display
Fixed 2 decimal places	5678 −123.45	5678.00 −123.45
Scientific 2 decimal places	5678 −123.45	5.68E+03 −1.23E+02
Currency 2 decimal places	5678 −123.45	$5,678.00 ($123.45)
, (Comma) 2 decimal places	5678 −123.45	5,678 (123.45)
General	5678 −123.45	5678 −123.45
+/−	4 3 0	++++ −−−
Percent	5 .1	500% 10%
Date (D1)	31679	24-Sep-86
Time (T1)	.5	12:00:00 PM
Text	+A2*A3	+A2*A3

Table 3.1   1-2-3's format options

Scope of the Formatting Change

You can also choose how extensive an impact you want a particular format command to have by formatting the entire worksheet or a range of cells in one area of the worksheet. First you will examine the procedure for changing the default format for a section of the worksheet.

CHANGING THE FORMAT FOR A RANGE OF CELLS   Everything you have accomplished with 1-2-3 so far has focused on individual cells. However, 1-2-3 also allows you to work with any contiguous rectangle of cells, called a *Range*, to accomplish tasks such as formatting. Figure 3.1 shows groups of cells that are valid ranges as well as some groups that are not. The groups on the left are

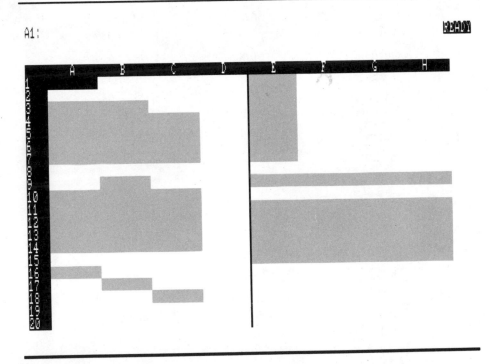

FIGURE 3.1   Valid and invalid ranges

invalid ranges because they do not form one contiguous rectangle. The cell groups on the right are valid ranges because they form a contiguous group. As long as this rule is met, the range can be as large as you wish or as small as one cell.

You can use several methods to specify cell ranges. You can type them in like a cell address or highlight them with the cell pointer. Any two diagonally opposite corners can be used to specify the range as long as they are separated by one or more decimal points. For example, the range of cells shown in the following illustration can be specified as B4.C8, B4..C8, B8.C4, B8..C4, C8.B4, C8..B4, C4.B8, or C4..B8.

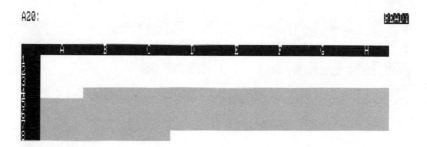

The most common way to specify a range is to use the upper left-most cell first and the lower rightmost cell last. Also, since 1-2-3 will supply the second period, you might as well save a keystroke and just type B4.C8. If you plan to specify a range by highlighting it, you can save yourself some time by positioning the cell pointer in the upper leftmost corner of the range before beginning.

Retrieve your investment model by typing /**FRREALEST** and pressing RETURN. The model should match the one shown in Figure 3.2. To try out the range specifications as you add some formats to this model, follow these steps:

1. Move the cell pointer to D13, the upper leftmost cell in the range you will format.

2. Type / to activate the menu.

3. Use the RIGHT ARROW key, and move the cursor to Range, and press RETURN.

A1:   READY

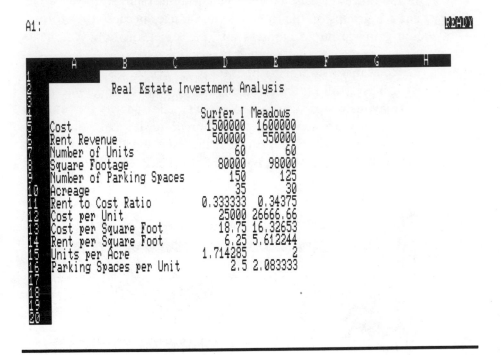

FIGURE 3.2   Investment model

4. Press RETURN to select the Format option that is currently highlighted.

5. Select the Fixed format option by typing **F**.

6. Press RETURN to select the default of two decimal places.

7. Use the RIGHT ARROW and the DOWN ARROW to position the cell pointer in E16, highlighting the entire area to be formatted as shown in Figure 3.3. Then press RETURN.
   The format should immediately change to two decimal places for each of the entries in this section and match the display in Figure 3.4. The other range that needs to be formatted is D11..E11. This time you will not position the

cell pointer first so that you can experience the extra steps involved.

8. Enter / Range Format Fixed and press RETURN.
   This command sequence will accept the default of two decimal places. You cannot expand the range at this point, as it has the incorrect beginning location. You must first free the beginning of the range.

9. Press ESC. Now you will find that you can move the cell pointer to D11 without altering a range specification.

10. Type . (period). This will anchor the beginning of the range again.

11. Expand the range by moving the cell pointer to E11.

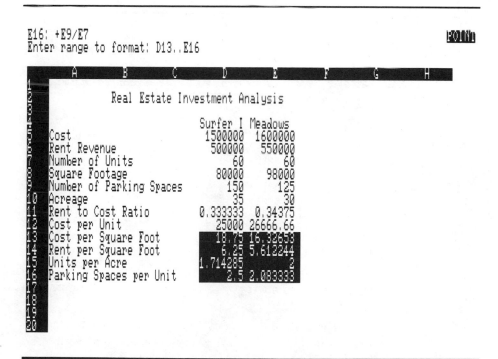

FIGURE 3.3   Area to be formatted highlighted

If you move the cell pointer to any cell that has been formatted with a range command, you can tell the format that has been assigned to the cell, even if it is empty. This information is displayed as a single character representing the format type in the control panel. Table 3.2 presents examples of some of the commonly used format abbreviations. These format specifications are enclosed within parentheses and are placed immediately after the cell address, as in the following:

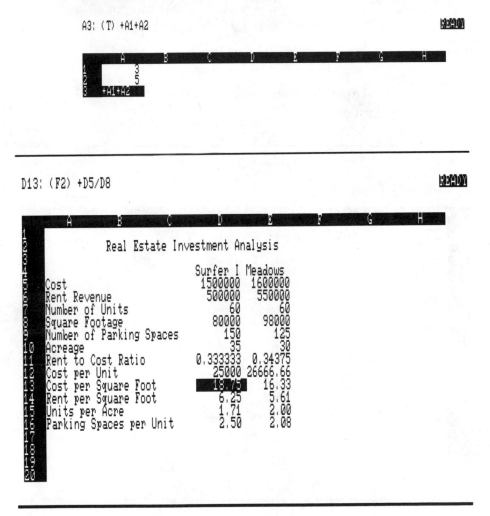

FIGURE 3.4   Changing the format to two decimal places

Abbreviation	Format in Effect
(P2)	Percent with two decimal places
(T)	Text to display formulas as they are entered
(G)	General
(C0)	Currency with zero decimal places
(,2)	Comma with two decimal places
(D1)	Date format 1
(T1)	Time format 1

TABLE 3.2   Examples of format abbreviations

For formats that allow you to specify the number of decimal places, a numeric digit follows, as in this illustration:

The model still is not presented in the optimal format. The numbers in the cells at the top would be easier to read if they had commas inserted after the thousands position. There are two formats that will add these commas. One is refered to as the *Comma format* (,); the other is the *Currency format*. The only difference between the two is whether or not a dollar sign is inserted at the front of the entry. Either of these two formats could be added with another range request but since the cells that you wish to change include all the remaining value entries on the worksheet, you will use the Global formatting option covered in the next section.

MAKING A GLOBAL FORMAT CHANGE   When you wish to alter the format of the entire worksheet or even most of it, a *Global format* change is the ideal solution. A Global format change alters

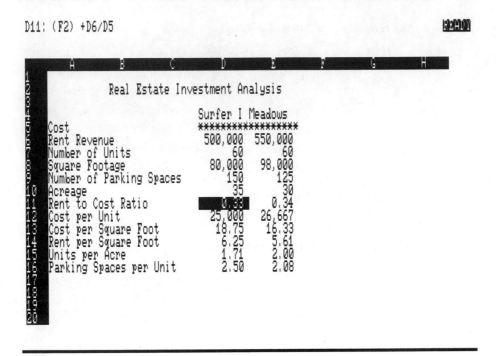

FIGURE 3.5   Asterisks indicating column not wide enough

the default format for every cell on the worksheet including both cells with entries and cells that are currently empty. As long as the worksheet cells have not had their formats altered with Range format commands, the new default format will take effect. For an empty cell, this format will be used as soon as a value entry is placed in the cell. The Global formatting option is especially useful when most of the worksheet is formatted with the same option. You can choose a Global format that meets the requirement for most of the cells, and then go back and format the exceptions with a range format command.

To alter the Global format for the model, follow these steps:

1. Type / to activate the menu.

2. Press RETURN to select the Worksheet option.

3. Press RETURN to select the Global option.

4. Press RETURN to select the Format option.

5. Type **,** to select the Comma format.

6. Type **0** to specify zero decimal places, and press RETURN to finalize this entry. The display will change to match the one in Figure 3.5. Everything looks fine except that the two cost figures are now displayed as asterisks. The values that were stored there are still in memory and are replaced only by the asterisks to indicate that once the new formats are used, the numeric values in these cells require more space than the column width allows. You can correct this quickly by increasing the Global width. This command will be explained later in the chapter; for now, the command will be entered as shown.

7. Enter **/WGC10** and press RETURN. The columns will be

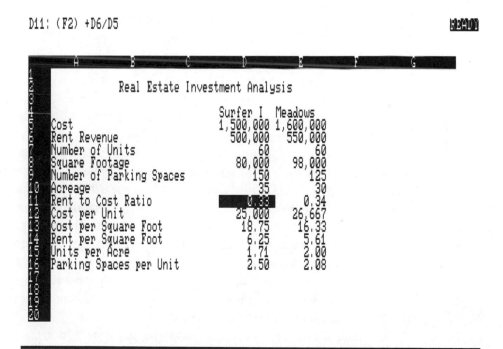

FIGURE 3.6 Column widened to 10

widened to 10 characters, producing the display shown in Figure 3.6. The columns are now wide enough to display the cost figures with commas.

CHECKING A FORMAT SETTING   If you move the cell pointer to one of the cells that has been formatted with the Global option, you notice that there is no format code in the control panel. Only Range formats will display in the control panel. To check the Global format setting, you have to check the Worksheet status. The Worksheet status screen provides information on all the worksheet default settings. Check it now by following these directions:

1. Enter **/W** to select the Worksheet menu.

2. Type **S** to display the status.
   Your screen will look like the one in Figure 3.7. Notice that the indicator has changed to STAT. Don't be concerned if your screen is slightly different. The status screen for Release 1A screen is different and the amounts of conventional and standard memory installed vary from system to system. If you look at the format you should see (,0).

3. Press ESC or RETURN. This last step will return you to the Worksheet and READY mode.

You can use the Format option to look at the formulas within worksheet cells by using a display format of Text. This means that you can review all the formulas at once rather than having to move the cell pointer to each cell and view the control panel to see the formula. The Text format displays formulas in the cells where you entered them rather than showing the result of the formulas within the cell. To make this change, you must use both the Global format change and a Range format change. The Global change will alter the default setting for all worksheet cells; however, since Range formats take priority, some of the cells will ignore the default. This means that you must reset the format of these cells with the Range format command before the cells use the default setting.

Before beginning, replace the copy of the investment model on disk with the formatted copy now in memory.

STAT

```
Available Memory:
   Conventional...... 291962 of 292848 Bytes (99%)
   Expanded......... (None)

Math Co-processor: (None)

Recalculation:
   Method.......... Automatic
   Order........... Natural
   Iterations...... 1

Circular Reference: (None)

Cell Display:
   Format.......... (,0)
   Label-Prefix..... '
   Column-Width..... 10
   Zero Suppression. Off

Global Protection: Off
```

FIGURE 3.7   Status screen

1. Type /**FS** and press RETURN.

2. A prompt message will display. Type **R** in response.
   This will replace the file on disk. It is important to save the file at this time, because the reformatting process used to view the formulas will eliminate the Fixed and Comma formats that you wish to retain permanently. Since you are becoming familiar with menu selections, from now on you will be given only the entries that you should make for each exercise. Directions will no longer tell you to point to a selection and press RETURN or type the first letter of the selection. You can use whatever method you prefer, as long as you enter the menu selections specified.

3. Enter /**Worksheet Global Format** to select the Global

format menu or press RETURN as each menu is presented until you are looking at the menu that provides format options.

4. Select **Text** as the format option.

5. Move the cell pointer to D11 then enter **/Range Format Reset** to reset the Range format to the Global default.

6. Move the cell pointer to E16 and press RETURN to view a display of the formulas like the one in Figure 3.8.

Since the formulas in this particular model are short, you can view the complete formula within each cell. If the formulas were longer, the columns would need to be widened to see the entire formula. In the next section you will learn all about tailoring the column width to meet your particular needs.

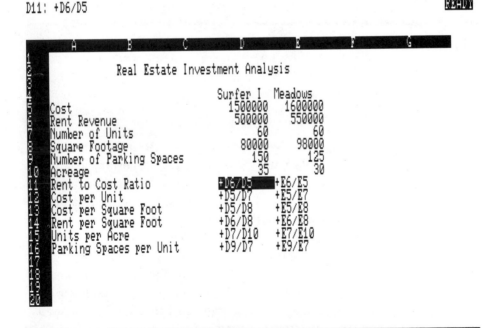

D11: +D6/D5   READY

```
              A         B         C         D         E         F         G
 1
 2                      Real Estate Investment Analysis
 3
 4                                          Surfer I  Meadows
 5   Cost                                   1500000   1600000
 6   Rent Revenue                            500000    550000
 7   Number of Units                             60        60
 8   Square Footage                           80000     98000
 9   Number of Parking Spaces                   150       125
10   Acreage                                     35        30
11   Rent to Cost Ratio                      +D6/D5    +E6/E5
12   Cost per Unit                           +D5/D7    +E5/E7
13   Cost per Square Foot                    +D5/D8    +E5/E8
14   Rent per Square Foot                    +D6/D8    +E6/E8
15   Units per Acre                          +D7/D10   +E7/E10
16   Parking Spaces per Unit                 +D9/D7    +E9/E7
17
18
19
20
```

FIGURE 3.8   Formula display

CHANGING WORKSHEET COLUMNS

You have examined some of the changes you can make to the appearance of individual entries in cells. There are also several commands that allow you to make changes to one or more columns at one time. 1-2-3 provides options that let you determine the width you wish to use for columns. With the addition of Release 2, you can also hide or display columns on your worksheet.

Altering Column Widths

The default width of columns is nine when you begin a new 1-2-3 worksheet. This is adequate for values displayed with the general format; often, however, it is not wide enough when you want to display numbers with commas, dollar signs, and decimal places or some labels and most of the formulas you wish to display with the text format option. At other times, the opposite might be true. Even though you may have a column that never contains more than one character, the full width of nine is always reserved for the column. If you could make some columns narrower, you might be able to view a few more columns on the screen. 1-2-3 will let you handle both types of changes by altering the column width. In fact, it even lets you choose whether to change the width of all the columns at once or to alter the width of a single column.

CHANGING THE WIDTH OF ONE COLUMN   The ability to alter the width of individual columns lets you tailor your display to meet your exact needs. This is the preferred approach when you only have a few columns to change, since columns are neither wider nor narrower than the requirements of your data. Any change you make for a single column will take precedence over the Global default column width setting that you establish. This means that you can make both types of changes to your worksheet.

The investment model created in Chapter 2 provides an opportunity for changing a column width. Follow these steps for making the changes:

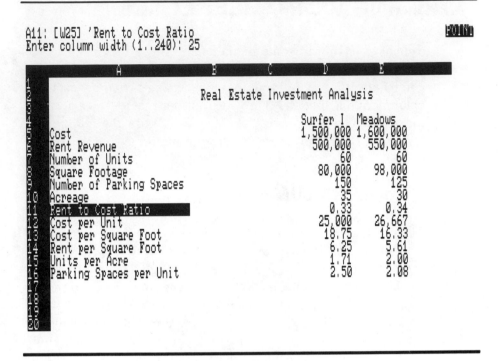

A11: [W25] 'Rent to Cost Ratio
Enter column width (1..240): 25

```
                     A              B       C        D        E
1                                 Real Estate Investment Analysis
2
3
4                                           Surfer I  Meadows
5  Cost                                     1,500,000 1,600,000
6  Rent Revenue                               500,000   550,000
7  Number of Units                                 60        60
8  Square Footage                              80,000    98,000
9  Number of Parking Spaces                       150       125
10 Acreage                                         35        30
11 Rent to Cost Ratio                            0.33      0.34
12 Cost per Unit                               25,000    26,667
13 Cost per Square Foot                         18.75     16.33
14 Rent per Square Foot                          6.25      5.61
15 Units per Acre                                1.71      2.00
16 Parking Spaces per Unit                       2.50      2.08
17
18
19
20
```

FIGURE 3.9   Widening columns

1. Enter **/File Retrieve REALEST** and press RETURN.

2. Move the cell pointer to column A.
   Notice the list of long label entries in that column. They extend beyond the boundaries of column A and borrow space from column B. You can widen column A so that the entries will completely fit within the column.

3. Enter **/Worksheet Column Set-Width**.

4. Press the RIGHT ARROW key until column A is wide enough to display the entire entry, as in Figure 3.9.

5. Press RETURN.

This finalizes the width change. Column A will remain at a width of 25 unless you make another change. Adjusting the width of this column makes it clear where the data is entered. Adjusting the column width can also be important in Release 2 if you ever print a copy of the worksheet to a disk file. Release 2 will write data only to the disk that fits within the column where it was entered.

CHANGING THE WIDTH OF ALL THE COLUMNS For certain models, all the column widths need to be altered. If you have a model like the following one and wish to narrow the column width, it is tedious to make this change a column at a time.

```
A1:                                                            READY

          A         B       C       D       E       F       G       H
1                           Employees Hired By Month
2
3                 Jan      Feb     Mar     Apr     May     Jne     Jly
4  Region 1         1        7       7       6       0       3       8
5  Region 2         4        3       8       6       4       6       9
6  Region 3         5        0       5       6       8       5       6
7  Region 4         6        7       4       6       4       2       0
8  Region 5         2        3       0       9       0       6       8
9  Region 6         9        3       7       0       4       4       4
10 Region 7         4        5       2       8       8       8       5
11 Region 8         5        3       3       7       6       2       2
12 Region 9         3        8       8       6       8       9       2
```

Since each entry under the "Month" heading is so small, it is better to narrow the columns and view all the months on the screen at once. The / Worksheet Global Column-Width command can make this change for you easily: Only one command is required to change all the columns. After entering the command sequence you can type the new width or use the LEFT ARROW key to make the width narrower by one each time you press it. When you have adjusted the column to the desired width, you need only press RETURN to finalize the current selection. These entries will alter the preceding report so that all the months can be viewed. If you wish, you can make the entries in the worksheet shown above and follow these steps to make this change:

1. Enter **/Worksheet Global Column-Width**.
2. Enter **5** for the width. Press RETURN.

This produces the following results:

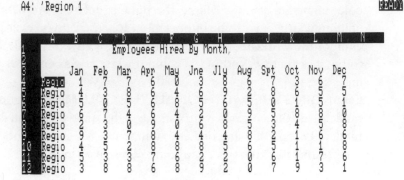

A4: 'Region 1

The only problem with this display is that column A has also become smaller and will not display the region numbers. To fix this problem, the following steps are required:

1. Move the cell pointer to column A.

2. Enter **/Worksheet Column Set-Width 9** and press RETURN.

This change to an individual column width fixes the problem and produces the following result:

A4: [W9] 'Region 1

A Worksheet Global Column-Width change can also be used to make all the columns wider. This is often useful when you are displaying the model as text to view its formulas. If all the formulas are approximately the same length, you may want to widen the column width to accommodate the longest formula entry.

If you want to check the default column width, you cannot point to one of the cells and see it displayed. The width is displayed in the control panel only when the change has been made to a single column with the Worksheet Column Set-Width command. You must give the same status instruction used to check the format by entering **/Worksheet Status**. Remember that you can always change this default; or, if you prefer, you can use the Worksheet Column command to alter the width of one column.

Inserting and Deleting Columns

No matter how thoroughly you plan your worksheet applications, sometimes you need to make substantial changes to a worksheet model. You might need to add an employee to a model, to delete accounts that are no longer used, or to add some blank space to make the worksheet more readable. 1-2-3 will accommodate each of these needs by means of commands that let you insert or delete blank rows or columns in the worksheet.

INSERTING ROWS AND COLUMNS   You can insert blank rows and columns at any location in the worksheet you choose. Before beginning your request, tell 1-2-3 where to place the blank rows or columns by positioning the cell pointer. If you will be adding rows to the worksheet, they will be placed above the cell pointer's location. If you will be adding columns, they will be placed to the left of the cell pointer. Once you make the request to insert rows or columns, you cannot alter the site where they will be placed. If you realize that you forgot to position the cell pointer, your only option is to press ESC to return to READY mode, move the cell pointer, and start the process over again.

When 1-2-3 inserts rows into a worksheet, the cell addresses of the data below this location are changed. It is as though 1-2-3 pushes the data down on the worksheet to make room for the new blank rows. Under normal circumstances, 1-2-3 automatically adjusts all

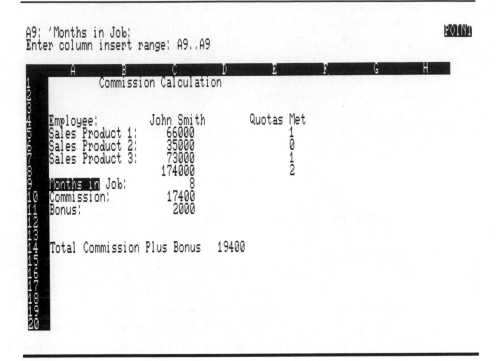

FIGURE 3.10   Inserting a column

the formulas that reference this data. The same is true for data that resides to the right of the location where columns were inserted.

The insert command is invoked by entering /**Worksheet Insert Rows**. 1-2-3 prompts you for the number of rows to insert but does not use a straightforward question such as, "How many rows would you like to add?" Instead, it asks for the range where you want the insertion to occur. It does not use this range to control the placement of the insertion, only to control the number of rows to insert. If you specify a range that includes three rows, three rows will be inserted. If you specify a range of one row, only one row will be inserted. Seeing this in action will clarify the way it works.

Let's add a few blank rows to the commission calculations you created in Chapter 2. Follow these steps to complete the changes:

1. Enter **/File Retrieve.**

2. Type **COMM** and press RETURN.

3. Move the cell pointer to C8.
   Notice that the formula that totals sales is entered as
   +C5+C6+C7. Look at this formula again after inserting a
   column, and notice how 1-2-3 has automatically adjusted it
   for you.

4. Position the cell pointer in A9 (anywhere in column A
   would work just as well).

5. Enter **/Worksheet Insert Column** to produce the display in
   Figure 3.10.

6. Press RETURN to restrict the insertion to one column.
   The results are shown in Figure 3.11. If you move the cell

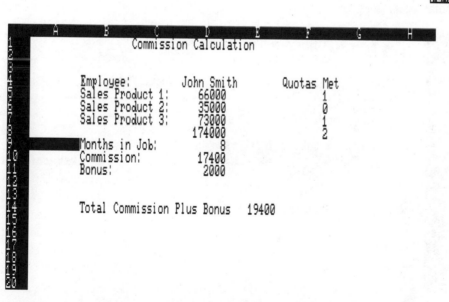

FIGURE 3.11   Result of insertion

pointer to D8, you will find that the formula has been changed and the formula for summing sales now reads +D5+D6+D7 to reflect its new location in the worksheet.

Inserting rows is just as easy. Let's insert two blank rows above the section that begins with Months in Job, to separate the sections of the model.

1. Move the cell pointer to D9. Any place in row 9 would work just as well.

2. Enter /**Worksheet Insert Rows** and expand the range to include two rows as shown in Figure 3.12.

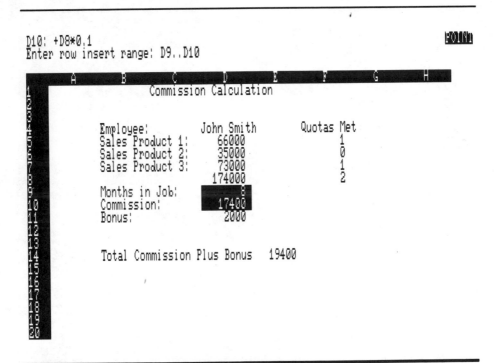

FIGURE 3.12 Inserting rows

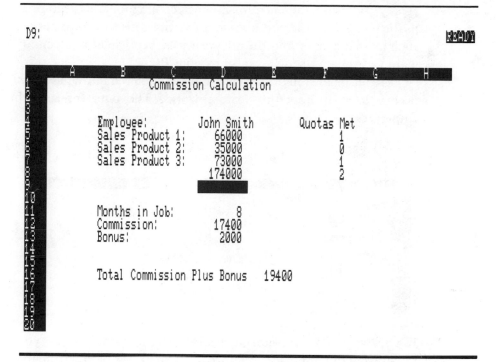

FIGURE 3.13   Result of adding two rows

3. Press RETURN.

     You will find that two blank rows have been added, pro-
     ducing the results shown in Figure 3.13. Notice that the
     addition of some blank space on the side and between the
     two sections makes the model more appealing.

4. Save these changes by entering /**File Save**, pressing RE-
     TURN, and typing **R**.

Hiding and Displaying Columns

Release 2 adds a new feature to 1-2-3, which allows you to conceal
columns from view on the display screen temporarily. The data in
these columns is not altered in any way and can be displayed again

at any time with the entry of another command. This feature is particularly useful if you are working with sensitive information such as salary data and do not wish it to be visible onscreen, in plain view of anyone who walks by your PC.

Use an expansion of the salary data you entered in Chapter 2 to take a look at how this feature works. The data for several employees follows:

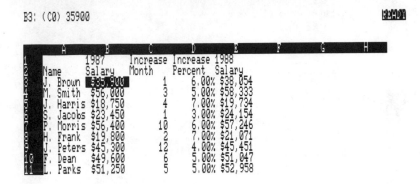

If you wanted to correct misspellings in the name entries, you might want to temporarily remove the salary information from the screen. This can be accomplished by following these steps:

1. Enter **/File Retrieve**.

2. Type **SALARY** and press RETURN.

3. Enter **/Worksheet Column Hide**.

4. Point to column B, and press RETURN, as follows:

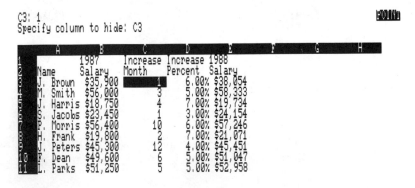

Your model will not match this exactly as you have only one row of salary entries. You will be able to see the column disappear from view.

5. Enter /**Worksheet Column Hide**.

6. Move to column E.

7. Press RETURN. The result is a worksheet with both salary columns temporarily hidden, like this:

A3: 'J. Brown

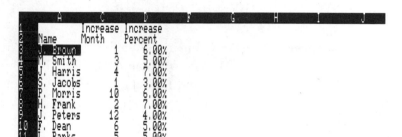

To bring these columns back into view, another set of menu entries is required.

8. Enter /**Worksheet Column Display**.

9. Point to column B and press RETURN.
   Notice that all the hidden columns are marked as an asterisk. Another command sequence is required to restore the second salary column.

10. Enter /**Worksheet Column Display**, point to column E, and press RETURN.

CHANGING THE ALIGNMENT OF LABEL ENTRIES

You already learned one method for changing the alignment for a label in Chapter 2, when you entered a few of the labels by beginning them with a ″ symbol. This method works; but if you have a large number of labels to enter, it is time consuming. It also requires you to edit the entries and replace the label indicator at the front of the label if you want to change its alignment. Fortunately, there are several alternatives that can be real time savers. One option allows you to change the alignment of labels that are currently on the worksheet; the other changes the default for the current worksheet so that any new labels you enter will use the new alignment setting.

Changing Previously Entered Labels

Two methods for altering the alignment of labels are already recorded on the worksheet. You can use the EDIT method, or you can use a Range command that alters the label alignment of the rows in the range. The EDIT method follows these simple rules for editing the entry in any cell.

1. Move the cell pointer to the cell whose alignment you wish to change.

2. Press **F2** (EDIT), followed by HOME, to move to the front of the entry.

3. Press the DEL key to eliminate this label indicator. Then type the indicator that corresponds to the type of alignment you want to use.

The second method requires less work; many cell indicators can be changed with a single command. In this case, the command is **/Range Label**. When you enter this command, it presents the following menu for your selection:

You can choose the type of alignment you want and specify the range of entries that are affected. The major differences between this approach and a global change is the scope of the change and the fact that the / Range Label command affects only the cells that contain entries. Empty cells do not retain this information. If you subsequently place entries in these empty cells, the entries will be aligned in accordance with the default label prefix. To check this default, enter **/Worksheet Status** to view by-now-quite-familiar display screen.

Look at the effect of altering the alignment of the labels in this example:

1. Move your cell pointer to A1.

2. Type **Jan** then press the RIGHT ARROW key.

3. Type **Feb** then press the RIGHT ARROW .

4. Type **Mar** then press the RIGHT ARROW key.

5. Continue entering month abbreviations across until you place **Aug** in H1.

6. Press the **HOME** key.
   Your display should look like this:

```
A1: 'Jan                                              READY

        A       B       C       D       E       F       G       H
1   Jan     Feb     Mar     Apr     May     June    July    Aug
2
3
```

The labels are currently left aligned in accordance with the default.

7. Move the cell pointer to A1.

8. Enter **/Range Label Right**.

9. Use the RIGHT ARROW key to move to H1 and press RETURN.

Each of the entries in row 1 is now right aligned in its cell, although subsequent entries in these cells would not be affected.

10. Enter /**Worksheet Erase Yes** to erase this example.

Changing Alignment on a Global Basis Before Making Entries

If you change the default label alignment, any new entries you make on the spreadsheet will use this setting. Existing entries will not be affected. This option is especially useful when you wish to enter a series of column headings or other information with a different alignment. You can alter the default alignment without concern for the data already on the worksheet, then make your entries and change the alignment back to its original setting, if you wish.

Let's enter some month names as column headings, using center alignment to see how this might work.

1. Enter /**Worksheet Global Label-Prefix Center**.

2. Move the cell pointer to B2 and type **Jan**, then press the RIGHT ARROW key.

3. Enter **Feb** and press the RIGHT ARROW key.

4. Continue entering the month abbreviations across until you have entered **July** in H2.

Each of your entries will be center aligned in its cell, as follows:

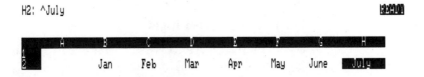

Each entry has a caret symbol at the front of the entry, automatically generated by 1-2-3.

ERASING WORKSHEET DATA

You have learned how to change worksheet entries and completely replace them with other data. However, there are times when you will want to eliminate the entries completely; they may be mistakes or old data that is no longer required. Whatever your reason for wanting to eliminate them, 1-2-3 provides a quick solution. 1-2-3 does not even care what type of entry the cell contains; it erases labels, numbers, and formulas with equal ease. The most common way to eliminate data is to erase a range of cells. This will eliminate all their contents. A second approach is more extensive and thus more dangerous, since it eliminates all the entries on the entire worksheet.

To erase a range of cell entries, the easiest approach is to move the cell pointer to the upper leftmost cell you wish to erase and enter /**Range Erase**. In response to the prompt, move the cell pointer to the lower right corner of the range you wish to erase and then press RETURN. This eliminates not only the cell entry but also any label prefix assigned to the cell with a Range command. Formats assigned with a Range command are retained when the cell contents are erased and will be applied to any new entries placed in the cell.

The following data shows two entries that were made on the worksheet and finalized.

Pressing ESC will not help you eliminate either entry; both have been finalized. To eliminate the x that was entered in error, do the following:

1. Place the cell pointer in B1.

2. Enter /**Range Erase**.

3. Press RETURN to erase the single cell-entry.

A worksheet erase command packs much more destructive capability, since it eliminates everything from the worksheet. It is useful mainly if you make a complete mess and want to erase it. In that case, you can enter **/Worksheet Erase Yes** to effectively remove the entire worksheet from memory and start over with your entries on a blank worksheet.

SUMMARY

In this chapter, you have learned how to access 1-2-3's menus, thereby opening a whole new realm of opportunities for customizing your models to meet your exact needs. You can create a more professional-looking worksheet with the commands for formatting, changing the column width and the changing label alignment. Now that you understand the options that are available, you will want to plan out the worksheet format before you start entering your next model.

WORKING
WITH FILES

New computer users always find the concept of files a little difficult to understand. This is partly because you cannot *see* a file, the way you can see entries that you place on the worksheet. But files are really quite simple to work with. They use concepts that are very similar to those you use every day for storing written documents in your office. The main difference is that computer files are stored on a disk instead of in a drawer. In this chapter you will learn about basic file concepts and explore the basic file commands that 1-2-3 has to offer. You will then learn about Release 2's new features that allow you to temporarily exit 1-2-3 and access the file-handling features of your computer's operating system. There are a few additional differences between Release 1A and Release 2, most of them very subtle and relating to the use of directories or the display of files stored on the disk. If you are using Release 1A, check the special information in the examples that describe some of these differences.

FILE CONCEPTS

Every day you undoubtedly work with a number of different pieces of paper. Periodically, you probably place some of these papers into file folders in a cabinet or desk drawer to make space for new information on your desktop. Then, when you want to review these papers again, you search for them in the cabinet, or you ask your secretary to bring you the file folder you wish to see. Assuming that you have an organized filing system, the papers you want will arrive back on your desk.

Your computer uses very similar procedures to maintain its information. Taking a look at the similarities and differences will help you understand the important role that files can play for you.

Storing Information on Disk

When you store information in your computer, you provide the machine with an organizational challenge similar to the one faced by you or your secretary. In the computer's case, the "desktop" is the memory of the system; and, like your desktop, it has a limited amount of space. How much space it has available in memory will dictate how much information you can place in it at any one time. Part of this space can be used for a program such as 1-2-3; another part can be used to store a worksheet that you are building with the package. Only one worksheet can be on your computer's desktop at any one time; this keeps things organized for you. Just as you use file folders to store papers, so your computer uses disk files to store information. The computer's files are maintained on disk rather than in a cabinet. When you build a model, it will be stored in the computer's "desktop"—its temporary memory. You generally will want to store a copy of this model in memory before you exit 1-2-3 or before you start creating a second model. This storage makes it possible for the computer to recall the first model another time so that you can work on it again.

TEMPORARY NATURE OF MEMORY When working with a computer, you need to save your model before you complete it, as 1-2-3 does not automatically maintain a permanent record of your model. As soon as you turn your system off or exit 1-2-3 (whether deliberately or accidentally), the model is lost from memory. In order to use this model again, you must already have stored a copy of it in a file on your disk. As long as you have done this, you can retrieve a copy of the file from disk and place it in the memory of your computer system again.

DISK MAINTAINS ITS COPY When you are working with data in the form of papers stored in your office files and you retrieve a copy so you can work with it again, the file no longer contains a copy. But storing data in computer disk files works differently. Once you store a copy of a model on disk, it remains there until you take some special action to remove it from the disk. Even when you retrieve a copy of the model to place it in memory again, the original copy is maintained on the disk. This feature offers a tremendous advantage over paper storage methods: If you accidentally destroy the copy in the computer's memory, you can always retrieve another copy of the model from the disk.

Organizing the Disk Data

When you create file folders for your office, you probably have a system — even a rudimentary one — for labeling these files. One rule of your system is probably that no two folders have exactly the same label. If they did, you would have a lot of difficulty finding the papers you need once they were filed. Perhaps your system for labeling file folders is quite organized. It may include color coding or some other scheme that makes it easy to categorize your files.

Storing files on disk also uses a system. Part of this system involves rigid rules you must follow; there is also room for some flexibility, however, so that you can personalize the system to suit your needs. You need not be concerned with the specifics of how the data is stored on disk. Your only concern is the rules that you need to follow when working with these files, especially those rules that center around the names you use for your files and the location of these files when they are stored.

FILENAMES   Before you can store a file on your disk, you must determine what to name it. Since the naming process follows particular, although somewhat flexible, rules, first review the options before considering the mechanics for storing the file.

Each file on a disk must have a unique name. This name will consist of from one to eight characters. You can create a name using the alphabetic characters, numeric digits, and some of the special symbols. Since it can be difficult to remember which symbols are permissible and which are not, it is best to limit your use of special symbols to the _ (underline symbol). This symbol is particularly useful as a separator in a filename. For example, the name 87_Sales might be used to store the sales data for 1987. Be aware that spaces are not allowed in filenames; 87 Sales would not be a valid name.

Although there is no flexibility in the rules already discussed, you can assign the eight allowable characters any way you like. It is best to develop some consistent rules for naming your data, as consistency can help you determine a file's contents when you see the filename later on. If you are storing sales data for a number of years, keeping one year's worth of data in each file, you could use the method already described and create names such as 87_Sales and 88_Sales. You could also use names such as Sales_87 or Sls1987. It really does not matter what pattern you select for your names. What is important is that once you decide on a naming pattern, you apply it consistently for each file that you create. It is not a good strategy to name files 85_Sales, Sales_86, Sls_1987, and Sales88; this pattern is too inconsistent. You can enter filenames in either upper case or lower case letters, or even a combination of the two. Regardless of which type of entry you make, it will be translated into upper case. All filenames are stored in upper case on the disk.

You can also add filename extensions. These are one to three optional characters that you add at the end of a filename. They too can be entered in upper or lower case. They are separated from a filename by a period. For example in 87_Sales.WK1, the filename extension is .WK1. These extensions can be used to categorize files or to provide an extra three characters of description. Some programs automatically add extensions for you. 1-2-3 does this. Table 4.1 shows some of the most common filename extensions that you will encounter and the type of files they are used for.

If you are working with Release 1.0 or 1A, the extension that is added is .WKS. With Release 2.0 and 2.01, the extension that is added is .WK1. 1-2-3 has other filename extensions that it uses when data other than models are stored in files. Later in this book you will learn that you can create a graph on the screen and save a copy of this graphic image on disk. These files are automatically assigned the filename extensions of .PIC. You will also learn that you can print a copy of your model to the printer, or to the disk if you prefer. When you print to the disk, the print output is stored in a file with the extension .PRN. You do not need to memorize this information; 1-2-3 handles it all for you. You need to realize what these extensions are only when you want to work directly with with the data stored on your disk, using commands from your operating system. These

Filename Extension	Use
.WK1	Worksheet files in Release 2
.WKS	Worksheet files in Release 1A
.PIC	1-2-3 graph files
.PRN	Print files
.DRV	1-2-3 driver files
.COM or .EXE	Executable program files
.BAT	DOS batch files

TABLE 4.1   Common filename extensions

filename extensions appear when you use operating-system commands. They could cause confusion if you were not at least aware that 1-2-3 was creating them and using them to distinguish different types of files.

LOCATION OF YOUR DATA   Files can be stored on either hard or floppy disks. The lower-cost hard disks, thanks to today's technology, are a popular storage medium for business computer systems. A floppy disk holds from 360,000 to over 1,440,000 characters, depending on whether you are using the standard double-sided, double-density disks or the new high-density disks. Today's typical hard disk installed in a computer system has a capacity of over 20,000,000 characters of information.

When new files are added to floppy disks, their names are added to a directory on the disk that keeps track of every file on the disk. Although you could use a single directory to maintain a hard disk, such a directory could become so lengthy that it would be difficult to work with. This would be like having a single index to catalog a whole library of reference volumes; it would take a long time to read. More likely, each book in the collection has its own index. Some books may even have chapter outlines that can be referenced for contents. To lessen the burden of the main disk index, you can set up subdirectories for your hard disk. Subdirectories function as a second-level index to group files that are related. You can create these groupings on any basis you like, including for each individual that uses the system, for each application category on the system, or by application program. In all cases, common files such as DOS utilities normally are maintained in the root directory (the main directory on the disk). When subdirectories are added, their names are placed in the root directory; however, the names of the files they contain are kept in the subdirectory, not in the root directory. Subdirectories are organized in a hierarchical structure, as shown in Figure 4.1. Here, the entries in the main directory include two references to subdirectories. These subdirectories must be created through commands in your operating system. Although 1-2-3 can-

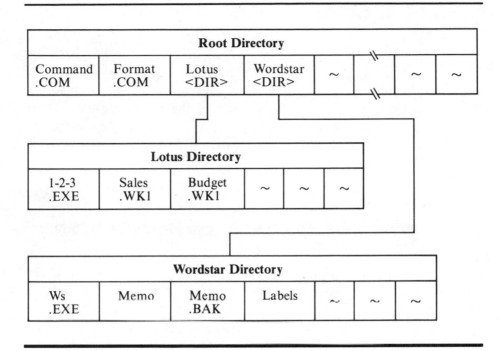

FIGURE 4.1   Directory and subdirectories

not create the directories, it will use whichever directory is current on the hard disk, and it gives you commands that let you activate another directory.

1-2-3 always assumes that you want to work with files on the current or default directory. This means that if you are content to use the current directory, you do not need to specify it when saving your data. However, if you want to use a different disk drive or a directory other than the current default, you must either change the default or enter the file location along with the filename (depending on which release of 1-2-3 you are using). We will look at both of these possibilities in the section on 1-2-3 commands, which follows.

1-2-3 FILE COMMANDS

You can use commands on 1-2-3's menu to handle your file-management tasks. There are menu selections for saving your data into disk files and retrieving copies of these files to place in memory. 1-2-3 has grouped each of the file-management commands under the selection FILE in the main menu. You can bring this menu to your screen by entering /**File**. The following will appear:

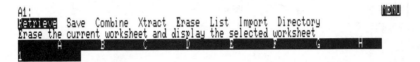

You will have an opportunity to try many of these commands in the following sections.

File Save

1-2-3 does not save your files automatically. It is your responsibility to save the data you enter in memory. It is best to do this periodically; do not wait until you are ending your 1-2-3 session before you save data for the first time. A good guideline is to save every 20 to 30 minutes. If you save with that frequency, you can never lose more than 20 to 30 minutes of your work, even if the power goes off unexpectedly.

SAVING THE FIRST TIME   You use a slightly different procedure to save your data the first time. Since you have never saved the data before, you need to enter a filename to identify your data on the disk. If you are saving onto floppy disks, you also need to ensure that a formatted disk is placed in the current drive. At this point, make a few entries on the current screen and then save the data.

1. Erase memory by entering /**Worksheet Erase Yes**.

2. Move the cell pointer to B2 and type **Qtr1**. Press the RIGHT ARROW key. Type **Qtr2** through **Qtr4** in C2 through E2, as follows:

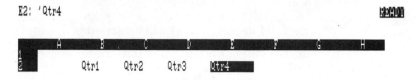

3. Enter /**File Save** to produce the following display:

The exact appearance of your screen will depend on which drive you are using as the default and the names of the files you have already stored on this drive.

4. Type **QTRSALES** and press RETURN to supply the name to use when storing your data.

After you have completed the last entry, the disk drive light will come on momentarily while your data is being written to disk. When the file has been placed on the disk, the indicator light will change from its WAIT status back to READY. At this point you can continue to work on this model or start a new one, since you know that this one has been saved to the disk. For now, you will want to make some additions to this model to see how the process differs for subsequent saves.

SUBSEQUENT SAVES   Each time you save a model that is already on the disk, you have the option of replacing the copy on the disk with the information that is currently stored in memory or of entering a new name. If you have saved the model previously, 1-2-3's default will be to save the model under this name. Make the following changes to the model and save the model again with these steps:

1. Move the cell pointer to A3 and type **Sales**. Press the DOWN ARROW key. Type **Expenses** in A4 and **Profit** in A5.

2. Enter **/File Save**. 1-2-3 will present this display:

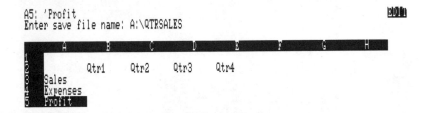

Notice that 1-2-3 is suggesting that the file be saved under the same name you used previously. If you are working with Release 1A your display will be slightly different, as Release 1A does not display the drive and directory.

3. Press RETURN. 1-2-3 will present this menu:

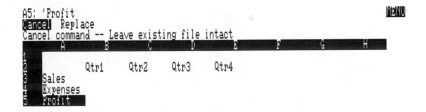

1-2-3 is asking if you wish to cancel the save request or replace the copy of the model stored on disk with the current contents of memory.

4. Enter **Replace**. 1-2-3 will save the updated model under the name you used previously.

If you want to save a model under a new name, 1-2-3 makes this possible. When 1-2-3 suggests that you use the original name, all you need to do is type a new name. Then, when you press RETURN, the file will be saved under the new name. This feature is especially useful when you need to create two similar copies of a model. You can create a file, then save the model under two different names before entering the changes on the duplicate file.

If you are working with Release 2, you can save a file to a directory other than the current one. To do this, specify the directory you want when you use / File Save. If 1-2-3 suggests that you use C:\LOTUS\QTRSALES but you wish to use A:SALES, when 1-2-3 presents its suggestion do the following:

1. Press ESC.

2. Press ESC two more times to remove the entire suggestion.

3. Type the complete pathname, which includes the drive, directory and filename (A:SALES for this example).

File Retrieve

A file-retrieve operation reads a worksheet file from disk and places it in the memory of your computer. When it places the model in memory, it erases the memory's previous contents. This means that you must always save a copy of your worksheets in memory in order to retain a copy, before you bring another worksheet into memory.

RETRIEVING FROM THE DEFAULT DRIVE When you want to bring a worksheet file into memory, most of the time you will want to use the default drive, since this is the same drive you have been using for data storage. If you don't take any special action, 1-2-3 assumes that this is where it should look for worksheet files and automatically displays a list of all the worksheet files on this drive. Release 2 even displays the file list in alphabetic sequence to make it easy for you to find the file you want. You can select a file by pointing to it with the highlighted bar it will provide you. You can also type the name of the file from your keyboard, either before or after 1-2-3 displays its list. However, one thing you cannot do is use the first letter entry. This feature will work with all of 1-2-3's other menus, but not with a file-retrieve operation.

Follow these steps to retrieve the file QTRSALES from the disk in the current directory:

1. Enter **/File Retrieve**. A list of file names similar to this display will appear, as follows:

2. Use the arrow keys to move the highlighted bar through the list until it is on QTRSALES. Then press RETURN.

If you need additional information about the files to make a selection and you are using Release 2.0, you can press F3 before you make a selection. 1-2-3 will expand the list to provide information on the size of each file and the date and time each file was created, as shown in Figure 4.2.

RETRIEVING FROM ANOTHER LOCATION   Release 2 lets you retrieve a file that is not on the current disk or in the current directory but the retrieve procedure changes slightly. Release 1A does not allow you to change directories without first using the /File Directory command (this will be discussed later in this chapter). After using this command to change the directory, you can use

FIGURE 4.2   Expanding the list for files to retrieve

the standard command sequence for a file retrieve to achieve your goal.

To change the directory for a retrieve operation, you must override the default directory setting for this one activity. The difference in the process is subtle: You begin and end the same way as usual, but you change the directory in the middle.

Assuming that you have data disks that you can place in two of your drives and that the default drive is drive A, use these steps to try the procedure.

1   Enter **/File Retrieve**.

2.   Press ESC twice to delete the reference to the default drive and directory. The following display appears:

3.   Type in the full name of your file, including its path and directory, and press RETURN.

Determining What Files Are on Your Disk

Just as you might look at the names of the different file folders in an office file cabinet, sometimes you may wish to look through the names of the files on your disk. The /File List command will handle this type of request for you. It lets you determine what types of files you want to view, by offering this menu selection:

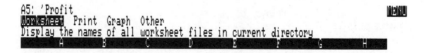

Since 1-2-3 stores worksheet, print, graph, and other types of files on the disk, these are your options when entering the command from Release 2. Release 1A ignores other file types and displays only the first three selections. 1-2-3 checks the files whose filename extension corresponds to the type of file you choose. Enter the following sequence of commands to view all the worksheet files on your disk.

1. Enter **/File List**.

2. Enter **Worksheet**.

3. If you have Release 2, move the highlighted bar around in the list to point to various filenames. As each filename is highlighted, an expanded description of the file entry appears at the top of the screen, as shown in Figure 4.3.

4. Press ESC to return to READY mode.

To list files on another disk or in another directory, use the same approach described in the preceding discussion for retrieving from another disk. If you have Release 2, this means that when you are presented with the list, press ESC twice to delete the reference to the current directory, and type in a new drive or directory designation before pressing RETURN. For Release 1A, as always, the only way to access a different directory is to activate it by using /File Directory.

Removing Files from the Disk

The files that you save on your disk are retained indefinitely. In fact, 1-2-3 never eliminates any of them; it will remove a file only if you make a specific request for it to do so. The command used for eliminating files is /File Erase. To remove a file from your disk, follow these steps. (Execute them only if you have a file you wish to eliminate—these steps work!)

1. Enter **/File Erase**. This produces the following display for you to select the type of file you want to erase:

FIGURE 4.3   Exploring the list of files on your disk

The display is slightly different for Release 1A, since it does not support the Other option.

2. Enter **Worksheet** to produce a list of your worksheet files like this:

If you wish to expand this list to include file sizes and date and time stamps, press F3.

3. Use the arrow keys to position the highlighted bar on the file that you want to permanently remove from the disk, and press RETURN.

Once you have deleted a file, there is no practical way to restore it. There are utility programs that can restore a file that has been deleted in this fashion, but they are not part of 1-2-3 and most of them require some technical expertise to use effectively. Therefore, you must be extremely cautious when removing files from the disk.

Changing the Directory

1-2-3's dependence on a default directory — the drive and subdirectory you are using — saves you a considerable amount of time. If you are working with a hard-disk system, your data will probably be stored in a subdirectory. To work in it for a period of time, you need to be able to change to another one. A default directory means that 1-2-3 assumes that the directory you are referencing is the current default, unless you specify otherwise. If you keep this default set to the drive containing your data, you will not need to enter the directory in order to make most of your file requests. The package does provide capabilities that let you alter the directory setting. This feature means that when you want to work with worksheet files that are on the floppy disk in drive A, it will be easy to have the directory set at drive C and alter it to a floppy drive.

USING ANOTHER FLOPPY DRIVE   If you are currently working with a floppy-disk-based system with two drives, your only option is to switch the other drive. If the default drive is A, you cannot keep the 1-2-3 system disk and all its HELP information in the drive. Rather than remove the 1-2-3 system disk from drive A, you can set the default data disk to drive B. Before beginning, make sure that the system disk is in drive A, since 1-2-3 will attempt to read the current directory before allowing you to change it. Before making the change, insert a formatted disk in drive B for data storage; 1-2-3 will check this drive as it changes the directory. To make the directory change, follow these steps:

1. Enter **/File Directory**.
2. Enter **B:** then press RETURN.

When you switch drives in Release 1A you will get an erroneous ERROR MESSAGE, which reads, "Directory does not exist". Ignore this message. Press RETURN a second time to change the directory.

CHANGING HARD-DISK DIRECTORIES   You have already seen how, if you have Release 2, you can access data on another disk or in another directory on a one-time basis with the /File Retrieve and /File Save commands. Each time you wish to use a directory other than the current one you must enter the complete pathname for the file. The pathname includes the disk drive and an optional subdirectory along with the filename. This approach is cumbersome if you have to use information in these other locations repeatedly. A better solution is to make the other disk or directory the active one. You also use the /File Directory command to change the active directory on your hard disk. First the entry /File Directory is required. The current directory would be displayed as follows:

```
A1:
Enter current directory: A:\
```

In this example, the current directory is C:/HALDIR/. Next type the new directory. If the new directory were C:/ACCT/, you would type **C:/ACCT/** — the new directory. With a hard disk, you can also type a drive if you want to start using one of the floppy disks for storage and retrieval.

A TEMPORARY EXIT
TO THE OPERATING SYSTEM

In Release 2, 1-2-3's /System command allows you to temporarily exit from 1-2-3 to perform file-management tasks directly with the operating system. Since 1-2-3 provides a number of file-management commands directly in its menu structure, it is easier to use 1-2-3's menu selection where these commands are available. The DOS commands are especially useful for performing tasks that 1-2-3's menu does not support. Before examining how the system feature works, let's cover a few basics about your computer's DOS operating system.

What is the Operating System?

The operating system that your computer uses is in some ways similar to a foreman in a production environment. A foreman manages the operation of the production line and coordinates the resources required to complete a job. The operating system in your computer is a program that manages the tasks that your computer performs and coordinates the resources required to complete a task. The operating system must always be in memory along with 1-2-3 or any other application program, to ensure that these programs can access the resources of the computer system.

The operating system you will be using on your computer is MS/DOS or PC/DOS or, in the latest computers, OS/2. The letters in the OS or DOS portion of these names stand for Operating System.

BASIC FEATURES

Some of the basic tasks that the operating system performs are reading and writing data to and from the disk. The operating system also contains a variety of utility programs that copy files or disks, prepare disks for data storage, and check the directory of a disk. You can use these utility features before you enter a program like 1-2-3 to handle many tasks relating to file and disk information. After you place an application program like 1-2-3 into the memory of your machine, you usually cannot access the operating system features any longer. With Release 2 of 1-2-3, Lotus has provided a temporary exit from 1-2-3 that retains all of your current worksheet data in memory while you work with DOS tasks.

Types of DOS Tasks to Perform

Normally once you are in 1-2-3 you want to forget about the operating system and enjoy the ease with which you can use 1-2-3's menu to handle tasks. But there are exceptions. One of the most important exceptions is when you want to save data on a disk and don't have a formatted disk available to save on. Without the /System feature, if you do not have a formatted disk available, you will lose all the data that is in memory. With the /System feature, you can exit temporarily and format another disk. You can then use this newly formatted disk to save your data. You can also make a copy of a file on your disk to give to another business associate: You can remain in 1-2-3, temporarily switch to DOS to complete your task, and switch back again. The steps for each of these special uses are covered in the following sections.

USING /SYSTEM TO PREPARE A DISK The DOS command for preparing a disk is FORMAT. In the following exercise, you will use this command to format a blank disk that you will place in drive A. Follow these steps to complete the exercise and return to 1-2-3.

1. Type /**System**.
2. If you are working with a floppy-disk-based system, place the DOS disk in drive A.
3. Type **FORMAT A:** and press RETURN.
4. Place a blank disk in drive A in response to the following prompt on your screen:

   Insert a new diskette for drive A:
   and strike any key when ready

   With Release 3.0 of DOS and higher, the message will be a little different. Here, you must use RETURN to confirm that you are ready to proceed with the format operation.
5. Press RETURN to begin formatting.
6. Type **N** and press RETURN to indicate that you do not want to format additional disks.
7. Type **EXIT** to return to 1-2-3.

A transcript of the entries for this process through step 6 is shown in Figure 4.4. Your display will look similar. However, if any bad sectors were encountered in your disk, FORMAT will skip them and notify you that it has done so with a message about the number of bad sectors excluded.

When DOS formats a disk it uses the program FORMAT. COM, which is supplied on your operating-system disk. If you are working with a floppy-disk system and follow the instructions in this exercise, everything will work fine. If you are working with a hard disk, the directory that contains FORMAT.COM must be the active directory when you type the format instructions. For a hard-disk system where FORMAT.COM is not in the current directory, replace step 2 in the instructions with "Type **CD**." This changes the directory to the root directory on your hard disk where, presumably, you will have a copy of FORMAT.COM stored.

USING /SYSTEM TO COPY A FILE   You can use the DOS COPY command to copy a file on your disk to another disk without leaving 1-2-3. To copy the file SALES from the disk in drive A to a

---

```
(Type EXIT and press [RETURN] to return to 1-2-3)


The IBM Personal Computer DOS
Version 3.20 (C)Copyright International Business Machines Corp 1981, 1986
            (C)Copyright Microsoft Corp 1981, 1986

C)FORMAT A:
Insert new diskette for drive A:
and strike ENTER when ready

Format complete

    362496 bytes total disk space
    362496 bytes available on disk

Format another (Y/N)?N
C)_
```

FIGURE 4.4   Using the /System feature to prepare a disk

formatted disk in drive B and return to your task in 1-2-3, follow these steps:

1. Enter /**System**.

2. Place the disk containing SALES in drive A and the formatted disk in drive B.

3. Type **COPY A:SALES.WK1 B:** and press RETURN.
   The filename extension .WK1 was used in this example. If you are using Release 1A, the proper extension is .WKS.

4. Type **EXIT** and press RETURN.

USING /SYSTEM TO CREATE A NEW DIRECTORY   You can create a new subdirectory for your hard disk without leaving 1-2-3. This option lets you create a logical section on the disk, which you can begin to use for specialized storage of worksheet data or other information. In the following example, the subdirectory will be added directly to the root directory of the disk, which is the main directory. In most cases, this is where directories should be added. Using too many levels causes confusion and makes it difficult to locate individual files. Follow these steps if you have a hard disk and wish to establish a subdirectory called BUDGET.

1. Save your current worksheet and clear memory with /**WEY**, if data from a previous task remains on your screen.

2. Enter /**System**.

3. Type **cd** to make the root directory active.

4. Type **md\budget** to create a subdirectory named budget.

5. Type **cd\budget** to make your new directory active.
   Figure 4.5 shows the transcript of your DOS entries on the screen up to this point.

6. Perform any DOS tasks you wish in this directory.

7. Type **Exit** to return to 1-2-3.

```
(Type EXIT and press [RETURN] to return to 1-2-3)

The IBM Personal Computer DOS
Version 3.20 (C)Copyright International Business Machines Corp 1981, 1986
               (C)Copyright Microsoft Corp 1981, 1986

C)cd \

C)md \budget

C)cd \budget

C)_
```

FIGURE 4.5   Creating a subdirectory

Note that the current 1-2-3 directory would now be C:/BUDGET/, since that directory remained active after it was created.

Returning to 1-2-3

You may have noticed in the previous examples that when you finished entering DOS commands you returned to 1-2-3 by typing **Exit** and pressing RETURN. When you exit to DOS and return, everything is the same as it was before you entered the System request. The same worksheet will be on the screen and 1-2-3 will be ready to continue where you left off.

SUMMARY

In this chapter you have learned that you can create permanent copies of your data in files on disk. You have also learned that there are two methods for working with files. You can use 1-2-3 menu commands to save and retrieve the data, determine what files the disk contains, and change the default disk or directory. And, if you are using Release 2, you also have the option of temporarily setting your 1-2-3 tasks aside and using operating-system commands to prepare diskettes, copy files or disks, change or create directories, and carry out other DOS tasks. Because disk files protect the investment you have made in your data, practice with the file commands presented until you are confident that you have added them to your toolkit of 1-2-3 skills.

5

MAKING
1-2-3 DO MOST
OF YOUR WORK

Until now, you have had to enter every worksheet entry that you needed for your models by yourself. While that is similar to using a columnar pad for your entries, it does not take advantage of the productivity features offered by a package like 1-2-3. In this chapter, you will be introduced to some of these features. Making only a few entries, you often can complete your model by putting 1-2-3 to work.

In this chapter, you will be introduced to commands that can move worksheet data to a new location. This means that if the requirements of your application change, it will be easy to restructure the worksheet. You will also learn how to restructure data stored in a column to a row orientation and vice versa. Again, this is quite an improvement over the eraser method that manual spreadsheets provide.

1-2-3's *Copy* command, also covered in this chapter, has more potential than any other command to increase your productivity with 1-2-3. You will learn the ins and outs of copying both label and formula data. You will also learn about other 1-2-3 features, such as repeating label entries and generating a series of numeric entries. Once you have mastered the Copy feature, you will want to master some of the tools that can help you monitor your expanded worksheet. For example, you will learn how to control the recalculation of formulas stored on the worksheet. In addition, you will be introduced to commands for splitting your screen display into two windows and for freezing certain information on the screen.

COPYING WORKSHEET DATA

Copying entries on a manual worksheet is a laborious task. To make an additional set of entries that duplicate existing ones, you must pick up your pencil and physically copy each entry that you wish to make. Naturally, duplicate entries take just as long to make as the original entries.

When you make duplicates with 1-2-3, however, this is not the case. For any entry that you wish to duplicate, you can have 1-2-3 complete 95 percent of the work for you. Just tell 1-2-3 what you want to copy and where you want it copied to. 1-2-3 does all the remaining work. It can take a column of label entries and copy it to ten new columns. It can even take a row of formulas that calculate all your sales projections for the month of January and copy it down the page to the next eleven rows, thus giving you all the calculations for February through December. The truly amazing part of this process is that it even knows to adjust the formulas as it copies them.

We will use a building-block approach in covering all the features of the Copy command. First, we will look at how to use Copy to duplicate a label entry. Then we will look a little closer at Copy's inner workings, as we examine its ability to adjust formulas.

Copying Labels

There are many situations in which copying labels can save you time. Perhaps you want to create a worksheet that uses account titles or months of the year in two different locations. Rather than typing them in again, you can use the Copy option. Not only does it save you time, but it also guarantees that both sets of entries are identical. Copy is also useful when you have a number of similar entries to make. Often, you can copy your original entries and make minor editing changes in less time than it would take to type each of the complete entries.

INVOKING COPY TO DUPLICATE LABELS   Copy is a little different from the other menu commands you have used. It does not have a submenu like /Range Format Currency or /Worksheet Insert Rows. Instead of using a multi-layered menu approach, the Copy command uses prompts. You must respond to these prompts in order to define the source location you wish to copy information from and the target location you wish to copy information to. When you invoke copy by entering /Copy, this is the first prompt message you see:

1-2-3 is asking what cells you wish to copy from. Think of this "from" range as the source of information to be copied. It suggests a range that encompasses only one cell. This suggested location is always the location of the cell pointer at the time you invoke Copy. If the location that 1-2-3 suggests is acceptable, you can press RETURN to accept it. If you like the beginning of the range but wish to enlarge it to include a row or column of cell entries, you can expand it with your pointer movement keys. If you don't like the beginning of the range, you must unanchor the start by pressing ESC. You will then be free to move the beginning of the range. When you want to anchor it again, use the same strategy that worked with the Format commands and type a period. Of course, you will then be free to expand the range with the arrow keys. Once you have finalized the source selection, 1-2-3's interest shifts to the target location (the location the data is copied to).

The prompt message displayed by 1-2-3 Release 2 for the target range looks like this:

When you request Copy, 1-2-3 initially again suggests the location of the cell pointer. The suggested location is not a range but a single cell, since you will almost always need to move the cell pointer to define the target range. And this is *all* you need to do, since it is displayed as a cell address rather than a range. You do not have to press ESC, as there is no range to unanchor. Once you select a location to start the copy, either you must press RETURN to finalize the location or you must modify it to represent a range. You can create a range with the standard method of typing a period and using the arrow keys to mark the end of the range.

Release 1A presents the same information in a different format. Here, the target range prompt appears at the right of the screen and the source range remains on the left.

Reviewing an example will help clarify how easy it is to copy a label entry. Follow these steps:

1. Move the cell pointer to A1 and type **Sales Product A**, then press RETURN.

2. Enter **/Copy** to generate this prompt message:

Notice that the suggestion for the source range is A1, the

location of the cell pointer when you invoked the Copy command.

3. Press RETURN.

The prompt message generated next also suggests the original location of the cell pointer as the target range. However, you must change it.

4. Move the cell pointer to A2 and press RETURN to generate these results:

The new label generated is identical to the original entry, but it required far fewer keystrokes to create. Later, you will learn how to extend this productivity even further by copying to many locations with one command. For now, here are a few additional hints for the simplest case of copying—copying an entry to one new location.

Modifying Copied Labels   The entry in A2 is currently identical to the original. Sometimes this situation is exactly what you need; other times, however, a slight modification might be required. If you wanted the label "Sales Product B" in A2, the Copy approach is still best. However, fixing the label would require these extra steps:

1. Move the cell pointer to A2.

2. Press F2 (EDIT).

3. Press the BACKSPACE key, type **B**, and press RETURN to finalize.

The results will look like this:

Keep this possibility in mind when you look for opportunities to copy. A Copy followed by a quick edit can still be much quicker than making new entries. Since you can use this feature with numbers as well, one potential application of Copy is to generate a list of numbers with only one digit different.

Making Copy Work Smoothly   Because of the way in which 1-2-3 suggests a location for the source range, the most efficient way to work with Copy is to position your cell pointer on the cell you wish to copy before requesting the command. If more than one cell is being copied, select the upper leftmost cell in the range being copied. This strategy will allow you to expand the cell range downward and to the right, once you are prompted for the source range.

Copying Formulas

In one sense, copying formulas is no different from copying label or number entries. It is accomplished with the same / Copy command. You respond to the prompts the same as when you are copying label and number entries. With formulas, however, you need to be able to control how 1-2-3 copies the cell addresses in formulas. If you have one constant interest rate and want all formulas to refer to it, you must be able to direct 1-2-3 to carry out that direction. On the other hand, you need a different approach if you enter a formula for January profit that subtracts the cost of goods sold in January from the sales for January and want to copy this formula to generate formulas that calculate profit for the other eleven months. You cannot calculate February's profit by subtracting the January cost-of-goods-sold figure from January sales. You need to subtract February's cost of goods sold from February sales. Fortunately, 1-2-3 can handle this type of situation as well. These situations are handled by the type of references contained in the original formula and are not an option selected after the copy operation begins. Let's examine an example of Copy for different reference types to help clarify this.

ADDRESS TYPES   All the cell addresses you have entered in formulas thus far have contained a column name immediately followed by a row number — for example, A1, E4, IV2000. This is the cell address specification that is used most frequently with 1-2-3. This type of address is called a *relative address*. There are two additional types of addresses: *absolute* and *mixed addresses*. They are distinguished by the way they are recorded in your formulas and the way in which 1-2-3 performs a copy operation for each of the three types. It is important to master the differences in the three types of addresses; the type of address references you use is critical in determining how your formulas are copied to new worksheet locations.

Relative Addresses   Relative addresses are the only type of cell address used until this chapter. They are easy to enter in formulas, whether you use the typing or the pointing method of formula creation. When 1-2-3 records your entry, it appears to store the formula exactly as you entered it. In fact, if you move your cell pointer to any cell that holds one of the formulas you have entered, you will see the exact formula you entered in the control panel.

However, 1-2-3 remembers your instructions in a slightly different way from what it displays. If you store the formula +A1+A2 in cell A3, 1-2-3 will interpret your instructions in this way: "Take the value that is located two cells above the location that will store the result and add that value to the value that is located one cell above the cell which will contain the result." Everything is remembered as relative direction and distances from the cell that will contain the result when your formula contains relative references.

These relative references will mean that when you copy this type of formula to another location, 1-2-3 will adjust the formula in the new locations to reflect the same relative distances and directions. For example, if you were to copy the formula stored in A3 to B3, the formula you would see in the control panel for B3 would be

A1:   READY

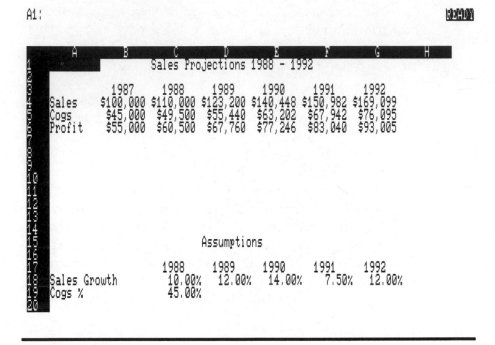

FIGURE 5.1   Completed sales projection model

+B1+B2. This formula uses different cell addresses from the original, but it still records the same relative directions: "Take the value that is two cells above the cell that will contain the results and add this value to the value that is one cell above the cell that will contain the results." This adjustment is handled automatically as long as you use relative references when you build your formulas. Since you have not learned about other types of address yet, this should be easy.

You will build a model that allows you to practice the formula copy process. This model records profits for the current year and projects them for the next five years. The final result of your entries will look like Figure 5.1. Follow these steps to create the model:

1. Enter **/Worksheet Erase Yes** to start with a clean worksheet.

2. Move the cell pointer to C1 and type **Sales Projections 1988–1992**, then press RETURN.

3. Move the cell pointer to A4, then make these entries:

A4:	**Sales**
A5:	**Cogs**
A6:	**Profit**
B3:	**˄1987**
C3:	**˄1988**
D3:	**˄1989**
E3:	**˄1990**
F3:	**˄1991**
G3:	**˄1992**

The caret (˄) symbols in front of the year entries will cause the numeric digits to be treated as labels and will center them within the cell.

4. Move the cell pointer to B4 and make these entries for 1987:

B4:	**100000**
B5:	**45000**
B6:	**55000**

These entries are not computed, as they are assumed to be the actual numbers at the end of 1987. They will appear as follows

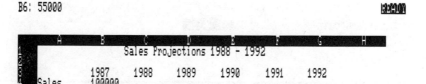

It is time to begin thinking about how you want to project sales for the remaining years. You can use a constant growth rate that would apply to all years, or you can assume that sales will grow at varying percentages each year. There are also a number of choices for computing the cost of the goods sold each year. One method is to use a percentage of sales. Even if you select this method without evaluating other options, you must again decide if one percentage will be used for all years or if the percentage will vary by year. The profit calculation does not require you to make a decision, since it is always equal to Sales minus Cost of Goods Sold. This model assumes that sales will grow at varying rates but that cost of goods sold will be the same percentage of sales each year. You must enter these assumptions before projections can be made.

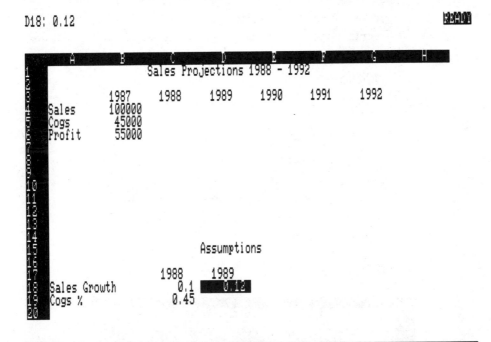

FIGURE 5.2   Entering numbers and labels for the sales projection model

D18: 0.12

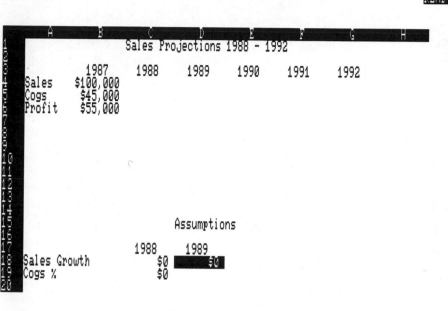

FIGURE 5.3 Using a global format

5. Move the cell pointer to D15 and type **Assumptions**, and press RETURN.

6. Complete these entries:

A18:	**Sales Growth**
A19:	**Cogs %**
C17:	**^1988**
C18:	**.1**
C19:	**.45**
D17:	**^1989**
D18:	**.12**

Your entries should appear like those shown in Figure 5.2.

C18: (P2) 0.1

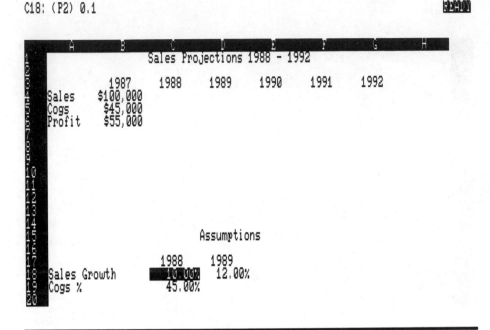

FIGURE 5.4   Adding a range format

7. Enter **/Worksheet Global Format Currency**. Type **0** and press RETURN. The percentages will display as zeros, like the ones in Figure 5.3.

   This instruction will set the Global format to Currency, but you will also need to use a Range format for the percentages that will be used in the model.

8. Move the cell pointer to C18, then enter **/Range Format Percent** and press RETURN to accept two decimal places. Use the RIGHT and DOWN ARROW keys to move the cell pointer to G19, then press RETURN.

   The range of cells you just selected includes all the values you wish formatted as percent. It also includes a few blank cells — but they have to be included, unless you wish to apply the format with separate commands for the sales growth and cost-of-goods-sold percentage. The reformatted percentage entries are shown in Figure 5.4.

9. Move the cell pointer to C4, type **+B4*(1+C18)**, and press RETURN.
   This will compute the sales projection for 1988. Rather than typing this formula for each year, a better option is to copy it.

10. Enter **/Copy**. Press RETURN in response to 1-2-3's prompt message, which appears as shown in Figure 5.5.

11. Move the cell pointer to D4 and press RETURN.
    The cell pointer will remain in C4, which was the beginning of the source range.

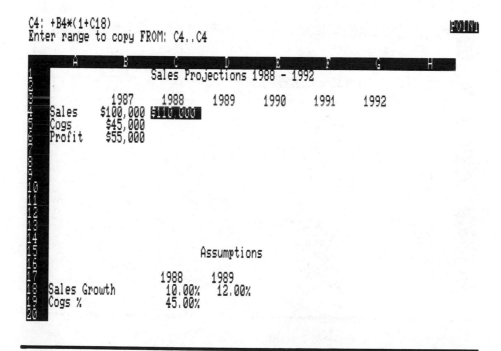

FIGURE 5.5 Specifying the source or from range for copy

12. Move the cell pointer to D4 to look at the new formula
    shown in Figure 5.6.

Notice that 1-2-3 has adjusted each of the cell references to take the
new location of the result into account. Each reference in the formula is the same distance and direction from the result in D4 as the
original references were from C4, where the original result was
computed. Before completing the copy process for sales, you will
want to take a look at an absolute reference — a reference that will
not be updated by a copy operation.

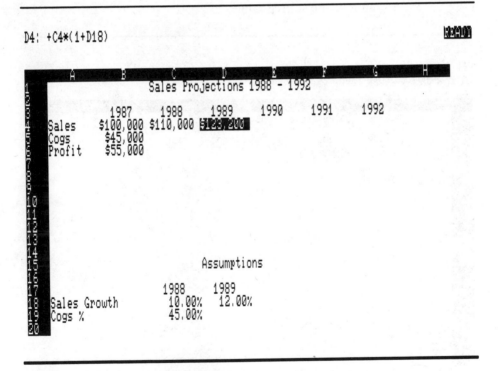

FIGURE 5.6   The completed formula

Absolute Addresses   Absolute cell references are references that remain the same regardless of where the formula is copied to. The formula reference is effectively frozen in place and not allowed to change. Some special action must be taken to create these references, since they have a $'s in front of both the row and column portion of the address. $A$3 or $D$8 are examples of absolute cell references.

You can create an absolute reference in one of two ways— by typing or pointing. Both parallel the creation method for relative references. If you choose to build the formula by typing, you will need to type the $s. If you choose to build the formula by pointing, you can press F4; 1-2-3 will then add the $s in front of the row and column portion of the address.

Let's use this approach to build the cost-of-goods-sold data, to clarify how the feature works. Follow these steps to enhance the sales projection model you were working on earlier in the chapter:

1. Move the cell pointer to C5.

2. Type +.

3. Move the cell pointer to C4 with the UP ARROW key.

4. Type *.

5. Move the cell pointer to C19 with the DOWN ARROW key.

6. Press (F4) ABS once to add the $s.
   Your display should match Figure 5.7. Since you were in POINT mode, you could add the $s with F4. If you want to type the cell address, you cannot use F4 to add the $s, so you will have to type them.

7. Press RETURN to complete the formula.

8. Enter /**Copy** and press RETURN to accept C5 as the source range.

9. Move the cell pointer to D5 and press RETURN.

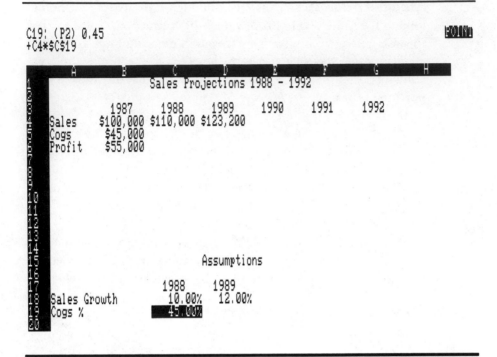

FIGURE 5.7   Using an absolute reference

If you move the cell pointer to D5, you will see that the new formula also references C19 for its cost-of-goods-sold percent, as shown in Figure 5.8.

Mixed Addresses   Mixed addresses borrow something from each of the other two types of addresses. A mixed address is "mixed" in that one part is fixed and the other part is relative. This means that either the row or the column portion of the address is fixed, but never both. During the Copy process the fixed portion behaves like an absolute address, and the other portion functions like a relative address and is adjusted based on the location it is being copied to.

A mixed address can be written like A$5 or $D7. In the first example, the column portion of the address will be adjusted as the formula is copied to different columns, yet the row portion will remain fixed if the formula is copied to other rows. In the second example, the exact opposite takes place: The column portion of the address will always remain fixed regardless of where the formula containing it is copied. The row portion of this address will be updated when the formula is copied to a different row.

The mixed-address feature is seldom used—only if you are building complex models. Still, it is important to know that this is possible, in case you ever see a mixed address in a formula. For now, it is enough just to know that this feature exists. A more productive way to spend your time is to put the relative and absolute address types to the test with additional Copy commands.

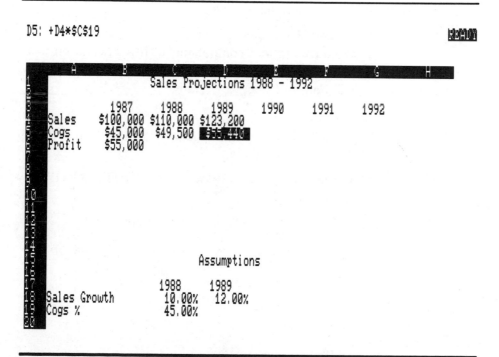

FIGURE 5.8 Copy operation completed for the cogs formula

SCOPE OF COPY   You have learned how to copy a formula to a new location on the worksheet, using the exercises you have completed thus far. This is just one of the ways you can use Copy. Other options are copying the contents of one cell to many additional locations and copying many locations to many additional locations.

Copy One Entry to One New Location   You have already used this facet of the Copy operation. You used it to copy the sales and cost-of-goods-sold projections for 1988 to create the same projections for 1989. Now you will use it one more time to copy the profit calculation from 1988. But first, you must enter the formula for 1988 profit and complete the assumption area. Follow these steps to add a formula for profit and then to copy the formula to one additional location.

1. Move the cell pointer to C6.

2. Type **+C4-C5** and press RETURN.
   Since you wish both components of this calculation to be updated for the appropriate year when the formula is copied, both references are relative.

3. Enter /**Copy**.

4. Press RETURN to accept the source range generated by 1-2-3.

5. Move the cell pointer to D6 with the RIGHT ARROW key and press RETURN.

6. Enter the following in the assumption area:

E17:	^**1990**
F17:	^**1991**
G17:	^**1992**
E18:	**.14**
F18:	**.075**
G18:	**.12**

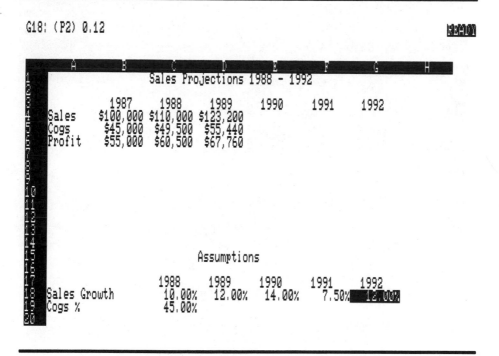

FIGURE 5.9   Profit formula added and assumptions extended

The model should look like the one in Figure 5.9. You have been making slow but steady progress in completing it. Now it is time to step up the pace and copy to more than one location at a time.

Copy One Entry to Many New Locations   1-2-3's Copy command is not restricted to the single copy approach we have been using. By expanding the size of the target range, you can copy the entry in one cell to a range that is as large as a row or column of the worksheet. You can put this expanded version of Copy to use in completing the sales projections for the remaining years of the model. Follow these steps:

1. Move the cell pointer to D4.

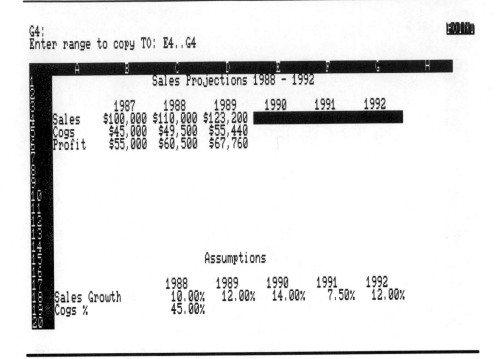

```
G4:                                                              POINT
Enter range to copy TO: E4..G4

          A       B       C       D       E       F       G       H
                     Sales Projections 1988 - 1992

                    1987    1988    1989    1990    1991    1992
       Sales    $100,000 $110,000 $123,200
       Cogs      $45,000  $49,500  $55,440
       Profit    $55,000  $60,500  $67,760






                              Assumptions

                    1988    1989    1990    1991    1992
       Sales Growth 10.00%  12.00%  14.00%   7.50%  12.00%
       Cogs %       45.00%
```

FIGURE 5.10   Copying to a target range of more than one cell

2. Enter /**Copy** and press RETURN to accept the source range.

3. Move the cell pointer to E4 in response to the prompt for the target range.

4. Type **.**
   The period will anchor the beginning of the range and allow you to expand it.

5. Move the cell pointer to G4.
   The target range you are copying to is highlighted, as shown in Figure 5.10. This one command will copy the sales projection formula into E4, F4, and G4.

6. Press RETURN to produce the results shown in Figure 5.11.

Copy Many Locations to Many New Locations   You can step up the pace a little faster and copy a column or a row of formulas to many columns or many rows all in one step. To accomplish this, you must expand both the source and target ranges to include a range of cells. You can use this approach to complete the formulas for your model. Although the column of formulas you need to copy includes only two cells, it is still a column. You will be able to copy this column of formulas to columns E, F, and G. Follow these directions to complete the Copy operation:

1. Move the cell pointer to D5.
   This location is the upper leftmost cell in the range to be copied. As long as you remember to place the cell pointer

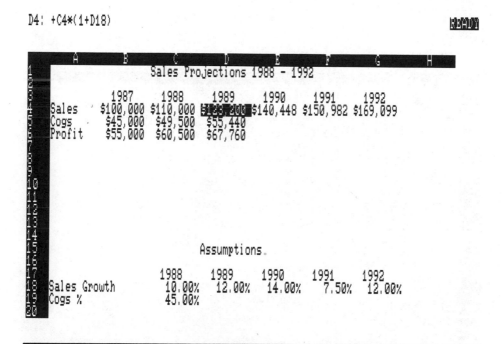

FIGURE 5.11   Copy completed

in the upper leftmost cell in the range to be copied, the Copy process will be easy to follow for either rows or columns.

2. Enter /**Copy**.

3. Expand the source range to D6 by moving the cell pointer with the DOWN ARROW key.

   The cells you are copying from should be highlighted, as shown in Figure 5.12.

   The location where you should place the cell pointer when expanding the source range is always the lower rightmost ~ell in the range to be copied. Again, keeping the lower rightmost cell in mind will make these directions work even when you wish to copy a row of data

4. Press RETURN, move the cell pointer to E5, and type . (period). This anchors the upper leftmost cell in the target range.

```
D6: +D4-D5                                              [READY]
Enter range to copy FROM: D5..D6

      A        B        C        D        E        F        G        H
                    Sales Projections 1988 - 1992
1
2
3           1987    1988     1989     1990     1991     1992
4    Sales  $100,000 $110,000 $123,200 $140,448 $150,982 $169,099
5    Cogs    $45,000  $49,500  $55,440
6    Profit  $55,000  $60,500  $67,760
7
8
9
10
11
12
13
14
15                          Assumptions
16
17          1988     1989     1990     1991     1992
18   Sales Growth   10.00%   12.00%   14.00%    7.50%   12.00%
19   Cogs %         45.00%
20
```

FIGURE 5.12   Copying a source range of more than one cell

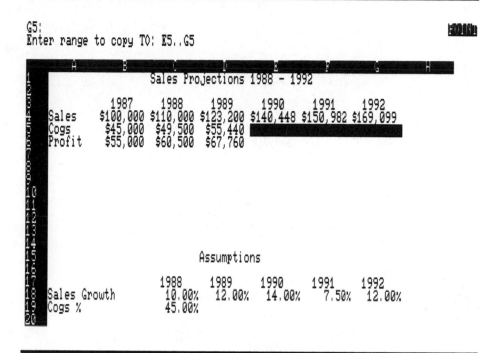

G5:
Enter range to copy TO: E5..G5

Sales Projections 1988 - 1992

	1987	1988	1989	1990	1991	1992
Sales	$100,000	$110,000	$123,200	$140,448	$150,982	$169,099
Cogs	$45,000	$49,500	$55,440			
Profit	$55,000	$60,500	$67,760			

Assumptions

	1988	1989	1990	1991	1992
Sales Growth	10.00%	12.00%	14.00%	7.50%	12.00%
Cogs %	45.00%				

FIGURE 5.13   Defining the target range for the copy

5. Move the cell pointer to G5.
   You are probably thinking that G6 would have been the correct location. Since 1-2-3 already knows from your definition of the target range that you are copying a column of formulas, it only needs to know how far across the worksheet you wish to copy this column. G5 answers that question. The target cells you are copying to should be highlighted and should match the display in Figure 5.13.

6. Press RETURN to see the results in Figure 5.14.

Copying a row of cell entries will follow the same basic pattern as this example. First you must define which row of cells is in the source or from range. Next, you must tell 1-2-3 where to begin copying this row to and how far down the worksheet to copy it.

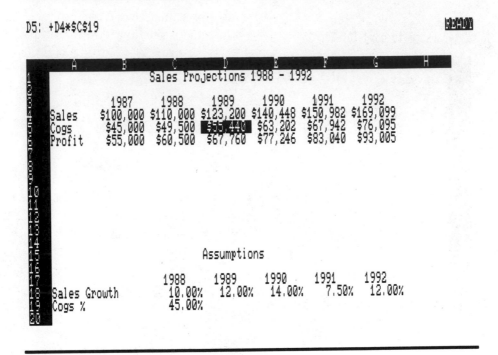

D5: +D4*$C$19

FIGURE 5.14   Result of the copy operation

Keep in mind that all these copy methods can be used for values and labels just as easily as for formula entries.

REARRANGING THE WORKSHEET

Planning is your best assurance that your completed model will both look good and meet your business needs. But even when you plan, there still will be occasions when you want to rearrange the data contained in your model. 1-2-3 has commands that will reorganize the worksheet for you. This means that you do not have to reenter and erase entries the way you would with a manual version of your model. These special commands include one that can move any range of data to another range that is the same size and shape. A second command allows you to take a row of data and place it in a column or to take a column of data and place it in a row.

Moving Worksheet Data

The /*Move* command is used to move data in one range of the worksheet to another range. This range can be a single cell, a row of cells, a column of cells, or a rectangle with multiple rows and columns. The size and shape of the relocated data are determined by the original location of the data. This means that a row of data can only be moved to another row, not placed into a column of cells.

You can use the Move command to relocate labels, values, and formulas. When Move relocates formulas, it adjusts the cell references in the formulas being moved to account for the new location of these formulas on the worksheet. Move also adjusts absolute references to conform to the new worksheet location.

The Move command is very similar to the Copy command, except that here the original location of the data is not retained. To use this command, enter /**Move**. 1-2-3 prompts you for the source range. Just as with the Copy command, it is easiest to specify the range if you position your cell pointer in the upper leftmost cell in the range before requesting Move. And, also like the Copy command, you can press RETURN to specify a single cell as the source or you can move the cell pointer to expand the size of the range.

After you finalize the source range with RETURN, 1-2-3 prompts you for the target range, the new location for your data. Unlike the Copy command, the source range determines the size and shape of the data being moved. Therefore, all you need is a beginning location for the relocated data, which you can define by specifying the upper leftmost cell of the new area. Once you have specified the target range and finalized it with RETURN, the Move operation is complete.

You can use Move to relocate your assumptions on the current model by following these steps:

1. Move the cell pointer to A15.
   This is the upper leftmost cell in a rectangle that will include all the entries in the assumption section, including the label in row 15.

2. Enter **/Move**.

3. Move the cell pointer to G19.
   Everything to be moved will be highlighted, as shown in Figure 5.15.

4. Press RETURN to finalize the source or from range.

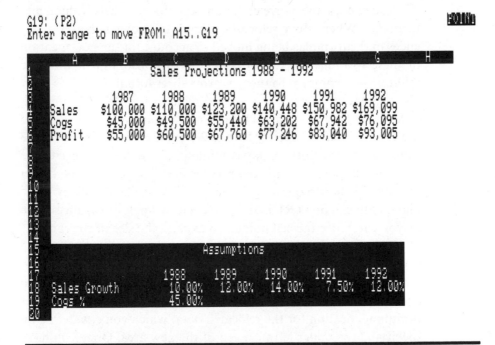

FIGURE 5.15   Highlighting the area to move

5. Move the cell pointer to B22 and press RETURN.

6. Press PGDN to see where the range was moved.
   The entire range of cells containing assumption data will
   be relocated to B22 . . . H26, as follows:

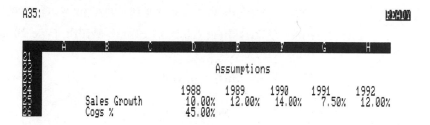

7. Enter **/File Save**, type **SALESPRJ**, and press RETURN
   to save this worksheet.

Transposing Data

1-2-3's *Transpose* features are new options for Release 2. Not only do
they copy data but they also alter its orientation. Transpose places
data with a row orientation into a column. Likewise, it places data
with a column orientation into a row. The power of this command
will become apparent the first time you need to do major restructuring of a worksheet. You will have an opportunity to try both types of
transposition.

Both versions of Transpose can be used with labels and numbers,
but neither version should be used with formulas that contain
relative references. Since the Transpose command is actually a
special form of Copy, the references in the formulas will be altered as
they are written to the new cells. However, the data they reference
will still be in its original position and will cause disastrous results in
your formulas.

ROWS TO COLUMNS   /Range Transpose makes it easy to change
data that was entered in a row to a column orientation. You do not
even need to tell 1-2-3 whether the data you are transposing is in a

row or column. 1-2-3 can figure it out from the range that you define. All you need to do is define the data to transpose, then tell 1-2-3 the upper leftmost cell where you wish to place the data. The following example illustrates how this command works:

1. Enter /**Worksheet Erase Yes** to clear the worksheet.

2. Enter /**Worksheet Global Column-Width**, type **20**, and press RETURN.

3. Make these entries in cells B2..K2:

B2:	**Sales-Widgets**
C2:	**Sales-Kites**
D2:	**Sales-Wind Surfers**
E2:	**Sales-Rockets**
F2:	**Sales-Blocks**
G2:	**Sales-Sand**
H2:	**Sales-Jacks**
I2:	**Sales-Rafts**
J2:	**Sales-Balls**
K2:	**Sales-Dolls**

4. Press the HOME key.
   A few of the entries appear as follows:

A1:

The entries are so wide that only a few are visible on the screen at once. You may decide to try a different orientation using the Transpose command.

5. Move the cell pointer to B2 and enter /**Range Transpose**.

6. Select B2..K2 as the source or from range and press RETURN. This selection can be accomplished quickly by using the END key, followed by the RIGHT ARROW key.

7. Move the cell pointer to A4 and press RETURN.
   This will place the entries in column A but the original entries are still in row 2.

8. Enter /**Range Erase** and expand the range by pressing the END key, followed by the RIGHT ARROW key until it reads B2..K2. Then press RETURN.
   Your screen should match the display shown in Figure 5.16.

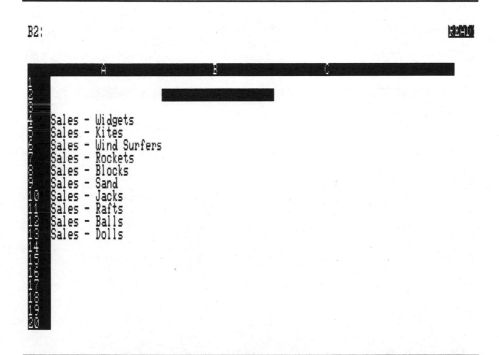

FIGURE 5.16   The transposed data

COLUMNS TO ROWS   Transposing a column data to a row is just as easy as the other way around. Try this example with the months of the year:

1. Using Figure 5.17 as your guide, enter abbreviations for each of the months in A5..A16.

2. Move the cell pointer to A5 by pressing the END key, followed by the UP ARROW key. Then enter **/Range Transpose**.

3. Select the range A5..A16 and press RETURN.

4. Move the cell pointer to B3 and press RETURN.
   Although you can only see the first seven month names in Figure 5.18, the remainder have been transposed as well.

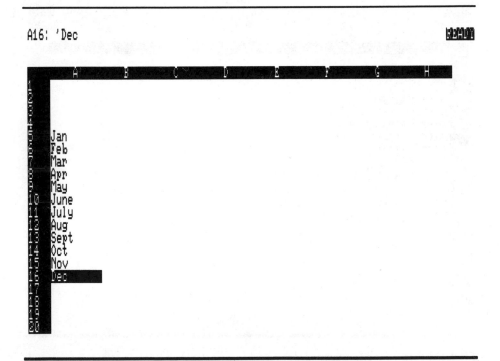

FIGURE 5.17   Data entered in a column

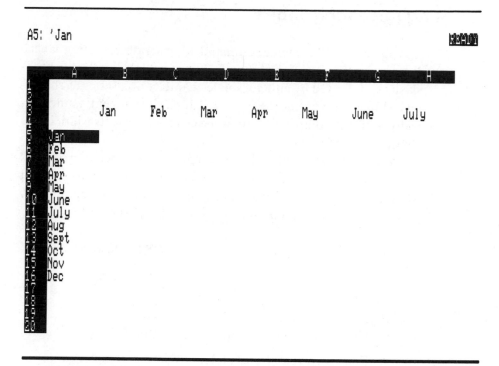

FIGURE 5.18   The result of transposing it to a row

The months are in the range B3..M3. The original entries will remain unless you use the / Range Erase command to remove them.

GENERATING CELL ENTRIES

This section covers the entries that you can have 1-2-3 generate for you. The generating features are so easy to use that it is like having someone perform data entry for you free of charge. 1-2-3's *repeating label* feature can generate dividing lines and other quick entries in worksheet cells. The other feature can generate a series of numbers that have the same increment between each value in the series — for example, 1, 2, 3, 4 or 25, 50, 75, 100.

Creating Repeating Labels

You do not need a menu command to generate repeating labels. Instead, you accomplished it with the special label indicator back-slash (\), followed by either a single character or a series of characters. Whichever you choose, 1-2-3 will duplicate your entry automatically to fill the complete width of the cell and adjust its width if you change the cell width.

You can use this feature to make a dividing line between sections of a worksheet or to create the top and bottom lines when you want to draw a box around your assumptions. Follow these steps to draw a box around the assumptions section of the worksheet:

1. Enter /**File Retrieve**, type **SALESPRJ**, and press RETURN.

2. Move the cell pointer to A21.

3. Enter * and press RETURN.
   Notice how the *s completely fill A21.

4. Enter /**Copy** and press RETURN.

5. Move the cell pointer to B21, type ., move the cell pointer to I21, and press RETURN.

6. Move the cell pointer to A22 and type *, then press Return.

7. Enter /**Copy** and press RETURN.

8. Move the cell pointer to A23, type ., then move the cell pointer to A27 and press RETURN.

9. Move the cell pointer to A21, then enter /**Copy**.

10. Move the cell pointer to I21 with the END key, followed by the RIGHT ARROW key, and press RETURN.

11. Move the cell pointer to A28 and press RETURN.

12. Move the cell pointer to I22 and type '   *.
    Leave eight spaces before the * to form the right edge of the

box. Since you are entering spaces, you can omit the label indicator; 1-2-3 will automatically consider it a label and add the '.

13. Enter /**Copy** and press RETURN.

14. Move the cell pointer to I23, type **.**, then move the cell pointer to I27 and press RETURN.

15. Move the cell pointer to A21.
    The final result of your entries is a line of asterisks on all four sides of the assumptions. Since the display is wider than the screen width you can view only three sides of this box, as follows:

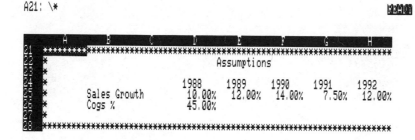

16. Enter /**File Save**, press RETURN, then enter **Replace**.

17. Enter /**Worksheet Erase Yes**.

Generating a Series of Numbers

It can be tedious to enter a long list of numbers. In one special situation you can assign this task to 1-2-3: when the list of numbers is a series with equal intervals. The interval can be either positive or negative, but it must be the same between every number in the series. This means that lists such as 10, 20, 30, 40; 7, 9, 11, 13, 15; 52609, 52610, 52611; and 30, 29, 28, 27 can be generated by the package. A list such as 1, 3, 7, 15 could not be generated because the intervals between the numbers in the list are not the same.

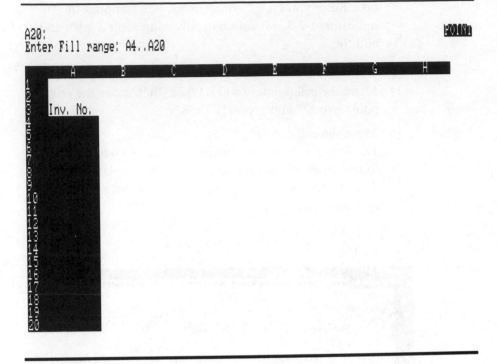

FIGURE 5.19 Highlighting the fill range

Follow these instructions to try this feature to generate a list of invoice numbers:

1. Type **Inv. No.** in A3.

2. Move the cell pointer to A4. This is the upper leftmost cell in the range where you will have 1-2-3 generate numbers.

3. Enter **/Data Fill**, type **.**, and use the DOWN ARROW key to highlight the fill range to A20, as shown in Figure 5.19. Then press RETURN.

4. Type **57103** and press RETURN in response to the prompt for the start number.

5. Press RETURN to accept 1 for the "step" increment number.
This is the value that is added to each value in the list to create the next entry.

6. Type **59000**.

The entries in the control panel should look like this:

The stop value must always be as large as the last value in the list. This means that there are two factors that can end a list. The fill numbers stop being generated at the end of the range selected. They can also stop sooner if the stop value is not large enough to accommodate the numbers you are generating.

7. Press RETURN.

The list of numbers generated is shown in Figure 5.20.

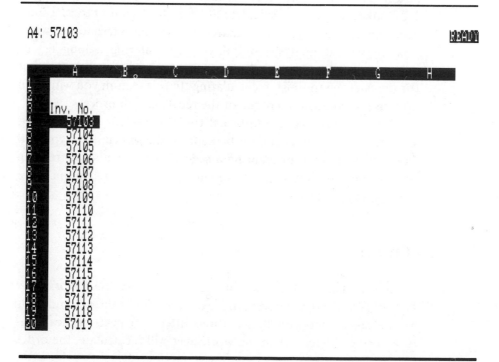

FIGURE 5.20   Numbers generated by fill

Naturally, you can make your range larger to generate a larger list of numbers. You can also choose a horizontal range of cells and create an entry for each cell in the row.

8. Enter /**Worksheet Erase Yes**.

OTHER WORKSHEET COMMANDS TO HANDLE EXPANDED DATA

Now that you have learned the secrets of creating these models quickly, you will find that you can create many more models as well. Some of the models you create will contain data for many months or years. You will also want to learn some of the tricks that make working with these models easier, such as controlling recalculation. This is a helpful trick, because as your models grow larger, 1-2-3 takes longer to recalculate after each of your entries. 1-2-3's speed seems quite good, compared to manual alternatives, when you do what-if analysis; but if you are entering a long list of account names or invoice numbers, it is annoying to have to wait for the package to finish recalculating. In this section you will learn how to put yourself in charge of the recalculation process.

You will also need additional tools to use for large models, since the entire model cannot be kept on the screen. And you will learn the technique of creating a second window and of freezing certain information on the screen. Both these techniques are covered in this section.

Recalculation

1-2-3's recalculation options are accessed with the /*Worksheet Global Recalculation* command. Actually this is three commands in one, since it lets you change three different aspects of recalculation. You can select when the worksheet will recalculate, the order in which it will recalculate formulas, and how many times it recalculates the worksheet. The latter two options are advanced features of recalculation that are seldom required. If you are curious about these, check your 1-2-3 manual. The first option affects when the recalculation occurs. This is a real time-saver that can be used with any large worksheet.

To alter the timing of recalculation for the sales projection worksheet, follow these steps:

1. Enter /**File Retrieve**, type **SALESPRJ**, and press RETURN.

2. Enter /**Worksheet Global Recalculation**.
   The following menu will display:

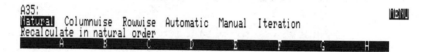

The first three options in this menu refer to the order of recalculation. The last option refers to the number of times the worksheet recalculates. The other two options, *Automatic* and *Manual*, let you determine whether the package will automatically update the model after a change or whether you wish to control recalculation.

3. Enter **Manual**.
   This selection means that 1-2-3 will not recalculate formulas after a worksheet change. To recalculate them you will need to press the F9 (CALC) key.

4. Move your cell pointer to C4 and type **120000**.
   Notice that this change does not affect the results in any category, although it does turn on the CALC indicator at the bottom of your screen. This indicator is a warning that changes have been made and the worksheet has not been recalculated.

5. Press F9 (CALC).
   Now you will see the results of the change.

6. Change the value in C4 back to 110000 by typing **110000**.
   Again the results are not affected.

7. Press F9 (CALC).
   Your display should again show the results you started with.

8. Enter /**Worksheet Global Recalculation Automatic**.
   From this point on, every worksheet entry will cause recalculation. Keep this easy-to-make change in mind; it is a
   great option when you have a significant amount of data
   to enter.

Using Windows to Help Monitor Data

1-2-3 allows you to split the screen into two different sections and
to view a different portion of the worksheet in each section. You
have the option of splitting the screen vertically or horizontally.
Which method to select will depend on how your worksheet is
arranged and which sections you want to view. If you want to see
columns in two different areas, you will split the screen vertically. If
you want to view rows from two different locations, you will want
to choose a horizontal split.

The command that you use to create the split is /*Worksheet
Window*. It is different from any other 1-2-3 command you have
used: It requires that you position your cell pointer before invoking it. The location of the cell pointer determines the size of the two
windows, and the cell pointer cannot be moved after the command
is invoked.

After invoking the /Worksheet Window command, you must
select *Horizontal* if you want two horizontal windows. The split
will be made above the cell pointer at the time the command is
invoked. Selecting *Vertical* will draw two vertical windows, the
first of which ends immediately to the left of the cell pointer's
location when the command was invoked.

Once the screen is split into two windows, you can use the F6

(WINDOW) key to move to the other window. Regardless of which window you are in, F6 always takes you to the opposite window.

The /Worksheet Window menu has some additional selections. The only other command that is not an advanced option is the selection *Clear*. This option allows you to return to a display with one window. Cursor position is not important when you plan to choose Clear.

Try this exercise with your sales projection model to clarify how it works. Follow these steps:

1. Press the HOME key.

2. Use the DOWN ARROW key to move the cell pointer to A10.

3. Enter /**Worksheet Window**.
   This menu should appear:

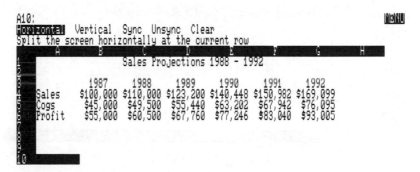

4. Enter **Horizontal**.

5. Press F6 (WINDOW) to move the cell pointer to the lower window.

6. Move the cell pointer to A29 to view the assumptions in the lower window.
   Your screen should match the display in Figure 5.21.

7. Enter /**Worksheet Window Clear**.
   The display will return to a single window.

Using Titles with Large Worksheets

One of the problems with large worksheets is that you cannot see all the data on the screen at one time. This problem is magnified when you move your cell pointer to the right or down and find that the labels at the left of the rows and the top of the columns scroll off the screen. Essentially you can find yourself in a sea of numbers with no visible indication of what each of these numbers represents. The solution in 1-2-3 is to fix some of this label information on the screen.

The command that freezes label information on the screen is the /*Worksheet Titles* command. As with the /Worksheet Window

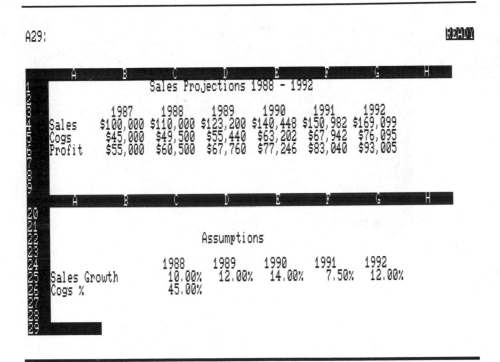

FIGURE 5.21   Two horizontal windows

command, the position of the cell pointer at the time you invoke this command is critical. The cell pointer location defines what information will be frozen on the screen. The command has four options: to fix titles both vertically and horizontally; to fix them vertically; to fix them horizontally; or to clear all fixed titles from the screen. This last option does not eliminate the titles themselves, but it ensures that neither vertical nor horizontal titles are frozen any longer.

If you choose to freeze vertical titles with either the *Vertical* or *Both* options, when you invoke / Worksheet Titles any columns to the left of the cell pointer will become fixed on the screen. You will not be able to move your cell pointer into these columns with the arrow keys. If you move to the right of the point where columns would normally scroll off the screen, only columns to the right of the fixed titles will scroll off the screen. The columns defined as titles will always be visible.

The situation is similar for horizontal titles, whether you choose Horizontal or Both. All rows above the cell pointer at the time / Worksheet Titles is invoked will remain frozen on the screen, even when the cell pointer moves far enough down on the worksheet to cause rows to scroll off the screen. The rows below the frozen titles can scroll off the screen but not the titles you have fixed on the screen.

Looking at an example of this command with the sales projection worksheet will show you how it works. If you wanted to bring the right edge of the assumptions box into view, the left edge would scroll off the screen unless you first fixed the titles. Use these steps for fixing columns A through C:

1. Press the HOME key, then press PGDN. Move the cell pointer to D25.
   You may think you could have just moved the cell pointer to D25, but the instructions given are the only way to ensure that you have just the desired rows and columns above and to the left of the cell pointer.

2. Enter /**Worksheet Titles** to produce this display:

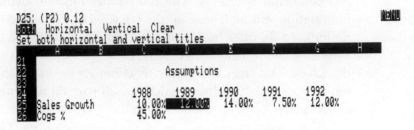

3. Enter **Vertical**.

4. Move the cell pointer to K25 to produce this display:

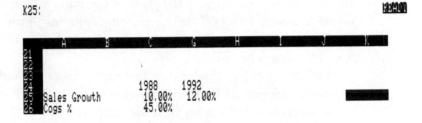

Notice that columns A, B, and C are frozen on the screen, yet columns D, E, and F scrolled off the screen.

5. Enter /**Worksheet Titles Clear**.
   This will unfix the titles, and columns A through C will scroll off the screen. These title-fixing features will be useful in situations where the total is at the bottom of a long column or to the right side of a long row. By fixing the titles you can check the total yet keep the corresponding labels on the screen for readability.

SUMMARY

In this chapter you have been introduced to a variety of tools that can dramatically increase your productivity with 1-2-3. Rather than having to type in each of your formulas, you have learned several ways to copy formulas as well as other data quickly. In addition, you have learned techniques for reorganizing the worksheet. This will allow you to salvage a worksheet that no longer meets you needs. You have also learned other techniques, including generating a series of numeric entries and creating repeating labels with only a few keystrokes. And you received new commands to help you manage the worksheets that you can now create so rapidly, including commands to create windows or freeze label information on the screen. You also learned how to control the recalculation features of the package, thus reducing the time required to enter data.

PRINTING
YOUR
WORKSHEET

In this chapter you will have an opportunity to explore 1-2-3's *Print* features. You can use them to create a quick draft copy of your worksheet, using only a few instructions. When you are ready for a final copy, you can create a professional-looking report with a few new commands. These commands will allow you to control the print margins, access the special Print options offered by your printer, and even add headers and footers to every page.

First, you will learn to use the basic Print options. Then, you will learn more complex Print options, via the building-block approach, until you have a full set of Print features that you can use. You will also have the opportunity to explore options for printing formulas and using worksheet commands to further customize your print output.

PRINT BASICS

The basic Print features are designed to give you quick access to a printed copy. This quick access is made possible by default values that 1-2-3 has set for options such as margins and page length. Later you will learn to override these default settings, but for now you might as well appreciate their presence; they make it easy for you to print out your files.

Determining the Destination

What is the destination for 1-2-3's Print features? At first the answer seems obvious. After all, if you are printing, you would expect to use the printer. But 1-2-3 offers you a choice: you can print to a printer or to a file on disk. The unexpected option of using a disk to capture print output adds considerable flexibility to the Print features.

To select a destination, first access the Print features by typing **/Print**. This will cause the following submenu to display:

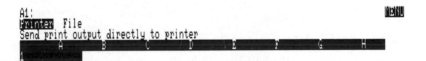

1-2-3 is asking whether to direct your output to the printer or to write it to a file. If you want to create printed hard copy immediately, choose the printer.

THE FILE OPTION   The *File* option is designed to let you write your print output to a file. Unlike the files that contain worksheets, this file contains print data and is referred to as an *ASCII text file*. It will automatically be assigned the filename extension .PRN. Once you have stored the information in the file you can do various things with it: print it at a later time, modify it with many word processors, and use it as input to some application programs. It is good to be aware of the printing-to-a-file special feature. However, since you will want to print to a printer most of the time, this chapter will focus on this option, giving relevant examples. Should you want to write your file to a disk, you can use any of the options presented here, just as well.

THE PRINTER OPTION   When you select the *Printer* option, 1-2-3 assumes that the output device is the printer you selected when 1-2-3 was installed. As long as this printer is attached to your system and online when you tell 1-2-3 to begin printing, your print output will be sent to this device. Normally, the top or front of the printer has a series of small lights to indicate that the printer is online and ready to accept data. Verify that the printer is turned on and is online before you start to work with the Print commands. It is also a good idea to understand the defaults that will apply to your output before you learn about the instruction that actually starts the printing.

THE DEFAULT SETTINGS   One of the things that simplifies printing the first time you use a worksheet is the default settings that are provided for some of the Print options. These defaults affect the length of a page of output and the amount of white space, or the margin, on all four sides of a printed page. The defaults also apply to the printed pages you write out to disk.

The default page that is predefined to 1-2-3 has several areas affecting the amount of data that prints on a page. The layout of a printed page defining these areas is shown in Figure 6.1. Notice that a page of output is defined as 66 lines. Yet not all these lines will contain Print data; some of them are reserved for top and bottom margins. Once two lines are deducted for a top margin and two more are deducted for a bottom margin, only 62 lines will print on a page. In addition to the top and bottom margins, 1-2-3 allows three lines at both the top and bottom for a header or footer, even if you choose not to use either one. This means that of the 66

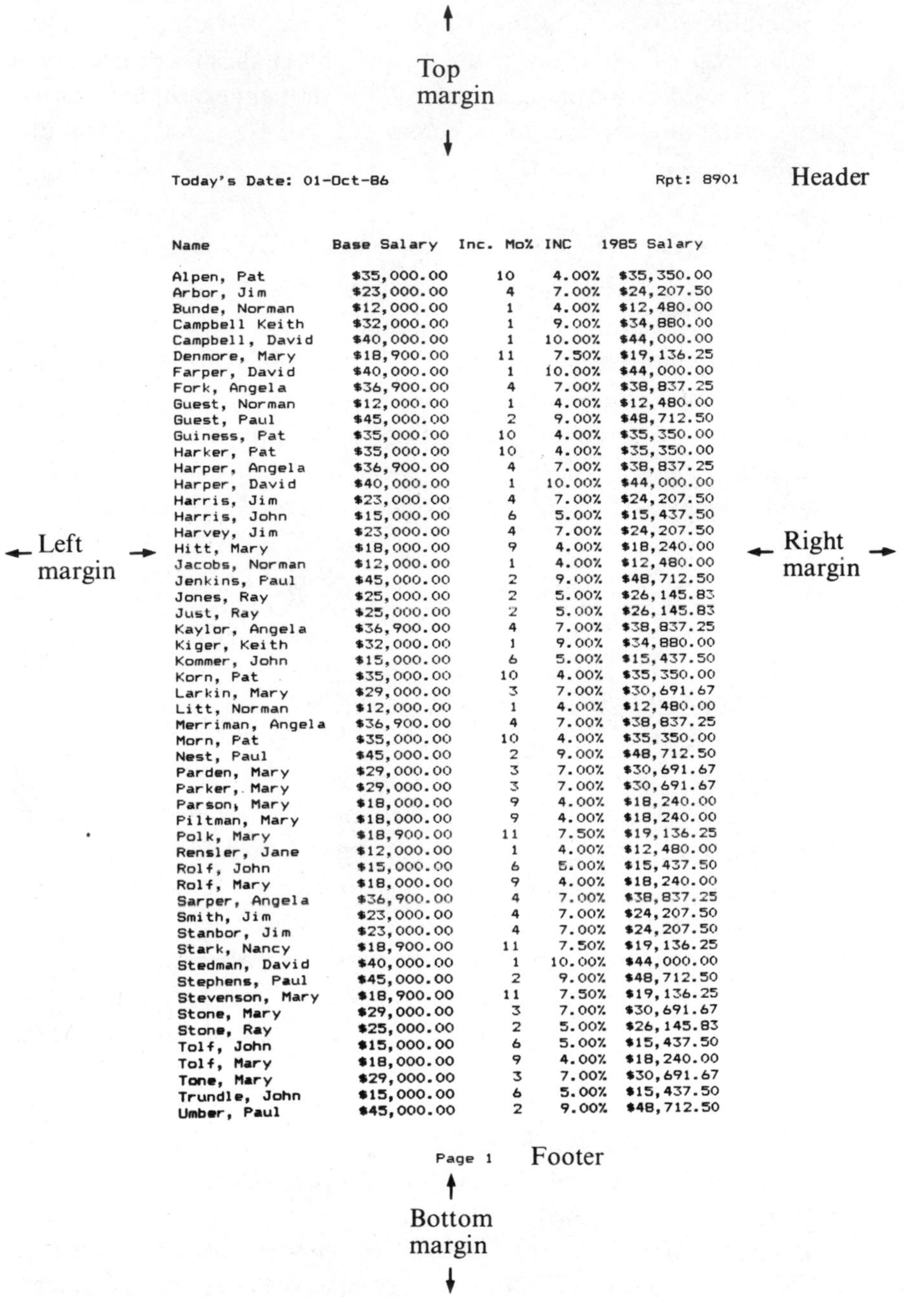
Top margin
Header
Left margin
Right margin
Footer
Bottom margin

Today's Date: 01-Oct-86 Rpt: 8901

Name	Base Salary	Inc. Mo	% INC	1985 Salary
Alpen, Pat	$35,000.00	10	4.00%	$35,350.00
Arbor, Jim	$23,000.00	4	7.00%	$24,207.50
Bunde, Norman	$12,000.00	1	4.00%	$12,480.00
Campbell Keith	$32,000.00	1	9.00%	$34,880.00
Campbell, David	$40,000.00	1	10.00%	$44,000.00
Denmore, Mary	$18,900.00	11	7.50%	$19,136.25
Farper, David	$40,000.00	1	10.00%	$44,000.00
Fork, Angela	$36,900.00	4	7.00%	$38,837.25
Guest, Norman	$12,000.00	1	4.00%	$12,480.00
Guest, Paul	$45,000.00	2	9.00%	$48,712.50
Guiness, Pat	$35,000.00	10	4.00%	$35,350.00
Harker, Pat	$35,000.00	10	4.00%	$35,350.00
Harper, Angela	$36,900.00	4	7.00%	$38,837.25
Harper, David	$40,000.00	1	10.00%	$44,000.00
Harris, Jim	$23,000.00	4	7.00%	$24,207.50
Harris, John	$15,000.00	6	5.00%	$15,437.50
Harvey, Jim	$23,000.00	4	7.00%	$24,207.50
Hitt, Mary	$18,000.00	9	4.00%	$18,240.00
Jacobs, Norman	$12,000.00	1	4.00%	$12,480.00
Jenkins, Paul	$45,000.00	2	9.00%	$48,712.50
Jones, Ray	$25,000.00	2	5.00%	$26,145.83
Just, Ray	$25,000.00	2	5.00%	$26,145.83
Kaylor, Angela	$36,900.00	4	7.00%	$38,837.25
Kiger, Keith	$32,000.00	1	9.00%	$34,880.00
Kommer, John	$15,000.00	6	5.00%	$15,437.50
Korn, Pat	$35,000.00	10	4.00%	$35,350.00
Larkin, Mary	$29,000.00	3	7.00%	$30,691.67
Litt, Norman	$12,000.00	1	4.00%	$12,480.00
Merriman, Angela	$36,900.00	4	7.00%	$38,837.25
Morn, Pat	$35,000.00	10	4.00%	$35,350.00
Nest, Paul	$45,000.00	2	9.00%	$48,712.50
Parden, Mary	$29,000.00	3	7.00%	$30,691.67
Parker, Mary	$29,000.00	3	7.00%	$30,691.67
Parson, Mary	$18,000.00	9	4.00%	$18,240.00
Piltman, Mary	$18,000.00	9	4.00%	$18,240.00
Polk, Mary	$18,900.00	11	7.50%	$19,136.25
Rensler, Jane	$12,000.00	1	4.00%	$12,480.00
Rolf, John	$15,000.00	6	5.00%	$15,437.50
Rolf, Mary	$18,000.00	9	4.00%	$18,240.00
Sarper, Angela	$36,900.00	4	7.00%	$38,837.25
Smith, Jim	$23,000.00	4	7.00%	$24,207.50
Stanbor, Jim	$23,000.00	4	7.00%	$24,207.50
Stark, Nancy	$18,900.00	11	7.50%	$19,136.25
Stedman, David	$40,000.00	1	10.00%	$44,000.00
Stephens, Paul	$45,000.00	2	9.00%	$48,712.50
Stevenson, Mary	$18,900.00	11	7.50%	$19,136.25
Stone, Mary	$29,000.00	3	7.00%	$30,691.67
Stone, Ray	$25,000.00	2	5.00%	$26,145.83
Tolf, John	$15,000.00	6	5.00%	$15,437.50
Tolf, Mary	$18,000.00	9	4.00%	$18,240.00
Tone, Mary	$29,000.00	3	7.00%	$30,691.67
Trundle, John	$15,000.00	6	5.00%	$15,437.50
Umber, Paul	$45,000.00	2	9.00%	$48,712.50

Page 1

FIGURE 6.1 Layout of a printed page

possible lines, only 56 lines will be used for printing with the default settings.

Similarly, standard print on an 8½ by 11 sheet of paper allows 80 characters to print across the page; yet the default settings will reduce this number. 1-2-3 has a default left margin setting of 4 and a default right margin setting of 76. This means that a maximum of 72 characters can print across the page without modifying the defaults. Initially, try the Print operation without modifying any of these defaults.

The Basic Print Options

The second level of the Print menu is the same, whether you have chosen Printer or File. It is actually the main Print menu since it is the root from which all the other Print options can be selected. Here is what it looks like:

This menu is different from any of the other menus you have used, which all disappear as soon as you make your first selection. In contrast, this Print menu stays on your screen so you can make additional selections. For this reason, it frequently is referred to as a "sticky menu." You will find it a real convenience; most Print operations require more than one menu selection.

Another important distinction is that 1-2-3 can remember the results of any command that affects the Print setting. To have 1-2-3 remember what you want to print or any changes that you make to the Print settings, first complete the definition of your Print specifications, then save the worksheet.

DEFINING THE RANGE TO PRINT   At this point you want to tell 1-2-3 how much of the worksheet you wish to print. Therefore, select the Range option from the main Print menu. The next step depends on whether the worksheet already has a Print range defined. If not, just move to the beginning of the Print range, type a period, and move to the end of the Print range. If the worksheet was printed previously, the Range address used from that time will probably still be defined. Before you can move the cell pointer to a new beginning location, press ESC to unlock the beginning of the range. Whether you have printed previously or not, you can type a Range reference by entering the address of the beginning of the range, followed by a period and the cell address of the end of the range—for example, B3.H15. If a current range exists, 1-2-3 will immediately replace it with the range you enter; you do not need to press ESC.

The size of the range you define will affect how 1-2-3 prints your data when you request printing. If your defined range contains more data than will fit on one page, 1-2-3 will break the data into more than one page when you print. If the width of the range selected exceeds the number of characters that will print across one page, 1-2-3 will print as many columns across the first page as possible without exceeding the right margin setting. It will then break the output into more than one page. If the number of rows in the range selected exceeds the number of rows that can print on one page, 1-2-3 will generate a page break when the data prints.

To enter some data for printing and try several options for specifying the Print range, experiment with the following exercise. You could print worksheets you entered for other chapters, but you might not have one readily available. Therefore, this section offers instructions for creating employee data to be printed. You need to make quite a few entries to create this model, but it is designed to let you try each of the Print options covered in this chapter without having to enter data again. You will use entries more than once to build a large file quickly. You will use the Copy command extensively to further reduce these entry requirements. Follow these steps to enter the model and define the Print range.

1. Enter the following labels across row 1:

   A1:   SS#

   B1:   **Last Name**

C1:	**First Name**
D1:	**Salary**
E1:	**Location**
F1:	**Phone**
G1:	**Position**
H1:	**Increase %**
I1:	**'1988 Salary**

2. Enter **/Worksheet Global Column-Width 11** and press RETURN.

3. Move the cell pointer to column A, enter **/Worksheet Column Set-Width**, then type **13**, and press RETURN.

4. Make these entries in the cells shown:

A2:	**'516-75-8977**
B2:	**Jones**
C2:	**Paul**
D2:	**45900**
E2:	**DAL**
F2:	**980**
G2:	**2301**
H2:	**.05**
I2:	**+D2*(1+H2)**
A3:	**'541-78-6754**
B3:	**Parker**
C3:	**Mary**
D3:	**32100**
E3:	**CHI**
F3:	**541**
G3:	**1605**

H3:   .04

A4:   '897-90-8769

B4:   Smith

C4:   Larry

D4:   61250

E4:   ATL

F4:   342

G4:   1402

H4:   .05

A5:   '213-78-5412

B5:   Appel

C5:   Tom

D5:   22300

E5:   BOS

F5:   219

G5:   1750

H5:   .06

5. Move the cell pointer to I2, enter /**Copy**, and press RETURN. Move the cell pointer to I3, type ., move the cell pointer to I5, and press RETURN.
This completes the first four records. You need more rows of data to get the full effect of the Print features, but typing the entries would take too long. Instead, copy these entries until you have a sufficient number to print more than one page. You will have many duplicates, but you will have the opportunity to print more than one page.

6. Move the cell pointer to A2 and enter /**Copy**. Then press END and the DOWN ARROW key, followed by END and the RIGHT ARROW key. Press RETURN to finalize the source range. Next move the cell pointer to A6 and

press RETURN.

This time you copied the first four rows of the worksheet to create another four. Next time you will copy the eight existing data rows. After that you will copy the 16 entries and then the 32 entries (the number of records become larger each time you make a copy).

7. Proceed with the copy by entering /**Copy**. Then press END and the DOWN ARROW key, followed by END and the RIGHT ARROW key. Press RETURN, then move the cell pointer to Al0 and press RETURN.

8. Continue copying in this manner until you have entries in cells A1..I65, using the same procedures described in the previous step.

A1: [W13] 'SS#   READY

```
        A          B          C         D          E        F
1  SS#        Last Name  First Name Salary    Location  Phone
2  516-75-8977 Jones      Paul       $45,900  DAL          980
3  541-78-6754 Parker     Mary       $32,100  CHI          541
4  897-90-8769 Smith      Larry      $61,250  ATL          342
5  213-78-5412 Appel      Tom        $22,300  BOS          219
6  516-75-8977 Jones      Paul       $45,900  DAL          980
7  541-78-6754 Parker     Mary       $32,100  CHI          541
8  897-90-8769 Smith      Larry      $61,250  ATL          342
9  213-78-5412 Appel      Tom        $22,300  BOS          219
10 516-75-8977 Jones      Paul       $45,900  DAL          980
11 541-78-6754 Parker     Mary       $32,100  CHI          541
12 897-90-8769 Smith      Larry      $61,250  ATL          342
13 213-78-5412 Appel      Tom        $22,300  BOS          219
14 516-75-8977 Jones      Paul       $45,900  DAL          980
15 541-78-6754 Parker     Mary       $32,100  CHI          541
16 897-90-8769 Smith      Larry      $61,250  ATL          342
17 213-78-5412 Appel      Tom        $22,300  BOS          219
18 516-75-8977 Jones      Paul       $45,900  DAL          980
19 541-78-6754 Parker     Mary       $32,100  CHI          541
20 897-90-8769 Smith      Larry      $61,250  ATL          342
```

FIGURE 6.2 The right side of the entries

9. Move the cell pointer to column D and enter /**Range Format Currency 0**, press RETURN, then press END followed by the DOWN ARROW key. Press RETURN.

10. Move the cell pointer to H2 then enter /**Range Format Percent**. Press RETURN, then press the END key followed by the DOWN ARROW key. Press RETURN again.

11. Move the cell pointer to I2. Enter /**Range Format Currency**. Type **0** and press RETURN.
Press the END key followed by the DOWN ARROW key. Press RETURN. The upper portion of your entries should match Figures 6.2 and 6.3.

A1: 'Position

```
          G         H          I         J       K       L
1   Position    Increase %  1988 Salary
2       2301       5.00%    $48,195
3       1605       4.00%    $33,384
4       1402       5.00%    $64,313
5       1750       6.00%    $23,638
6       2301       5.00%    $48,195
7       1605       4.00%    $33,384
8       1402       5.00%    $64,313
9       1750       6.00%    $23,638
10      2301       5.00%    $48,195
11      1605       4.00%    $33,384
12      1402       5.00%    $64,313
13      1750       6.00%    $23,638
14      2301       5.00%    $48,195
15      1605       4.00%    $33,384
16      1402       5.00%    $64,313
17      1750       6.00%    $23,638
18      2301       5.00%    $48,195
19      1605       4.00%    $33,384
20      1402       5.00%    $64,313
```

FIGURE 6.3   A look at the left side of the entries

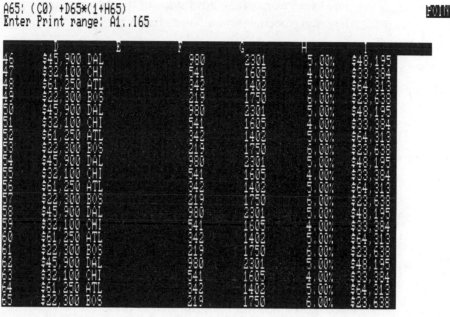

FIGURE 6.4 Selecting a print range

12. Press the F5 (GOTO) key, type **A2,** and press RETURN to bring the left side of the worksheet into view on your screen.

13. Enter **/Print Printer Range**, then press the HOME key. Type **.** (period). Press END followed by the RIGHT ARROW key, then END followed by the DOWN ARROW key to highlight the range A1..I65, as shown in Figure 6.4. Press RETURN.
    You can use the DOWN ARROW and END RIGHT ARROW approach since there are no blank cells within the data. If there were, you would have to use the pointer movement keys by themselves. Notice that the main Print

menu is still in the control panel to let you make additional selections. Take advantage of its presence and enter the range specification a few different ways.

14. Enter **Range**, press ESC to unlock the beginning of the range, then move the cell pointer to B1. Type **.**, then press the END key followed by the DOWN ARROW key. Press the RIGHT ARROW key twice, then press RETURN to select the range B1..D65.

15. Enter **Range**, then type **A1.I65** and press RETURN. When you type the address of a replacement range you do not have to press the ESC key first.

TELLING 1-2-3 TO BEGIN PRINTING   Once you have defined the range, simply select Go from the Print menu. Use the following single step to immediately send the range you just defined to the printer:

1. Check to be sure that your printer is turned on and is online. Then enter **Go**.

This will cause 1-2-3 to print the worksheet row by row and increment its internal line count with each line printed. When all the data in the defined range has been printed, 1-2-3 will return to the Print menu. The Print output is shown in Figure 6.5. If you want a second copy you can type GO again, but 1-2-3 will not move to the top of a page before it starts printing again. You cannot solve this problem by paging with the formfeed or linefeed button on your computer, since 1-2-3 maintains its own line count to tell it how much more space it has on a page. If you were to physically advance the paper in your printer without zeroing the line count, the new page would only contain data part of the way down the page; the line count would increment to 66 before reaching the bottom of the page. Look at the basic Control options before printing a second time.

ADVANCING A LINE   Sometimes you want to print more than one Print range. Depending on the size of each range of data, you may want to place it on a single page or separate pages. If you placed it on the same page it would merge together unless you added one or more blank lines after printing the first range. 1-2-3 will do this for you when given the command /Print Printer Line. Normally you need only enter Line, since the Print menu is likely to be on your screen. Each time you enter Line, 1-2-3 causes the printer to advance the paper one line and add one to the internal line count.

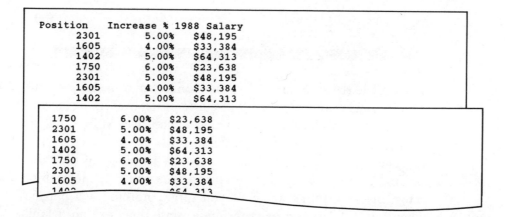

FIGURE 6.5 Output from the print operation

ADVANCING A PAGE   Advancing a line is fine for a small separation; but when you want data on separate pages you might have to request Line too many times to make this solution a practical one. Instead, use the command / Print Printer Page. It will quickly advance the paper to the top of the next page. Try this now:

1. Enter **Page**.

Only Page is needed since you are already in the main Print menu.

SETTING 1-2-3'S LINE COUNT TO ZERO   When the paper in your printer is set at the top of a form, you will want 1-2-3's line count to be set to zero. The command for this is *Align*. Try it with this entry:

1. Enter **Align.**

It looks like nothing has happened, but 1-2-3 has completed its housekeeping chore of zeroing the line count.

CLEARING THE PRINT SETTINGS   The Print menu has a special command for clearing Print settings from a previous operation. If you select Clear from the Print menu, these options will appear:

The first selection clears everything connected with the previous printing, and is appropriately labeled *All*. It sets everything back to the defaults. This means that you must define the next Print operation, just as if you had never printed before.

The second option only eliminates the definition of the Print range. After executing this command, you must define a Print range before printing again. If you forget, nothing will happen when you tell 1-2-3 to begin printing, since there are no default settings for the Print range.

The last two options, *Borders* and *Format*, will be discussed along with the more advanced features they relate to. Like the other options, they eliminate any special settings that have been made and leave the worksheet as if these special features had never been invoked.

QUITTING THE PRINT MENU   Since the Print menus do not disappear after you make your selections, you need a way to let 1-2-3 know you are finished selecting Print options. The *Quit* option in the Print menu is designed to do this. Once you select Quit you will be back in READY mode. Try it now with this command:

1. Enter **Quit**.

SAVING YOUR PRINT SPECIFICATIONS   When you decide to print a worksheet, you probably will want to produce updated copies of the same report when your worksheet data changes. It is easy to print a report on subsequent occasions if you save the worksheet file after printing. The *Save* operation saves any updates to worksheet data, as well as your Print definition. This means that the Print range and any special settings you may have entered for margins or page length will still be available the next time you need to print. You will be able to enter /Print Printer Go to produce the output.

ADDING A FEW OPTIONS

You have already mastered the basics of printing. You do not need any other commands to get a printed copy of your data. Soon your expectations will increase and you will not be content with just any old printout of your data. You will want to improve it. This is where the Print options can assist you significantly. You can access them by entering Options from the main Print menu to produce this menu:

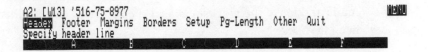

This is another "sticky menu," like the main print menu. It will stay around until you choose Quit or press ESC.

Margin Settings

To change margin settings, select *Margins* from the Options menu. You will be presented with a submenu, which looks like this:

Each option on this menu represents one of the four areas where margins can be specified.

Whatever values you enter for margins will change the print defaults for this one worksheet. If you save the worksheet file after making changes to the margins, the changed values will be in effect for this worksheet the next time you retrieve it. If you want to make a temporary change, don't save the worksheet after changing the margins.

The limitations placed on potential margin settings are different for Release 1A and Release 2. In Release 2, the limits on top and bottom margins are from 0 lines to 32 lines for each of these margin choices. In Release 1A, the settings for both margins can be between 0 and 10 lines each. To enter a new margin setting, select the type of margin you wish to specify, then type a new value and press RETURN.

The range of acceptable values for the right and left margins are the same under all releases of the product. You can use settings of from 0 to 240 characters for both right and left margins.

Try the following exercise with the employee data to see how margins can affect the output:

1. Enter **/Print Printer Options Margins**.

2. Enter **Left**, type **10**, and press RETURN.

3. Enter **Right**, type **70**, and press RETURN.

4. Enter **Quit**.
   This Quit exits the Options menu and returns you to the main Print menu.

5. Enter **Go**.
   You should find that one fewer column prints across the page because you have reserved more space for the right and left margins.

6. Enter **Page Align**.

Defining Headers and Footers

Headers and footers are lines that appear at the top or bottom of every page of print output. Information placed in the header, at the top of a page, typically may include the date or time, an identifying report number, a report title, the preparer's name, or a page number. The most frequent entry in a footer, at the bottom of the page, is the page number.

Headers and footers can be up to 240 characters. However, do not make them any longer than the number of characters that will fit on a page bounded by your left and right margin settings, or else 1-2-3 will truncate the extra characters. So if you use the default left and right margin settings of 4 and 76, do not enter a header longer than 72 characters.

USING SPECIAL SYMBOLS Two special symbols can be used anywhere in a header or footer to add special information. The @ makes 1-2-3 substitute the current system date at that location when it prints the header or footer line. The # makes 1-2-3 insert the current page number at the location in the header or footer.

Either of these special symbols can be used alone or combined with text characters. If you wanted the words Page Number to appear in front of the actual page number, you would place "Page Number #" in the header. Likewise, if you wanted to label the date you could enter "Today's Date: @".

THE THREE SECTIONS   1-2-3 allows you to define entries for the left, middle, and right sections of a header or footer. In other words, each header or footer has the potential to be divided into three sections. The sections are separated by the vertical bar symbol (¦).

When you ask to enter a header by entering / Print Printer Options Header, this is the display you will see:

A2¦ [W13] '516-75-8977

Enter Header Line¦

Whatever you type will appear left aligned in the header line. When you are finished entering information for the left section, type a vertical bar (¦) to indicate that you would like to begin entering the

```
Report No: 2350                                    Page 1

SS#            Last Name   First Name Salary        Location
516-75-8977    Jones       Paul       $45,900 DAL
541-78-6754    Parker      Mary       $32,100 CHI
897-90-8769    Smith       Larry      $61,250 ATL
213-78-5412    Appel       Tom        $22,300 BOS
      Report No: 2350                               Page 2

      213-78-5412   Appel     Tom        $22,300 BOS
      516-75-8977   Jones     Paul       $45,900 DAL
      541-78-6754   Parker    Mary       $32,100 CHI
      897-90-8769   Smith     Larry      $61,250 ATL
      21                                 $22,300 BOS
```

FIGURE 6.6   Header at the top of two pages

center section. When you have completed the center section, type another vertical bar (¦) to indicate the beginning of the entries for the right section. You can omit any section by entering the vertical bar to end the section without entering anything in it. For example, the header "¦¦Report Number: 3405" would not place anything in the left or middle sections of the header. It would place Report Number: 3405 right aligned in the header line printed at the top of every page. You can also enter everything on the left side by not using any vertical bar characters in your header.

Try this exercise to see how adding a header can affect your output:

1. Enter **Options Header**, then type **Report No: 2350 ¦¦Page #**, and press RETURN.

2. Enter **Quit.**

3. Enter **Go**.

4. Enter **Page Align**.
   Figure 6.6 shows the header at the top of the first two printed pages.

Using Borders

The labels you enter at the top and/or left side of a worksheet provide descriptive information on the first page of a printed report. When the rows in the worksheet exceed the length of one page, the rows at the top are not repeated automatically, and the second page contains data that is meaningless without labels. Similarly, when the columns in the worksheet exceed the width of one page, the columns at the left will appear only on the first page. Data further to the right will be printed on subsequent pages but will be meaningless without labels.

The Borders command allows you to select rows or columns that will appear at the top or left side of every page. The columns or rows you select as borders should not be included in the Print range. Otherwise, this data will print twice on the first page of the report: once as part of the border and once as part of the Print range.

To use the Borders option, enter /Print Printer Options Borders. The following menu will display:

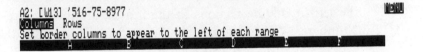

When you want to place information at the top of the worksheet on every page, choose Rows and select a range that includes at least one cell in each row you want to use. To use column information on each page, select Column and choose a range with at least one cell from every column you want to use.

You can put the Borders option to use for the employee file you created earlier in the chapter; the worksheet has more rows than will fit on one page and the second page has no labels. Follow these steps to add the top row as a border:

1. Type **A2.F65** and press RETURN. Notice that the row

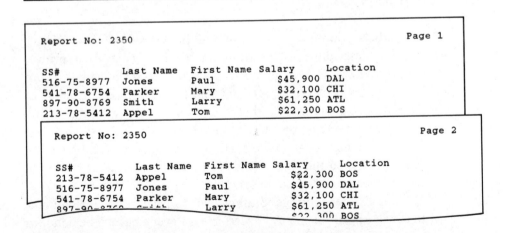

FIGURE 6.7   Borders option places labels on all pages

containing the labels is not included in the Print range, since you will use it as a border row.

2. Enter **Options Borders Rows**.

3. Move the cell pointer to A1 and press RETURN.

4. Enter **Quit**.

5. Enter **Go** followed by **Page Align Clear All Quit** when the printing stops.

The output contains labels at the top of both pages 1 and 2, as shown in Figure 6.7. The Clear All command eliminated all of the print settings, including the Print range and borders.

Changing the Page Length

The page length is sct at a default of 66 lines for most printers. This is perfect for 8½ by 11 paper on most printers when you are printing at six lines to the inch. But if you change to eight lines to the inch or use a different size paper, you need to change the page length.

Which length to choose depends on which release of 1-2-3 you are using. Release 1A supports page lengths of any size between 20 and 100 lines. Release 2 has the same upper limit but supports a page size as small as ten lines.

To make this change, enter **/Print Printer Options Pg-Length** (Page-Length in Release 1A) and type any acceptable length before pressing RETURN. This change in length affects only the current worksheet. If you bring a new worksheet into memory and want it to use a page length other than the default, you need to invoke the command again.

Setup Strings

Setup strings are special character sequences that you can transmit to your printer to activate special features. These special features allow you to override standard settings such as printing six lines per inch or using standard typeface. Depending on the features of your printer, you can access alternate fonts. Print can be eight lines to the inch, or it can be compressed to allow more characters per inch horizontally than the standard setting of 10 or 12.

Unfortunately, print setup strings are specific to the different brands of printers. The commands that activate the features of one printer would not necessarily communicate the same information to another. The examples in this section use codes that will function for an Epson LQ-1500. This printer was chosen because it is one of the most popular currently being marketed. Before you try any of the examples, first check the manual for your printer and substitute the proper setup strings.

To add a setup string, enter **/Print Printer Options Setup**. This display will be presented for your entry:

```
A2: [W13] '516-75-8977                                    MENU
Enter Setup String:
          A        B        C        D        E        F
```

The characters you enter are generally a three-digit number preceded by a backslash. Supposing that when you look in your manual, you find that the code for compressed print is 15. In that case, type **\015** and press RETURN. This Print feature will be in effect for the entire worksheet when it is printed. It will also be used the next time you retrieve the file containing this worksheet, as long as you remember to save the file after entering the setup string. Also, since most printers have a memory feature, this Print feature will be in effect until you turn the printer off or send a string that turns off compressed print. Keep in mind that the size of characters affect the number that can fit across a line. If you choose an option that changes the character size, you might need to adjust your margin settings.

Try this example with the print control codes to have your printer produce compressed print:

1. Enter **/Print Printer Range**, type **A1..I65**, and press RETURN.

```
Report No: 2350                                                        Page 1

SS#         Last Name First Name Salary      Location  Phone    Position  Increase % 1988 Salary
516-75-8977 Jones     Paul       $45,900 DAL           980      2301      5.00%    $48,195
541-78-6754 Parker    Mary       $32,100 CHI           541      1605      4.00%    $33,384
897-90-8769 Smith     Larry      $61,250 ATL           342      1402      5.00%    $64,313
213-78-5412 Appel     Tom        $22,300 BOS           219      1750      6.00%    $23,638
516-75-8977 Jones     Paul       $45,900 DAL           980      2301      5.00%    $48,195
541-78-6754 Parker    Mary       $32,100 CHI           541      1605      4.00%    $33,384
897-90-8769 Smith     Larry      $61,250 ATL           342      1402      5.00%    $64,313
213-78-5412 Appel     Tom        $22,300 BOS           219      1750      6.00%    $23,638
516-75-8977 Jones     Paul       $45,900 DAL           980      2301      5.00%    $48,195
541-78-6754 Parker               $32,100 CHI           541      1605      4.00%    $33,384
                                                       342      1402      5.00%    $64,313
```

FIGURE 6.8 Using compressed print

2. Enter **Options Setup**.
   You do not have to enter / Print Printer again since you are already in the main Print menu.

3. Type **\015** or your control codes and press RETURN.
   You will need to substitute the proper code for your printer at this point.

4. Enter **Margins Right**, type **132**, and press RETURN.

5. Enter **Quit**, then **Go**, to print, as in the example shown in Figure 6.8.

6. Enter **Options Setup**.

7. Type **\018** and press RETURN.
   This setup string tells the printer to suspend compressed print. You will want to check your manual for the proper string for your printer.

8. Enter **Quit** then **Go**.

9. Enter **Quit** to exit the Print menu.

To delete printer setup strings, enter **/Print Printer Clear Format**. Do not use the Clear All option; it does eliminate printer setup strings, but it affects other worksheet entries as well.

SPECIAL PRINT OPTIONS

The Print features you have worked with up to now are the back-bone of 1-2-3's print capabilities. You will want to master them because you will use them every day to produce printed copies of all your models. A few additional Print features are used less fre-quently but are still important. They can help you solve the occa-sional problems for which the regular Print features offer no solu-tion. The additional Print features include special commands for printing print data to a file, printing cell formulas, and Print options that are hidden away in the worksheet menu.

Special Preparation for Writing to a File

You can write all your print output to a file by entering /**Print File** rather than / Print Printer. When this is the only change you make, the file that is created is identical to the data printed to a printer. Since the file data is frequently used for a purpose other than printing, this may not be appropriate. When writing data to a file, ask yourself whether page breaks, borders, and other formatting options should be applied. If you decide that you do not want the format options included—that you want your data written to the file without regard to page breaks or any other formatting such as margins, headers, or footers—enter the following command:

/Print File Options Other Unformatted

Later, if you decide to again include formatting when you print the worksheet data to your printer, you will first need to enter /**Print Printer Options Other Formatted** to restore formatting for the worksheet.

Printing Cell Formulas

1-2-3 provides a quick way to print a list of the contents of worksheet cells. This means that rather than displaying the result of a formula, the formula you originally entered will be displayed. Other attributes of the cell, such as width and format, will also be included in the list. Cells that are blank will be excluded from the list. Since 1-2-3 only prints the contents of one cell on a line, you can see how long this list might be for even a medium-sized worksheet.

You can try this technique for a section of the current worksheet. Follow these steps:

1. Enter /**Print Printer Range**.

2. Type **G2.I10** and press RETURN.

3. Enter **Options Other Cell-Formulas**.

4. Enter **Quit** to leave the Options menu and enter **Go**.

5. Enter **Options Other As-Displayed Quit**.
   This command sequence will set the display back to the normal mode where the printout of the worksheet matches the display you see on the screen.

6. Enter **Page Align Quit**.
   The list produced should look like the one in Figure 6.9.

Worksheet Features to Enhance Control

All the Print options you have reviewed thus far have been located within the Print menu. This is exactly where you would expect to look for this type of feature. There are several additional options that can significantly affect print results, but they are activated in

```
G2:  2301
H2:  (P2)  0.05
I2:  (C0)  +D2*(1+H2)
G3:  1605
H3:  (P2)  0.04
I3:  (C0)  +D3*(1+H3)
G4:  1402
H4:  (P2)  0.05
I4:  (C0)  +D4*(1+H4)
G5:  1750
H5:  (P2)  0.06
I5:  (C0)  +D5*(1+H5)
G6:  2301
H6:  (P2)  0.05
I6:  (C0)  +D6*(1+H6)
G7:  1605
H7:  (P2)  0.04
I7:  (C0)  +D7*(1+H7)
G8:  1402
H8:  (P2)  0.05
I8:  (C0)  +D8*(1+H8)
G9:  1750
H9:  (P2)  0.06
I9:  (C0)  +D9*(1+H9)
G10: 2301
H10: (P2)  0.05
I10: (C0)  +D10*(1+H10)
```

FIGURE 6.9 Printing cell formulas

unexpected ways. Two of the commands are found in the worksheet; the other is entered directly in worksheet cells.

ADDING PAGE BREAKS If you have Release 2, you can add a page break at any location within a worksheet to ensure that the information following the page break starts a new page. This feature can prevent awkward breaks that can occur, for example, between the last number in a column and the total for a column. Once 1-2-3 has processed the manual page break that you insert, it will again begin processing the automatic page breaks from the location of the manual page break to the end of the document. If you do not wish this, you must insert additional manual breaks to again interrupt the automatic page processing feature.

To insert a page break in the worksheet, move your cell pointer to the leftmost cell in the Print range in the row that you want to force to the top of a new page. Then enter /**Worksheet Page**. This causes 1-2-3 to insert a blank line above the cell pointer and to place a double colon symbol (::) in the cell that contained the cell pointer. The cell pointer then moves down a line and stays on the line that has the data it was originally with. If the double colon symbol is anywhere but at the left edge of the print range, 1-2-3 will ignore the page break request. If this symbol is at the left edge of the range and if you choose a range that is more than one page across, the break will occur across all pages in the range.

If you are using Release 2, follow these steps to insert a page break in the employee listing:

1. Move the cell pointer to A25.

2. Enter / **Worksheet Page**.
   The entries in row 25 and subsequent rows were moved down a row. The reason is that this command inserted a blank row and placed the page break symbol in the cell where the cell pointer was located when you requested the command.
   Figure 6.10 presents a look at a similar example where

B26: 'Appel   READY

	B	C	D	E	F	G
8	Smith	Larry	$61,250	ATL	342	1402
9	Appel	Tom	$22,300	BOS	219	1750
10	Jones	Paul	$45,900	DAL	980	2301
11	Parker	Mary	$32,100	CHI	541	1605
12	Smith	Larry	$61,250	ATL	342	1402
13	Appel	Tom	$22,300	BOS	219	1750
14	Jones	Paul	$45,900	DAL	980	2301
15	Parker	Mary	$32,100	CHI	541	1605
16	Smith	Larry	$61,250	ATL	342	1402
17	Appel	Tom	$22,300	BOS	219	1750
18	Jones	Paul	$45,900	DAL	980	2301
19	Parker	Mary	$32,100	CHI	541	1605
20	Smith	Larry	$61,250	ATL	342	1402
21	Appel	Tom	$22,300	BOS	219	1750
22	Jones	Paul	$45,900	DAL	980	2301
23	Parker	Mary	$32,100	CHI	541	1605
24	Smith	Larry	$61,250	ATL	342	1402
25	::					
26	Appel	Tom	$22,300	BOS	219	1750
27	Jones	Paul	$45,900	DAL	980	2301

FIGURE 6.10   Inserting a page break

the range began in column B. Placing the page break in column B would not work for the current example since column A is also used.

3. Enter /**Print Printer Go**.
   Since the range was already established in any earlier exercise, there is no need to reenter it.

4. Enter **Page Align Quit**.

ADDING SETUP STRINGS IN THE WORKSHEET   You have already seen how you can add a setup string through the Print options menu. These setup strings activate features on your printer and stay in effect while the entire worksheet is printing. With Release 2, you can also embed these same setup strings within the worksheet. This approach allows you to turn setup strings on and off in different parts of a document, and to use bold printing for a heading or important information.

Embedded setup strings must be in a row by themselves. Therefore, you must insert blank rows above the area where you want the setup string activated. Place the embedded setup string to the far left of the inserted row, and make sure that it starts with two vertical bar symbols (||). Follow these bars with the specific setup strings you want to use. Use the same format for the setup strings that you use when you add a single string through the Print options menu. The string always starts with a backslash (\) and is followed by a three-digit number that represents an acceptable setup string for your particular printer.

Use the following instructions to boldface the heading for the employee listing. When you enter the example, substitute the setup string for your particular printer.

1. Call up the employee worksheet on your screen and press HOME.

2. Enter /**Worksheet Insert Row** and press RETURN.

3. Type ||.

4. Continue typing **027069** and press RETURN.

```
SS#           Last Name   First Name  Salary    Location  Phone
516-75-8977   Jones       Paul        $45,900   DAL              980
541-78-6754   Parker      Mary        $32,100   CHI              541
897-90-8769   Smith       Larry       $61,250   ATL              342
213-78-5412   Appel       Tom         $22,300   BOS              219
516-75-8977   Jones       Paul        $45,900   DAL              980
541-78-6754   Parker      Mary        $32,100   CHI              541
897-90-8769   Smith       Larry       $61,250   ATL              342
213-78-5412   Appel       Tom         $22,300   BOS              219
516-75-8977   Jones       Paul        $45,900   DAL              980
541-78-6754   Parker      Mary        $32,100   CHI              541
897-90-8769   Smith       Larry       $61,250   ATL              342
213-78-5412   Appel       Tom         $22,300   BOS              219
516-75-8977   Jones       Paul        $45,900   DAL              980
541-78-6754   Parker      Mary        $32,100   CHI              541
897-90-8769   Smith       Larry       $61,250   ATL              342
213-78-5412   Appel       Tom         $22,300   BOS              219
516-75-8977   Jones       Paul        $45,900   DAL              980
```

FIGURE 6.11   Highlighting by adding print strings to the worksheet

This is the control code for boldface printing on an Epson LQ-1500 printer. Substitute the correct control code for boldface pointing on your printer; check your printer manual if you are not familiar with the codes.

5. Move the cell pointer to row 3.

6. Enter /**Worksheet Insert Row** and press RETURN.

7. Type ¦¦ **\027\064** and press RETURN.
   This entry represents the two vertical bars and the backslash that starts all setup strings, and the control code, which indicates that you want your printer to use its default setup string again. Only the control code portion of this entry varies from printer to printer. You will need to select the correct code from your printer manual.

8. Enter /**Print Printer**.

9. Enter **Range**, then type **A1.F25**.

10. Enter **Go**. A portion of the output showing the highlighted entries from row 1 appears in Figure 6.11.

11. Enter **Page Align Quit**.

HIDING COLUMNS   1-2-3's / *Worksheet Column Hide* in Release 2 can enhance the features of the Print commands by letting you define a wide print range and hide those columns that you do not want printed. The Print range command allows you to define only one contiguous print range. With the Column Hide option you can effectively extend this to many separate columns of information by hiding the columns that lie between the areas you want to print.

This feature is especially advantageous when a worksheet contains confidential information. You can hide a column that contains salary information or a projected increase percentage. Yet you can still create a list of employee names, locations, and phone numbers, even when the salary information is in the midst of the data columns you need. The Hide feature will not destroy the salary data, merely temporarily remove the unwanted data from view. When you want to restore hidden data, use the / Worksheet Column Display command and select one or more adjacent columns that are marked by asterisks to indicate their hidden status.

If you have Release 2, follow these steps to print a copy of the employee data without the salary or social security number columns:

1. Move the cell pointer to column A.

2. Enter / **Worksheet Column Hide**.
   The control panel asks that you specify the columns to be hidden as shown below:

```
A2: [W13] '516-75-8977                                    
Specify column to hide: A2

        A          B          C          D          E          F
1  SS#        Last Name  First Name Salary     Location   Phone
2  516-75-8977 Jones      Paul       $45,900 DAL                980
3  541-78-6754 Parker     Mary       $32,100 CHI                541
```

3. Press RETURN to select column A.

4. Move the cell pointer to column D, where the salary information is stored.

5. Enter /**Worksheet Column Hide** and press RETURN.

6. Enter /**Print Printer Clear All** to remove any prior print settings.

7. Enter **Range** , press Home, and type .. Then move with the RIGHT and DOWN ARROW keys until the cell pointer is in G10, and press RETURN.

8. Enter **Go**.
   The printed report will appear like the one in Figure 6.12.

9. Enter **Page Align Quit**.
   This command will position the paper at the top of a form, zero the line count, and exit from the Print menu, placing you back in READY mode.

10. Enter /**Worksheet Column Display** and position the cell pointer in column A before pressing RETURN.

11. Enter /**Worksheet Column Display** and select column D. The last two instructions prove that your original data is still intact even though it was not visible on the screen.

Last Name	First Name	Location	Phone	Position
Jones	Paul	DAL	980	2301
Parker	Mary	CHI	541	1605
Smith	Larry	ATL	342	1402
Appel	Tom	BOS	219	1750
Jones	Paul	DAL	980	2301
Parker	Mary	CHI	541	1605
Smith	Larry	ATL	342	1402
Appel	Tom	BOS	219	1750
Jones	Paul	DAL	980	2301

FIGURE 6.12   Hiding worksheet columns

SUMMARY

In this chapter you learned how to use a few simple commands to create a quick printed copy of work in progress. You found out the importance of monitoring the Print housekeeping tasks, which include page and line advancing and aligning your pages with 1-2-3's internal line count. After mastering the basics, you learned how to give a professional appearance to your output by controlling page length, margins, printer features, headers, and footers. You also discovered how to make a few changes not normally thought of as Print options because they are not found in the Print menu. These special features include adding page breaks, hidden columns, and setup strings.

7

BASIC
WORKSHEET
FUNCTIONS

Your 1-2-3 models have already shown you the importance of formulas. Formulas are actually the power behind a spreadsheet package like 1-2-3: They record your calculations and use them over and over again. But there is a problem with formulas: It takes a long time to record them, and when you are recording a long series of calculations, it is easy to make a mistake. Fortunately, 1-2-3 has built-in functions to reduce these drawbacks. These functions are prerecorded formulas that have already been verified for accuracy. All you need to do is specify which data they should operate on, each time you use them. The built-in functions also provide features that go beyond the capabilities of formulas and let you access the system date as well as calculations such as the square root and tangent.

In this chapter you will examine how 1-2-3's built-in functions are recorded on the worksheet. You will learn the syntax and the rules that provide a powerhouse of almost 90 prerecorded calculations that you can access easily. You will learn about the seven categories into which all 1-2-3 functions are grouped. There is an eighth category as well, with specialized application in the data-management environment. This subject will be covered in Chapter 9, when data-management features are discussed. In this chapter, however, you will examine a variety of functions from the different categories and learn how to use them in application models. This chapter is longer than previous ones because it explains the many diverse functions and exposes you to some of the variety offered by these functions.

BUILT-IN FUNCTION BASICS

A few general rules apply to all functions, regardless of their type. In some cases there are differences in how individual functions expect you to convey the data being used. You need to know the general rules and the individual exceptions, as well as which category of function is likely to handle the task you wish to address. This section provides such information. Read it before addressing the individual-function categories; it is an important first step.

General Rules

Since built-in functions are formulas, they are value entries in worksheet cells. There are several new rules that do not apply to formulas, all pertaining to the syntax of recording the different components of a function. A diagram of these components is shown in Figure 7.1. The first rule for function entry is that all functions must start with an @. After entering the @ symbol, you must include the special keyword that 1-2-3 uses to represent the

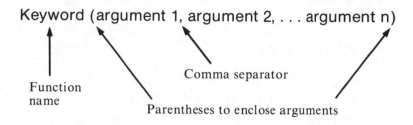

FIGURE 7.1   Function format

function. This keyword is the function's name. You can enter it in either upper case or lower case, but it must follow 1-2-3's spelling exactly.

RULES FOR FUNCTION ARGUMENTS   The next component within a function is the *arguments*. Arguments specify the data with which the function will work. Arguments are required by most functions, since most functions must be defined exactly in order to be used. However, there are a few exceptions to this rule. Arguments must be enclosed within parentheses; but if the function you are using does not require arguments, you do not need to use parentheses.

When using a function that requires multiple arguments, use a comma (,) to separate the arguments. With Release 2, a semicolon (;) is an acceptable alternative. Spaces cannot be used within a function; therefore, they are not valid as a separator character.

Function arguments can be provided as cell addresses, a name that you assign to one or more cells, constants, and even other built-in functions. The examples you enter in this chapter may include some constants in functions to expedite data entry. However, it is preferable to store the data needed by the function in worksheet cells and to reference these cells within the function, since a change in an argument's value will not require that you edit the function. Much variety is possible; look at these examples of the @SUM function, which total the values you provide as arguments:

@SUM(9,4,8,7)

@SUM(A1;D3;Y6;Z10)

@SUM(Salaries,RentExp,Equipment)

@SUM(A1..H4)

@SUM(A1,@SUM(B2..B3),Z2)

All five would be valid function entries, although you would need Release 2 for the semicolons in the second example. As you progress through the exercises in this chapter, you will have an opportunity to use different types of arguments.

Most of the built-in functions expect value entries for arguments. Release 2 has built-in functions that require string or character data for arguments. You cannot substitute a type of data for an argument that is different from what 1-2-3 is expecting. For example, if you use 1-2-3's @SUM function, you will need to provide value entries as arguments. @SUM will add these together to produce a total. If you substitute label entries for the arguments, @SUM will return an error.

DIFFERENT TYPES OF FUNCTION ARGUMENTS Different functions require different arguments and use them in different ways. The three basic types of functions are those that require no arguments, those that expect a list of arguments in any sequence, and those that require a specific number of arguments in a specific order.

Examples of functions that require no arguments are @RAND, @NA, and @PI. @RAND is used to generate a random number and does not require any input. @NA is used when data is missing and you want to mark its position as not available at the current time. @PI is used to represent the special mathematical constant 3.14159265, which is used in geometric problem solving.

There are also a number of functions that expect a list of values for arguments. The entries in the list can be single cells or ranges of cells and can be provided in any order you like. All the statistical functions fall within this category of argument types. For example, these two functions are equivalent:

@SUM(A1,B4,C5,D2..D10,F1,H2..M4)

@SUM(F1,H2..M4,A1,C5,D2..D10,B4)

In both cases all the individual values, as well as each of the values in the ranges, will be totaled to produce a single sum. Functions that allow this interchangeability of argument order specify "list" as their argument. For example, since @SUM accepts this type of argument, you can expect to see @SUM(list) when we discuss the syntax of this function in detail.

The last type of function argument is position dependent. Functions that require arguments in a specific order cannot have their arguments reordered without erroneous results occurring. For example, the @PMT function is designed to calculate the amount of a loan payment. The function requires three arguments: the principal, the interest, and the term of the loan. Later in the chapter you will see the functions specified like this:

@PMT(principal,interest,term of loan)

When using the function, you must provide the three arguments in this exact order.

Chapter Organization

There are seven categories of functions in 1-2-3, excluding the special database functions. The various function categories form the organizational structure of the rest of this chapter. You can use the remainder of the chapter in two ways. The preferred approach is to work through the exercises in each function category to become familiar with their use. There may be function categories that apply to your models, but unless you take an in-depth look at what they can do, you might not realize their potential. A second alternative, if your time is limited, is to focus on those function categories for which you have immediate use, then to come back and take a look at the other categories as you need them.

A CLOSE-UP LOOK AT EACH OF THE FUNCTION CATEGORIES

The built-in functions are grouped into categories in which each of the functions within a category has some similarity of purpose. This logical grouping of functions allows you to focus easily on the special requirements of a category. It can also help you increase your knowledge of new functions whose purpose might be similar to some functions you are already using. For example, if you are working with the @PMT and @FV functions from the financial category, it is wise to look closely at the other financial functions. Many of them may provide useful features in your models. Although this chapter covers only a subset of the functions, a comprehensive list of all the functions can be found in Appendix C.

As you work through this section you will find that Release 2 has functions that do not occur in Release 1A. Release 2 was given a whole new category of functions for working with string data. Within individual categories, these new functions for Release 2 users are appropriately marked.

Statistical Functions

"Statistics" is a word that causes many people to be apprehensive. They recall statistics as complicated mathematical procedures from a required college math course. But 1-2-3's statistical functions need not invoke this sense of alarm. They are simple to use, and they compute the most basic statistical measures. These are computations that you perform everyday without even thinking about them as "statistical." They include computations such as the average, sum, count, minimum value, and maximum value.

1-2-3's statistical functions perform their magic on lists of values. Frequently these lists are a contiguous range of cells on the worksheet. They can also be a series of individual values or a combination of a range and individual values. Blank cells can be included within the list, but all the values in the blank range will count as zeros. When a range contains multiple blank cells, 1-2-3 will ignore the cells that contain blanks.

The @COUNT function is an exception to the others in the statistical category. It counts the number of nonblank entries in the list. It can accept string values within its argument list in addition to numeric values.

You will use one model to test all the statistical functions. It will contain information on the monthly sales for all the High Profits Company sales personnel in region 4, as shown in Figure 7.2. Follow these steps to create the basic model before continuing:

1. Enter /**Worksheet Global Format Currency**. Type **0** and press RETURN.
    This command establishes a global format for the model before you enter data. Next you will format a section of the model that requires whole numbers to be displayed without the dollar sign.

2. Enter /**Range Format Fixed**. Type **0** and press RETURN. Type **B6.C13** and press RETURN.

3. Move the cell pointer to column A and enter /**Worksheet Column Set-Width**. Press the RIGHT ARROW key four times and press RETURN.
    This action widens this column to 13 positions in preparation for the data to be entered. There is one more column to be widened. You could have entered these commands, like the formatting command, after you entered the data in the worksheet. However, if you know what your final

G6: [W11] @SUM(D6..F6)

```
          A          B         C         D         E         F         G
1                        High Profits Quarterly Sales Figures
2                                   Region 4
3
4                                    Jan       Feb       Mar       Qtr.
5    Salesperson District Branch    Sales     Sales     Sales     Total
6    Jason Rye         1     1705  $95,800  $105,650  $114,785  $316,235
7    Paul Jones        3     3201  $56,780   $52,300   $48,750  $157,830
8    Mary Hart         1     1705  $89,675  $108,755  $135,400  $333,830
9    Tom Bush          2     4250  $91,555   $87,600   $92,300  $271,455
10   Gary Lowe         2     4250  $76,900   $82,600   $83,500  $243,000
11   Karen Stein       3     2950  $68,565   $76,500   $82,300  $227,365
12   Cindy Boyd        2     4590 $110,800  $153,400  $105,665  $369,865
13   Jim Rogers        1     1921  $98,000  $114,785  $114,785  $327,570
14
15               TOTAL SALES       $688,075 $781,590  $777,485 $2,247,150
16
17
18
19
20
```

FIGURE 7.2   Using the financial functions

report will look like, it is often best to perform the house-keeping tasks first.

4. Move the cell pointer to column G and enter /**Worksheet Column Set-Width**. Press the RIGHT ARROW key twice for a width of 11, then press RETURN.

Once you have completed the housekeeping tasks, you are ready to begin entering the data for the model. You can use Figure 7.2 as a guide to obtain the entries, or you can use the detailed entries in step 5.

5. Place the following entries in the worksheet cells listed:

C1:	**High Profits Quarterly Sales Figures**
D2:	**Region 4**

A5:	Salesperson
A6:	Jason Rye
A7:	Paul Jones
A8:	Mary Hart
A9:	Tom Bush
A10:	Gary Lowe
A11:	Karen Stein
A12:	Cindy Boyd
A13:	Jim Rogers
B5:	District
B6:	1
B7:	3
B8:	1
B9:	2
B10:	2
B11:	3
B12:	2
B13:	1
B15:	TOTAL SALES
C5:	Branch
C6:	1705
C7:	3201
C8:	1705
C9:	4250
C10:	4250
C11:	2950
C12:	4590
C13:	1921

D4:	Jan
D5:	Sales
D6:	95800
D7:	56780
D8:	89675
D9:	91555
D10:	76900
D11:	68565
D12:	110800
D13:	98000
E4:	Feb
E5:	Sales
E6:	105650
E7:	52300
E8:	108755
E9:	87600
E10:	82600
E11:	76500
E12:	153400
E13:	114785
F4:	Mar
F5:	Sales
F6:	114785
F7:	48750
F8:	135400
F9:	92300
F10:	83500
F11:	82300

F12:	**105665**
F13:	**114785**
G4:	**Qtr.**
G5:	**Total**

6. Move the cell pointer to D4 and enter /**Range Label-Prefix Right**. Move the cell pointer to G5 and press RETURN.

Your model should match the one in Figure 7.3. You are now ready to use it in testing the statistical functions.

D4: "Jan   READY

	A	B	C	D	E	F	G
1			High Profits Quarterly Sales Figures				
2			Region 4				
3							
4				Jan	Feb	Mar	Qtr.
5	Salesperson	District	Branch	Sales	Sales	Sales	Total
6	Jason Rye	1	1705	$95,800	$105,650	$114,785	
7	Paul Jones	3	3201	$56,780	$52,300	$48,750	
8	Mary Hart	1	1705	$89,675	$108,755	$135,400	
9	Tom Bush	2	4250	$91,555	$87,600	$92,300	
10	Gary Lowe	2	4250	$76,900	$82,600	$83,500	
11	Karen Stein	3	2950	$68,565	$76,500	$82,300	
12	Cindy Boyd	2	4590	$110,800	$153,400	$105,665	
13	Jim Rogers	1	1921	$98,000	$114,785	$114,785	
14							
15		TOTAL SALES					
16							
17							
18							
19							
20							

FIGURE 7.3 Right aligning the labels

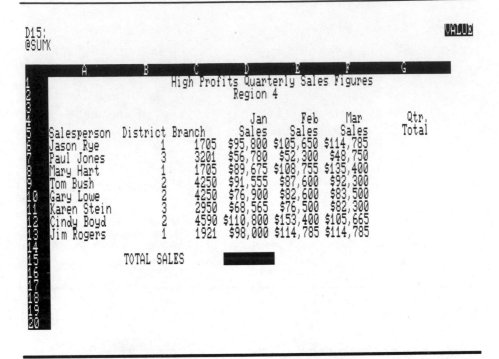

D15:   VALUE
@SUM

	A	B	C	D	E	F	G
1			High Profits Quarterly Sales Figures				
2			Region 4				
3							
4				Jan	Feb	Mar	Qtr.
5	Salesperson	District	Branch	Sales	Sales	Sales	Total
6	Jason Rye	1	1705	$95,800	$105,650	$114,785	
7	Paul Jones	3	3201	$56,780	$52,300	$48,750	
8	Mary Hart	1	1705	$89,675	$108,755	$135,400	
9	Tom Bush	2	4250	$91,555	$87,600	$92,300	
10	Gary Lowe	2	4250	$76,900	$82,600	$83,500	
11	Karen Stein	3	2950	$68,565	$76,500	$82,300	
12	Cindy Boyd	2	4590	$110,800	$153,400	$105,665	
13	Jim Rogers	1	1921	$98,000	$114,785	$114,785	
14							
15		TOTAL SALES		▓▓▓▓▓			
16							

FIGURE 7.4   Entering @SUM

@SUM   The @SUM function totals a list of values. The syntax for the function is @SUM(list). The list can be a range of values, a list of individual values separated by commas, or a combination of the two.

@SUM is one of the most frequently used functions. It easily performs the laborious task of adding each of the numbers in a range without having to enter a long formula to add each value separately. It can be used just as easily to total a row of values. As with any other formula, once you have entered it for one row or column, you can easily copy it to other locations where you have similar needs.

Using @SUM to Total Sales   You will use the @SUM function to compute the total sales in each month and the total sales for each salesperson during the quarter. Follow these steps to add the sum computations:

1. Move the cell pointer to D15 and type **@SUM(**, as shown in Figure 7.4.

2. Move the cell pointer to D6 and type **.** to lock the beginning of the range in place. Then move the cell pointer to D13 to highlight all the entries, as shown in Figure 7.5.

3. Type **)** and press RETURN to display the results shown in Figure 7.6.

You have just entered your first @SUM function using the pointing method for specifying the range. If you prefer you can always type

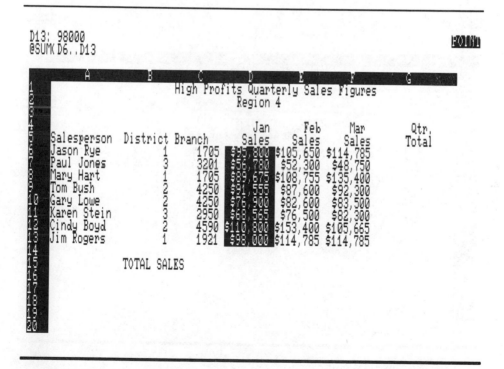

FIGURE 7.5 Highlighting the range

the range address rather than pointing to it, but the pointing method helps prevent errors. As you point to the beginning of the range you want to sum, you get visual verification that this is the correct beginning location for the calculation. The same is true when you point to the end of the range, since 1-2-3 highlights everything in the range. Either way you choose to enter the @SUM function, this function is a lot quicker than typing +D6+D7+D8+D9+D10+D11+D12+D13 — the alternate method for computing the desired result.

4. With the cell pointer in D15, enter /**Copy**. Press RETURN then move the cell pointer to E15 and type **.** before moving the cell pointer to G15 and pressing RETURN.

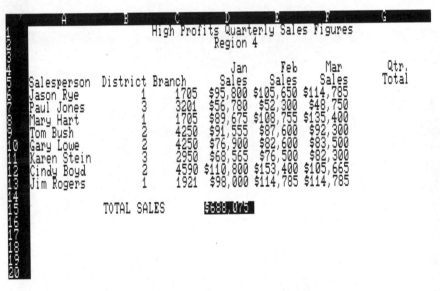

FIGURE 7.6   @SUM completed

This Copy command totaled all the columns for you, giving you maximum use from the one function you entered.

5. Move the cell pointer to G6. Type **@SUM(**, then move the cell pointer to D6. Type **.**, then move the cell pointer to F6. Type **)** and press RETURN.

   This formula produced a quarterly sales figure for Jason Rye.

6. Enter **/Copy** and press RETURN. Move the cell pointer to G7 and type **..** Then move the cell pointer to G13 and press RETURN.

   This last instruction copies the totals down the column so that you now have a total sales figure for each salesperson for the quarter, as in the model shown earlier in Figure 7.2.

Allowing for Expansion The example you just completed computes the monthly sales totals correctly. But if you want to add another salesperson to the bottom of the list, you need to revise the @SUM formulas at the bottom of the columns so they include a reference to the cell containing the figure for the new employee. You don't need to do this, however, if you insert the blank row in the middle of the sum range and enter the new data there. In that case, the new row will be included automatically since 1-2-3 will expand the range. The problem is that most of your additions are at the very top or bottom of the range and 1-2-3 does not stretch the range to include these new rows. However, you can overcome this revision requirement by entering your initial sum formula a little differently.

Leaving a blank row at the top and the bottom of the column you are summing will give you the expansion capability you need. If your original @SUM range includes a blank row at the top and bottom of the range, you can insert blank rows at the top or bottom and 1-2-3 will adjust the range for you. The blank rows do not affect the @SUM results since 1-2-3 treats them as zero. To alter the original @SUM formula, then copy it across again in preparation for adding a new salesperson, follow these steps:

A6: [W13]   READY

```
                 A         B        C        D        E        F        G
                         High Profits Quarterly Sales Figures
                                     Region 4

                                       Jan      Feb      Mar      Qtr.
                 Salesperson District Branch  Sales    Sales    Sales    Total

                 Jason Rye          1    1705  $95,800 $105,650 $114,785 $316,235
                 Paul Jones         3    3201  $56,780  $52,300  $48,750 $157,830
                 Mary Hart          1    1705  $89,675 $108,755 $135,400 $333,830
                 Tom Bush           2    4250  $91,555  $87,600  $92,300 $271,455
                 Gary Lowe          2    4250  $76,900  $82,600  $83,500 $243,000
                 Karen Stein        3    2950  $68,565  $76,500  $82,300 $227,365
                 Cindy Boyd         2    4590 $110,800 $153,400 $105,665 $369,865
                 Jim Rogers         1    1921  $98,000 $114,785 $114,785 $327,570

                 TOTAL SALES             $688,075 $781,590 $777,485 $2,247,150
```

FIGURE 7.7   Inserting a blank row to facilitate expansion

1. Move the cell pointer to A6 and enter **/Worksheet Insert Row**, then press RETURN to produce a display like the one shown in Figure 7.7.

2. Move the cell pointer to D16 and type **@SUM(D6..D15)**, then press RETURN.

3. Enter **/Copy** and press RETURN. Move the cell pointer to E16 and type **.**, then move the cell pointer to G16 and press RETURN.
   These new @SUM entries will allow you to expand your entries at either the top or the bottom of the database by placing the cell pointer in either row 6 or row 15 and using /Worksheet Insert Row to add a new blank row for the new employee information.

4. Move the cell pointer to A7 and enter **/Worksheet Insert Row** and press RETURN.

5. Make these entries to add the new salesperson:

A7:	**Jane Hunt**
B7:	**2**
C7:	**4590**
D7:	**87650**
E7:	**92300**
F7:	**93415**
G7:	**@SUM(D7..F7)**

Notice in Figure 7.8 that the totals for each month have been adjusted to show the new results. This means that you will be able to add new entries in any location within the data and have the formula updated for you automati-

---

G7: [W11] @SUM(D7..F7)   READY

```
              A         B       C        D         E         F          G
                        High Profits Quarterly Sales Figures
                                    Region 4
                                        Jan       Feb       Mar       Qtr.
      Salesperson  District Branch      Sales     Sales     Sales     Total
  7   Jane Hunt        $2    $4,590  $87,650   $92,300   $93,415   $273,365
  8   Jason Rye         1     1705   $95,800  $105,650  $114,785   $316,235
  9   Paul Jones        3     3201   $56,780   $52,300   $48,750   $157,830
 10   Mary Hart         1     1705   $89,675  $108,755  $135,400   $333,830
 11   Tom Bush          2     4250   $91,555   $87,600   $92,300   $271,455
 12   Gary Lowe         2     4250   $76,900   $82,600   $83,500   $243,000
 13   Karen Stein       3     2950   $68,565   $76,500   $82,300   $227,365
 14   Cindy Boyd        2     4590  $110,800  $153,400  $105,665   $369,865
 15   Jim Rogers        1     1921   $98,000  $114,785  $114,785   $327,570
 16
 17   TOTAL SALES             $775,725 $873,890 $870,900 $2,520,515
```

FIGURE 7.8 Total for the quarter

cally. Also notice that the district and branch values in this new line are formatted as currency, since the original ranges that were formatted did not include these cells.

6. Move the cell pointer to B7 and enter /**Range Format Fixed**, type **0**, and press RETURN. Move the cell pointer to C7 and press RETURN.

@COUNT   The @COUNT function returns the number of non-blank entries in a list. Its syntax is @COUNT(list), where list can represent a range or it can represent individual cells, just as it did in the @SUM function. Unlike the other statistical functions, @COUNT does not require value entries. It can count employee names as well as entries in the sales column.

Entries that contain zero are not equivalent to blanks and will be counted. You must carefully choose which column or row of a worksheet to count since you want to select data where mandatory entries are required for each record. Otherwise, the computed count may be artificially low due to the blank values in certain fields.

Follow these steps to count the number of sales personnel for region 4 of High Profit:

1. Move the cell pointer to B18 and type **'# SALES PERSONNEL**.

2. Move the cell pointer to D18, type **@COUNT(A6.A16)**, and press RETURN.
   The name field was chosen for counting the number of entries since it is assumed that all sales personnel have a name entry. It is possible that some salespeople who were not employed for the full quarter might not have all the months of sales data, and that counting these other fields could cause results to be computed lower than they should be.

3. Enter /**Range Format Fixed**, type **0**, and press RETURN twice.
   Your model should match the display in Figure 7.9.

```
D18: (F0) @COUNT(A6..A16)                                          READY
```

```
          A        B        C        D        E        F        G
              High Profits Quarterly Sales Figures
                         Region 4

                                 Jan      Feb      Mar      Qtr.
Salesperson  District Branch    Sales    Sales    Sales    Total

Jane Hunt        2     4590   $87,650  $92,300  $93,415  $273,365
Jason Rye        1     1705   $95,800 $105,650 $114,785  $316,235
Paul Jones       3     3201   $56,780  $52,300  $48,750  $157,830
Mary Hart        1     1705   $89,675 $108,755 $135,400  $333,830
Tom Bush         2     4250   $91,555  $87,600  $92,300  $271,455
Gary Lowe        2     4250   $76,900  $82,600  $83,500  $243,000
Karen Stein      3     2950   $68,565  $76,500  $82,300  $227,365
Cindy Boyd       2     4590  $110,800 $153,400 $105,665  $369,865
Jim Rogers       1     1921   $98,000 $114,785 $114,785  $327,570

          TOTAL SALES        $775,725 $873,890 $870,900 $2,520,515
          # SALES PERSONNEL        9
```

FIGURE 7.9   Using @COUNT

   4. Enter **/File Save**, type **SUMCOUNT**, and press
      RETURN.

The @COUNT function has widespread applicability. You can use
it to count the number of loan payments that have been received.
You can count the number of items in your inventory. Once you
have mastered the basics you will find many worksheets where the
@COUNT feature is useful.

@MIN   The @*MIN* function searches a list of values and returns
the smallest value in the list. Its syntax is @MIN(list). You could
use this function to find the lowest contract bid if all your bid
figures were listed on a worksheet. You could also use it to find the
lowest recorded temperature, the lowest-price supplier for an item,

G19: [W11] @MIN(G6..G16)   READY

```
         A          B        C        D        E        F        G
                            High Profits Quarterly Sales Figures
                                     Region 4
                                     Jan      Feb      Mar       Qtr.
                                     Sales    Sales    Sales     Total
  Salesperson  District  Branch
  Jane Hunt       2       4590    $87,650  $92,300  $93,415   $273,365
  Jason Rye       1       1705    $95,800 $105,650 $114,785   $316,235
  Paul Jones      3       3201    $56,780  $52,300  $48,750   $157,830
  Mary Hart       1       1705    $89,675 $108,755 $135,400   $333,830
  Tom Bush        2       4250    $91,555  $87,600  $92,300   $271,455
  Gary Lowe       2       4250    $76,900  $82,600  $83,500   $243,000
  Karen Stein     3       2950    $68,565  $76,500  $82,300   $227,365
  Cindy Boyd      2       4590   $110,800 $153,400 $105,665   $369,865
  Jim Rogers      1       1921    $98,000 $114,785 $114,785   $327,570

            TOTAL SALES          $775,725 $873,890 $870,900 $2,520,515
            # SALES PERSONNEL         9
                            LOWEST QTR SALES FIGURE          $157,830
```

FIGURE 7.10   Using @MIN

the individual who is paid the lowest salary, or in the case of the High Profit model, the lowest sales amount for a month or the quarter.

Add a label and a calculation to show the sales for the worst performer in region 4:

1. Move the cell pointer to D19 and type **LOWEST QTR SALES FIGURE** and move the cell pointer to G20.

2. Type **@MIN(G6.G16)** and press RETURN to produce the results shown in Figure 7.10.
   You could use this low sales amount to help you establish incentive programs or minimum sales standards.

The @MIN function will ignore blank cells. Cells that contain characters are evaluated as zero and could therefore erroneously be considered the lowest value in a list. Unfortunately, the function does not highlight the entry that produced the lowest value; it only returns it. If you want to find the entry that matches the returned value, you must visually scan the values in the cells that comprise the list.

@MAX The @*MAX* function examines a list of values and returns the largest value in the list. It returns the exact opposite of @MIN but uses an identical syntax of @MAX(list). You can use it to find the amount sold by the top performer, the highest hourly wage or annual salary, or the highest temperature in the month of August (assuming that the worksheet contains appropriate data values for these items). You can use @MAX to determine the highest sales for the quarter by making the following entries:

1. Move the cell pointer to D20 and type **LARGEST QTR SALES FIGURE**, then move the cell pointer to G20.

2. Type **@MAX(G6.G16)** and press RETURN.
   Like the @MIN function, @MAX ignores blank cells. It also treats labels as zeros. The results are shown in Figure 7.11.

3. Enter **/File Save**, type **MINMAX**, then press RETURN.

@AVG The @*AVG* function returns one value: the arithmetic average of all the values in a list. It is computed by summing all the values in the list and then dividing this sum by the number of entries in the list. @AVG is equivalent to the calculation @SUM (list)/@COUNT(list), and it uses the syntax @AVG(list).

You can use this new function to determine the average sales for each month. Follow these steps:

1. Enter **/File Retrieve**, type **SUMCOUNT**, then press RETURN.
   This will bring the original @SUM example into memory.

2. Move the cell pointer to B19 and type **AVERAGE SALES**. Then move the cell pointer to D19.

3. Type **@AVG(D6.D16)**, then press RETURN.

4. Enter **/Copy** and press RETURN. Move the cell pointer to E19 and type **.**, then move the cell pointer to G19 and press RETURN.
   You should now have the average for all three months and the quarter total in your model, as shown in Figure 7.12.

Date and Time Functions

Date and time information are an important part of many business decisions. Date information is needed to tell if a loan is overdue or

---

G20: [W11] @MAX(G6..G16)

```
                    High Profits Quarterly Sales Figures
                               Region 4
                                  Jan      Feb      Mar      Qtr.
     Salesperson District Branch Sales    Sales    Sales    Total

     Jane Hunt        2    4590  $87,650  $92,300  $93,415  $273,365
     Jason Rye        1    1705  $95,800 $105,650 $114,785  $316,235
     Paul Jones       3    3201  $56,780  $52,300  $48,750  $157,830
     Mary Hart        1    1705  $89,675 $108,755 $135,400  $333,830
     Tom Bush         2    4250  $91,555  $87,600  $92,300  $271,455
     Gary Lowe        2    4250  $76,900  $82,600  $83,500  $243,000
     Karen Stein      3    2950  $68,565  $76,500  $82,300  $227,365
     Cindy Boyd       2    4590 $110,800 $153,400 $105,665  $369,865
     Jim Rogers       1    1921  $98,000 $114,785 $114,785  $327,570

              TOTAL SALES       $775,725 $873,890 $870,900 $2,520,515
              # SALES PERSONNEL          9
                                LOWEST QTR SALES FIGURE    $157,830
                                LARGEST QTR SALES FIGURE   $369,865
```

FIGURE 7.11   Using @MAX

D19: @AVG(D7..D15)   READY

```
            A         B        C         D        E        F         G
                          High Profits Quarterly Sales Figures
                                   Region 4

                                       Jan      Feb      Mar       Qtr.
                                      Sales    Sales    Sales     Total
  Salesperson District Branch

  Jane Hunt        2      4590    $87,650  $92,300  $93,415   $273,365
  Jason Rye        1      1705    $95,800 $105,650 $114,785   $316,235
  Paul Jones       3      3201    $56,780  $52,300  $48,750   $157,830
  Mary Hart        1      1705    $89,675 $108,755 $135,400   $333,830
  Tom Bush         2      4250    $91,555  $87,600  $92,300   $271,455
  Gary Lowe        2      4250    $76,900  $82,600  $83,500   $243,000
  Karen Stein      3      2950    $68,565  $76,500  $82,300   $227,365
  Cindy Boyd       2      4590   $110,800 $153,400 $105,665   $369,865
  Jim Rogers       1      1921    $98,000 $114,785 $114,785   $327,570

            TOTAL SALES           $775,725 $873,890 $870,900 $2,520,515
            # SALES PERSONNEL            9
            AVERAGE SALES          $86,192  $97,099  $96,767   $280,057
```

FIGURE 7.12   Using @AVG

if there is still time remaining in the discount period for an invoice. Time information can be used to calculate the service time for various tasks or to log the delivery time for various carriers. Release 1A contains functions that support the date-stamping of worksheets and the use of dates in various calculations. Release 2 has added time functions that allow you to time-stamp a worksheet and perform calculations that involve time differences.

WORKING WITH DATES   1-2-3 can work with dates between January 1, 1900 and December 31, 2099. A unique serial number is assigned to each date: The number for January 1, 1900 is 1 and the number for December 31, 2099 is 73050. This serial-date number represents the number of days since December 31, 1899. Although representing every date in terms of its distance from December 31, 1899 may seem strange, this is what provides the date arithmetic features of the package. Since all dates have the same comparison point, you can subtract one date from another to determine how many days apart they are. If a loan is due on a date whose serial date number is 32980 and today's serial date number is 32990, then it is obvious that the loan is overdue since the serial number for the due date is less than today's serial date number.

All of this may seem a little confusing, but 1-2-3 can reduce some of the difficulty. You will not need to calculate or enter serial date numbers. 1-2-3 does that for you with its date functions. 1-2-3 also provides a format command that formats serial date numbers so they look presentable. You can choose from a variety of date formats that are familiar to you in the Range format menu.

Date-Stamping the Worksheet   Both releases of 1-2-3 provide a way for you to put a *date stamp* on the worksheet. With Release 1A, the function you will use is @*TODAY*. This function does not require arguments; when you enter it in a worksheet cell, it always accesses the system date and displays the serial date number for the system date in the worksheet cell where you entered the function. You can use / Range Format to change the appearance of this serial date number to something more familiar. Release 2 provides the identical feature, except that the function you enter is @*NOW*. You will learn some additional features of @NOW later, but for the moment the only important information about @NOW is that it enters a serial number in the worksheet cell. The serial number contains two parts with @NOW. It consists of a whole number and a decimal fraction. The whole number represents the serial date number and the decimal fraction represents the current time. Both the date and time will be updated every time the current model is recalculated. If you save your worksheet file after entering the @NOW function, it will be available the next time you use the worksheet. Every time you boot your system, you will want to ensure that the correct date is being used so that your models can be time-stamped accurately.

You can try out this date-stamping feature with these instructions, but remember to adjust them for Release 1A by substituting @TODAY for @NOW:

1. Enter /**Worksheet Erase Yes**.

2. Type **@NOW** and press RETURN.
   If you are using Release 2, you should see a serial-date number display that looks something like this:

A1: @NOW   READY

| A | B | C | D | E | F | G | H |
1   32126.00

Your display will be slightly different, since it will be based on the date when you are using the worksheet. There will be an even greater difference if you are using Release 1A, as the options are not the same. In fact, once entered, this function will be updated every time the worksheet is recalculated; so if you work with the spreadsheet past midnight, you will see the date change. If you save the worksheet to disk, the next time you retrieve the worksheet an updated date will appear in the cell that contains @NOW.

3. Enter /**Worksheet Column Set-Width** and press the RIGHT ARROW key. Then press RETURN.
   This instruction widens the display so that you can view date and time display in this column.

4. Enter /**Range Format Date** to produce this display:

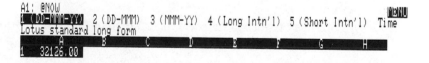

A1: @NOW   MENU
1 (DD-MMM-YY) 2 (DD-MMM) 3 (MMM-YY) 4 (Long Intn'l) 5 (Short Intn'l) Time
Lotus standard long form
| A | B | C | D | E | F | G | H |
1   32126.00

This display shows the various date-formatting options.

5. Use the RIGHT ARROW key and move to each of the menu options to view the date pattern that would be produced by selecting that option. Then select option 1 by typing **1** and pressing RETURN.
   The serial date number should now be formatted with a pattern like this:

```
A1: (D1) [W10] @NOW                                                    READY
      A            B       C       D       E       F       G
1   15-Dec-87
```

> Remember that your display will look a little different,
> since your date is probably different from the one used for
> this example.

If you include @NOW in an area of your worksheet that you
normally print, you will have an automatic date-stamp on every
printed report you create. Since you must retrieve the worksheet in
order to print it, the date will automatically be updated every time
the worksheet is printed.

Time-Stamping the Worksheet   The *time-stamp* feature is
accessed with the @NOW function and is only available for
Release 2. The difference between using @NOW to date-stamp the
worksheet or to time-stamp it is the format that you place on the
result of the function. @NOW returns both a whole number and a
decimal fraction. The whole number represents the number of
days; the decimal fraction represents the portion of the current day
that has already elapsed. If the decimal is .25, that would represent
a quarter of the day as having elapsed, or 6 a.m. A decimal fraction
of .5 represents noon and .75 represents 6 p.m. Naturally, all the
fractions between the ones listed also represent specific times
within the day.

To see these time displays as other than decimal fractions, you
will need to format the entries as time. Do this by using / Range
Format Date Time, producing the following display for your
selection:

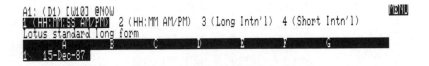

```
A1: (D1) [W10] @NOW                                                    MENU
1 (HH:MM:SS AM/PM)  2 (HH:MM AM/PM)  3 (Long Intn'l)  4 (Short Intn'l)
Lotus standard long form
      A            B       C       D       E       F       G
1   15-Dec-87
```

The variety of time displays will allow you to create a report that
closely matches the organizational standards you are currently
using.

You can time-stamp your worksheet by following these steps:

1. Move the cell pointer to A2, then type **@NOW** and press RETURN.

2. Enter **/Range Format Date Time 2** and press RETURN. Your display will be formatted like the following one, although the hour and minutes in the display will depend on the time of day when you make your entry.

A2: (D7) [W10] @NOW

Entering Dates Many times when you want to work with dates, you do not want the current date. You want to record the date of hire, loan due date, or an upcoming anniversary date. 1-2-3 provides a way for you to record this date information in the worksheet. You use the @*DATE* function and supply arguments that represent the year, month, and day.

This function is the first one you have worked with where the arguments needed to be supplied in a specific order, as shown in this syntax:

@DATE(YR,MO,DA)

The first argument, *YR*, can be any number from 0 to 199, with 1900 represented by 0, 1988 by 88, and 2099 by 199. The month argument, *MO*, can be any number from 1 through 12. The day argument, *DA*, can be a number from 1 to 31 but it must be a valid day number for the month you select. For example, September cannot have 31 because 30 is the largest number of days in September. Since you will want the function to generate the correct serial-date number for you, you must adhere exactly to the order shown for the three arguments.

You can put the @DATE function to work in a model that calculates the charges for video rentals. In this example, the charges will depend on the number of days that a patron has had the video.

You will enter the customer number in column A, the video number in column B, the date the video was checked out in column C, and the date it is returned in column D. These last two entries will be used to compute the charges. The formula you use will subtract the date when the video was checked out from the date when it was returned and multiply the number of days by $2.25. Follow these steps to make the entries and apply the formats shown in Figure 7.3.

1. Enter /**Worksheet Erase Yes** and make these entries in the worksheet cells listed:

A4:	**Customer-id**
A5:	**'21-876**
A6:	**'23-765**
A7:	**'34-651**
A8:	**'11-223**
A9:	**'56-675**
A10:	**'77-990**
A11:	**'11-983**
B4:	**Video**
B5:	**350**
B6:	**610**
B7:	**212**
B8:	**443**
B9:	**551**
B10:	**215**
B11:	**623**
C1:	**Every Rental Videos**
C3:	**Checked**
C4:	**Out**

D3:	**Checked**
D4:	**In**
E3:	**Amount**
E4:	**Due**

2. Now enter these dates using the @DATE function/:

C5:	**@DATE(87,11,6)**
C6:	**@DATE(87,09,26)**
C7:	**@DATE(87,10,27)**
C8:	**@DATE(87,10,31)**
C9:	**@DATE(87,11,5)**
C10:	**@DATE(87,11,16)**
C11:	**@DATE(87,11,17)**
D5:	**@DATE(87,11,9)**
D6:	**@DATE(87,09,27)**
D7:	**@DATE(87,11,1)**
D8:	**@DATE(87,11,2)**
D9:	**@DATE(87,11,6)**
D10:	**@DATE(87,11,18)**
D11:	**@DATE(87,10,18)**

3. Move the cell pointer to E5 and type **(D5-C5)*2.25**.
   This entry is the computation for the cost of the rental.
   This computation is the number of days times the daily
   charge of $2.25. But first you must calculate the number of
   days by subtracting the two dates.

4. Enter **/Copy**, press RETURN, then move the cell pointer
   to E6 and type **..** Then move the cell pointer to E11 and
   press RETURN.

5. Move the cell pointer to column A, press HOME and

E5: (C2) (D5-C5)*2.25

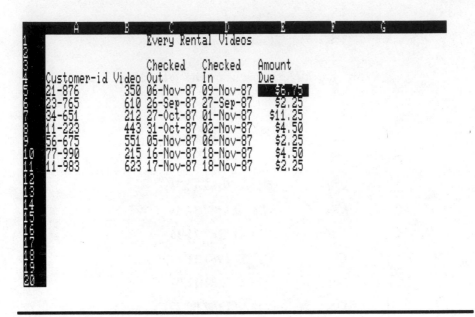

FIGURE 7.13   Result of subtracting two dates

enter /**Worksheet Column Set-Width**. Then type **12** and press RETURN.

6. Move the cell pointer to C5. Enter /**Range Format Date 1**. Type **C5.D11** and press RETURN.

7. Enter /**Worksheet Column Set-Width**, then press the RIGHT ARROW key so that the dates display properly. Then press RETURN.

8. Move the cell pointer to D5. Enter /**Worksheet Column Set-Width**, then press the RIGHT ARROW key followed by RETURN.

9. Move the cell pointer to E5. Enter /**Range Format Currency**. Press RETURN, then type **E5.E11** and press RETURN to produce the completed model shown in Figure 7.13.

Your model is now complete. However, you may be thinking that it would be just as easy to type the date in the way you want to see it by using a label entry such as "Apr-14-88". While this solution seems reasonable, the problem is that your entry would be a label and labels cannot be used in arithmetic operations. You would not be able to subtract two dates or compare the date against the current date without converting these label entries to dates. You will learn more about this conversion process in Chapter 10. For now, use @DATE anywhere you need to record a date on the worksheet.

Extracting a Portion of a Date   There are three functions that allow you to extract part of a date. You have the choice of extracting the year, month, or day from a serial date number. The syntax of the three functions are:

@YEAR(serial date number)

@MONTH(serial date number)

@DAY(serial date number)

Try all three functions by adding new columns to the existing model for the video rentals. Follow these steps:

1. Move the cell pointer to H5. Type **@YEAR(D5)** and press RETURN.
   The year number "87" should now display in this cell.

2. Move the cell pointer to I5. Type **@MONTH(D5)** and press RETURN.
   The month number should now appear in the cell.

3. Move the cell pointer to J5. Type **@DAY(D5)** and press RETURN.
   The day number should now appear in the cell, as shown in Figure 7.14.

4. Move the cell pointer to H5, enter **/Copy**, and press the RIGHT ARROW key twice to move the cell pointer to J5.

Then press RETURN. Move the cell pointer to H6 and type ., then move the cell pointer to H11 and press RETURN.

The model should match the data shown in Figure 7.15.

5. Press HOME, then enter **/File Save**, type **VIDEOS**, and press RETURN.

6. Enter **/Worksheet Erase Yes**.

Entering Times   Just as you need to use a function to enter dates, you must also use one for making time entries on the worksheet. If you enter time representations without using the special function

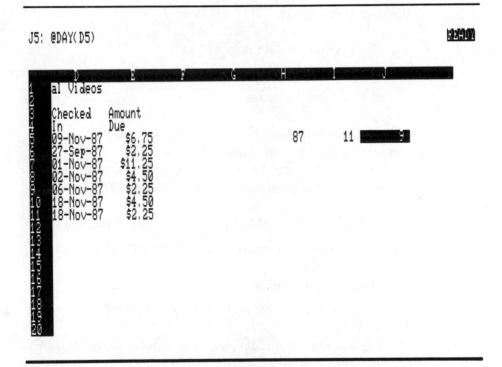

FIGURE 7.14   Extracting date components

H5: @YEAR(D5)

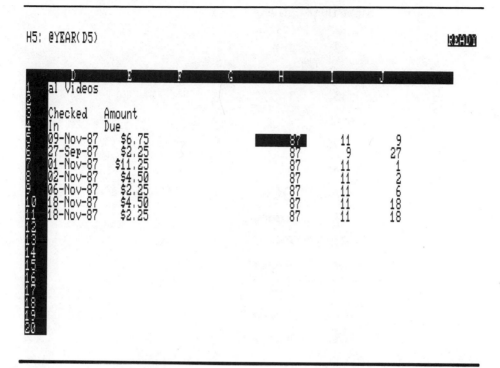

FIGURE 7.15   Copy the date functions

you will not be able to use it in time computations. The function available in Release 2 and above, used to make a time entry on the worksheet, is @*TIME*. This is the syntax it uses:

@TIME(hour,minute,second)

In this function, *hour* is a number between 0 and 23, with 0 representing midnight and 23 representing 11 P.M. *Minute* is a number between 0 and 59, and *second* has the same acceptable value range as minute.

Follow these instructions to create a worksheet that times the elapsed time between when a vehicle is logged in for repair and when it leaves the service facility.

1. Make these entries:

A3:	**Job**
A4:	**Number**
A5:	**1**
A6:	**2**
A7:	**3**
A8:	**4**
B1:	**QUICK CAR REPAIR November 12, 1987**
B3:	**Time**
B4:	**In**
C4:	**Repair**
C5:	**Tire**
C6:	**Brakes**
C7:	**Steering**
C8:	**Lube**
D3:	**Time**
D4:	**Out**
E3:	**Elapsed**
E4:	**Time**

Your model should now look like this:

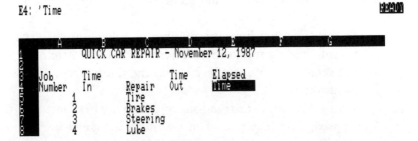

2. Move the cell pointer to B5, then enter **/Range Format**

Date Time 2. Move the cell pointer to B8 and press RETURN.

3. Move the cell pointer to D5 then enter /**Range Format Date Time 2**. Move the cell pointer to D8 and press RETURN.

4. Move the cell pointer to E5 then enter /**Range Format Date Time 4**. Move the cell pointer to E8 and press RETURN.

5. Move the cell pointer to B5, type **@TIME(8,5,0)**, and press the DOWN ARROW key.
Notice the zero entry for seconds. It is used as a place marker even when you do not have a special value to enter.

6. Move the cell pointer to B6, type **@TIME(8,10,0)**, and press the DOWN ARROW key.

7. Move the cell pointer to B7 and type **@TIME(8,30,0)** and press the DOWN ARROW key.

8. Move the cell pointer to B8 and type **@TIME(8,32,0)** and press RETURN to produce this display:

B8: (D7) @TIME(8,32,0)

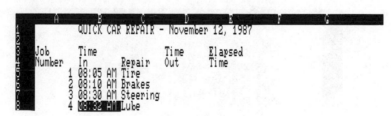

9. Complete the remaining time entries for the times the vehicles were completed by making these entries in column D:

D5:	**@TIME(9,17,0)**
D6:	**@TIME(10,34,0)**
D7:	**@TIME(13,18,0)**
D8:	**@TIME(9,44,0)**

Notice the use of a twenty-four-hour clock representation, with the number 13 used to represent 1 P.M., as shown below:

D8: (D7) @TIME(9,44,0)

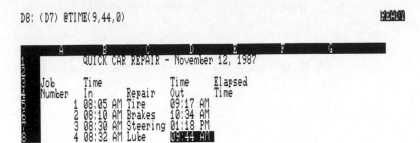

10. Move the cell pointer to E5, type **+D5-B5**, and press RETURN.
This computes the elapsed time for the repair of the first vehicle. When you copy this formula for the remaining entries, your job will be finished.

11. Enter **/Copy** and press RETURN. Move the cell pointer to E6, type **.**, then move the cell pointer to E8 and press RETURN to produce these results:

E5: (D9) +D5-B5

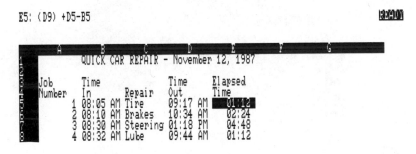

12. Enter **/File Save**, then type **TIME** and press RETURN.

13. Enter **/Worksheet Erase Yes**.

Extracting Part of a Time Entry   There are three functions available in Release 2 and above that can extract any part of a time serial number. They are @HOUR, @MINUTE, and @SECOND. All three use a time serial number as their argument, as in

@HOUR(time serial number). Since all three follow the same pattern, you will only need to take a close look at one to understand how each of them works.

The @*HOUR* function is used whenever you wish to work with only the hour portion of a time entry. The function always returns a value between 0 and 23. You can use this function to track the delivery hour for packages if the @TIME function was used to record the time of receipt. Follow these steps to enter the information on the packages and use the @HOUR function to extract the delivery hour:

1. Complete these entries:

A1:	**Time**
A2:	**Received**
A3:	**@TIME(8,4,6)**
A4:	**@TIME(9,11,0)**
A5:	**@TIME(9,30,0)**
A6:	**@TIME(9,45,0)**
B1:	**Package**
B2:	**Number**
B3:	**1761**
B4:	**3421**
B5:	**2280**
B6:	**7891**
C2:	**Recipient**
C3:	**B. Jones**
C4:	**R. Gaff**
C5:	**J. Bowyer**
C6:	**J. Kiger**
D2:	**Hour**

2. Move the cell pointer to A3 and enter **/Range Format Date Time 1**. Press the END key, followed by the DOWN ARROW, key then press RETURN.

3. Enter **/Worksheet Column Set-Width**, type **14**, and press RETURN.

4. Move the cell pointer to column C and enter **/Worksheet Column Set-Width**, type **16**, and press RETURN.

5. Move the cell pointer to D3, type **@HOUR(A3)**, and press RETURN.
   This extracts the hour number, which is 8.

6. Enter **/Copy** and press RETURN. Move the cell pointer to D4, type **.**, move the cell pointer to D6, then press RETURN. This produces the following display:

D3: @HOUR(A3)   READY

```
              A            B            C              D       E      F
   1  Time          Package
   2  Received       Number    Recepient          Hour
   3     08:04:06 AM     1761  B. Jones                    8
   4     09:11:00 AM     3421  R. Gaff                     9
   5     09:30:00 AM     2280  J. Bowyer                   9
   6     09:45:00 AM     7891  J. Kiger                    9
```

7. Enter **/File Save**, type **HOUR**, and press RETURN.

8. Enter **/Worksheet Erase Yes**.

String Functions

String functions are a new feature for Release 2.0. They provide a variety of character-manipulation formulas that give you flexibility in rearranging text entries. You can work with the entire label entry for a cell with the string functions, or with just a part of it. The functions in this category can be real life savers when you have to correct data-entry errors. You will work with abbreviated examples that correct errors in one or two entries; but the same formula you create for one entry could be copied down a column to correct a large portion of a worksheet. You will have the opportunity to work with functions that change the case of an entry from upper to lower or even proper. You will also learn how to extract one or more characters from the beginning or the end of a character string.

When the string values you are working with are used as arguments for the string functions, they must be enclosed in quotation marks ("). However, when these same entries are referenced by a cell address, no quotation marks are required. For example, the function @UPPER converts text entries to upper case. If you want to include the string jim smith as an argument in this function, you need to record it as @UPPER("jim smith"). However, if you store jim smith in A5, you can write @UPPER(A5), without quotation marks.

Some string functions produce another string as a result of the function. Other string functions produce numeric results that are equivalent to a position number within the string.

@UPPER The @*UPPER* function will change all the characters to upper case. This feature allows you to convert worksheet text data to all capital letters, if that is your preference. The syntax of the function is @UPPER(string).

Make these entries to try the function:

1. Move the cell pointer to A1, then enter **jim smith** and move the cell pointer to A2.

2. Type **Bill Brown**, then move the cell pointer to A3.

3. Type **JANE JONES**, then move the cell pointer to B1.

4. Enter **/Worksheet Global Column-Width**, type **12**, and press RETURN.

5. Type **@UPPER(A1)** and press RETURN.

6. Enter **/Copy** and press RETURN. Move the cell pointer to B2, type **.**, move the cell pointer to B3, and press RETURN.

The converted data appears like this:

B1: @UPPER(A1)

```
        A          B          C          D          E          F
1   jim smith    JIM SMITH
2   Bill Brown   BILL BROWN
3   JANE JONES   JANE JONES
```

@LOWER   The @*LOWER* function converts text entries to all lower case. Regardless of whether the text is upper case, lower case, or proper name format (with the first letter capitalized), the @LOWER function produces a string that is guaranteed to be in lower case.

You can use the example you created to test the @UPPER function for the @LOWER function. Follow these steps to add a new column to the model:

1. Move the cell pointer to C1, type **@LOWER(A1)**, and press RETURN.

2. Enter **/Copy** and press RETURN. Move the cell pointer to C2, type **.**, move the cell pointer to C3, and press RETURN to produce this display:

C1: @LOWER(A1)

```
        A          B          C          D          E          F
1   jim smith    JIM SMITH    jim smith
2   Bill Brown   BILL BROWN   bill brown
3   JANE JONES   JANE JONES   jane jones
```

@PROPER   The @*PROPER* function converts text into the format you expect to see for proper nouns. The first letter in each word is capitalized and the remaining letters of the word are displayed in lower case. This is another function you can use to establish consistency in the data on your worksheet. The model that was used to test the @UPPER and @LOWER functions can be used with @PROPER. Add another column to this model by following these instructions:

1. Move the cell pointer to D1, type **@PROPER(A1)**, and press RETURN.

2. Enter /**Copy** and press RETURN. Move the cell pointer to D2, type **.**, move the cell pointer to D3, and press RETURN to produce this display:

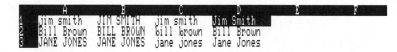

3. Enter /**File Save**, type **CASE**, and press RETURN.
4. Enter /**Worksheet Erase Yes** to clear the worksheet.

@RIGHT   The @*RIGHT* function extracts one or more characters from the right of a string entry. The function has two arguments: the function you want to extract from and the number of characters to extract. The syntax of the function looks like this:

@RIGHT(string,number of characters)

Examples of this function and the results it produces are:

@RIGHT("Lotus 1-2-3",5) equals 1-2-3

@RIGHT("ABC COMPANY   ") equals Y with seven trailing blanks.

You can use this function to extract a warehouse location represented by the last three characters in every part number. Make these entries on your worksheet to see how this function works:

1. Enter:

A1:	**Part No.**
A2:	**TY-3452-DAL**
A3:	**ST-67-CHI**
A4:	**JV-893-DAL**
B1:	**Warehouse**

2. Move the cell pointer to column A, then enter /**Worksheet Column Set-Width**, type **12**, and press RETURN.

3. Move the cell pointer to B2 and type **@RIGHT(A2,3)**, then press RETURN.

4. Enter /**Copy**, press RETURN, then move the cell pointer to B3. Type **.**, then move the cell pointer to B4 and press RETURN to produce this result:

B2: @RIGHT(A2,3)

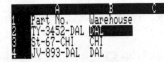

The warehouse locations have been filled with the result of the @RIGHT function. The last three characters of each part number represent the location, which is now displayed in column B. This feature is useful if you need to create a report that displays the warehouse locations but does not require the full display of the part numbers. Because the warehouse location is extracted from the longer entry, it is now much easier to focus on the information of interest (assuming that it is the warehouse location).

5. Enter /**File Save**, type **RIGHT**, and press RETURN if you want to save this model.

@LEFT   The @*LEFT* function removes characters from the front of a string. You can use it to reference strings in separate first name, last-name, and middle-initial columns of the worksheet, and to combine the result of these three functions with the string operator for concatenation (&). Concatenation will join all three into a set of initials. Make these entries to try the @LEFT function:

1. Enter /**Worksheet Erase Yes**.

2. Make the following entries on the worksheet:

A1:	**F Name**
A2:	**Sally**
A3:	**Joe**
A4:	**Sam**
A5:	**Kim**
B1:	**M Init**
B2:	**T.**
B3:	**L.**
B4:	**P.**
B5:	**D.**
C1:	**L Name**
C2.	**Smith**
C3:	**Harris**
C4:	**Polk**
C5:	**Jackson**
D1:	**Initials**

3. Move the cell pointer to D2 and type **@LEFT(A2,1)&@LEFT(B2,1)&@LEFT(C2,1)**, then press RETURN to see the first set of initials displayed:

D2: @LEFT(A2,1)&@LEFT(B2,1)&@LEFT(C2,1)

In this string formula the & serves as a means of combining strings, just as a + is used with numbers.

4. Enter **/Copy**, then press RETURN. Move the cell pointer to D3, type **.**, and move the cell pointer to D5. Press RETURN to complete the Copy operation.
The results look like this:

D2: @LEFT(A2,1)&@LEFT(B2,1)&@LEFT(C2,1)

	A	B	C	D	E	F	G	H
1	F Name	M Init	L Name	Initials				
2	Sally	T.	Smith	STS				
3	Joe	L.	Harris	JLH				
4	Sam	P.	Polk	SPP				
5	Kim	D.	Jackson	KDJ				

5. Enter **/File Save**, type **LEFT**, and press RETURN.

@REPEAT   The @*REPEAT* function is used to duplicate a character string a specified number of times. The primary purpose of this function is to improve the appearance of the worksheet. @REPEAT can create dividing lines between the assumptions of a report and the display of the final results. In one sense, @REPEAT is similar to the backslash character (\), since it repeats labels. It differs in the sense that \ is restricted to filling a single cell, whereas @REPEAT can extend across many worksheet cells. In addition, @REPEAT can complete the dividing line with the entry of one function, whereas the \ character normally requires repeated entries or copying to complete its task.

If you wish, you can go back to the sales projections you entered in an earlier chapter and replace the asterisks with the backslash, using a new character sequence. For now, enter @REPEAT in a worksheet cell to see how it works. Follow these steps:

1. Move the cell pointer to A7.

2. Type **@REPEAT("+-",36)** and press RETURN.
Your display should match this:

A7: @REPEAT("+-",36)

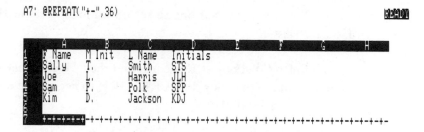

Notice that quotation marks were required in the function, since a string value was placed in the function as an argument.

Math Functions

1-2-3's math functions perform both simple calculations and more complex operations suited to an engineering or manufacturing application. Rather than look at the trigonometric functions and more complex operations, you will benefit most from the general purpose examples emphasized by the exercises in this section. You will learn how to overcome rounding problems, look at the absolute value of a number, and to work with only the integer portion of a number.

@ABS   The @*ABS* function returns the positive or absolute value of a number, without regard to whether the number is positive or negative. The function is useful when you are concerned with the relative size of numbers and do not care if the number is positive or negative.

An example of this function is illustrated by the need of retail establishments to monitor cash overages and shortages in their registers. Consistent cash overages and shortages indicate a cash-control problem that should be corrected. Simply adding the overages and shortages doesn't always work: They might cancel each other out. However, examining the absolute value of the overages and shortages reveals the total amount of the differences.

Follow these instructions to set up a model for the Hot Dog House Register:

1. Enter /**Worksheet Erase Yes** and then /**Worksheet Global Format Currency**. Press RETURN to accept the default of two decimal places.

2. Place these entries in worksheet cells:

A5:	**Monday**
A6:	**Tuesday**
A7:	**Wednesday**
A8:	**Thursday**
A9:	**Friday**
A10:	**Saturday**
A11:	**Sunday**
A13:	**TOTAL DIFFERENCE FOR THE WEEK:**
C1:	**' Hot Dog House Register**
C2:	**Week of November 10, 1987**
C4:	**Over/Under**
C5:	**42**
C6:	**-35**
C7:	**22.78**
C8:	**-57**
C9:	**12.58**
C10:	**.58**
C11:	**-2.10**
E4:	**Absolute Value**

3. Move the cell pointer to E5, then enter **@ABS(C5)** and press RETURN.
   This step computes the absolute value of the entry in C5.

4. Enter /**Copy** and press RETURN. Move the cell pointer to E6, type **.**, move the cell pointer to E11, and press RETURN.

Once you have completed this step, all the daily cash differences have been converted to their absolute values and stored in column E.

5. Move the cell pointer to E13, then type **@SUM(E5.E11)** and press RETURN to produce the results shown in Figure 7.16.

This step computes a total of the cash differences without regard to whether they were positive or negative, by using the absolute value of each day's total in the sum calculation. This method prevents the cash differences from partially canceling each other out and seeming like less of a problem than they actually are.

E13: (C2) @SUM(E5..E11)   READY

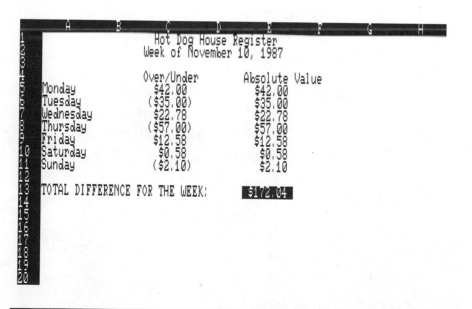

FIGURE 7.16   Using @ABS

@INT   The @*INT* function lets you truncate the decimal places in a number to produce a whole number or integer. You can use it when you work with date computations in Release 2 and wish to truncate the decimal fraction that represents the time portion of the current date. You can also use it when calculating the number of complete items that can be produced on a production line. To see how this function works, create a model similar to this second example.

This model will determine how many complete items can be produced from a given volume of raw material. The raw material is cowhide, and the product being produced is wallets. It has been determined that one wallet will require 0.6789 square feet of cowhide. Partially completed items will not be considered, since they cannot be shipped. It does not work to round the calculated result; the decimal fraction computed could be rounded upward and would no longer represent completed items. The only solution is to truncate the decimal portion of the number.

The @INT function that you will use when creating your model follows this syntax:

@INT(NUMBER)

Follow these steps to create your model:

1. Enter **/Worksheet Erase Yes** and make the following entries:

A1:	**Cowhide needed for 1 wallet –**
A3:	**Available sizes**
A4:	**1**
A5:	**5**
A6:	**10**
A7:	**15**
A8:	**20**

A9:	**25**
D3:	**Wallets Produced**
E1:	**.6789**
F1:	**Sq. ft.**

2. Move the cell pointer to D4 and type **@INT(A4/$E$1)**. Notice that the argument for the @INT function is the formula A4/$E$1. This formula divides the size of the piece of raw material by the square footage requirements. The reference to the requirements of one piece is absolute; this one value will be referenced in all the calculations and should not change if this formula is copied. The second part of the formula adds the @INT function, which will cause any decimal fraction resulting from the computation to be truncated. This result will then represent the actual number of wallets that can be produced.

3. Enter **/Copy** and press RETURN. Move the cell pointer to D5, type **.**, move the cell pointer to D9, and press RETURN.
   You now have the integer portion of each of the calculations, as shown below:

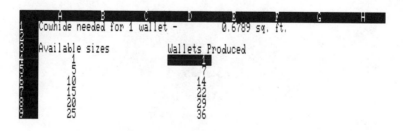

4. Enter **/File Save**, type **INTEGER**, and press RETURN.

5. Enter **/Worksheet Erase Yes**.

@ROUND   The *@ROUND* function actually alters the way a number is stored internally by letting you specify the number of decimal places you want. This function can solve some of the problems caused by the discrepancy between how numbers are stored and the format you use to display them. In Chapter 3 you learned that you could use the format commands (/ Worksheet Global Format and / Range Format) to display numbers with a varying amount of decimal places. But the problem with these changes is that the full internal accuracy is still maintained despite the change in the display appearance. This can cause totals at the bottom of a column to appear as though they do not add properly. This is caused by the greater internal storage accuracy of the numbers being added.

Use the following steps to create a model that shows this discrepancy, then apply the @ROUND function to the formulas in the model so that the internal accuracy is equal to the numbers that are displayed.

1. Make these entries:

A2:	**Product 1 Sales**
A3:	**Product 2 Sales**
A4:	**Product 3 Sales**
C1:	**Price**
C2:	**33.3333**
C3:	**67.5068**
C4:	**3.3335**
D1:	**Quantity**
D2:	**100**
D3:	**50**
D4:	**100**
E1:	**Total $$Tc1**

2. Move the cell pointer to C2 and enter **/Range Format Currency**, type **4**, and press RETURN. Press the END key, followed by the DOWN ARROW key, then press RETURN.

3. Move the cell pointer to E2 and enter **/Range Format Currency**, type **0**, and press RETURN. Type **E2.E5** and press RETURN.

   The END and DOWN ARROW sequence will not work for this format operation, since the cells are empty at this time and it would format to the bottom of the column.

4. Type **+C2*D2** and press RETURN.

   This formula computes the total cost of the purchase. A whole number is displayed; however, a decimal fraction exists in the number stored internally because of the decimals in the price.

5. Enter **/Copy** and press RETURN. Move the cell pointer to E3, type **.**, then move the cell pointer to E4 and press RETURN.

6. Move the cell pointer to E5 and type **@SUM(E2.E4)**. Press RETURN to produce the results below:

E5: (C0) @SUM(E2..E4)   READY

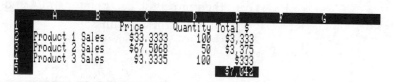

Looking at the column E figures suggests that the total should be $7,041, not the $7,042 shown. The difference of 1 is due to the rounding discrepancy that occurs when the total $ numbers are displayed. The @SUM function is computed from the numbers that are stored, not those that are displayed. The @ROUND function can solve this problem. But first you need to learn a little more about its syntax.

The format of the @ROUND function is:

@ROUND(number to be rounded, place of rounding)

The number to be rounded can be a number, a reference to a cell that contains a number, or a formula that evaluates as a number. The place of rounding is a positive or negative number that specifies the place of rounding. Rounding to the nearest whole number uses 0 as the place of rounding. Rounding to decimal places to the right of a whole number uses positive integers for each place further to the right. Rounding to the left of the whole-number position is represented by negative integers. Table 7.1 shows the effect of some of the rounding options on a number.

You can apply this @ROUND function to the total $ computations with these steps:

1. Move the cell pointer to E2, then press F2 (EDIT).

2. Press the HOME key to move to the front of the entry. Press DEL to delete the +.

3. Type **@ROUND(**.

4. Press the END key, then type **,0)** and press RETURN.

5. Enter **/Copy**, then press RETURN. Move the cell pointer to E3, type **.**, then move the cell pointer to E4 and press RETURN to produce these results:

E2: (C0) @ROUND(C2*D2,0)

The addition of @ROUND to each formula makes the column total agree with the numbers displayed. This is because you altered the internal accuracy of each of the numbers to force it to match the display.

6. Enter /**File Save**, type **ROUND**, and press RETURN.

7. Enter /**Worksheet Erase Yes**.

Many worksheets will have @ROUND added to most of the formulas. To use it, follow the same procedure used in this example, making each formula an argument to the @ROUND function.

Special Functions

1-2-3's special functions are grouped together because they do not fit neatly into any of the other function categories. Some of them are used to trap error conditions; others count the number of rows in a range or allow you to choose a value from a list of options. Still others let you examine the contents of worksheet cells closely, thus providing information about a cell's value or other attributes. For the most part, this group can be thought of as a smorgasbord of sophisticated features. Because of these functions are so complex, only one of them will be introduced at this time. More sophisticated examples will be deferred until Chapter 10.

Number	Rounded Number	Formula for Rounding
12345.678123	12345.6781	@ROUND($A$3,4)
	12345.68	@ROUND($A$3,2)
	12345.7	@ROUND($A$3,1)
	12346	@ROUND($A$3,0)
	12300	@ROUND($A$3,-2)
	10000	@ROUND($A$3,-4)

TABLE 7.1   Effect of various rounding options

@NA   This function causes *NA* ("not available") to appear in the cell where @NA is entered. Its impact does not stop there: All worksheet cells that reference this cell will also have the value NA. There are no arguments for this function: Its syntax is @NA.

@NA is used as a flag to remind you to complete missing entries before finalizing a report. Since cells that reference this cell take on the value NA, there is no way for you to erroneously assume that a total reflects all data entries. The presence of NA in the total area acts as a flag to remind you to enter the missing value before you finalize a report.

Create a model that uses the @NA feature to flag missing grades for an instructor. All students who miss an exam have their grade entered as @NA rather than as a test score. This means that their final grade-point average will show as @NA since it will reference each of the exam grades, including the one recorded as @NA. An instructor could use this model at the end of a semester to identify those students who had not yet made up missing exams. The instructor would have the option to change the missing exam grade to a 0, or to record an Incomplete for the student's final grade. Follow these steps to complete the model:

1. Make these entries to add a heading for each category and to place the students' names in the model:

C1:	**Fall Semester 1987**
A3:	**Student**
A4:	**B. Black**
A5:	**S. Conners**
A6:	**F. Dalton**
A7:	**G. Limmer**
A8:	**S. Melton**
A9:	**P. Stock**
A10:	**J. Zimmer**

B3:	**Exam 1**
C3:	**Exam 2**
D3:	**Exam 3**
E3:	**Final**
F3:	**Average**

2. Record these grades for the first exam:

B4:	**75**
B5:	**67**
B6:	**78**
B7:	**88**
B8:	**67**
B9:	**67**
B10:	**91**

3. Record these entries for the second exam:

C4:	**@NA**
C5:	**78**
C6:	**90**
C7:	**81**
C8:	**55**
C9:	**89**
C10:	**82**

Since B. Black did not take exam 2, @NA was recorded for that student's score. Recording NA will not give you the same effect. @NA is a value entry that will affect calculations referencing the cell. NA is a label entry and cannot be used in arithmetic calculations.

4. Record these grades for exam 3 and the final exam:

D4:	82
D5:	72
D6:	89
D7:	93
D8:	40
D9:	@NA
D10:	75
E4:	88
E5:	81
E6:	92
E7:	87
E8:	60
E9:	78
E10:	89

5. Move the cell pointer to F4 and type **@AVG(B4.E4)** and press RETURN.

6. Enter **/Copy** and press RETURN. Move the cell pointer to F5, type **.**, and move the cell pointer to F10. Then press RETURN.
   The results are shown in Figure 7.17. Notice that the average for B. Black and P. Stock display as NA. These averages are not available, since one of the values needed to compute them is missing.

7. Enter **/File Save**, type **NA**, and press RETURN.

8. Enter **/Worksheet Erase Yes**.

Financial Functions

1-2-3 provides an entire category of functions to use in investment calculations and other calculations concerned with the time value of money. You can use these financial functions to monitor loans, annuities, and cash flows over period of time. With Release 2, some depreciation calculations are also included in these financial functions. You can quickly compare various financial alternatives since you can rely on the function to supply the correct formulas. As

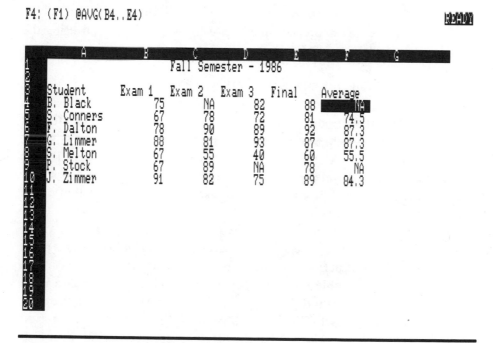

FIGURE 7.17   Using @NA

with the other functions, all you need to supply are arguments to tailor the calculations to your exact needs.

When you use financial functions, it is very important that all the arguments and the result use the same unit of time. For example, a function to compute a loan-payment amount will require you to decide whether you want to calculate the payment amount on a yearly, quarterly, or monthly basis. Once you decide on one of these or some other unit of time, you must apply it consistently across all arguments. If you choose to compute a monthly payment amount, the interest rate must be expressed as a monthly rate. Likewise, the term should be expressed as a number of months. You will work with three of the built-in functions in this section.

@DDB   The @*DDB* function, available in Release 2 and above, computes the depreciation expense for a specific period using the double declining balance method. The format of the function is:

@DDB(cost,salvage,life,period)

Cost is the amount you paid for the asset you are depreciating. It must be a value or a reference to a cell that contains a value. *Salvage* is the value of the asset at the end of its useful life. Like the cost, this argument must be a value or a reference to a cell that contains one. *Life* is the expected useful life of the asset; that is, the number of years needed to depreciate the asset from its cost to its salvage value. Normally the life of the asset is expressed in years, but it must always be a value or a reference to a value. *Period* is the specific time period for which you are computing the depreciation. Since the double declining balance method of depreciation is an accelerated method that allows you to depreciate more in the early years of an asset's life, it is important to specify the correct period for your calculations. Like the other arguments, period must be a value or a reference to one.

Use the @DDB function to build a model that calculates the depreciation expense for each year in an asset's five-year life. Follow these steps:

1. Make these entries:

A1:	**Depreciation Expense Using the Double Declining Balance Method**
A3:	**Cost:**
A4:	**Salvage Value:**
A5:	**Useful Life:**
A6:	**Year 1:**
A7:	**Year 2:**
A8:	**Year 3:**
A9:	**Year 4:**
A10:	**Year 5:**
A12:	**Total Depreciation:**
C3:	**11000**
C4:	**1000**
C5:	**5**

2. Enter /**Worksheet Global Format Currency** and press RETURN.

3. Move the cell pointer to C3 and enter /**Range Format Currency**, type **0**, and press RETURN. Move the cell pointer to C4 and press RETURN.

4. Move the cell pointer to C5, then enter /**Range Format Fixed**. Type **0** and press RETURN twice.

5. Enter /**Worksheet Column Set-Width**, press the RIGHT ARROW key twice, and press RETURN. Move the cell pointer to column A, enter /**Worksheet Column Set-Width**, type **11**, and press RETURN.

6. Move the cell pointer to C6 and type **@DDB($C$3,$C$4,$C$5,1)**, and press RETURN. This formula computes the depreciation expense for the

C6: [W11] @DDB($C$3,$C$4,$C$5,1)   READY

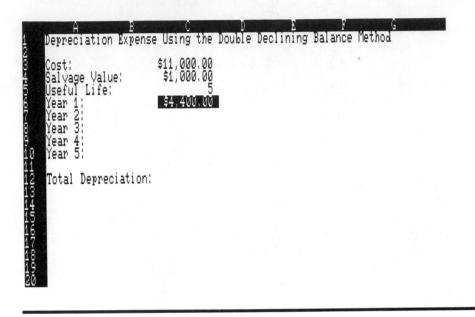

FIGURE 7.18   Depreciation for Year 1

first year, as shown in Figure 7.18. The $s were used so that the formula could be copied, even though it will need to be edited to change the year number.

7. Enter **/Copy** and press RETURN. Move the cell pointer to C7, type **.**, move the cell pointer to C10, then press RETURN.
   The formula has been copied but each formula needs to be edited to reference the proper year.

8. Move the cell pointer to C7 and press F2 (EDIT). Press the RIGHT ARROW key, then press the BACKSPACE key to delete the 1. Type a 2 and press RETURN.

9. Use this same edit technique to change the formulas in C8..C10 to reference the proper year.

10. Move the cell pointer to C12, type **@SUM(C6.C10)**, and press RETURN to produce the results shown in Figure 7.19.

11. Enter **/File Save**, type **DEPREC**, and press RETURN.

12. Enter **/Worksheet Erase Yes**.

FIGURE 7.19   Copying @DDB

@PMT   The @*PMT* function calculates the appropriate payment amount for a loan. The syntax for this function is:

@PMT(principal,interest,term of loan)

The *principal* is a numeric value that represents the amount of money borrowed. *Interest* is a numeric value that represents the interest rate. To specify a nine percent interest rate, you can use 9% or .09. *Term* is the number of payments for the loan. It is a numeric value and should be expressed in the same time period as the interest.

You can test this function in building a model that determines whether you can afford the monthly payments on your dream home. Complete these steps:

1. Make the following entries:

A1:	**Principal:**
A2:	**Interest:**
A3:	**Term:**
A5:	**Monthly Payments:**
C1:	**150000**
C2:	**.09**
C3:	**20**
D3:	**years**

2. Move the cell pointer to C1, enter /**Range Format Currency**, and press RETURN twice.

3. Move the cell pointer to C2 and enter /**Range Format Percent**. Press RETURN twice.

4. Move the cell pointer to C5 and enter /**Range Format Currency** and press RETURN twice.

5. Enter /**Worksheet Column Set-Width**, type **12**, and press RETURN.

6. Type **@PMT(C1,C2/12,C3*12)** and press RETURN. The interest rate must be divided by 12 to convert the annual percentage to a monthly figure. The term is expressed in years and must be multiplied by 12 to express it as months. The result is shown below:

C5: (C2) [W12] @PMT(C1,C2/12,C3*12)

7. Enter /**File Save**, type **PAYMENT**, and press RETURN.

8. Enter /**Worksheet Erase Yes**.

Logical Functions

1-2-3's logical functions allow you to build conditional features into your models. The functions in this category return logical (true or false) values as the result of the condition tests they perform. They are a powerful addition to 1-2-3 because they allow you to alter calculations based on conditions in other locations of the worksheet. This flexibility lets you construct models patterned after "real world" business conditions, where exceptions are prevalent.

These functions let you have more than one calculation for commission payments, purchase discounts, FICA tax, or any other computation requiring multiple calculations that depend on other values in the worksheet. Because these functions frequently use both simple and compound operators and because they are frequently used in combination when making an entry, none of them is covered in this chapter. However, many logical functions will be introduced in Chapter 10 when advanced functions are discussed.

SUMMARY

In this chapter you have explored the time-saving features of 1-2-3's built-in functions. By now you should be familiar with the different categories of functions and the types of features they can offer you as you build your models. The functions in this chapter are the simpler functions from each of these categories, but they can still add significant power to your models. After mastering the examples in the categories of interest you will want to study the more sophisticated function examples in Chapter 10.

8

CREATING GRAPHS

The worksheet is an excellent way to *perform* all your financial projections, but it is not always the best way to *present* the results from these calculations. Important numbers that you want to highlight often get lost in a sea of other figures. How can you make sure that you and others who read your report, which contains hundreds of numbers, will focus on those conditions and trends that you think are important?

One solution is to use 1-2-3's graphics features, which let you present your data in an easy-to-interpret format. Graphs do not present all the specific numbers; instead, they can summarize the essence of your data so that you can focus on general patterns and trends. And when you find something in a graph that warrants more detailed analysis, you can still return to the supporting worksheet figures for a closer look.

You do not have to reenter your 1-2-3 data to use the graphics features. You can use the data already entered for your spreadsheet application without making any changes. Nor do you need to learn a new system to create your graphs; 1-2-3's graphics features are accessed through menus that are just like 1-2-3's other menus. You only need to learn a few new commands. Once you have entered your worksheet data, you need make only a few menu selections to present this data in graphic format. (Incidentally, any changes you make to your data will be reflected in your graph.)

To view your graphs on the screen, you need a color monitor or

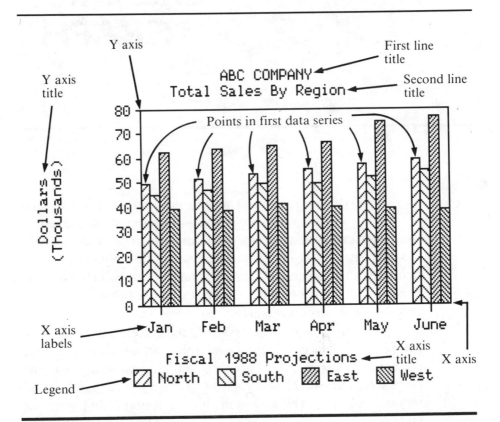

FIGURE 8.1   A bar graph with titles and legend

a monochrome (one-color) monitor with a graphics card. But even if you do not have a monitor that will support graphics, you can still make the menu selections that define the graph, and save it to disk for printing later on.

1-2-3 can never print a graph directly. Graphs must be saved to disk and printed with the separate *PrintGraph* program that is part of your 1-2-3 package. A separate program is required because 1-2-3's graphics features are so extensive. There are different fonts, different sizes, and color, as well as support for a variety of printers and plotters. If all these options had been placed within 1-2-3, so much memory would have been required that there would be no room for your own data.

This chapter will introduce you to the basic commands for defining a graph. You will learn about some of the special options that produce a more professional product. You will find out how to create and save multiple graphs on a single worksheet file. You will also learn how to obtain a printed copy of a graph.

CREATING A GRAPH

Creating a basic graph is really quite simple. There are three basic steps. First, decide what type of graph you wish to see. Second, tell 1-2-3 what data to place in this graph. And third, tell 1-2-3 to display the graph for you. Once you have completed these basics, you may want to add further enhancements.

Basic Graphics Technology

Before you can begin to create your first graph, there are a few basic terms to understand. A sample graph, with the key terms and components marked, is shown in Figure 8.1. A discussion of each of the basic terms follows. More specialized terms are covered along with the implementation of specific features, discussed later in the chapter.

DATA SERIES   1-2-3's graphs are designed to show from one to six sets of data values, depending on the type of graph that you select. A set of data values is referred to as a *series* and must consist of a range of contiguous cells on the worksheet. A series can represent sales of a product for a period of six months, the number of employees within the company each year for the last ten years, or the number of rejects on a production line for each of the last 16 weeks.

X AXIS   The individual values in the series are represented as data points along the *X axis*, which is the horizontal X axis at the bottom of the graph. Each point along this axis might represent a year, a month, or a quarter. It could also represent a division, a product, or a project. The points along this X axis can be labeled to make it clear what they represent. In addition, a title can be placed along the X axis that describes the general category of data shown along the X axis. For example, if each of the points on the X axis represents a month between January and December, an appropriate title for the X axis might be Fiscal 87, to describe the category to which each of these months belongs.

Y AXIS   The *Y axis* is the vertical axis found on most of the graphs that 1-2-3 produces. It is used to measure the relative size of each value within a series. Once you tell 1-2-3 which data to display on the graph, this axis is labeled automatically. 1-2-3 will sometimes represent graph data in thousands or millions and label the Y axis appropriately. You can also add a title for this axis; you might describe the units of measure as dollars, number of employees, or some other appropriate unit of measure for the quantities shown on this axis.

LEGEND   If you choose to show more than one data series on a graph, you can describe each of the series with a legend at the bottom of the graph. The legend will show the symbol or pattern used to represent each series in the graph and will describe the data represented by that symbol or pattern.

Entering Some Data for a Graph

If you have worked through the examples in this book from Chapter 1, you already have a number of worksheets that 1-2-3's graphics features could represent nicely. Even though you have some data for a graph, you will enter a short new worksheet designed to let you work with a small amount of data, yet still experience the maximum number of graphics features. Follow these steps to enter the required data for the examples in this chapter:

1. Make the following entries in the worksheet cells shown:

D1:	' ABC COMPANY
D2:	SALES BY REGION
A5:	North
A6:	South
A7:	East
A8:	West
B4:	Jan
B5:	50000
B6:	45000
B7:	62800
B8:	39550
C4:	Feb
C5:	+B5*1.035
C6:	+B6*1.05
C7:	+B7*1.02
C8:	+B8*.98
D4:	Mar
E4:	Apr
F4:	May
G4:	June

2. Enter /**Worksheet Global Format Currency**, type **0**, and press RETURN.

3. Move the cell pointer to B4, then enter /**Range Label Right**, move the cell pointer to G4, and press RETURN. This aligns the labels on the right side of the cell as the numbers are aligned.

4. Move the cell pointer to C5, then enter /**Copy** and move the cell pointer to C8. Press RETURN, then move the cell pointer to D5, type ., move the cell pointer to G5, and press RETURN again.

5. Move the cell pointer to the following cells and type these numbers:

E6:	**50000**
F7:	**75000**
D8:	**41000**

Adding these numbers overlays the formulas in those cells and provides more variety in the graph than growth at a constant rate.

6. Move the cell pointer to C5.
   Your entries should look like this:

C5: +B5*1.035

Notice that the original formula is not altered by the addition of several numeric constants to the model. You are now done entering the data you will use with the graphics examples. Now it is time to define your requirements for the graph.

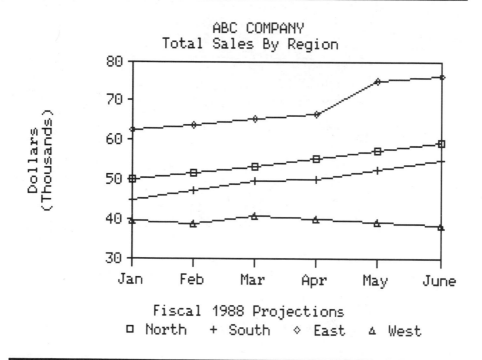

FIGURE 8.2   A line graph

Deciding on a Graph Type

1-2-3 offers you five different graph types. Your options are line, bar, stacked bar, XY, and pie. A *bar graph* looks like the one shown in Figure 8.1. It uses bars of different heights to represent the data ranges you wish to graph. Bar graphs are especially appropriate when you wish to contrast the numbers in several series.

A *line graph* shows the points in the data range you specify, plotted against the Y axis. The points may be connected with a line, shown as symbols, or both. This type of graph is an excellent choice for plotting trend data over time, such as sales or expenses. An example of a line graph is shown in Figure 8.2.

A *stacked bar graph* places the values in each of the series you

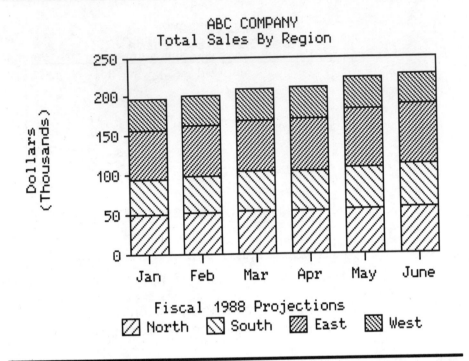

FIGURE 8.3   A stacked bar graph

select on top of each other for any one point on the X axis. A stacked bar is a good choice whcn you wish to see the level of the total as well as each of its components. You might use this type of graph to show the contribution to profit from each of the company's subsidiaries, as shown in Figure 8.3.

An *XY graph* plots the values in one series against the values from a second series. You might use this graph type to plot age against salary, time against temperature, or machine repairs against the age of the machinery. Figure 8.4 shows an example of an XY graph.

A *pie graph* shows only one range of values. It represents the percent that each value is of the total by the size of the pie wedge assigned to that value. A pie chart is an effective way to show the relative size of different components of a budget or the contribution to profit from different product lines. An example of a pie chart is shown in Figure 8.5.

If you do not choose one of the graph types for your graph, 1-2-3 will use the default type of a line graph. Your first example will be of a bar graph, so use the following steps to make that selection.

1. Enter /**Graph**.

   This will display the main graph menu as shown below:

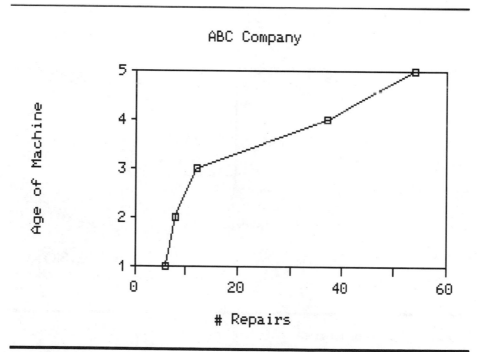

FIGURE 8.4 An XY graph

2. Enter **Type** to see the following submenu:

3. Enter **Bar**.

   Notice that once you have made the type selection, you are
   returned to the main graph menu, not READY mode. The
   Graph menu is another "sticky" menu, like Print. It will
   stay around so you can make additional selections for
   defining your graph, disappearing only when you choose
   Quit.

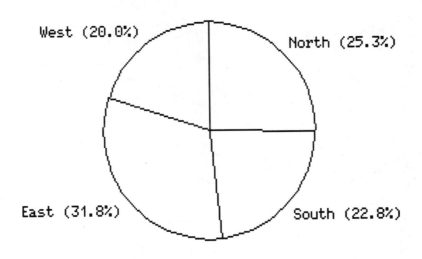

FIGURE 8.5   A pie chart

Specifying the Data to Use on the Graph

There are no defaults for the data to be shown in a graph. If you forget to tell 1-2-3 which data to display on the graph, your graph will be blank. Line, bar, and stacked bar graphs can each show up to six data series or ranges. These graph types can have data assigned to graph range A, B, C, D, E, and F in the graph menu. Pie and XY graphs are special; a pie chart can only show one data range, while an XY chart can show two. For a pie chart, data is assigned to graph range A; for an XY chart, graph range B is used.

Follow these steps to assign data to graph ranges A through D in the current graph to see how data is assigned to the various graph ranges:

1. Enter A to produce this display:

```
C5: +B5*1.035                                           POINT
Enter first data range: C5
```
```
      A       B       C       D       E       F       G       H
```

There is no need to enter /Graph since the graph menu is already on the screen.

2. Move the cell pointer to B5 and type ., then move the cell pointer to G5 and press RETURN.
This step assigns the range B5..G5 to the A range of the graph so that it will now represent the sales for the North region in the months of January through June.

3. Enter **B** and move the cell pointer to B6. Type ., move the cell pointer to G6, and press RETURN.
This assigns the data for the South region to the B range of the graph.

4. Enter **C** and move the cell pointer to B7. Type ., move the cell pointer to G7, and press RETURN.
This assigns the data for the East region to the C range of the graph.

5. Enter **D** and move the cell pointer to B8. Type ., move the cell pointer to G8, and press RETURN.

This assigns the data for the West region to the D range of the graph. This is the last region for ABC Company. The E and F ranges are currently unassigned. It is important to notice that all the ranges assigned have the same unit of measure — dollars. If some ranges were measured in units of products sold and others in dollars, both could not be shown on the same graph. The unit of measure must be the same for all of the data shown on a graph.

Viewing the Graph

Although the graph is not quite finished, you can still view it to see how the various data ranges stack up against each other. Sometimes if one range is either extremely large or small in comparison to the others, it is not practical to graph the data together; the values in the smaller range will seem to blend with the X axis. To view your graph and return again to the menu, follow these steps:

1. Enter **View**.

If your monitor can display graphics, this command will produce an image that looks like the one in Figure 8.6. All four data ranges are shown on the graph; the A range values are represented by the leftmost bar in each grouping. There are six different points on the X axis, each representing one month in the range.

2. Press ESC to return to the menu display.

Enhancing the Display

The current graph is not useful. The bars are all hatch-marked to distinguish them but the only way to tell which set of bars represents which set of data is by remembering the sequence in which the

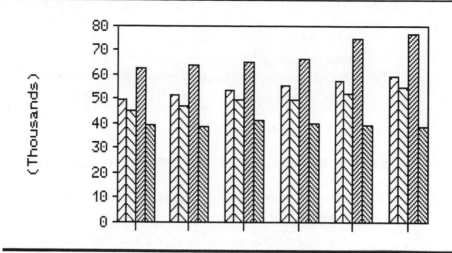

FIGURE 8.6   Displaying the data in bar graph format

different regions were assigned to the graph ranges. Nor can you tell whether the points on the X axis represent years, months, or days and whether the numbers graphed are sales, expenses, or number of employees. Obviously some additional information must be added to the graph. In this section you will learn how to add titles to the graph, label the X axis points, and add legends and grid lines.

LABELING THE X AXIS DATA POINTS   Without labels along the X axis it is impossible to tell what each group of values represents. You can overcome this problem easily by assigning a range of labels to be displayed along this axis. This range of labels should correspond to the values in the data ranges that have been assigned and should have the same number of entries in the range. Normally you will already have values like this in a column or row of the worksheet. For the current example, the labels that you need for the X axis are in B4..G4.

You can assign these labels to the X axis with the X range

option from the graph menu. Follow these steps to make the assignment:

1. Enter **X**.
   This will produce a display similar to the one used for the graph data ranges:

```
C5: +B5*1.035                                              POINT
Enter X axis range: C5
```

| A | B | C | D | E | F | G | H |

You must enter the range address you want to use either by typing it or by using the pointing method.

2. Move the cell pointer to B4, type **.**, and move the cell pointer to G4 before pressing RETURN.

3. Enter **View** to see the graph with the addition of labels along the X axis.
   Your display should match the one shown in Figure 8.7.

4. Press ESC to return to the graph menu.

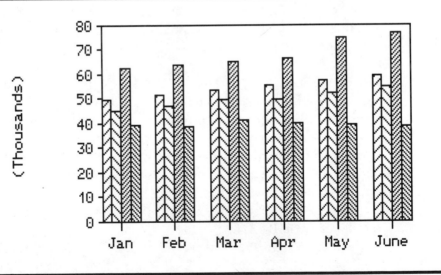

FIGURE 8.7   Adding X axis labels to the bar graph

ADDING TITLES Titles can be added to your graph in four different locations to improve its appearance. You can add a title along either of the axes or at the top of the graph in one or two lines. The menu you will see when you select / Graph Options Titles looks like this:

You will have 39 characters in which to enter any one of these four titles, once you select the option you want. The title can be even longer if you make it by using data that is already stored in a worksheet cell. Follow these steps to enhance your current graph with titles in all four locations:

1. Enter **Options** to produce the following menu:

2. Enter **Titles First** to add a title at the top of the graph.

3. Enter **\D1** and press RETURN.
    This will use the current entry in D1 as the title at the top of the graph. Notice how the Options menu returns to the screen. It too is a "sticky" menu: you must choose Quit in order to leave.

4. Enter **Titles Second**, type **Total Sales by Region**, and press RETURN.
    This time the title was added by typing, since there was no entry on the worksheet that exactly matched the desired title.

5. Enter **Titles X-axis**, type **Fiscal 1988**, and press RETURN.

6. Enter **Titles Y-Axis**, type **Dollars**, and press RETURN.

7. Enter **Quit**.
    This will exit the graph Options menu and place you in the main graph menu.

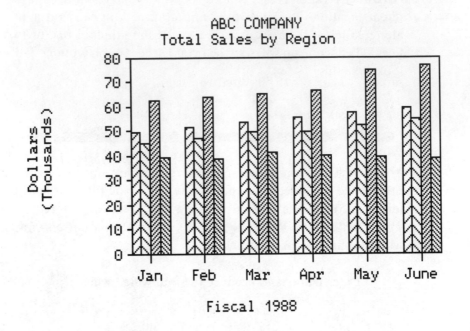

FIGURE 8.8   Adding titles to the bar graph

8. Enter **View** to produce a display with all four titles like the one shown in Figure 8.8.

9. Press ESC to return to the graph menu.

ADDING LEGENDS   Legends add clarity to a graph that presents more than one data series by identifying how each data series is represented on the graph. If symbols are used to distinguish the different data series, the legend will consist of the series indicator and a word describing the data shown by that series. If color or hatch-mark patterns are used, a small square of the color or pattern is placed at the bottom of the screen along with the one-word descriptor.

The Options menu presents the Legend alternative, as shown below:

When you select Legend you will be presented with a choice of the same six letters that you used to assign worksheet ranges to the different data series for the graph. Select each of the data series that you assigned and enter a legend for it. You will need to select Legend and the appropriate letter each time until you have assigned a legend entry to each of the data series you used in the graph. Follow these steps to assign the legends for the current graph:

1. Enter **Options Legend A**, type **\A5**, and press RETURN. The label stored in the cell A5 will be used for the legend. Your other option is to type "North" and press RETURN. The advantage of using the label entry in the cell is that if you decide to update it later, the graph title will automatically be updated for you the next time the graph is created.

2. Enter **Legend B**, type **\A6**, and press RETURN.

3. Enter **Legend C**, type **\A7**, and press RETURN.

4. Enter **Legend D**, type **\A8**, and press RETURN.

5. Enter **Quit**.

6. Enter **View** to create the display shown in Figure 8.9.

7. Type ESC to return to the graph menu.

ADDING GRID LINES   *Grid lines* are a series of lines that are parallel to either the X axis or the Y axis and that originate from the markers on the axis. They are designed to help you interpret the exact value of data points by extending either up or to the right from these markers. These lines are called grid lines since choosing to use them in both directions at once will create a grid pattern on your graph.

To get the menu for Grid, enter /Graph Options Grid. The Grid options can be used with all graph types except the pie chart;

grid lines across a pie chart would detract from your ability to interpret the graph. The grid menu contains these four options:

With a bar graph only the first option, Horizontal, is appropriate. This choice will let you interpret the top of each of the bars more accurately. Try it now for the current graph with these entries:

1. Enter **Options Grid Horizontal**.

2. Enter **Quit** to leave the options menu.

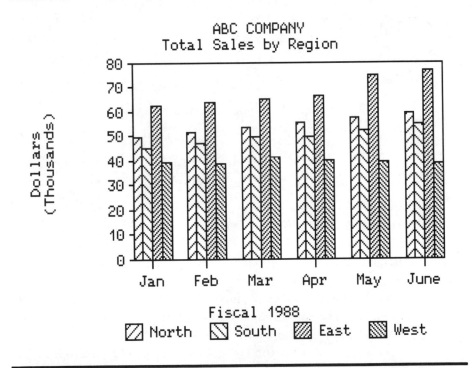

FIGURE 8.9   Adding a legend to the bar graph

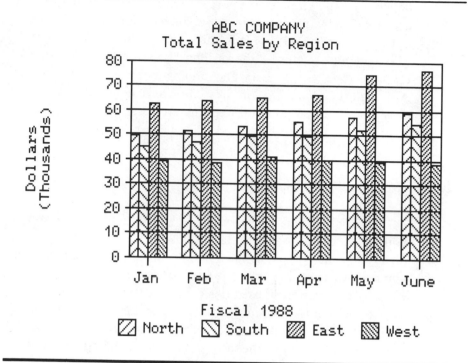

FIGURE 8.10   Adding horizontal gridlines to the bar graph

3. Enter **View** to produce the graph shown in Figure 8.10.

4. Press ESC to return to the graph menu.

5. Enter **Options Grid Clear Quit**.
   This will remove the horizontal grid lines and return to the graph menu. If you wish to verify that the lines have been removed, you can use the View command.

VIEWING THE GRAPH IN COLOR VS. BLACK AND WHITE   If you have a monitor that shows a single color, your only option is to view the graph from the B&W (black and white) option. If you have a color monitor, you can select Options Color and different colors will be used for the various data ranges. Whether you use three colors or a more extensive palette when coloring the graph depends on the graphics support supplied by your system. If you are able to view the system in color, you will want to use the B&W option to switch back to black and white before saving the graph. This option distinguishes the various data series by placing hatch-mark patterns within bars and adding symbols to line graphs. Although the Color Option uses color to distinguish the various data ranges, these color differences are lost when the graph is printed on a standard black and white printer.

Naming the Current Graph

1-2-3 can only maintain one set of graph definitions at a time unless you assign a name to these definitions. Now that you have completely defined a graph, assign a name to these specifications before you create a second graph. The command to use is /Graph Name Create. Once you have used this command to assign a name, you are free to reset the current graph settings. This lets you start fresh to define a new graph or make a few changes to create a second graph that has many of the same options as the first graph. Follow these steps to assign a name to the current graph settings so you can create additional graphs.

1. Enter **Name Create**.
   You do not need to enter /Graph, since you are already in the graph menu.

2. Type **Sls_bar** and press RETURN.

A Look at Some Other Graph Types

Working with several additional graph types will give you a close-up look at how easy it is to create additional graphs or to change the type for the existing graph. In this section you will use the current data series to create a line graph and a stacked bar graph. Then you will create a pie graph with a subset of this data. Follow these steps to create the three additional graphs:

1. Enter **Type Line**.

2. Enter **View** to display a graph like the one shown in Figure 8.11.
   Notice that different symbols are used for each series shown on the graph. The legend is automatically changed from the hatch mark patterns to these symbols.

3. Press ESC to return to the graph menu.

4. Enter **Name Create**, type **Sls_line**, and press RETURN.

5. Enter **Type Stacked-Bar**.

6. Enter **Options Titles Second-Line**, press ESC to remove the existing title, then type **Total Company Sales** and press RETURN.

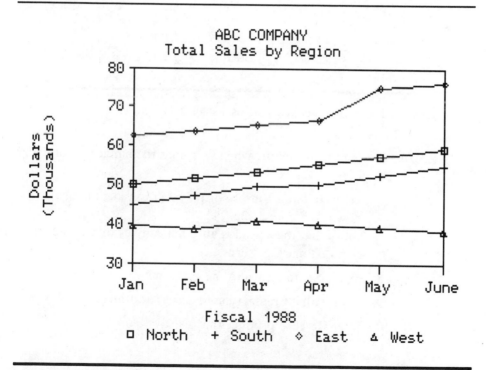

FIGURE 8.11 Displaying the same data as a line graph

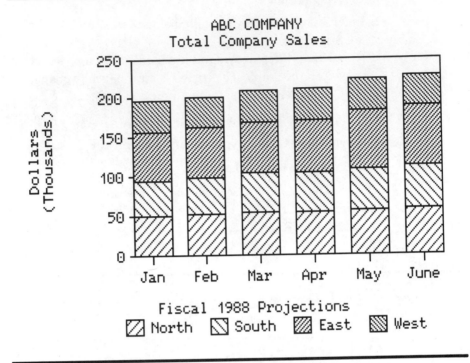

FIGURE 8.12   Displaying the same data as a stacked bar graph

You can use this technique when you want to change any of the
current graph specifications.

7. Enter **Quit** and **View** to display a graph like the one
    shown in Figure 8.12.
    Notice that the legend is automatically changed back to
    the hatch mark patterns.

8. Press ESC to return to the graph menu.

9. Enter **Name Create**, type **Sls_sbar**, and press RETURN.

10. Enter **Reset** to produce this display:

11. Enter **Graph**.
    This will eliminate all the previous graph settings.

12. Enter **A**, type **B5.B8**, and press RETURN.

13. Enter **X**, type **A5.A8**, and press RETURN.

14. Enter **Type Pie**.

15. Enter **Options Titles First**, type **ABC COMPANY**, and press RETURN.

16. Enter **Titles Second**, type **January Sales By Region**, and press RETURN.

17. Enter **Quit View** to view a graph like the one in Figure 8.13.

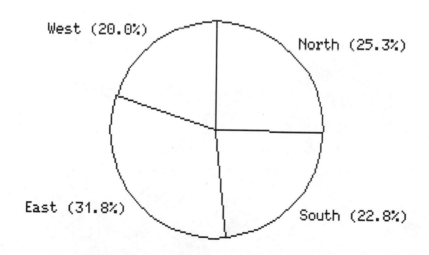

FIGURE 8.13   A pie chart

18. Press ESC, enter **Quit**, move your cell pointer to A12, and make these entries:

      A12:   1

      A13:   102

      A14:   3

      A15:   4

With Release 2, you can use these codes to change the appearance of a pie graph. First create a range with the same number of value entries as the range shown on the graph. Numbers 0 to 7 are used, each representing a unique hatch-mark pattern. Adding 100 to any one of

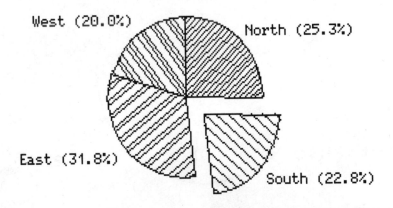

FIGURE 8.14 A pie chart with shading

these entries will explode that piece from the pie (that is, split it off from the pie sections that remained joined).

These values will show as currency, since that is the Global format. This will not affect their impact on the graph; however, if you find the $s confusing, you can eliminate them with / Range Format General.

19. Enter /**Graph B**, type **A12.A15**, and press RETURN.

20. Enter **View**.

If you are using Release 2, notice how the new graph shown in Figure 8.14 differs from the previous one. It is much easier to read and emphasizes the South's contributions.

21. Press ESC to return to the graph menu.

22. Enter **Name Create**, type **Janpie**, and press RETURN.

23. Enter **Quit** to return to READY mode.

SAVING A GRAPH

Several aspects of graphs must be saved. You must save the graph definition if you plan to use the graph the next time you work with the current worksheet. Since 1-2-3 cannot print a graph, you must also save the graphic or print image for printing with the Print-Graph program.

Saving the Worksheet File

After you have created one or more graph definitions, you will want them to be available the next time you work with the current worksheet. To save these graph definitions, save the worksheet file to disk after defining the graphs. Follow these steps to save the graphs for the Profit file:

1. Enter /**File Save**, type **Profit** and press RETURN.

Saving the Graph Image

When you save the worksheet file you do not automatically save the graphic or print image for the current graph. In order to save this image so that you can print it with the PrintGraph program, you must use /Graph Save. This menu option saves the file under the name that you specify and adds the filename extension of .PIC to distinguish the file from a worksheet file.

To save multiple graphs for later printing, you must save each one as the current graph, even though the graphs are all defined on the same worksheet. For each graph, use Graph Name Use, followed by Save.

Follow these steps to save the graphs created for the Profit worksheet:

1. Enter **/Graph Save**, type **Jan_pie**, and press RETURN. Since you exited the graph menu to save the worksheet, now you must reenter it. The current graphic image was not saved along with the graph definition stored in the worksheet file. Although you are using the same name as you used for the graph specifications on the worksheet, the step you just took creates a unique file. The file that is created with this instruction will be named JAN_PIE.PIC as it is stored on disk.

2. Enter **Name Use**, point to SLS_BAR, and press RETURN. The bar graph you created will now be the active graph. When you perform another graph save, this is the image that will be saved.

3. Press ESC, enter **Save**, type **Sls_bar**, and press RETURN. This will save the graphic image of the bar graph you created.

4. Enter **Name Use**, point to SLS_LINE, and press RETURN. The line graph you created will now be the active graph.

5. Press ESC, enter **Save**, type **Sls_line**, and press RETURN.

6. Enter **Name Use**, point to SLS_SBAR, and press RETURN. The stacked bar graph that you created will now be the active graph.

7. Press Esc, enter **Save**, type **Sls_sbar**, and press RETURN.

8. Enter **Quit** to exit the graph menu.

9. Enter **/Quit Yes**.
   Depending on how you entered 1-2-3, Quit will return you either to DOS or to the Lotus Access System. If quitting takes you back to DOS you can enter LOTUS to place yourself in the Lotus Access System. The following examples assume that you are in the Lotus Access System and are ready to learn how to print the graphs.

PRINTING A GRAPH

As mentioned, you will use the Lotus PrintGraph program to obtain a printed copy of your graphs. Before you can use this program, you must have previously saved the graph in a .PIC file. PrintGraph also must be configured for your system. This should have been completed when 1-2-3 was configured in the installation process. If not, return to Install to add the necessary information to the PrintGraph program. This process is described in Appendix A.

The Lotus Access System, which you will use to select the PrintGraph option, is shown for Release 2.01 as follows:

```
┌──────────────────────────────────────────────────────────────┐
│ 1-2-3  PrintGraph  Translate  Install  View  Exit             │
│ Enter 1-2-3 -- Lotus Worksheet/Graphics/Database program      │
└──────────────────────────────────────────────────────────────┘
```

The PrintGraph menu for Release 1A shown in Figure 8.15 is very different from the Release 2 menu shown in Figure 8.16. Yet despite this apparent difference, the features are very similar. It is just that the definition of the various settings is covered by the selection

```
Copyright 1982, 1983 Lotus Development Corp. All Rights Reserved.        MENU
---------------------------------------------------------------------------
Select Options Go Configure Align Page Quit
Select pictures
===========================================================================
SELECTED GRAPHS   COLORS              SIZE    HALF        DIRECTORIES

          Grid:      Black     Left Margin:     .750   Pictures
          A Range:   Black     Top Margin:      .395   B:\
          B Range:   Black     Width:          6.500   Fonts
          C Range:   Black     Height:         4.691   A:\
          D Range:   Black     Rotation:        .000
          E Range:   Black                             GRAPHICS DEVICE
          F Range:   Black     MODES
                                                       Epson FX80/1
          FONTS               Eject: No                Parallel
                              Pause: No
          1: BLOCK1                                    PAGE SIZE
          2: BLOCK1
                                                       Length  11.000
                                                       Width    8.000
```

FIGURE 8.15   The PrintGraph menu in Release 1A

Settings in Release 2 but by two different selections (Options and Configure) in Release 1A. With Release 1A, *Options* will provide access to changing colors, paper size, and action settings. *Configure* will address hardware configuration changes such as the directory to use and the output device. This chapter emphasizes the Release 2 selections for completing PrintGraph tasks; but if you are using Release 1A, these descriptions should help you make the correct selections.

Selecting Graph Files

Before you can print a graph you must have a copy of it saved as a .PIC file (the file type that 1-2-3 uses when you use / Graph Save). This file must be in the directory shown on the main PrintGraph menu screen under Graphs Directory. If this description of the directory location for your graph files does not match the location of your .PIC files, you must change the directory.

CHANGING THE GRAPH DIRECTORY To make this change, enter Settings Hardware to activate this menu:

```
Copyright 1986 Lotus Development Corp.  All Rights Reserved. Release 2.01  MENU

Set directory containing graphs
Graphs-Directory  Fonts-Directory  Interface  Printer  Size-Paper  Quit
```

The graph directory has a default setting of A:\. This means that 1-2-3 will expect to read your graph files from drive A. If you have graph files stored on another drive, change it to drive A. Check the current setting for your graph files now; if a change is required, follow these steps:

1. Enter **Settings Hardware Graphs-Directory**.

2. Type the path name for your graph files.
   For example, if your graph files are stored on drive C in

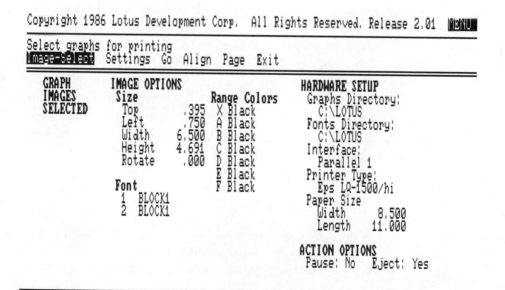

```
Copyright 1986 Lotus Development Corp.  All Rights Reserved. Release 2.01  MENU

Select graphs for printing
Image-Select  Settings  Go  Align  Page  Exit

GRAPH      IMAGE OPTIONS                      HARDWARE SETUP
IMAGES       Size                             Graphs Directory:
SELECTED       Top      .395   Range Colors      C:\LOTUS
               Left     .750   X Black        Fonts Directory:
               Width   6.500   A Black           C:\LOTUS
               Height  4.691   B Black        Interface:
               Rotate   .000   C Black           Parallel 1
                               D Black        Printer Type:
             Font              E Black           Eps LQ-1500/hi
             1  BLOCK1         F Black        Paper Size
             2  BLOCK1                           Width    8.500
                                                Length  11.000

                                             ACTION OPTIONS
                                               Pause: No   Eject: Yes
```

FIGURE 8.16 The PrintGraph menu in Release 2

the directory \123\GRAPHS, you would make this entry:

C:\123\GRAPHS

3. Press RETURN to finalize the new setting.

4. Enter **Quit** twice to return to the main menu.

TELLING PRINTGRAPH WHICH FILES TO PRINT   The Image-Select option on the main PrintGraph menu allows you to select graphs from the directory listed under Graph Directory on the left side of the main PrintGraph screen. Once you select Image-Select, the names of the graph files on this directory will be displayed for you, as shown in Figure 8.16. A highlighted bar will rest on the first file name in the list. The UP and DOWN ARROW keys will let you scroll through the list of file names, moving the highlighted bar through the list until you find a file that you wish to print.

To mark a file for printing, position the highlighted bar on the file name and press the space bar. If you change your mind, press the space bar again to undo the selection. After you select the first file you can move the highlighted bar up and down in the list to select as many additional files as you like. 1-2-3 will even remember the order in which you made your selections and print the graphs in the same sequence.

If you are uncertain what a graph file contains, you can move the highlighted bar to the file name and press F10. 1-2-3 will re-create the chosen graph on your screen for you to review. When you are finished viewing the graph, you can press ESC to return to the selection screen to make additional selections. Once you have marked all the graphs, press RETURN to select the graphs you want for printing. Use these steps to select the graph files created in this exercise:

1. Enter **Image-Select**.

2. Use the highlighted bar and move to JANPIE, then press the space bar to mark the graph with a #.
   Once it is marked you can make additional selections.

3. Move the highlighted bar to SLS_SBAR and press the space bar.

4. Move the highlighted bar to SLS_BAR and press the space bar.

5. Move the highlighted bar to SLS_LINE and press F10 to view the graph.

6. Press RETURN to return to the menu, then press the space bar.

7. Press RETURN to select the Settings menu.

Controlling the Settings

The PrintGraph program has a wide variety of settings that allow you to tailor the printing of a graph. Many of these settings are advanced features, best explored only once you have mastered the basics. This section presents the basic settings that you can work with to make PrintGraph respond to your needs. The following menu shows the various aspects of the graphic process that can be changed when you select Settings from the main PrintGraph menu:

```
Copyright 1986 Lotus Development Corp.  All Rights Reserved.  Release 2.01  MENU

Specify colors, fonts and size
Image  Hardware  Action  Save  Reset  Quit
```

IMAGE SETTINGS   The Image settings allow you to alter features such as size, color, and fonts. Although these features are nice to have available, since you can use the default settings they are not relevant to the basic set of skills you are initially trying to develop.

HARDWARE SETTINGS   You have already explored one hardware setting change: the change to the directory for your graph files. You can also alter the directory where the fonts are stored. The fonts affect the type of printing used for labels throughout the graph. To access these fonts you must be sure that the font files are in the directory shown at the right side of the main PrintGraph menu. If not, you can change this display by using the command /Graphs Settings Hardware Fonts-Directory and typing a new directory name.

CHECKING THE INTERFACE AND PRINTER TYPE   In order for your printer or plotter to produce graphs correctly, the proper interface and printer type must show on the PrintGraph menu. Eight different interface options are available, although the first two are used most frequently since they represent standard parallel and serial interfaces. The first option, 1, represents a standard *parallel connection*, which is the most common way of connecting a printer to your system. The second represents a *serial connection*, which is commonly used to connect a plotter to your system. The default value for this setting is 1, which represents a standard parallel interface. If your output device is a plotter you may need to change this setting to serial. However, consult with your dealer or a knowledgeable expert before making these changes.

If you have installed PrintGraph to operate with a variety of printers, the Hardware Printer setting may require frequent change. Each time you want to use a different printer, select Print-Graph Settings Hardware Printer and the output device you want to use for your graphs. If your current setting is blank or needs to be changed, follow these steps:

1. Enter **Hardware Printer**.

2. Select the correct output device from the list of options specified during the install process. Press RETURN and enter **Quit**.
   If no options are displayed it means that you did not install PrintGraph. If the printer type you wish to select is not displayed as an option, return to Install to correct the problem.

SAVING THE CHANGES TO SETTINGS   All the changes you make to the settings are temporary; unless you save them, they will apply only to the current session. When you want to retain the new setting values for subsequent sessions, you must store them in the file PGRAPH.CNF (GRAPH.CNF in Release 1A). To make the new settings permanent you must choose Save from the Settings menu to store the settings in the file, PGRAPH.CNF. Follow these steps to save your changes:

1. Enter **Save** and **Quit** to return to the main menu. Unlike other save operations, here you do not need to enter a file name. 1-2-3 always uses the same file.

Printing the Graphs

Once you have made all the selections, printing the graph is quite simple. 1-2-3 will begin printing the graphs you have chosen with Image-Select when you choose Go from the PrintGraph menu. Pressing the Ctrl-Break keys simultaneously will stop the printing if you need to interrupt the process. However, the printer will not stop right away; it will continue to print the lines that have already been transmitted to it. Follow these steps to print the graphs you selected earlier:

1. Check to ensure that your printer is both on and online.

2. Enter **Go**.

3. Once all the graphs have been printed, enter **Exit**. Figure 8.17 shows one of the graphs that was printed.

If you have set the *Page Eject* option to Yes, the printer will advance to the next page after each graph is printed. If you have set the Eject option to No, the printer will use all the space on a page for graphs before advancing the paper. The *Pause* option allows you to change the paper when a graph is completed. The setting for pause must be Yes when you want to make this change for a device like a plotter. PrintGraph will continue the printing process until it has completed all the selected graphs, unless you choose to intervene with Ctrl-Break.

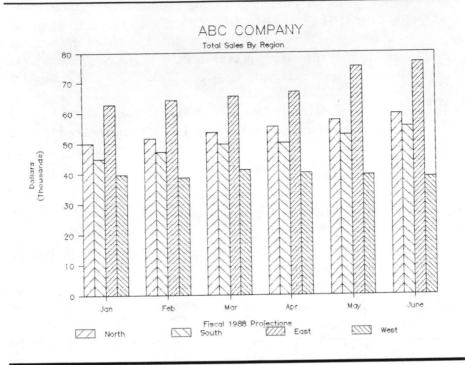

FIGURE 8.17   A graph printed with the PrintGraph program

SUMMARY

In this chapter you have learned how to present the results of your spreadsheet models in a graphic format. You are now familiar with the various types of graphs offered by 1-2-3 and can choose the one that presents your data clearly. You have also learned how to save your graph definition on the worksheet as well as to save a copy of the graphic or print image on the disk for later printing. You can then use the PrintGraph program and select the files containing the graphic images you wish to print. These various graphics options give you a second output format, which can surpass the printed report in conveying the meaning behind your information.

9

DATA
MANAGEMENT
BASICS

All the work you have done with 1-2-3 up to this point has been concerned with calculating some type of numeric result. This is the typical application for the 1-2-3 program. However, 1-2-3 also has other features — features that are more oriented toward the management of information than toward calculations. These data management features are a special group of commands that emphasize providing capabilities for the design, entry, and retrieval of information, with or without additional calculations. You can use these commands to keep track of information about your suppliers, clients, or employees.

Since this is a new area of 1-2-3 for you, the first step is to learn some new terms. A *database* is a collection of all the information you have about a set of things. These things can be customers, employees, orders, parts in your inventory, or anything else. If you created a database of employee information, you would place the information about each of your employees in it. All the information about one employee would be in one *record* of the database. A record is composed of all the pieces of information you want to record about each thing in the set, such as one employee. These individual pieces of information in the record are referred to as *fields*. Fields to include in each record in an employee database might contain name, job classification, salary, date of hire, and social security number. Every time you design a new database, you need to decide what fields will be included in each record.

A 1-2-3 database is a range of cells on the worksheet. The database can be in any area of the worksheet you want, but you must put the fields' names in the top row of the range. And the records in the database, which contain data for each field, go in the rows beneath the field names.

SETTING UP A DATABASE

To create a new database, first create a list of the fields you plan to use, then estimate the number of characters required for each field. To make this estimate, total the characters required to store one record in the database. If you then estimate the number of records that you will place in the database, you can multiply this number by the size of one record to get an estimate of how much memory is required for the database. Next, load 1-2-3 and enter /Worksheet Status to see how much memory is available. If the total you need exceeds the amount of memory available, another alternative is required — for example, splitting the database into two sections. Try this process for the employee file you will create.

1. Take a piece of paper and write down this list of field names:

   Last Name
   First Name

SS#

Job Code

Salary

Location

2. Write the size of each field next to the field name.
   For this example, use 12 characters for the last name, 12
   characters for the first name, 11 for the social security
   number, 4 for the job code, 8 for the salary, and 3 for the
   location. This makes a total of 50 characters for one
   record.

3. Estimate the number of records you plan to eventually
   enter into the database and multiply this number by the
   size of one record.
   For this example, 100 records is the estimate. Multiplying
   100 by 50 results in a product of 5000. This should be well
   within the limit of any system. However, for those occasions when it is larger, you can take a look at how to verify
   this calculation.

4. Enter /**Worksheet Status** and check the amount of available memory.
   The amount of memory shown in the worksheet status
   display in Figure 9.1 is 423,520 bytes — more than enough
   to accommodate 5000 characters, plus some extra for special options such as formatting. If the amount of available
   memory exceeds the size requirements of the database, it is
   safe to proceed. When the size of the database is larger
   than available memory, you must develop an alternative
   plan before beginning data entry.

Choosing a Location

Any area of the worksheet can be used for a database. Normally,
when your worksheet serves a dual purpose (both calculations and
a database), place the database below the calculations so it can

```
                                                                    STAT

Available Memory:
  Conventional..... 423520 of 423520 Bytes (100%)
  Expanded......... (None)

Math Co-processor: Present

Recalculation:
  Method.......... Automatic
  Order........... Natural
  Iterations...... 1

Circular Reference: (None)

Cell Display:
  Format.......... (G)
  Label-Prefix..... '
  Column-Width..... 9
  Zero Suppression. Off

Global Protection: Off
```

FIGURE 9.1   Using the Worksheet Status command to check available memory

expand easily. If nothing else is stored on the worksheet, row 1 is as good a starting location as any other.

Entering Field Names

Whatever area you select for your database, record your field names across the top row. Always choose *meaningful names*; they will be used again to invoke the data management features. Meaningful names can be *self-documenting meaning* (that is, they will help clarify what you are doing). Each field name must be contained within a single cell. Field names that span two cells are not acceptable. Neither are spaces at the end of a field name. Spaces or special characters in the cell immediately beneath the field name can also cause a problem with some of 1-2-3's data management features.

To enter the field names in the chosen area, simply type them in their respective cells and adjust the column widths.

1. Enter the field names for the employee database in these cells now:

A1:	**Last Name**
B1:	**First Name**
C1:	**"SS#**
D1:	**Job Code**
E1:	**"Salary**
F1:	**Location**

   These entries should create a display like this:

   F1: 'Location

   Pay special attention to the spelling, capitalization, and cell alignment of field names. When you use these in later tasks, everything must match exactly if the job is to be completed properly.

2. Move the cell pointer to column A and enter /**Worksheet Column Set-Width**, type **12**, and press RETURN.

3. Repeat step 2 for columns B, C, and E.

The label entries require a width equal only to the number of characters in the field. The salary field has been estimated at eight digits; however, 12 is allowed in the column width for the addition of a $, a comma, a decimal point, and one extra space to separate the entry from the adjacent fields.

Entering Data

Now that you have entered the field names, you can begin entering the data beneath them. The first record should be entered immediately beneath the field names. Each record will occupy one row; do not skip any row as you begin to enter records.

Make sure that the data you enter in each field is the same type. If a field contains value entries, the entries in all records for this field should contain value entries. If you do not have all the data for a record, you can leave the field blank as long as you do not leave the entire row blank. Except for these few simple guidelines, everything is exactly the same as entering data in the worksheet environment.

You will need to complete the data entry for the database used throughout the rest of this chapter. The normal procedure for entering records in a database is to enter a complete record at once; however, since it might be easier to complete the entries in one column before moving to the next one, the directions in this chapter are written from that perspective. You can either work from the screen display shown in Figure 9.2 or you can follow these explicit directions to complete the entries:

1. Place these entries in the Last Name field:

A2:   **Larson**

A3:   **Campbell**

A1: [W12] 'Last Name   READY

```
         A            B            C         D           E         F
 1  Last Name    First Name       SS#    Job Code     Salary   Location
 2  Larson       Mary         543-98-9876    23       $12,000      2
 3  Campbell     David        213-76-9874    23       $23,000     10
 4  Campbell     Keith        569-89-7654    12       $32,000      2
 5  Stephens     Tom          219-78-8954    15       $17,800      2
 6  Caldor       Larry        459-34-0921    23       $32,500      4
 7  Lightnor     Peggy        560-55-4311    14       $23,500     10
 8  McCartin     John         817-66-1212    15       $54,600      2
 9  Justof       Jack         431-78-9963    17       $41,200      4
10  Patterson    Lyle         212-11-9090    12       $21,500     10
11  Miller       Lisa         214-89-6756    23       $18,700      2
12
13
14
15
16
17
18
19
20
```

FIGURE 9.2 The employee database

A4:	**Campbell**
A5:	**Stephens**
A6:	**Caldor**
A7:	**Lightnor**
A8:	**McCartin**
A9:	**Justof**
A10:	**Patterson**
A11:	**Miller**

2. Make these entries in the First Name field:

B2:	**Mary**
B3:	**David**
B4:	**Keith**
B5:	**Tom**
B6:	**Larry**
B7:	**Peggy**
B8:	**John**
B9:	**Jack**
B10:	**Lyle**
B11:	**Lisa**

3. Make the following entries in the SS# field:

C2:	**'543-98-9876**
C3:	**'213-76-9874**
C4:	**'569-89-7654**
C5:	**'219-78-8954**
C6:	**'459-34-0921**
C7:	**'560-55-4311**
C8:	**'817-66-1212**
C9:	**'431-78-9963**
C10:	**'212-11-9090**
C11:	**'214-89-6756**

Notice that a single quotation mark was used at the beginning of each of these entries. The social security numbers must be labels because they include the dash character (-). If you forget to start these entries with a label indicator, a negative number will appear in the cell. You will then need to edit the cell entry and insert the label indicator at the front.

4. Enter the following Job Codes:

D2:	**23**
D3:	**23**
D4:	**12**
D5:	**15**
D6:	**23**
D7:	**14**
D8:	**15**
D9:	**17**
D10:	**12**
D11:	**23**

5. Move the cell pointer to E2, enter /**Range Format Currency**, type **0**, press RETURN, then move the cell pointer to E11, and press RETURN.

6. Make the following salary entries:

E2:	**12000**
E3:	**23000**
E4:	**32000**
E5:	**17800**
E6:	**32500**
E7:	**23500**
E8:	**54600**
E9:	**41200**
E10:	**21500**
E11:	**18700**

7. Enter the following Location codes:

F2:	**2**
F3:	**10**
F4:	**2**
F5:	**2**
F6:	**2**
F7:	**4**
F8:	**10**
F9:	**2**
F10:	**4**
F11:	**2**

This completes the entries required to create a database with 10 records.

Making Changes

Making changes to entries in the database is no different from making changes in the worksheet data you use. You have two good choices: retype any entry to replace it, or use the F2 (EDIT) technique to make a quick correction. To feel at home with making changes, just as if you were still making worksheet entries, carry out the following steps to change the salary and social security number for Mary Larson:

1. Move the cell pointer to C2, press the EDIT key (F2), and move with the RIGHT ARROW key until the small cursor is under the 7. Press the DEL key, type **4**, and press RETURN to correct the SS#.

2. Move the cell pointer to E2, press the EDIT key (F2), and press the HOME key. Next, press the DEL key, type 2, and press RETURN to produce the display shown in Figure 9.3.

```
E2: (C0) [W12] 22000                                      READY
```

```
         A           B            C        D          E        F
 1 Last Name    First Name        SS# Job Code    Salary Location
 2 Larson       Mary       543-98-9846       23   $22,000        2
 3 Campbell     David      213-76-9874       23   $23,000       10
 4 Campbell     Keith      569-89-7654       12   $32,000        2
 5 Stephens     Tom        219-78-8954       15   $17,800        2
 6 Caldor       Larry      459-34-0921       23   $32,500        4
 7 Lightnor     Peggy      560-55-4311       14   $23,500       10
 8 McCartin     John       817-66-1212       15   $54,600        2
 9 Justof       Jack       431-78-9963       17   $41,200        4
10 Patterson    Lyle       212-11-9090       12   $21,500       10
11 Miller       Lisa       214-89-6756       23   $18,700        2
12
13
14
15
16
17
18
19
20
```

FIGURE 9.3   Updating the database

The other way to update the entries in the database is to retype them, if the change is extensive.

SORTING THE DATABASE

1-2-3 provides sort features that can alter the sequence of the records in your database to any sequence you need. If you decide that you would like an employee list in alphabetical order, 1-2-3 can do this for you. If you decide that you want the records in order by job code, salary, or location, 1-2-3 can make this change easily. You will find 1-2-3's sort commands easy to work with, and you will be amazed at how rapidly 1-2-3 can resequence your data.

All the commands that you will need to specify the sort are located on this menu:

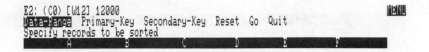

```
E2: (C0) [W12] 12000                                              MENU
Data-Range  Primary-Key  Secondary-Key  Reset  Go  Quit
Specify records to be sorted
         A           B           C           D           E           F
```

You can activate this menu by entering / Data Sort.

Defining the Database Location

The first step in resequencing your database is to tell 1-2-3 where the data is located. When you are sorting data, 1-2-3 is not interested in the field names, only in the data values that you expect it to sort. If you accidentally include the field names in this range, 1-2-3 will sort them just as if they were intentionally included as data values.

In defining the area to be sorted, you have the choice of defining some of the records or all of them. Always include all the fields, even if you want to exclude some of the records. This is because excluded fields remain stationary and do not remain with the other portion of the record to which they belong, thus jeopardizing the integrity of your file. Therefore, it is a good idea to save the file before sorting in case you accidentally exclude some of the field names. Follow these steps to tell 1-2-3 where the employee records are located:

1. Enter **/File Save**, type **EMPLOYEE**, and press RETURN.

2. Enter **/Data Sort**.

3. Enter **Data-Range** to produce this display:

```
E2: (C0) [W12] 12000                                             POINT
Enter Data-Range: E2

         A           B           C           D           E           F
```

4. Press the HOME key. Press the DOWN ARROW key. This will position you in A2, right below the first field name. If you had sorted this database previously, you would first have to press ESC to free the beginning of the range before moving the cell pointer.

5. Type ., press the END key followed by the DOWN ARROW key. Press the END key followed by the RIGHT ARROW key.
   At this point the database range should be highlighted like the one shown in Figure 9.4.

6. Verify that the range you wish to sort is highlighted and press RETURN.

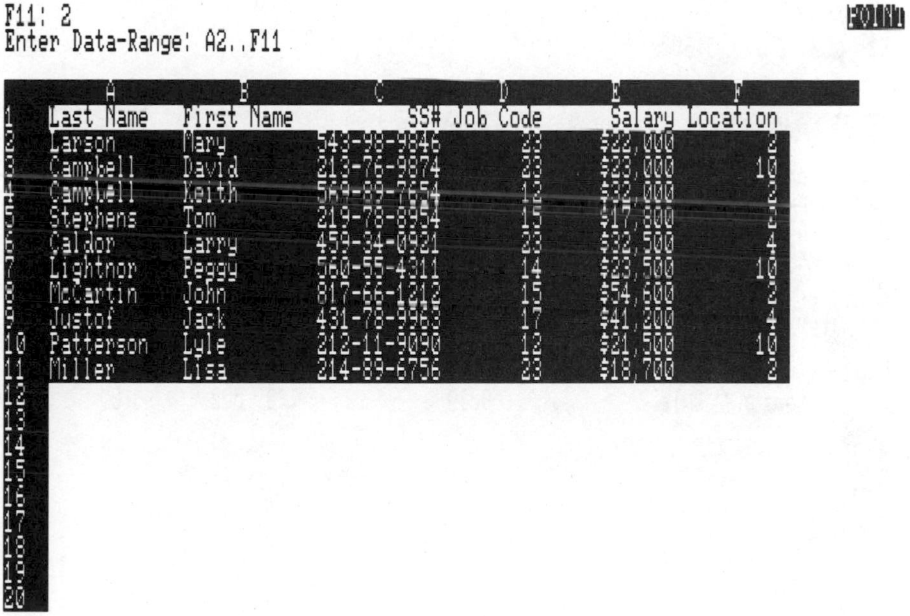

F11: 2   POINT
Enter Data-Range: A2..F11

	A	B	C	D	E	F
1	Last Name	First Name	SS#	Job Code	Salary	Location
2	Larson	Mary	543-38-9846	23	$22,000	2
3	Campbell	David	213-76-9874	23	$23,000	10
4	Campbell	Keith	569-89-7654	12	$32,000	2
5	Stephens	Tom	219-78-8854	15	$17,800	2
6	Caldor	Larry	459-94-0921	23	$22,500	4
7	Lightnor	Peggy	560-55-4311	14	$23,500	10
8	McCartin	John	817-66-1212	15	$54,600	2
9	Justof	Jack	431-78-9563	17	$41,200	4
10	Patterson	Lyle	212-11-9090	12	$21,500	10
11	Miller	Lisa	214-89-6756	23	$18,700	2

FIGURE 9.4 Highlighting the range to sort

Defining the Sort Sequence

You can sort your data in sequence by any of the database fields. If you sort by the contents of column D, the database will be in sequence by Job Code. If you sort by column C, social security number will determine the sequence. Whichever field you choose to sort on, you will also have to decide whether you want the entries to be sequenced from highest to lowest (descending) or lowest to highest (ascending).

1-2-3 refers to the field that determines the sequence of the records after the sort as the *primary key*. It also allows you to establish a *secondary key*. This secondary key, which is optional, is a precaution against duplicates in the primary key. 1-2-3 ignores the

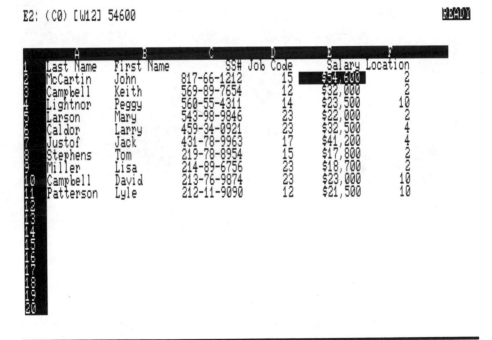

FIGURE 9.5   Records in SS# sequence

secondary key even when you specify one, except where the primary key contains duplicate entries. In that case, the secondary key is used to break the tie.

CHOOSING A PRIMARY KEY   There are two ways to specify the sort sequence. One is to enter /Data Sort Primary-Key and point to a cell that contains an entry for the field you want to control the order of the records. The other is to type the address of this cell. In either case, the next prompt you will see asks for the sort order, for which A and D are the only acceptable choices. An A represents ascending sequence and a D represents descending sequence. When 1-2-3 asks for the sort order, a default choice is present on the screen. If you want to use it, just press RETURN.

Follow these steps to see /Data Sort Primary-Key in action:

1. Enter **Primary-Key** to create this prompt:

```
E2: (C0) [W12] 12000                                        EDIT
Primary sort key: E2
```
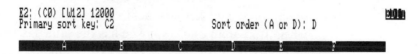

2. Move the cell pointer to C2 and press RETURN.
   This selects the social security number as the primary sort key.

3. Type **D** to create this display:

```
E2: (C0) [W12] 12000                                        EDIT
Primary sort key: C2                  Sort order (A or D): D
```

4. Press RETURN to request descending sequence.

5. Enter **Go** to activate the sort and change the sequence of the records to match Figure 9.5.
   Just defining the sort key does not change the data sequence. You must enter **Go** to specifically tell 1-2-3 that you are ready for the sort to take place.

CHOOSING A SECONDARY KEY The secondary key is the tie breaker. It resolves duplicate entries and determines which one of the duplicates should be listed first, based on the value of the secondary field. In situations like the last example where social security number was the controlling sequence, a secondary key is not needed. Since the social security number field does not contain legal duplicates, there is no need for a tie breaker. On the other hand, if you want to sort the employee file by last name, a secondary key is appropriate since last names sometimes are duplicated.

The process for specifying the secondary key is the same, except that you enter /Data Sort Secondary-Key. Try this feature by sorting the employee database in name order, following these steps:

1. Enter **/Data Sort Reset**.
   This cancels the current settings for the Data-Range and the Primary and Secondary sort keys.

2. Enter **Data-Range**, type **A2.F11**, and press RETURN.

3. Enter **Primary-Key**, type **A2**, press RETURN, type **A**, and press RETURN.
   The top cell in the last name field was selected as the sort key.

4. Enter **Secondary-Key**, type **B2**, press RETURN, type **A**, and press RETURN.
   The top cell in the first name field was selected as the secondary key. This key will be used to resolve the tie only when more than one employee has the same last name. In that case, the first name field will determine which record is placed first.

5. Enter **Go** to resequence the data to the alphabetical name list shown in Figure 9.6.
   There is no need to quit the sort menu. Entering Go to execute the sort will place you back in READY mode after the data has been resequenced. The Quit option is available for occasions when you want to exit the menu without performing the sort.

E2: (C0) [W12] 32500   READY

	A	B	C	D	E	F
1	Last Name	First Name	SS#	Job Code	Salary	Location
2	Caldor	Larry	459-34-0921	23	$32,500	4
3	Campbell	David	213-76-9874	23	$23,000	10
4	Campbell	Keith	569-89-7654	12	$32,000	2
5	Justof	Jack	431-78-9963	17	$41,200	4
6	Larson	Mary	543-98-9846	23	$22,000	2
7	Lightnor	Peggy	560-55-4311	14	$23,500	10
8	McCartin	John	817-66-1212	15	$54,600	2
9	Miller	Lisa	214-89-6756	23	$18,700	2
10	Patterson	Lyle	212-11-9090	12	$21,500	10
11	Stephens	Tom	219-78-8954	15	$17,800	2
12						
13						
14						
15						
16						
17						
18						
19						
20						

FIGURE 9.6   Records in sequence by name

When you save the worksheet with / File Save, 1-2-3 will save the sort specifications you just entered. The next time you use the worksheet you can execute the sort and change only those options that are different. Be especially careful when updating the Data Range if you add more fields to the end of the database. If you do not adjust the range, the new fields will remain stationary while the rest of the record is shifted to a new row.

SEARCHING THE DATABASE

As your database increases in size, it becomes increasingly important to review the information it contains selectively. Once the employee file contains 500 records, it becomes extremely time con-

suming to locate all the records that have a job code of 23 by
scanning the Job Code column visually.

1-2-3 gives you a way to work with information in your database selectively by means of an *exception reporting* capability. This
means you will have a method of selectively presenting information
that falls outside of a norm you establish. The selective review
feature can also provide an easy way to clean up the database or to
create reports in response to unexpected requests.

Working with 1-2-3's selective reporting features requires that
you enter your specifications for record selection on the worksheet.
These specifications are known as criteria and must be entered on
the worksheet before invoking 1-2-3's commands.

Once the criteria are entered, you must make various menu
selections. All the commands required for working with 1-2-3's
selective reporting features are found in the /Data Query menu,
which follows:

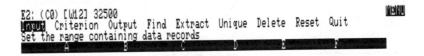

Like the Sort menu, /Data Query is "sticky"; in most situations,
you will have to make more than one selection from the menu
before 1-2-3 will complete your task.

Since the /Data Query features have a number of steps, the
best approach is to look at each step and then try a few examples
that combine all of the features. You will begin by exploring the
rules for entering your criteria on the worksheet.

Entering Criteria

You enter criteria on the worksheet to tell 1-2-3 which records you
want to work with. 1-2-3 will ignore records that do not match
these criteria when you ask the Data Query features to perform a
task with the database.

The first step in creating criteria is choosing a blank area on the worksheet in which to enter them. The rules for entering criteria differ, depending on whether you are working with *label data* or *value data*. Regardless of which type of data you want to enter, the criteria will represent the field name you are attempting to match against in the existing records. If you want to search against the Job Code field, you enter Job Code in the blank area that you chose. You must enter the field name exactly as it is in the database; that is, with identical spelling, capitalization, and alignment. You will then place the criteria specification immediately beneath this field name.

CRITERIA FOR VALUE DATA   You can enter two different types of criteria for matching records when you use a field that contains value entries. One option is to use an *exact entry match criteria*, which places a value that could occur in the field beneath the field name. If you want to search for all records with a 23 in Job Code, all you need to do is place 23 beneath the entry Job Code in the criteria area. Make the following entries to set up the exact match criteria:

1. Move the cell pointer to A13 and type **Job Code**, then move the cell pointer to A14 to finalize.

2. Type **23** and press RETURN to create the criteria entry shown in Figure 9.7.
   These entries do not select any records. They only enable you to use the Data Query commands to select the records you want. Before moving on to the remaining steps, look at the other types of criteria that are available. In fact, you can set up examples of some of these on the worksheet. You can make multiple-criteria entries in different locations on the worksheet as long as you use them one at a time.

The other type of value criterion is a *comparison formula*. This can be more powerful because it not only performs an exact match but can also identify records whose values are less than, greater

A14: [W12] 23   [READY]

	Last Name	First Name	SS#	Job Code	Salary	Location
1	Last Name	First Name	SS#	Job Code	Salary	Location
2	Caldor	Larry	459-34-0921	23	$32,500	4
3	Campbell	David	213-76-9874	23	$23,000	10
4	Campbell	Keith	569-89-7654	12	$32,000	2
5	Justof	Jack	431-78-9963	17	$41,200	4
6	Larson	Mary	543-98-9846	23	$22,000	2
7	Lightnor	Peggy	560-55-4311	14	$23,500	10
8	McCartin	John	817-66-1212	15	$54,600	2
9	Miller	Lisa	214-89-6756	23	$18,700	2
10	Patterson	Lyle	212-11-9090	12	$21,500	10
11	Stephens	Tom	219-78-8954	15	$17,800	2
12						
13	Job Code					
14	23					

FIGURE 9.7   Entering criteria to select records with a Job Code of 23

than, and not equal to an established value. The variety of logical operators that can be used to express these conditions is shown in Table 9.1.

You can still place the field name on the worksheet at the top of the criteria area, although 1-2-3 really does not care what field name you use when you are entering formula criteria. However, it is worth entering the correct field name even though it is not required; this helps document the basis of your selection.

The second entry is the formula. The formula is designed to compare the first value in a field against another value. For example, to select those records where the salary was greater than $25,000 you could enter the formula +E2>25000. You must use E2 as the cell reference in this formula, since you must use the first value in a field. You can use column C for this criteria by following these directions:

1. Move the cell pointer to C13, type **Salary**, and move the cell pointer to C14 to finalize.
   Actually, any field name would work equally well. However, Salary is the recommended entry as it clarifies which field you are using in the comparison.

2. Type **+E2>25000** and press RETURN.
   Do not be alarmed that your entry displays as a one rather than the formula. The one means it is true — E2 is greater than 25,000. If you are intent upon seeing it display as you entered it, you can use /Range Format Text on the cell. However, that is not really necessary.

CRITERIA FOR LABEL DATA There are both similarities and differences between the value and label criteria. Exact match entries work the same way as for value entries. You can place a field name in the criteria area and place the label entry you are looking for immediately beneath it. The one thing you must be careful with in label entries is to preserve capitalization and align-

=	Equal
>	Greater than
>=	Greater than or equal to
<	Less than
<=	Less than or equal to
<>	Not equal to

TABLE 9.1   Logical operators for building criteria formulas

ment of label entries. However, the data stored in the database should look the same as in the criteria area.

Wildcard characters are a new option with label entries. You can make a partial entry and use the asterisk (*) to tell 1-2-3 that you do not care which characters come at the end of the entry as long as the characters you have specified match. For example, to find all the records where the last name begins with C, you would enter Last Name for the field name in the criteria area and immediately beneath it you would enter C*. To find all the records where the last name starts with Camp, you would enter Camp*. Enter a sample for this type of criterion:

1. Move the cell pointer to A16, type **Last Name**, and move the cell pointer to A17 to finalize.

2. Type **Camp*** and press RETURN.
   In Release 2, there is one additional type of label criterion. The last type uses string formulas. Since this is an advanced topic, we will address the use of the ones you have already entered.

Defining the Database Location

You must tell 1-2-3 where your data is stored before it can search the database for the information you need. In this case, you must include the field names in the range that you provide, since they are an integral part of identifying the information you want to select.

The command by which you specify the location of the database is /Data Query Input. After you enter this command, you can point to your data range or type the required cell references as a range address. In both cases the field names must be included. You can select the employee database with these steps:

1. Enter **/Data Query Input**.

2. Press HOME to move the cell pointer to A1, type **.**, press the END key followed by the DOWN ARROW key, then press the END key followed by the RIGHT ARROW key.

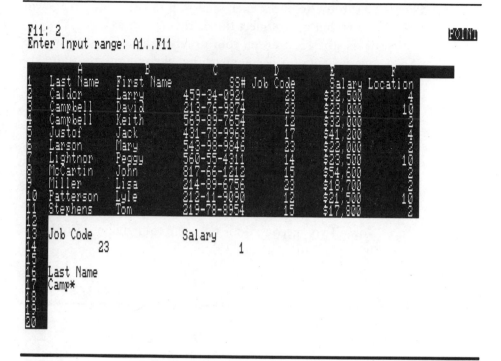

F11: 2
Enter Input range: A1..F11

	A	B	C	D	E	F
1	Last Name	First Name	SS#	Job Code	Salary	Location
2	Caldor	Larry	459-34-0921	23	$32,500	4
3	Campbell	David	213-76-9874	23	$23,000	10
4	Campbell	Keith	569-89-7654	12	$32,000	2
5	Justof	Jack	431-78-9963	17	$41,200	4
6	Larson	Mary	543-98-9846	23	$32,000	2
7	Lightnor	Peggy	560-55-4311	14	$23,500	10
8	McCartin	John	817-66-1212	15	$54,600	2
9	Miller	Lisa	214-89-6756	23	$18,700	2
10	Patterson	Lyle	212-11-9090	12	$21,500	10
11	Stephens	Tom	219-78-8954	15	$17,800	2
12						
13	Job Code		Salary			
14	23		1			
15						
16	Last Name					
17	Camp*					
18						
19						
20						

FIGURE 9.8   Selecting the area for Data Query Input

The database area should be highlighted as shown in Figure 9.8. Notice that the field names are included in this area.

3. Press RETURN to finalize.

The menu will remain on the screen for additional selections, such as the criteria location and the type of selection you want performed.

Telling 1-2-3 Where You Have Stored the Criteria

1-2-3 uses criteria to determine which records from the database will be used to fill your request. You have already entered several sets of criteria on the worksheet. Now you need to choose one set that 1-2-3 can use to check each record in the database. 1-2-3 will reject records that do not meet these criteria.

To define the location of your criteria on the worksheet, use / Data Query Criterion. Remember that the criteria must already be stored on the worksheet from the READY mode before you can use this command effectively. First use the criterion that searches all the records to find those that contain a Job Code of 23. Follow these steps:

1. Enter **Criterion**.

2. Move the cell pointer to A13, type **.**, press the DOWN ARROW key once, and press RETURN.

   Now all you need to do is tell 1-2-3 to highlight records that match the criteria.

A2: [W12] 'Caldor

	A	B	C	D	E	F
1	Last Name	First Name	SS#	Job Code	Salary	Location
2	Caldor	Larry	459-84-0921	23	$32,500	4
3	Campbell	David	213-76-9874	23	$23,000	10
4	Campbell	Keith	569-89-7654	12	$32,000	2
5	Justof	Jack	431-78-9963	17	$41,200	4
6	Larson	Mary	543-98-9846	23	$22,000	2
7	Lightnor	Peggy	560-55-4311	14	$23,500	10
8	McCartin	John	817-66-1212	15	$54,600	2
9	Miller	Lisa	214-89-6756	23	$18,700	2
10	Patterson	Lyle	212-11-9090	12	$21,500	10
11	Stephens	Tom	219-78-8954	15	$17,800	2
12						
13	Job Code		Salary			
14	23		1			
15						
16	Last Name					
17	Camp*					
18						
19						
20						

FIGURE 9.9   Finding the first matching record

Finding Matching Records

1-2-3's / Data Query Find command highlights records that match the criteria you have defined. If there are multiple entries that match, the records are highlighted one at a time. 1-2-3 begins at the top of the database, highlighting the first record that matches, and lets you use the UP and DOWN ARROW keys to move to other records that match the criteria. If the number of fields exceeds the width of the screen, you can also use the RIGHT and LEFT ARROW keys to view other fields within a highlighted record. You cannot move to records that do not match the criteria; the highlighted bar automatically skips over them.

You have already completed the preliminary steps for Find when you entered your criteria on the worksheet and then defined its location as well as the location of the data. Now whenever you enter Find, the criteria that was defined and referenced with Criterion will be used. The data referenced with the range Input will be searched for matching records. Since the preliminaries have been completed, only one step is needed to highlight the first record:

1. Enter **Find** to produce the display shown in Figure 9.9. Notice that the first record containing a job code of 23 was classified as matching the criteria, and that it is currently highlighted.

2. Press the DOWN ARROW key to move to the next record with a Job Code of 23, as shown in Figure 9.10.

3. Press the UP ARROW key to move back to the previous record.

4. Press ESC to return to the / Data Query menu.

Extracting Matching Records

The Find operation is useful when you need to answer a question quickly or to take a quick look at someone's record. You can specify the criteria to have these records selectively highlighted for you. The problem with Find is the data does not stay on the screen.

Often when you move to the second record, the first record disappears from view (the database is probably larger than your small example). The *Extract* operation can solve this; it permits you to selectively copy fields from the database to a new area on the worksheet. As you extract this information, you can also use the fields in any sequence in the output area you are building.

To use Extract, you must complete a preliminary step from READY mode. This step involves constructing an output area in a blank area of the worksheet. You create the output area by placing the field names you wish recorded in this area at its top. Any sequence is acceptable as long as the names are an exact match with the ones in the top row of the database in terms of spelling, capitalization, and alignment.

SETTING UP AN OUTPUT AREA   You must choose a location for the output of the Extract command and prepare it to receive data. One approach is to leave some blank rows at the bottom of the database and place the output area beneath this area. This way you will not find yourself moving the output area as the database expands. Another approach is to place the output area to the right of the database so you do not need to worry about the amount of expansion that will be required. Once you have selected the location, enter the names of the fields you want copied from matching records. Remember, you will not need to include every field, and the fields you choose do not need to be sequenced the same as in the database. You may want to copy the field names to the output area from above the database. This strategy eliminates all possibilities of a difference in spelling, capitalization, or alignment. Complete this task now for the employee file by following these steps.

1. Enter **Quit** to return to READY mode.
   You cannot build the output area from the / Data Query menu. You must exit it and return after you have completed the needed cell entries.

2. Move the cell pointer to A41, type **First Name**, and move the cell pointer to B41 to finalize the entry.

3. Enter **Last Name** and move the cell pointer to C41.

A3: [W12] 'Campbell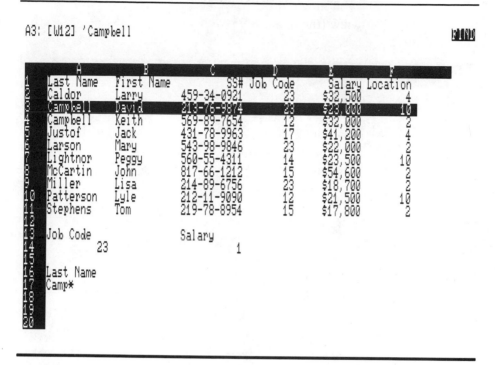

FIGURE 9.10   Finding the second matching record

4. Enter **"Salary** and move the cell pointer to D41 to finalize.

5. Enter **Job Code** and press RETURN.
   This is all that is required to set up the output area like the following:

You are ready to take a look at the remaining menu commands required to complete the Extract operation. The first command you need is /Data Query Output so that you can tell 1-2-3 where the output area is located. You can define the row containing the fields names you just entered as the output area. This would be row

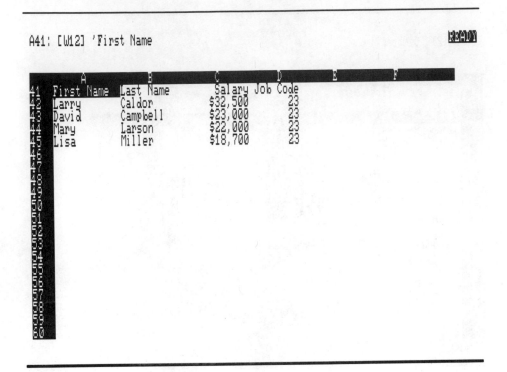

A41: [W12] 'First Name   READY

	A	B	C	D	E	F
41	First Name	Last Name	Salary	Job Code		
42	Larry	Caldor	$32,500	23		
43	David	Campbell	$23,000	23		
44	Mary	Larson	$22,000	23		
45	Lisa	Miller	$18,700	23		

FIGURE 9.11   Extracting matching records

41 in the current example. Be aware that 1-2-3 will use all the rows
from this point to the end of the worksheet to write matching
records. You can also select the row containing the field names and
an appropriate number of rows beneath it. If you choose the latter
approach, the output area you choose must be large enough to
contain all the selected records or you will get an error message
rather than the results you are looking for.

PERFORMING THE EXTRACT   Actually, once you have completed the preliminaries you have done all the difficult work. Now
all that is required is selecting Extract from the menu. Try this now
with your data:

1. Enter **/Data Query Output**. Move the cell pointer to A41,
    type a **.**, press END, then press the RIGHT ARROW key.

2. Enter **Extract**.

Move the cell pointer so you can view the entries that have been copied to the extract area. They should look like the ones in Figure 9.11.

3. Enter **Quit** to return to READY mode.

Trying a Few More Examples

You entered more than one set of criteria as you looked at some of the ways that criteria could be entered in worksheet cells. You can try an extract with the remaining two sets of criteria, using just a few easy steps. First use the criteria that selects records where the

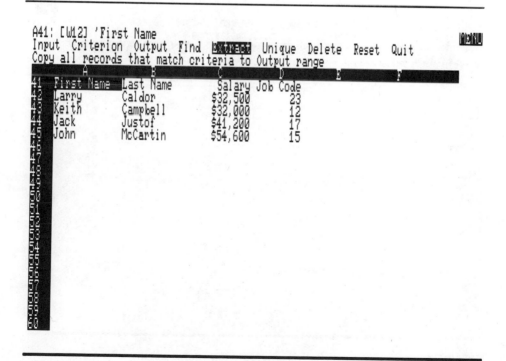

FIGURE 9.12 Extracting records with Salary greater than $25,000

salary entry is greater than $25,000, then use the criteria that selects records where the last name begins with Camp. Follow these steps:

1. Enter **/Data Query Criterion**, type **C13.C14**, and press RETURN.
   This is where you stored the criteria to select records by the salary field. You can use the same Input area and the same Output area as your previous request without making another entry.

2. Enter **Extract** to produce the list shown in Figure 9.12.

3. Enter **Criterion**, type **A16.A17**, and press RETURN.
   This will use the criterion you entered earlier, which selects last names that begin with Camp*. If you choose to point

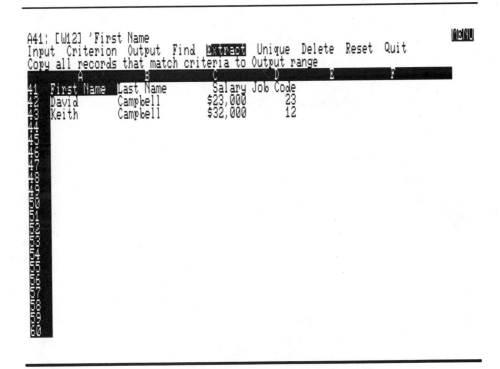

FIGURE 9.13   Extracting records where the last name begins with Camp

to this criterion rather than typing the range address, press
ESC first.

4. Enter **Extract** to produce the data shown in Figure 9.13.

5. Enter **Quit** to return to READY mode.

SPECIAL FEATURES

Now that you have completed the basics of data management, you
may want to take a look at some of 1-2-3's other data-management
features. These include: a short-cut approach to executing query
operation; referencing the database with a range name; and the
powerful database statistical function.

Using a Short-Cut Approach

There is a short-cut approach to reexecuting a Data Query command. However, it requires that certain conditions be met. The first
condition is that the database be the exact same size and location as
when the last query was executed. The second condition is that you
must be certain that your criteria are the same size and shape. They
can have new values or check new fields, just as long as the location
of these criteria is the same. The third condition is that if you are
performing Extract operations, the output area must be the same
size and shape. And the fourth and last condition is that you must
be performing the same data query operation. If you performed an
extract last time, you must perform an extract this time. If all of
these conditions are met you can reexecute the last query operation
by pressing F7 (QUERY).

Try this by carrying out the following directions to update the
criteria:

1. Move the cell pointer to A17 and type **L***, as shown in
Figure 9.14.

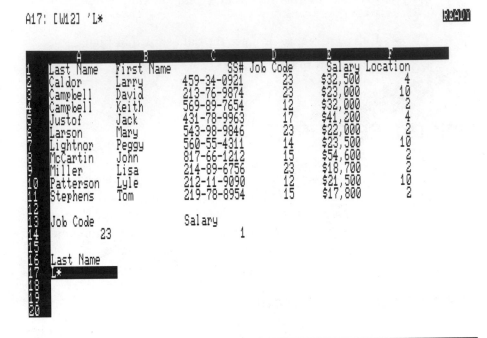

FIGURE 9.14 Changing the criteria to select records where the Last Name begins with L

2. Press F7 (QUERY), then press PGDN twice to produce the display shown in Figure 9.15.
    This is a handy feature if you need to perform multiple query operations. You only need to use the menu the first time. Then you can type new values in the criteria area if you wish, and press F* to have 1-2-3 use the new criteria.

Naming the Database

Using a name rather than a range address to refer to the database can provide flexibility. 1-2-3 permits you to assign a name to a range of cells. If you expand this range of cells by inserting blank rows or columns in the middle, the range referenced by the name will be expanded automatically. If a built-in function or formula references the name rather than an address, the built-in function is automatically adjusted for any change in the range.

You can assign names with the command /Range Name Create. Try it now with the employee database by following these steps:

1. Enter **/Range Name Create**, type **EMPLOYEE**, and press RETURN.

2. Press ESC then HOME, type **.**, then press END followed by DOWN, END followed by RIGHT, and RETURN. You will now be able to reference the range A1..F11 by the name EMPLOYEE. If you insert blank rows or columns in the middle of your database and make entries, the reference to EMPLOYEE will make these available immediately.

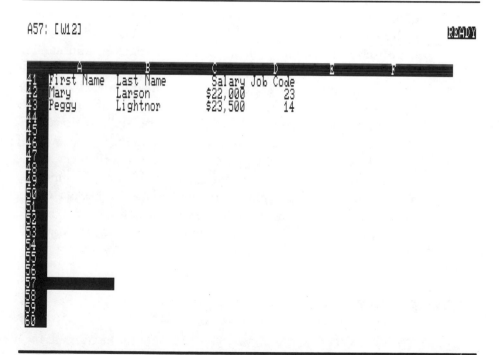

FIGURE 9.15   Extracting records with a Last Name that begins with L

USING THE DATABASE STATISTICAL FUNCTIONS

The database statistical functions are a special category of built-in functions that are designed to work exclusively in the data management environment. Like other built-in functions, they are prerecorded formulas that can perform calculations for you with a minimum of work on your part. Unlike other built-in functions, they operate on a database and require that you establish criteria for which records are to be included in the calculations they perform.

All the database statistical functions have the same format for their arguments. They are patterned after:

@DFUNCTION(database,offset in database,criteria location)

The first argument in all these functions is the location of the database. The range that you use to identify this location should include the field names as well as the data. The second argument, the offset, is the column number of the field that you want used in the calculations. This column number is always one less that what you would expect with the ordinary way of counting. 1-2-3 refers to the first column in the database as column zero and increments this by one for each column to the right. Since you have no control over 1-2-3's procedures, you will have to adjust your way of thinking when using these functions. The last argument is the location of the criteria. These criteria are defined in the same way as the ones you used with Extract and Find in the Data Query menu. You must record them on the worksheet before you include their location in the function. Putting a few of these to work will clarify exactly how you work with them.

Using @DAVG

The @DAVG function allows you to compute the average for a field in a selected group of database records. You can use this function to determine the average salary for employees in Job Code 23. You can use the criteria you entered for the / Data Query features. Just follow these steps:

1. Move the cell pointer to A21 and type **Average Salary for Job Code 23:** and move the cell pointer to D21 to finalize your entry.

2. Type **@DAVG(EMPLOYEE,4,A13.A14)** and press RETURN.

   Notice that the database reference uses the range name, EMPLOYEE, which includes the field names, all records, and all fields. The offset is 4 since you are referring to the fifth column and 1-2-3 starts with column 0 rather than column 1. The criteria location uses the entries in A13 and A14 to select the records whose salary entries will be included in the average. The results follow:

```
D21: @DAVG(EMPLOYEE,4,A13..A14)                                    READY

        A            B            C           D          E        F
21  Average Salary for Job Code 23:       24050
```

Using @DSUM

The @DSUM function follows the same pattern as the @DAVG function. If you want to total one of the fields in the database for all records with a job code of 23, you can use it without entering criteria again. Follow these steps:

1. Move the cell pointer to A22 and type **Total Salaries for Job Code 23:** and move the cell pointer to D22 to finalize your entry.

2. Type **@DSUM(EMPLOYEE,4,A13.A14)** and press RETURN.

   The results of this calculation follow:

```
D22: @DSUM(EMPLOYEE,4,A13..A14)                                    READY

        A            B            C           D          E        F
21  Average Salary for Job Code 23:       24050
22  Total Salaries for Job Code 23:       96200
```

Using @DCOUNT

The @DCOUNT function is used to selectively count the number of nonblank entries in records that match your criteria. It follows the same pattern as the other database functions and operates on the entries in the column specified by offset.

You can use this function to count the number of employees with a job code of 23. Follow these steps to enter the function:

1. Move the cell pointer to A23 and type **Number of Employees in Job Code 23:**, then move the cell pointer to D23 to finalize your entry.

2. Type **@DCOUNT(EMPLOYEE,3,A13.A14)** and press RETURN.

   The results of this calculation follow:

D23: @DCOUNT(EMPLOYEE,3,A13..A14)

The count operation is performed on the job code field. This will effectively give you a count of the records coded as Job Code 23. If the job code field were blank, the records could not be selected as matching the criteria for Job Code 23, making the count match exactly with the number of records that match.

Using @DMIN

The @DMIN function searches for the minimum value in the column specified. Only records that match your criteria are eligible for this minimum comparison. This provides a convenient way to determine the lowest salary paid to an individual in location 2 or the lowest salary paid to someone in Job Code 23. This time you will change the criteria and then enter the formula to determine the lowest salary in location 2. Follow these steps:

1. Move the cell pointer to A13 and type **Location**.

2. Move the cell pointer to A14 and type **2**.

3. Move the cell pointer to A24 and type **Minimum Salary for Location 2:**. Then move the cell pointer to D24 to finalize your entry.

4. Type **@DMIN(EMPLOYEE,4,A13.A14)** and press RETURN to produce these results:

```
D24: @DMIN(EMPLOYEE,4,A13..A14)                                    READY
```

```
        A            B            C            D        E        F
21  Average Salary for Job Code 23:          24050
22  Total Salaries for Job Code 23:          96200
23  Number of Employees in Job Code 23:          4
24  Minimum Salary for Job Code 23:          18700
```

SUMMARY

In this chapter you have learned to set up a database on 1-2-3's worksheet. After entering the data for the example, you learned how easy it is to change the sequence of your database records. You also learned that the query features can highlight matching records or extract a quick report for distribution. In addition, you found out about the database statistical functions, which you can now use to add power to your computations on a selective basis. In short, you learned all the basics of data management. After you have practiced with these commands for awhile, you will want to begin exploring some of the more advanced features on your own.

10

USING ADVANCED FUNCTIONS

You have already learned how to use some of the basic built-in functions that 1-2-3 has to offer. These provide an excellent way of handling everyday tasks such as totaling a column of numbers or rounding the result of a calculation to two decimal places.

In addition to these built-in functions, 1-2-3 also has a number of more sophisticated and specialized functions that can significantly help you to handle complex business needs. This chapter will show you how to use a number of these functions. In Chapter 7, the functions were organized by category. Here, although a particular category of functions is addressed, the focus is on the integration of the functions with an application example. In many instances, several functions are combined to resolve a specific application example. This is especially important for the more complex functions; new users need to understand how to apply these functions to the business problems they face.

ADDING LOGIC TO YOUR CALCULATIONS

According to 1-2-3's rules, you can place only a single entry into a worksheet cell. Therefore, only one formula can be stored in each worksheet cell. This can be limiting, especially considering the many exception conditions and special rules that apply to the calculations performed every day in a business setting. For example, when you give a customer a purchase discount, you may not want to multiply the purchase amount by a fixed percentage. The amount of the discount might depend on the size of the sale, whether the sale is cash or credit, and the amount purchased by the customer on an annual basis. Regular 1-2-3 formulas can calculate a discount based on a fixed percentage, but they cannot cope with all these conditions. Fortunately, 1-2-3 has a number of built-in functions that can step in to fill this need. These functions let you add logic processing to your calculations and let you make your calculations on the basis of on any conditions you wish to apply.

Creating a Salary Projection Model

The first example you will explore creates a salary model. With this model, you can estimate the various components of salary expense. After projecting a salary increase with a percentage growth factor, you can also estimate other salary expenses, such as your FICA contribution as an employer and the cost of the benefits you are supplying for different personnel classifications. You can easily adapt the model to meet other conditions and situations — either by adding new expense categories (patterning calculations after the examples provided) or by altering the formulas for the existing calculations. Since this model is dependent on the @IF function, it is a good idea to review how the @IF function works before starting the model.

USING @IF   The *@IF function* lets you test a condition to determine the appropriate value for a cell. @IF is one of the most powerful built-in functions because it frees you from the limitation of deciding on one formula for a cell. Now you can set up two different values for a cell and determine which one to use, based on other conditions in the worksheet. You can create two or more discount levels, payroll deductions, commission structures, or any other calculation that involves more than one alternative.

The @IF function uses three arguments in this sequence:

@IF(condition to test,value if true,value if false)

The first argument, the *condition to be tested*, can be any logical expression that can be evaluated as true or false. Examples are A1>9, C2=G10, and A2+B6>C3*H12. The expression returns a value of true only if the condition specified is met. For example, in the first expression, true will be returned only if A1 is greater than 9. If this expression evaluates as true, the cell will take on the value specified in the second argument of the function.

The second argument for the @IF function, the *value* the cell will use *if the condition is true*, can take several forms. It can be an actual numeric value, a formula that needs to be calculated, or another @IF statement to be checked if multiple levels of conditions must be met before an action is determined. In Release 2, this argument can be a string value as long as it is enclosed in double quotation marks.

The third argument is the *value* to be assumed by the cell containing the @IF statement *if the condition in the function is false*. All the conditions mentioned above for the value if true also apply here.

Release 2 also allows strings to be used with the logical IF condition. For example, you could have an entry such as @IF(A10="Chicago",F2,G2). If A10 contains Chicago, the cell containing this entry will take on the value of F2. If A10 contains anything else, the cell containing the function will be equal to G2.

MAKING THE ENTRIES IN THE SALARY MODEL   To minimize your entries, you need to enter data for only a few employees. Then, a simple copy operation and additional data entry allow you

G4: @IF(D4)=7,@IF(E4>50000,20000+(E4-50000)*0.02,E4*0.2),E4*0.14)

```
                    Salary Expense Projections
           1988              Job     1989
Name       Salary   Increase Class   Salary   FICA     Benefits
Jones, Ray $25,000    7.00%     3    $26,750  $1,913   $3,745
Larkin, Mary $29,000  5.00%     9    $30,450  $2,177   $6,090
Harris, John $45,000  6.50%     7    $47,925  $3,110   $9,585
Parson, Mary $55,900  5.50%     9    $58,975  $3,110   $20,179
```

FIGURE 10.1   Completed salary model

to expand this model to include as many employees as you want. The model you will be building is shown in Figure 10.1. You can follow these explicit instructions for your entries:

1. Enter **/Worksheet Erase Yes** to clear the worksheet.

2. Enter **/Worksheet Column Set-Width**, type **13**, and press RETURN.
    This will widen column A to accept the name entries.

3. Make these entries on the worksheet:

    A3: **Name**

    A4: **Jones, Ray**

    A5: **Larkin, Mary**

A6:	Harris, John
A7:	Parson, Mary
B2:	'1988
B3:	Salary
B4:	25000
B5:	29000
B6:	45000
B7:	55900
C1:	Salary Expense Projections
C3:	Increase
C4:	.07
C5:	.05
C6:	.065
C7:	.055
D2:	Job
D3:	Class
D4:	3
D5:	9
D6:	7
D7:	9
E2:	'1989
E3:	Salary
F3:	FICA
G3:	Benefits

4. Move the cell pointer to C4, enter /**Range Format Percent**, press RETURN, then move the cell pointer to C7 and press RETURN again.

5. Move the cell pointer to D4, enter /**Range Format Fixed**, type **0**, and press RETURN. Move the cell pointer to D7 and press RETURN again.

6. Enter **/Worksheet Global Format Currency**, type **0**, and
    press RETURN to produce this display:

D4: (F0) 3   READY

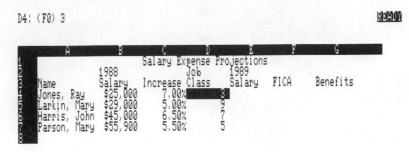

All the remaining entries in this model must be calculated.
Standard formulas will not work; various factors affect the computed results, and a regular formula cannot deal with these exceptions. After analyzing each of the required conditions, enter an
@IF statement that captures the essence of how you would perform these calculations manually under all circumstances.

FICA is not computed by the same method for all wage levels.
It is calculated at 7.15% unless the individual earns more than the
established cap amount for FICA. If earnings exceed the cap
amount, you will only pay an employer's FICA contribution on the
cap amount. You can record this with the @IF function if the
condition to be tested is recorded in the function and the two
different methods for performing the FICA computation are
recorded as the values for true and false conditions.

Follow these directions for making your entries:

7. Move the cell pointer to E4, type **+B4*(1+C4)**, and press
    RETURN.
    This formula calculates the projected salary for 1989,
    based on the increase percentage.

8. Enter **/Copy**, press RETURN, move the cell pointer to
    E5, type **.**, move to E7, and press RETURN.

9. Move the cell pointer to F4 and type **@IF(E4<
    43500,E4*.0715,43500*.0715)**, then press RETURN.

The essence of this function is to check whether the salary is less than $43,500 and, if it is, to multiply the salary by 7.15%. If it is not less than $43,500, the rate will be applied to $43,500, the amount chosen for this example as the arbitrary limit for FICA payments. You now have the rules for two different ways to perform the FICA calculation, depending on the amount of the salary.

10. Enter **/Copy**, press RETURN, move the cell pointer to F5, type **.**, then move the cell pointer to F7 and press RETURN.

The results will look like this:

F4: @IF(E4<43500,E4*0.0715,43500*0.0715)

	A	B	C	D	E	F	G
1			Salary Expense Projections				
2		1988		Job	1989		
3	Name	Salary	Increase	Class	Salary	FICA	Benefits
4	Jones, Ray	$25,000	7.00%	3	$26,750	$1,913	
5	Larkin, Mary	$29,000	5.00%	9	$30,450	$2,177	
6	Harris, John	$45,000	6.50%	7	$47,925	$3,110	
7	Parson, Mary	$55,900	5.50%	5	$58,975	$3,110	

Naturally if you had more records on your worksheet, you could copy this formula further down the worksheet than cell F7 before finalizing the copy.

In this case, the @IF function provided just the solution you needed. The next problem for the salary expense model involves calculating the cost of benefits. You can also solve this calculation with @IF, but due to its complexity you will require multiple levels of @IF statements.

The hypothetical model you are creating requires an answer to two different conditions concerning benefits. According to the company's specifications for the calculations, the first question concerns the job class of the employee. Executives have class greater than or equal to 7 and their benefits are calculated under different rules than for nonmanagement employees. Even after the job class is decided, however, there is still the salary factor, which can affect the estimated benefit amount.

In the current example, benefits for executive employees are calculated as 20% of the executive's salary unless the executive makes more than $50,000, which classifies the person as senior executive management. In this case, the computation is $20,000 plus 2% of the excess over $50,000. For nonexecutive employees, the calculation is a little different; it is always computed as 14% of the projected salary. All this may sound a little complex at first; but if you stop and think about it for a minute, you realize that you have no difficulty making these computations by hand. The trick is to record all these conditions in a worksheet cell. Following these directions will do this for you:

11. Move the cell pointer to G4 and type **@IF(D4>=7,@IF (E4>50000,20000+(E4−50000)∗.02,E4∗.2),E4∗.14)**.
   This formula examines all the necessary conditions. The condition in the first @IF checks to see if the job class is greater than or equal to 7. If this condition is true, the second @IF becomes the value of this cell and must be evaluated. This second @IF condition checks the salary to see if it is greater than $50,000 and, depending on the result of this condition test, computes the benefit expense to be either $20,000 plus 2% of the excess over $50,000 or 20% of the salary.

There is yet another condition, one that occurs when the job class is less than 7. In this case the benefit expense is 14% of the salary.

These multiple levels of conditions are frequently referred to as *nested if* statements. They are a little complicated but worth the time investment for the flexibility they offer.

12. Enter **/Copy**, press RETURN, and move the cell pointer to G5. Type **.**, move the cell pointer to G7, and press RETURN.
   Your salary model is now complete and should match the model shown earlier in Figure 10.1. If you have other salary expenses you can alter the model to include them and then save it.

13. Enter **/File Save**, type **SALARY**, and press RETURN. Or, if you do not wish to save this model, you can clear it by entering **/Worksheet Erase Yes**.

Calculating the Net Purchase Price

The next model you will build also needs the flexibility that occurs when logic is incorporated in worksheet cells. Since calculating a net purchase price involves calculating varying purchase discounts and applying shipping costs, numerous conditions need to be considered. In this case, the @IF function would be a cumbersome solution; many levels of nesting would be required to solve the problem. There are several additional functions within 1-2-3 that offer a wide range of options. The two that you will examine now are the @VLOOKUP function, which builds a table of codes and associated values on the worksheet for reference, and the @INDEX function (available in Release 2), which also builds a table of values but uses a different approach for finding the correct entry. First, you will examine each of the functions. Next, you will enter the basics of the model. Then you will apply the information you have obtained on the inner workings of two functions to complete the model.

USING @VLOOKUP   The @*VLOOKUP* function allows you to search a table that you have entered on the worksheet for an appropriate value to use in your worksheet. When you create the table that @VLOOKUP will be referencing, you must store the codes that will be looked up in a column on the worksheet. The values that you wish to correspond to each of these codes will be stored in the columns to the right of the codes. Figure 10.2 shows a table of codes in column A, and the associated return values for each code in column B. You must understand the way that @VLOOKUP works before you even enter the codes and associated values in the table.

The @VLOOKUP function expects three arguments, in this sequence:

@VLOOKUP(code to be looked up,table location,offset)

The first argument is *code to be looked up* — the entry in your worksheet, which will be compared against the column of table values. When numeric values are used, 1-2-3 looks for the largest value in the table that is not larger than the code you have supplied. The codes should be in ascending order. If the first code in the column is larger than the code you supply, you will get an ERR condition. When string values are used (permissible only with Release 2), the search is always for an exact match.

Since a table must be at least two partial columns on the worksheet, the second argument, *table location*, will always be a range reference to at least two partial columns on the worksheet. This reference must include the table codes as well as the return values.

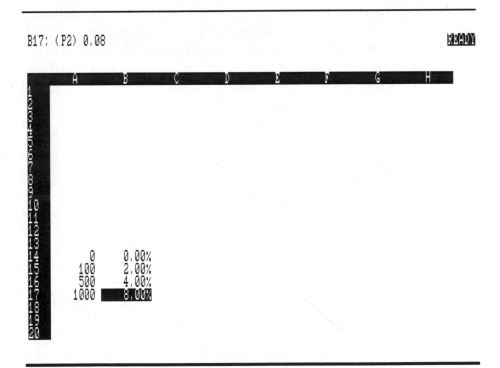

FIGURE 10.2   Entering the Lookup table codes and values

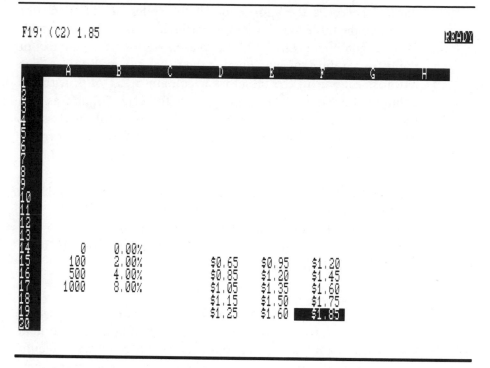

F19: (C2) 1.85   READY

	A	B	C	D	E	F	G	H
14	0	0.00%						
15	100	2.00%		$0.65	$0.95	$1.20		
16	500	4.00%		$0.85	$1.20	$1.45		
17	1000	8.00%		$1.05	$1.35	$1.60		
18				$1.15	$1.50	$1.75		
19				$1.25	$1.60	$1.85		

FIGURE 10.3   Entering the Index table values

The third argument, *offset*, tells 1-2-3 how many columns to the right of the code column to use when obtaining the return values. This function allows you to create tables that are more than two columns wide.

USING @INDEX   The @*INDEX* function also requires you to enter a table on the worksheet, but you do not enter values for matching. Every entry in the table is designed to be a return value. Which of these return values to use is determined by the row and column number you specify. You make your specifications known to 1-2-3 through this function:

@INDEX(table location,column number,row number)

Table location is the address of all the codes in the table. For example, the table location of the entries shown in the lower middle of Figure 10.3 is D15.F19. The *column number* is the number of the offset column, which contains the value you wish to use. The leftmost column in the table has a column offset of 0, with the column offset number increasing by 1 for each column as you move to the right. The row number is the number of the row you wish to use. The same numbering scheme is used: The upper row is row 0 and each row further down in the table is incremented by 1.

The type of application for which @INDEX is ideal is one where your data values can be used to access the correct value in the table. Computing shipping costs is a good example, if the cost is determined by weight and distance, and values can be assigned for each. Shortly, you can put the @INDEX function to work computing shipping costs.

CREATING THE PURCHASE MODEL   To compute a net purchase price, you need to know the basic components: the item purchased, a purchase price and quantity, a purchase discount amount, the shipping weight of the item, and the customer's shipping zone. All items weigh between 1 and 5 lbs and all customers are assigned a shipping zone from 1 to 3, depending on their distance from a regional warehouse.

Purchase discounts are computed on the extension of the item's cost — that is, you multiply the number of units by the unit price. Shipping costs are added after calculating purchase discounts. The discount rate applied increases with the size of the purchase. For a purchase of $100, a 2% discount is given; for $500, a discount of 4%; and for $1000 or more, an 8% discount. You can construct the @VLOOKUP table with these entries:

1. Move the cell pointer to A14, type **0**, and press
   RETURN.
   Normally, you would use a location further away from the data to allow for expansion. For now, however, you will find it easier to view the entries while building your formulas.

2. Enter these table codes and their associated values:

A15:	**100**
A16:	**500**
A17:	**1000**
B14:	**0**
B15:	**.02**
B16:	**.04**
B17:	**.08**

This completes the table entries for the @VLOOKUP table. You still need to enter the values for shipping costs, but this time you will use an index table. For purchase discounts, the index table is not an option because of the wide gap between entries. You would need an index table with 1000 entries, even though only three discounts needed to be stored. All these extra entries would be due to the @INDEX function's method of finding a return value based on the row and column location. Continue with the entries for the shipping table.

3. Move the cell pointer to D15 and type **.65**, and press RETURN.
   This is the value that will be used for the shipping cost of a one-pound item shipped to zone 1.

4. Complete the entries as follows:

D16:	**.85**
D17:	**1.05**
D18:	**1.15**
D19:	**1.25**
E15:	**.95**
E16:	**1.20**
E17:	**1.35**

E18:	**1.50**
E19:	**1.60**
F15:	**1.20**
F16:	**1.45**
F17:	**1.60**
F18:	**1.75**
F19:	**1.85**

Once you have entered the tables, enter the data in the main section of your model.

5. Move the cell pointer to A1 and begin making these entries:

A1:	**Item**
A2:	**Number**
A4:	**X5401**
A5:	**YT45**
A6:	**CF514**
A7:	**RT908**
A8:	**R4312**
B1:	**Units**
B2:	**Purchd**
B4:	**3**
B5:	**7**
B6:	**12**
B7:	**5**
B8:	**10**
C1:	**Unit**
C2:	**Cost**
C4:	**25.50**

C5:	38
C6:	47.50
C7:	150
C8:	12.50
D2:	Weight
D4:	1
D5:	3
D6:	4
D7:	1
D8:	2
E2:	Zone
E4:	2
E5:	0
E6:	1
E7:	2
E8:	1
F2:	Discount
G1:	Shipping
G2:	Costs
H1:	Net
H2:	Price

6. Move the cell pointer to C4, enter **/Range Format Currency**, press RETURN, move the cell pointer to C8, and press RETURN again.

7. Move the cell pointer to F4, enter **/Range Format Currency**, press RETURN, move the cell pointer to H8, and press RETURN.

8. Move the cell pointer to D15, enter **/Range Format Currency**, press RETURN, move the cell pointer to F19, and press RETURN.

B14: (P2) 0   READY

```
        A          B         C          D         E          F       G        H
1   Item       Units     Unit                                    Shipping  Net
2   Number     Purchd    Cost      Weight     Zone     Discount  Cost     Price
3
4   X5401          3     $25.50        1         2
5   YT45           7     $38.00        3         0
6   CF514         12     $47.50        4         1
7   RT908          5     $15.00        1         2
8   R4312         10     $12.50        2         1
9
10
11
12
13
14         0      0.00%
15       100      2.00%            $0.65     $0.95     $1.20
16       500      4.00%            $0.85     $1.20     $1.45
17      1000      8.00%            $1.05     $1.35     $1.60
18                                 $1.15     $1.50     $1.75
19                                 $1.25     $1.60     $1.85
20
```

FIGURE 10.4   Purchase model without formulas

9. Move the cell pointer to B14, enter **/Range Format Percent**, press RETURN, move the cell pointer to B17, and press RETURN.

This completes the data entry. The model is ready for the formulas and should now appear as shown in Figure 10.4. Naturally, other fields, such as customer name and shipping address, still need to be added. However, these are not important for your purposes at this time.

The formula for the purchase discount will use the @VLOOKUP function. The first argument will be the purchase amount, which must be computed by multiplying the units times the unit cost. This value will be looked up in the table stored in A14..B17. 1-2-3 does not attempt to find an equal match. It searches for the largest value in column A that is not greater than the purchase amount.

It then returns the value in column B from the same row. The table location will be specified as the second argument. The third argument instructs 1-2-3 which column in the table it should use for the return value. In the current example this number is a 1, indicating that it should use the values in column B, since they are one column to the right of the table codes.

10. Move the cell pointer to F4, type **@VLOOKUP(**.

11. Move the cell pointer to B4, type **∗**, move the cell pointer to C4, and type a **,**.

12. Move the cell pointer to A14, then press F4 (ABS). This will place $s in front of the row and column portion of the address, making it an absolute reference to the

---

F4: (C2) @VLOOKUP(B4*C4,$A$14,.$B$17,1)*(B4*C4)   READY

	A	B	C	D	E	F	G	H
1	Item	Units	Unit				Shipping	Net
2	Number	Purchd	Cost	Weight	Zone	Discount	Cost	Price
3								
4	X5401	3	$25.50	1	2	$0.00		
5	YT45	7	$38.00	3	0	$5.32		
6	CF514	12	$47.50	4	1	$22.80		
7	RT908	5	$150.00	1	2	$30.00		
8	R4312	10	$12.50	2	1	$2.50		
9								
10								
11								
12								
13								
14	0	0.00%						
15	100	2.00%		$0.65	$0.95	$1.20		
16	500	4.00%		$0.85	$1.20	$1.45		
17	1000	8.00%		$1.05	$1.35	$1.60		
18				$1.15	$1.50	$1.75		
19				$1.25	$1.60	$1.85		
20								

FIGURE 10.5 Computing purchase discounts

beginning of the table. You need an absolute reference, since you want the table reference to remain the same regardless of where you copy the formula.

13. Type a ., then move the cell pointer to B17.

14. Type **,1)*(B4*C4)** and press RETURN.
    This formula will look up a discount percentage appropriate for the purchase amount and multiply by the amount of the purchase. In this case the discount is zero, since the purchase amount is $76.50.

15. Enter **/Copy**, press RETURN, and move the cell pointer to F5. Type a ., move the cell pointer to F8, and press RETURN.
    The purchase discount has been computed for all the entries on the model that appears as shown in Figure 10.5.

16. Move the cell pointer to G4 and type **@INDEX(**.

17. Move the cell pointer to D15 and press F4(ABS).
    This will make the table reference absolute, which will allow the formula to be copied.

18. Type a **.** and move the cell pointer to F19.

19. Type a **,,** move the cell pointer to E4, type another **,,** and move the cell pointer to D4.
    In this step you have specified E4, the Zone, as the column to use for the return value and D4, the Weight, as the row.

20. Type **)***, move the cell pointer to B4, and press RETURN.
    This completes the formula, which will find the cost of shipping one item from the index table, then multiply it by the number of items.
       Note to Release 1A users: Since Release 1A does not have the @INDEX function, you can modify the application by adding a column of codes in column C to the left of the shipping costs. You can use this code and the offset option in @VLOOKUP to control the value returned from this table. Assuming you made this alteration to the

H4: (C2) +B4*C4-F4+G4   READY

```
      A        B        C        D       E        F        G        H
1  Item     Units    Unit                                Shipping Net
2  Number   Purchd   Cost    Weight   Zone   Discount  Cost     Price
3
4  X5401        3   $25.50      1       2     $0.00    $4.35   $80.85
5  YT45         7   $38.00      3       0     $5.32    $8.05  $268.73
6  CF514       12   $47.50      4       1    $22.80   $19.20  $566.40
7  RT908        5  $150.00      1       2    $30.00    $7.25  $727.25
8  R4312       10   $12.50      2       1     $2.50   $13.50  $136.00
9
10
11
12
13
14        0   0.00%
15      100   2.00%          $0.65   $0.95    $1.20
16      500   4.00%          $0.85   $1.20    $1.45
17     1000   8.00%          $1.05   $1.35    $1.60
18                           $1.15   $1.50    $1.75
19                           $1.25   $1.60    $1.85
20
```

FIGURE 10.6   Completed purchase model

to the worksheet entries, you could use a formula like this:

@VLOOKUP(D4,$C$15.$F$19,E4+1)*B4)

Notice that one is added to the zone to option values of 1, 2, and 3, which will access the table offset columns.

21. Enter **/Copy**, press RETURN, move the cell pointer to G5, type a **.**, move the cell pointer to G8, and press RETURN.

22. Move the cell pointer to H4, type **+B4*C4-F4+G4**, and press RETURN.
    This formula calculates the net purchase price by extending units times unit cost, subtracting the discount, and

adding the shipping cost. Once it is copied to the other rows, your model is complete.

23. Enter **/Copy**, press RETURN, move the cell pointer to H5, type a ., move the cell pointer to H8, and press RETURN.
   Figure 10.6 shows the resulting calculations in column H.

24. Enter **/Worksheet Erase Yes** to clear memory, or use **/File Save** to create a copy of the model on disk before clearing memory.

Checking Entries for Errors

Data entry errors can cause serious problems in worksheet accuracy. There are no facilities for validity checks; you make entries directly into each worksheet cell. However, there are a group of logical functions that can be used in combination with the @IF function to alert you to potential error situations in certain fields. These functions can check a cell to see if it contains a number or a string value. They can also check for the NA, which indicates that an entry is not available, or ERR, which indicates an error condition in a formula. The @ISNUMBER and @ISSTRING functions are only available in Release 2 and above.

These are the functions and the checks they perform:

@ISERR(value)-Checks for a value of ERR in a cell

@ISNA(value)-Checks for a value of NA in a cell

@ISNUMBER(value)-Checks for a numeric value in a cell

@ISSTRING(value)-Checks for a string value in a cell

In all four functions, the argument value is normally a cell address that references a cell you want checked. In the first function, a 1 representing true is returned if the cell has a value of ERR. In the second, a 1 is returned if the cell has a value of NA. The function @ISNUMBER returns a 1 if the cell contains a number. @ISSTRING returns a 1 if the cell contains a string.

Although these functions can be used alone, they are most frequently combined with the @IF statement, as in:

@IF(@ISNUMBER(A6),"A6 is numeric","A6 is not numeric")

This @IF statement checks to see if @ISNUMBER(A6) returns a 1 for true or a zero for false. If the result of this test is true, "A6 is numeric" will be placed in the cell containing the function. If the condition tests false because A6 does not contain a numeric value, the phrase "A6 is not numeric" will be placed in the cell that contains this function.

You will build two short models to look at the effect of two of these functions. You will see from these examples that it is easy to enter an error-checking formula once and copy it down the column. You can visually scan data for errors but it is much easier to scan a special column where messages are used to flag error conditions.

CHECKING FOR MISSING DATA   The first example you will enter works with the @NA function. This function serves as a place keeper for missing data. The model records the order number, order date, quantity, and price, and computes a total. If the price is missing, @NA is inserted in its place. When the order total is computed by multiplying quantity times price, if the value for a price is NA the total for that item is NA. To prevent this, insert a message that is more noticeable. Complete these steps to create the model:

1. Move the cell pointer to A1 and enter /**Worksheet Column Set-Width**, type **13**, and press RETURN.

2. Make these entries on the worksheet:

A2:	**Order Number**
A3:	**12760**
A4:	**12781**

A5:	12976
B2:	Date
B3:	'01-Oct-87
B4:	'01-Oct-87
B5:	'02-Oct-87
C2:	Quantity
C3:	3
C4:	4
C5:	12
D2:	Price
D3:	3.5
D4:	@NA
D5:	12.25
E2:	Total

Notice that the dates in column D were entered as labels. Normally this is not the approach to take with dates, since the @DATE function will create a serial date number that can be used in calculations. However, label entries were used because there is no need to use them in calculations. Later in this chapter, you will look at the features of another built-in function that can convert these labels to serial-date numbers.

3. Move the cell pointer to D3, enter /**Range Format Currency**, and press RETURN. Move the cell pointer to E5 and press RETURN.

Now that you have completed the preliminary entries, it is time to enter a formula in E3 that will test the price for the first entry for a value of NA. If a true condition is returned, the cell should take on the value NA; if a false condition is returned, the cell will have the value that is computed by multiplying price times quantity. Follow these steps to have the error-checking formula placed in column E.

4. Move the cell pointer to E3 and enter **@IF(@ISNA(D3), "Missing Unit Price",C3*D3)**, then press RETURN.

5. Enter **/Copy** and press RETURN. Move the cell pointer to E4, type a **.**, move the cell pointer to E5, and press RETURN.

   The following results should appear:

E3: (C2) @IF(@ISNA(D3),"Missing Unit Price",C3*D3)

Notice how the message, Missing Unit Price, flags the record that has no price entry. This is not necessary when you have only three records; but when you have hundreds, this message could offer a significant time savings.

6. Enter **/Worksheet Erase Yes** to clear memory.
   Remember to use / File Save if you want to retain a copy of this example.

CHECKING FOR NON-NUMERIC DATA You may have an application where you want to require your computer operators to enter numeric values in certain key fields. Although there is no direct way to lock out unacceptable input, you can display an error message if non-numeric data is entered. If you have Release 2 or above, you can use a combination of @ISNUMBER and @IF to handle this task for you. First, make a few entries in an address file. Then add a formula that checks the first zip code field to see if it contains a number, since the application is designed to accept a five-digit zip code for individuals living in the U.S. If the field does not contain a numeric entry, a message will be printed.

Follow these directions to make the entries in the file:

1. Move the cell pointer to A1 and enter /**Worksheet Column Set-Width**, then type **15**, and press RETURN.

2. Move the cell pointer to B1, enter /**Worksheet Column Set-Width**, type **20**, and press RETURN.

3. Make these entries in the worksheet cells shown:

A3:	**Name**
A4:	**John Smith**
A5:	**Jill Brown**
A6:	**Harry Olson**
A7:	**Mary Greene**
B3:	**Address**
B4:	**'1215 East 11th St.**
B5:	**'41 S. Main St.**
B6:	**'1111 G St. NW**
B7:	**'42 Stone Ct.**
C1:	**Client Listing**
C3:	**City**
C4:	**Towson**
C5:	**Akron**
C6:	**Austin**
C7:	**Berea**
D3:	**State**
D4:	**New York**
D5:	**Ohio**
D6:	**Ohio**
D7:	**Michigan**

E3:	**Zip Code**
E4:	**98765**
E5:	**45321**
E6:	**r567w1**
E7:	**44040**
F3:	**Zip Code Errors**

Notice that a single quotation mark was used at the front of the address entries to ensure that the entries were treated as labels. The only task remaining is to enter the error-checking formula:

4. Move the cell pointer to F4 and type **@IF(@ISNUMBER (E4),""," ERROR-Zip Code Must be numeric")**, and press RETURN.

   This formula bases the result of the @IF test on whether or not the referenced cell contains a number. If it docs, a blank (enclosed with the set of quotation marks) is placed in the cell. If the entry is not numeric, an error message is placed at that location.

5. Enter /**Copy**, press RETURN, move the cell pointer to F5, type a **.**, move the cell pointer to F7, and press RETURN again.

   The results follow:

F4: @IF(@ISNUMBER(E4),"","ERROR - Zip Code must be numeric")

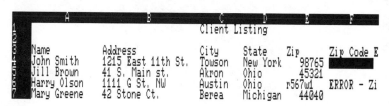

6. Enter /**Worksheet Erase Yes** to clear memory.

TURNING LABEL ENTRIES INTO SERIAL DATE AND TIME VALUES

Both date and time entries can require an extra effort, especially when you have an entire column of date entries to make. The @DATE and @TIME functions that you used in Chapter 7 each require three arguments. In addition, many users find the sequence of the date arguments to be different from their normal entry sequence, since the year, month, and day sequence is not normally used. There is a solution that allows you to enter either date or time as a label in one of the date or time display formats and then have another function convert the entry to a valid date or

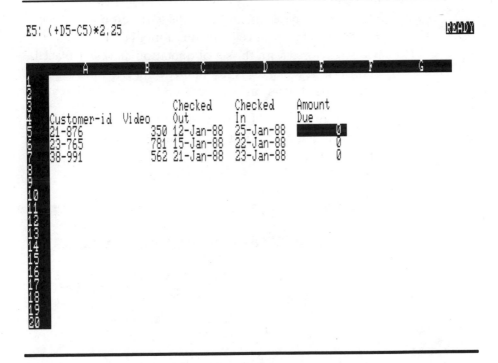

FIGURE 10.7   Dates stored as labels

time serial number. @TIMEVALUE is the function used to change a label entry in a valid time format to a time serial number. @DATEVALUE is the function used to convert a label that looks like a date to a valid date serial number. Both these functions are available only in Release 2 and above.

Using Dates From Label Entries to Compute Rental Fees

Figure 10.7 presents a few records that were entered with the dates stored as labels in columns C and D. As the entries in column E show, the fact that all the calculations are erroneously displaying as zeros suggests a problem with the calculation of the amount due. The cause of this problem is the manner in which the dates were entered. Since the formula for amount due subtracts the date in D5 from the date in C5, 1-2-3 is expecting values in these cells. A serial-date number would meet this requirement, but label entries do not. These dates were entered as labels, which means that they cannot be used in arithmetic calculations. You can correct this problem with a few modifications to the formula; but first enter the basic data that the model will use. Follow these steps to completion:

1. Move the cell pointer to column A and enter **/Worksheet Column Set-Width**, type **13**, and press RETURN. Use this same procedure to widen column C and column D to 11.

2. Make these entries:

A4:	**Customer-id**
A5:	**'21-876**
A6:	**'23-765**
A7:	**'38-991**
B4:	**Video**
B5:	**350**

B6:	781
B7:	562
C3:	Checked
C4:	Out
C5:	'12-Jan-88
C6:	'15-Jan-88
C7:	'21-Jan-88
D3:	Checked
D4:	In
D5:	'25-Jan-88
D6:	'22-Jan-88
D7:	'23-Jan-88
E3:	Amount
E4:	Due

The formula for the amount due in Figure 10.7 was entered as (D5-B5)*2.25. That figure already showed you that a different solution is required.

3. Move the cell pointer to E5, type **(@DATEVALUE(D5)-@DATEVALUE(C5))*2.25**, and press RETURN.

4. Enter **/Range Format Currency** and press RETURN twice.
   This format will be copied when you copy the formula to other cells in the range.

5. Enter **/Copy** and press RETURN. Move the cell pointer to E6, type a **.**, move the cell pointer to E7, and press RETURN.
   Now that the label entries are converted to actual date serial numbers, they can be used in formulas without causing an error, as the following illustration shows:

E5: (C2) (@DATEVALUE(D5)-@DATEVALUE(C5))*2.25

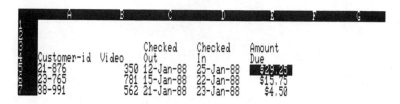

6. Use /**Worksheet Erase Yes** to clear memory or save the worksheet with the /**File Save** command.

Turning Time Labels Into Hours for Billing Clients

The @TIMEVALUE function converts labels that look like time entries into numeric time representation, which is suitable for use in any calculation. The format of the function to handle this conversion is @TIMEVALUE(time string). You can use it to convert time entries that are labels to numbers that can be involved in calculations. This conversion is one way to avoid the need for the three arguments that @TIME requires. It can also correct mistakes in data entry in which times were accidentally entered as labels. To try this function with a short example, follow these steps:

1. Move the cell pointer to column C, enter /**Worksheet Column Set-Width**, type **13**, and press RETURN.

2. Move the cell pointer to E5, enter /**Range Format Date Time**, type **4**, move the cell pointer to E7, and press RETURN.

3. Make these worksheet entries:

   A3:   **Job**

   A4:   **Number**

A5:	**1**
A6:	**2**
A7:	**3**
B3:	**Time**
B4:	**In**
B5:	**'8:05 AM**
B6:	**'8:10 AM**
B7:	**'8:30 AM**
C4:	**Repair**
C5:	**Tires**
C6:	**Brakes**
C7:	**Steering**
D3:	**Time**
D4:	**Out**
D5:	**'9:17 AM**
D6:	**'10:34 AM**
D7:	**'1:18 PM**
E3:	**Elapsed**
E4:	**Time**

It is possible to enter these times without the AM or PM designation for the entries before 1 PM. It is also possible to enter these designations in lower case, as in 9:05 am or 10:16 pm.

4. Move the cell pointer to E5, type @**TIMEVALUE(D5)-** @**TIMEVALUE(B5)**, and press RETURN.

5. Enter /**Copy**, press RETURN, move the cell pointer to E5, type a **.,** move the cell pointer to E7, and press RETURN.

The final results look like this:

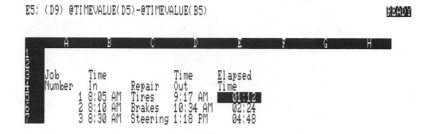

```
E5: (D9) @TIMEVALUE(D5)-@TIMEVALUE(B5)                          READY
```

	A	B	C	D	E	F	G	H
1								
2	Job	Time		Time	Elapsed			
3	Number	In	Repair	Out	Time			
4	1	8:05 AM	Tires	9:17 AM	01:12			
5	2	8:10 AM	Brakes	10:34 AM	02:24			
6	3	8:30 AM	Steering	1:18 PM	04:48			

6. Enter /**Worksheet Erase Yes** to clear memory.

MANIPULATING LABELS

Release 2 has an entire category of built-in functions that only operate on label or string entries. Release 1A, however, has none of these functions, so if you are working with Release 1A skip this section.

The string functions provide a variety of character-manipulation formulas that give you flexibility in arranging your text entries. They are extremely useful for correcting data-entry errors and for restructuring worksheet data for a new application.

The unique feature of the string functions is that many of them work with individual characters in the string. When 1-2-3 works with individual characters, its numbering system is different from yours. 1-2-3 considers the first character in the string to be in the 0 position of the string. Since 1-2-3 will not adjust its numbering scheme, in order to work 1-2-3's numbering method you will have to adjust your method of counting.

Replacing Incorrect Characters

You can replace characters with a text string without retyping the entire string. You can use this feature to change slashes to dashes, or to manipulate a part number into a warehouse location. The function is extremely flexible; you can replace multiple characters with one character, or you can replace one character with multiple characters.

The function you will use to make these replacements is @REPLACE. It uses four different arguments, in this fashion:

@REPLACE(original string,start location,# characters,new string)

The first argument is the *original string* or, more likely, a reference to the cell containing the original string.

The second argument is the *position number* in the original string where you want to begin the replacement. Remember that 1-2-3 calculates the position number, beginning with position 0 for the first character in the string.

The third argument is the *number of characters* to remove from the string. This argument offers considerable flexibility. You can specify 0 characters to have the new string inserted in the original string. When the number of characters is greater than the length of the new string, the string that is returned by this function will be shorter than the original. When the number of characters is the same as the number of characters in the original string, the entire string will be replaced.

The last argument is a series of characters enclosed in quotation marks, or a reference to a cell that contains a string. When the *new string* is empty — *" "* — @REPLACE will simply delete the characters from the original string.

You will work with an example that will alter a series of part numbers on the worksheet. The existing part numbers have three sections, each separated by slashes. @REPLACE will change the first slash to a dash and will delete the middle section of the entry. Follow these steps to take a look at @REPLACE in action.

1. Make the following entries:

A1:	**Part Number**
A2:	**AB/567/8907**
A3:	**VB/907/6754**
A4:	**JK/675/8752**

A5:   **LK/999/5544**

C1:   **Altered Part Number**

Your worksheet should now look like this:

C1: 'Altered Part Number

2. Move the cell pointer to C2, type **@REPLACE(A2,2,5,"-")**, and press RETURN.
   The character in position two is a slash, since position two refers to the third character in the string. The next argument tells the function to remove the / and the next four characters from the string. This removes both /s and the three characters between them. These five characters are replaced with a single -.

3. Enter **/Copy**, press RETURN, move the cell pointer to C3, type a **.**, move the cell pointer to C5, and press RETURN.
   The final results are as follows:

C2: @REPLACE(A2,2,5,"-")

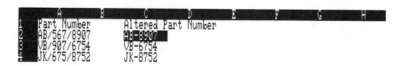

4. Enter **/Worksheet Erase Yes** to clear memory.

Using Part of a Name Entry

Some of the string functions allow you to dissect a string entry and restructure the original entry into a string that looks quite different. These features can be useful; they can alter names entered as

John Smith to Smith, John, or just Smith if you are only interested in the last name. Unfortunately, unless you have worked with the string functions for a while, you may have to experiment a bit to come up with the correct solution. The difficulty in creating the correct formula is partially because meaningful activities with these functions frequently require the use of a number of functions in one formula.

You will create a string formula that extracts the last name from an entry that looks like John Smith. This will require three built-in functions: @MID, @FIND, and @LENGTH. First you need to take a look at these functions and the arguments you will use with them.

USING @FIND   Use the @*FIND* function whenever you wish to locate the position of a string within a string. You can use it to locate the position of a blank space between first and last name, for example. When you combine the position of the blank space with the result of other functions, you can switch a name that is sequenced as first name/last name to a name that is sequenced as last name/comma/first name.

The @*FIND* function has three arguments and looks like this:

@FIND(search string,string to be searched,starting location)

The search string is a character sequence or a reference to a cell that contains a character sequence to be found in the second argument. As with the other string functions, when the characters are entered directly into the function, they must be enclosed within quotation marks. The length of the search string must be at least one less than the length of the string you plan to search. The function is case sensitive when it completes the search, so you will want to differentiate carefully between upper and lower case.

One option is to store the string directly within the function. The string can also be stored in a cell, and the cell address where it is stored can be used as a function argument. The maximum length of this string is 240 characters.

The last argument, *starting location*, is the position in the string to be searched where you want to begin your search. 1-2-3 counts the leftmost character in the string as zero, causing you to make a mental adjustment as you specify the place to begin.

If you were to enter "@FIND("-","213-28-78654), the result 6 would be returned. (Remember that 1-2-3 begins counting with position 0.) Even though 1-2-3 begins at position 4 when it determines what location the search string matches, it determines the position number based on its position from the far left of the string. After looking at the other two functions, you will use @FIND to build the formula that extracts the last name.

USING @MID   You can use the @*MID* function whenever you want to extract a portion of a string. Unlike @RIGHT and @LEFT, which only extract from the beginning or the end of a string, @MID can be used to extract a portion from the center of a string. This function offers the ultimate in flexibility; you can start anywhere in the string and extract as few or as many characters as you want.

The function looks like this:

@MID(string,start number,number of characters)

The first argument, *string*, is any group of characters, a reference to a group of characters, or a string formula.

Start number is the first character position you wish to extract from the string. If you choose to extract the first letter in the string, this is referred to a position 0.

The last argument, *number of characters*, is a number representing how many characters to extract from the string. An upper limit of 240 and a lower limit of 0 are the range of acceptable values. The entry @MID("abcdefghi",3,3) would return def.

USING @LENGTH   The @*LENGTH* function returns the number of characters in a string. It is a count of these characters. It is not the same as the position number of the last character, which will always be one less than the string length. @LENGTH is written as @LENGTH(string). For example, @LENGTH("Profit") equals 6, while the position number of the t is 5. Since this is the last function needed for your formula, you are ready to put all three together to access the last name.

COMBINING THE THREE FUNCTIONS Extracting the last name from entries that look like John Smith can be quite a challenge. The @RIGHT function cannot handle the task because last names have varying numbers of characters. You can use the three functions just discussed in combination to handle the task. Follow these steps to test the process:

1. Make these worksheet entries:

A1:	**John Smith**
A2:	**Jim Pearson**
A3:	**Rob Smithfield**
A4:	**Ken Horn**

2. Enter /**Worksheet Column Set-Width**, type **15**, and press RETURN.

3. Move the cell pointer to A10, press the SPACE BAR once, and press RETURN.
    This step will not appear to have an effect on the cell but it alters it to contain one blank space. This is quite important: It is the character you will be searching for within the name to identify the end of the first name.

4. Move the cell pointer to B1 and type **@MID(A1,@FIND($A$10,A1,0),@LENGTH(A1))**.

5. Enter /**Copy**, press RETURN, move the cell pointer to B2, type a **.**, move the cell pointer to B4, and press RETURN.
    Each of the entries in column B shows the last name of the individual listed in column A like this:

B1: @MID(A1,@FIND($A$10,A1,0),@LENGTH(A1))   READY

The formula will work for all first- and last-name entries, regardless of the length of each component. If the entries in column A contained middle names, a different formula would be required.

Combining Numbers and Strings

String and number entries cannot be combined into one cell, because string and numeric data have different attributes. String data cannot be used to perform calculations; numeric data is not affected by changes in label alignment. Although you cannot negate any of the basic attributes of strings or values, you can change one type of entry to the other type with the built-in functions.

There is one built-in function that turns string entries into numeric values and another function that converts values into strings. You can use them when you want to perform arithmetic operations on a string that looks like a number. After conversion with the @VALUE function, you will be able to perform the desired operation. These functions are also useful when you want to concatenate (combine) a numeric branch number or a date with some text data to produce a heading for a report. After conversion with the @STRING function this is possible.

The @*STRING* function uses two arguments with one representing the number to be converted and the other representing the number of decimal places that the string will display. It looks like this:

@STRING(number,number of decimal places)

The first argument, *number*, can be an actual numeric value or a reference to a value. The second argument, *number of decimal places*, is the number of decimal places that you want the converted string to display. If the original number has more decimal places than the number you specify, a string will be created by a rounded representation of the original number. If the number of decimal places in the original number is shorter, zeros will be used for padding.

You will make entries that allow you to test the workings of the @STRING function as it converts numeric data, so that it can be concatenated with character data to produce the report heading. These are the required steps to complete the test example:

1. Make these entries:

A3:	**Dept:**
A4:	**Headcount:**
B3:	**400**
B4:	**50**

2. Move the cell pointer to column A, enter / **Worksheet Column Set-Width**, type **10**, and press RETURN.

3. Move the cell pointer to B1 and type +**"January Budget Report for Department "&@STRING(B3,0)**, and press RETURN to produce these results:

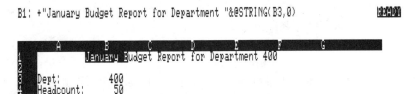

This formula starts with a + to make 1-2-3 use the entry as a value. This may seem contradictory, but all formulas are value entries even if they are string formulas. The string that is included in the formula is enclosed within quotation marks, which are required for all text not stored in a cell. The ampersand (&) joins (or concatenates) the two components of a string, and the @STRING function creates a string from the value in B3. The arguments for this function tell 1-2-3 to show zero decimal places when the conversion is made.

As you work with additional string entries, keep in mind that the conversion can take the opposite approach and turn strings that look like values into value entries.

SUMMARY

You have been introduced to some powerful functions in this chapter. In addition, you have learned how to apply some of these functions to common business tasks. Refer to the working examples you have created in the exercises for this chapter when attempting to incorporate some of these new options into your models. Once you have mastered these examples you can begin to explore the remaining built-in functions listed in Appendix C.

11

ADVANCED FILE-MANAGEMENT TECHNIQUES

By now you are probably an expert at the basic file-management features for saving and retrieving your worksheet files. These commands are the workhorses of the file commands because they play a central role in every worksheet session. A number of other file-management commands are used less commonly but provide some powerful options that you will want to incorporate into your set of skills.

In this chapter you will learn to use the Save feature to save a small portion of the worksheet in a worksheet file. This feature will let you transfer account names or end-of-period totals to another worksheet without having to reenter any of the data. You will also learn to use 1-2-3's Combine features, which let you combine an entire file or a range of data with the file currently in memory. This means that you can bring data into memory from disk without wiping out the current entries in the worksheet, as / File Retrieve does. Finally, you will explore a feature that enables you to import text data from a word processing program or other source into your 1-2-3 worksheet. This feature brings the lines of your word-processing document into the current worksheet as a column of long label entries. Or, if you prefer, you can use one of the / Data menu selections to split these long labels into individual cell entries. Together, these new commands provide ways to increase productivity by letting you reuse existing data rather than having to reenter it. The commands also let you consolidate the numbers in individual worksheets to compute a total automatically.

SAVING A SECTION OF THE WORKSHEET

In this section, you will examine the commands that let you save a range on a worksheet to a file without having to save the entire worksheet. You will have complete control over the amount of data that is saved to this file, and you can use it to start a new worksheet application. You can also add the data in this file to an existing application, using the 1-2-3 commands covered later in this chapter.

Why Would You Want to Save a Part of a Worksheet?

You may be wondering what purpose can be served by saving a portion of a current worksheet to a file. One of the advantages is that this approach lets you continue very large applications when you are running out of memory. Suppose that you have a model in which you are recording the detailed expenses by department for 1988. You have been monitoring the amount of available memory month by month and have come to the realization that you will not be able to fit an entire year's worth of information in memory at once. One approach open to you is to record expenses for the first quarter or six months in one worksheet and use other worksheets for the remaining periods. However, this strategy alone will not provide all the information you need. You will have all the detailed expenses but you will not have a total of all the expenses for the year. This is likely to be just as important as the detail.

1-2-3's File Xtract command will let you total each expense category on the worksheet that contains the expenses for the first quarter, and to save these totals separately in a worksheet file. The worksheet containing the totals can be used as the basis for the second-quarter worksheet. This same process can be used at the end of the second and third quarters so that the worksheet with the fourth quarter figures will be able to present a total for the entire year.

This same capability can be used in the data-management environment, as a database begins to grow too large for the worksheet. You can sort the worksheet and save one or more categories of data with the File Xtract command. This data can be used as the basis for a second database, containing only those categories of data that you have saved with File Xtract.

You could use the File Xtract feature on the employee database discussed in Chapter 9 to split the database by an alphabetical break if it became too large. Perhaps you could divide records by placing those records with last names beginning with the letters A through M in one database, and placing the others in a separate database. Other potential divisions would be by location codes or job codes.

The ability to extract information from a worksheet can also be useful when you wish to save data-entry time. You can use a worksheet containing a list of all your account names to save these names into a file by themselves. Anyone starting a new application requiring these names can retrieve the extract file to begin their application.

Different Options for Saving

There is more than one way to create the extract file. You can save just the values in the range selected, or if you prefer you can save the formulas. This chapter will help you examine both prospects so that you can become familiar with some of the potential sources of problems when saving formulas.

Whether you plan to save formulas or values, the command that you will use is / File Xtract. The spelling is a little different than you might expect, because of the commitment to have only a single command that begins with a given letter in a menu. The E is already used for the Erase command, thus the novel spelling for extract.

The menu that Xtract presents looks like this:

You can try each of these options in the next two sections.

SAVING VALUES   When you choose to save as Values, 1-2-3 will save the current values of the cells you select in a worksheet file. This file will have a filename extension of .WKS or .WK1, depending on which release of 1-2-3 you are using.

The extracted data is placed in the new file beginning in cell A1. The portion of the new file that contains data will be determined by the size and shape of the data being saved. It will retain its original size and shape, although each cell's address will be determined by its offset from the beginning of the range. The same offset will be used in the new file but the origin is always A1.

When you select the Values option, calculated results and labels will be retained in the new file. All formulas are replaced by the result of the formula calculations. This is a convenient way to carry the result of calculations forward to a new worksheet without needing to bring the data forward, as would be required when saving formulas.

When you enter / File Xtract Values, 1-2-3 asks for the name of the file to store the data in, using a prompt message like this:

You have the same options as with the / File Save command. You can type the name of a new file and 1-2-3 will store your data in that file. You can type the name of an existing file, specify the range to be saved, and 1-2-3 will prompt you with this message:

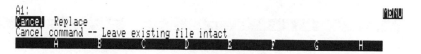

Building a small model is a good way to test the operation of the File Xtract command. The model will present the detailed sales data for each month in the first quarter and sum this data to provide an end-of-quarter figure. Although there is not enough data to cause a condition with insufficient memory, the concept and potential actions required are exactly the same as you would need with much larger models. Follow these steps to create this practice example:

1. Enter /**Worksheet Erase Yes** to ensure that the worksheet is blank.

2. Enter /**Worksheet Column Set-Width**, type **18**, and press RETURN.

3. Complete these entries:

A3:	**Sales-Product 1**
A4:	**Sales-Product 2**
A5:	**Sales-Product 3**
B2:	**"Jan**
B3:	**1200**
B4:	**4400**
B5:	**5400**
C2:	**"Feb**
C3:	**1500**
C4:	**5600**
C5:	**7800**
D2:	**"Mar**

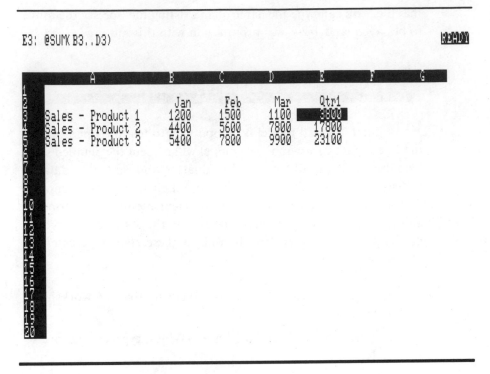

FIGURE 11.1   Data for the first quarter

D3:	1100
D4:	7800
D5:	9900
E2:	"Qtr1
E3:	@SUM(B3.D3)
E4:	@SUM(B4.D4)
E5:	@SUM(B5.D5)

These entries will produce the results shown in Figure 11.1.

4. Move the cell pointer to E3.

5. Enter /**File Xtract Values**.

6. Type **QTR1VALU** and press RETURN.
   QTR1VALU will be the name of the file used for this extract.

7. Expand the range by moving the cell pointer to E5 so that it looks like this:

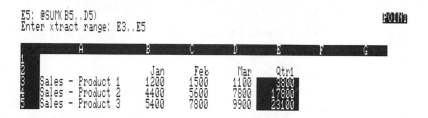

8. Press RETURN to finalize.
   The current value of these three cells will be written to the filename specified.

9. Enter **/File Save**, type **1ST_QTR**, and press RETURN to save the original file.

10. Enter **/File Retrieve**, type **QTR1VALU**, and press RETURN.
    This will place the three values in cells A1, A2, and A3. Your screen will look like this:

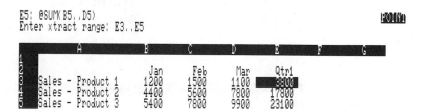

You will have an opportunity to work with this extract file again later. You will learn how to place its contents anywhere you like in the worksheet by combining it with an existing worksheet.

SAVING FORMULAS   Saving formulas is just as easy as saving values, but before you use this option you must consider how you will use this file and what it will contain. If you save the formulas without the data they need, will there be data on the new worksheet for them to operate on? Do they contain relative references that will be adjusted when they are placed in the new worksheet? Will the adjustments that are made be logical? In many cases, the answer to these questions is no, indicating that another approach would be preferred but there are situations where it is convenient to be able to save the formulas.

You will want to save the quarter totals as formulas to look at the differences. Follow these steps to complete the exercise:

1. Enter /**File Retrieve**, type **1STQTR**, and press RETURN to recall the original worksheet.

2. Move the cell pointer to E3.

3. Enter /**File Xtract Formulas**.

4. Type **QTR1FORM** and press RETURN.
   QTR1FORM will be the name of the file used for this extract.

5. Expand the range by moving the cell pointer to E5 and press RETURN to finalize.
   The formulas or values in these three cells will be written to the filename specified.

6. Enter /**File Retrieve**, type **QTR1FORM**, and press RETURN to produce this display:

A1: @SUM(IT1..IV1)

Notice that the formulas were adjusted for the new worksheet. This situation has a high potential for error, since the formulas might not be adjusted as you would expect. In this particular case, the Values option meets your needs better. Later, you will see the package work with formulas when you use the File Combine Add feature and only the current value of the formula.

COMBINING INFORMATION FROM OTHER FILES INTO THE CURRENT WORKSHEET

The File Retrieve operation has a Worksheet Erase feature built right into it. Every time you enter /File Retrieve, the file in memory will be replaced with the contents of the file you are bringing in from the disk. In many cases this is exactly what you need. But in many others, you might prefer to retain the current contents of memory and bring information into memory from disk to add to the current data. The File Combine command provides this capability.

In this section you will examine each of the File Combine Options separately in order to understand the function it serves. Each of these components will then be joined in examples to help you understand their sequence and their relationship with the File Combine menus.

Applications for the Combine Operation

There are many applications for the File Combine feature. This feature has three options, with a menu like this:

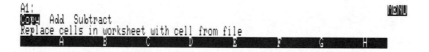

One option copies data from disk to an area of the worksheet and replaces the contents of this area with what is on the disk. This option would be useful for adding a list of account names that are stored in a file created with the Xtract command.

The second option adds the data on the disk to the data already in memory. Each value in the file will be added to a corresponding value in the current worksheet. The corresponding value is determined by the cursor location at the time the command is invoked. This command lets you automate the consolidation of sales or expenses for all the units within a company to produce a total company report.

The third option available is subtraction. This option can be used to remove the results for a subsidiary from the total company reports.

Deciding How Much Data to Combine

You have two options when combining a file with the current worksheet: to combine everything in the file, or — if the file contains range names — to combine the contents of a range name.

USING AN ENTIRE FILE   When you combine an entire file, everything in the file will be placed within the current worksheet. Which combining method to use depends on which selections you make.

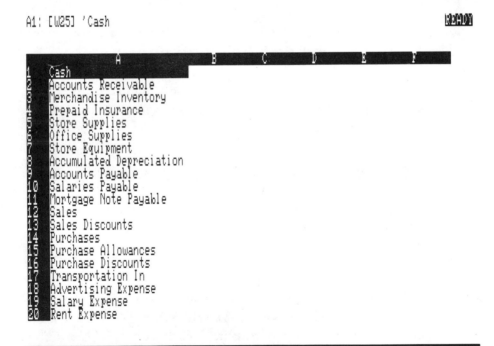

FIGURE 11.2   Account names

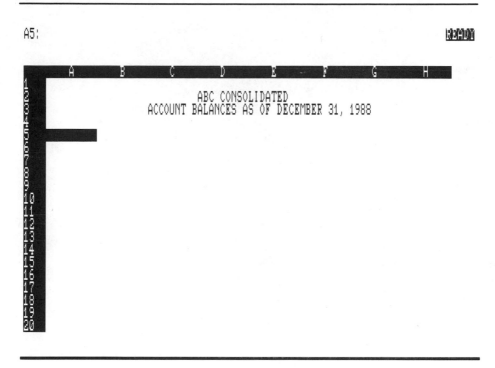

FIGURE 11.3   Worksheet requiring account names

Figure 11.2 shows a list of account names that are stored in a file named ACCOUNTS. The current worksheet shown in Figure 11.3 can use this list of names. The results of combining ACCOUNTS with the current worksheet is shown in Figure 11.4. The accounts were placed just where they were needed by the placement of the cell pointer in A5 before the combine operation was invoked with the menu.

USING A RANGE   You were introduced to range names in the database chapter. Ranges of cells can be assigned range names for a variety of reasons. For example, names can be added to improve the readability of formulas. They can also be used to let you combine less than an entire file with the current worksheet.

   If you want to use numbers in another worksheet, you can create an extract file for each group of numbers you wish to transfer. But a far easier approach is to use the /Range Name

A5: 'Cash   READY

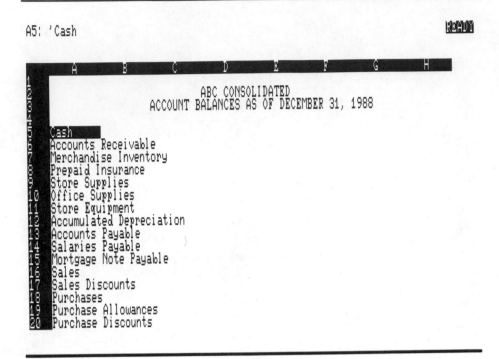

FIGURE 11.4   Worksheet with account names added

option in the sending file, save that file, and use the / File Combine command with the Named-Range option to obtain the data you need in a receiving file.

To try with the 1ST_QTR file you created earlier, follow these steps:

1. Enter **/File Retrieve**, type **1ST_QTR**, and press RETURN.

2. Move the cell pointer to E2 and enter **/Range Name Create**.
   You are including the label Total in this range so you can see how the label is handled.

3. Type **Total** and press RETURN.

4. Move the cell pointer to E5 to produce this display:

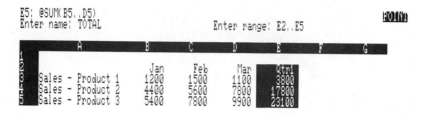

5. Press RETURN.

Both the label and formulas are now named Total. Later if you use this named range with File Combine, the combination method you select will determine whether the current value of the formula or the formula itself is used. The command you select will also determine whether the label at the top of the formulas is used. This will be more clear after you have examined the options for combining in more detail.

6. Enter **/File Save**, press RETURN, and enter **Replace**.

This save is required to save the assigned range names on the disk.

Methods for Combining

There are three different methods for combining data in a file with the current contents of memory. Each method has a completely different effect on the current worksheet, so be certain that you understand each one clearly before using these features on your own applications. Another recommendation is to save the current worksheet before you begin. That way, if you use the wrong method you can retrieve the worksheet from disk and try again.

You will need to build a new worksheet model to use with the /File Combine features. Follow these directions:

1. Move the cell pointer to B1, enter **/Range Erase**, move the cell pointer to E5, and press RETURN.

This is a short-cut approach to creating the new model, since you need the same entries and width for column A.

2. Make these worksheet entries:

B2:	**"Qtr1**
C1:	**Sales Summary by Quarter**
C2:	**"Qtr2**
D2:	**"Qtr3**
E2:	**"Qtr4**
F2:	**"Total**
F3:	**@SUM(B3.E3)**
F4:	**ASUM(B4.E4)**
F5:	**@SUM(B5.E5)**

This model shell is now ready to receive data from the various quarters and looks like this:

The Combine options provide the perfect solution because they do not destroy the current model as you bring the quarter totals in from other files. The data that you will be bringing in must be on disk, either as range names in a complete model or as an extract file that contains only the data you need.

COPYING TO THE CURRENT WORKSHEET   The / File Combine Copy command is used when you have data stored on disk, and you want to replace a section of the current worksheet. To bring this data into the current worksheet, position the cell pointer carefully; this is what will control the placement of the data. Use the values you stored in QTR1VALU for your first look at this command. Follow these directions:

1. Move the cell pointer to B3.

2. Enter **/File Combine Copy**.

3. Enter **Entire-File**.

4. Type **QTR1VALU** and press RETURN to produce these results:

Notice that each of the values in this small file are placed on the model and the entries are included in the total.

Try this same exercise with the formulas you stored in QTR1FORM, using these steps:

1. Move the cell pointer to B3, enter **/Range Erase**, move the cell pointer to B5, and press RETURN.

2. Enter **/File Combine Copy**.

3. Enter **Entire-File**.

4. Type **QTR1FORM** and press RETURN to produce these results:

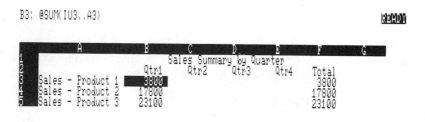

Notice that everything appears the same at first glance. But a look at the formula in the control panel shows that everything is not the same; this formula includes entries from most of the columns. In this instance, these formulas have the potential to cause nothing but trouble, as the CIRC status indicator at the bottom of the screen tells you. It says that the worksheet contains a formula reference to itself.

Another problem to be on the lookout for is incorrect cell-pointer placement or a lack of knowledge of the exact contents of an extract file or range name. If you were to position the cell pointer in the wrong place and use the Combine option, you could wind up with results like this:

Notice how everything is shifted off by one row, making the resulting model useless.

ADDING TO THE CURRENT WORKSHEET   When you use the /File Combine Add option, values will be added to the existing values. Which values are added is determined by cursor position and placement of the file values within the file. If the worksheet cells are blank, the only difference between Copy and Add is that Add ignores labels. Follow these steps to try the new command:

1. Move the cell pointer to B3, enter /**Range Erase**, move the cell pointer to B6, and press RETURN.

2. Move the cell pointer to B2.

You will be using the named range Total in the file 1ST_QTR this time. Since the label Qtr1 is included in the range, you need to position the cell pointer to B2 so that the first value in the file will be matched with B3.

3. Enter **/File Combine Add Named/Specified_Range**.

4. Type **Total** and press RETURN.

5. Type **1ST_QTR** and press RETURN to produce these results:

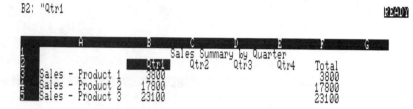

Try this again to see if it really adds.

6. Enter **/File Combine Add Named/Specified_Range**.

7. Type **Total** and press RETURN.

8. Type **1ST_QTR** and press RETURN. Move the cell pointer to B3 to see the value 7600:

You can see that that each of the numbers in the current worksheet doubled, as the numbers on the file were added to the current worksheet again.

SUBTRACTING FROM THE CURRENT WORKSHEET The /File Combine Subtract option is the exact opposite of the Add option. It subtracts the values stored on disk from the current worksheet cells. This option depends on the cursor location and the offset within the file that controls which numbers will be subtracted from which entries. You can try this by subtracting the last entry you added to the worksheet, following these steps.

1. Enter **/File Combine Subtract Entire-File**.
   Since you will use the file QTR1VALU, there is no need to have the cell pointer in B2. This file does not have a label before the numeric values the way the named range did.

2. Type **QTR1VALU** and press RETURN to produce these results:

Each of the entries returned to the original values as the subtract operation was completed.

IMPORTING TEXT DATA

1-2-3 provides a feature that allows you to transfer data from a word processor or any other program that can create ASCII text files. This data will be brought into 1-2-3 as a long label. Each line in the word processing document will be one label, with the end result of the transfer being an entire column of long labels. Although the entries may appear to reside in separate fields due to the data alignment in the original word processor, this is not the case. There is no automatic way to use a portion from the center of the long label without the Release 2 /Data Parse command, which you will examine later.

Why Put Text Data in the Worksheet?

The worksheet seems to be the place for calculations and other methods of rigorous analysis. Why would anyone want to put word processing data on the worksheet? One possible reason is a significant savings in data-entry time. If you have account names, employee numbers, inventory items, or other lists of text data in a word processing document and find that the same information is required in the spreadsheet environment, why retype it when you can have the package duplicate it for you? You will be ensured of data consistency between the two applications.

Bringing the Data Into the Worksheet

Bringing data into the worksheet involves several steps. Before you can enter 1-2-3 commands, you must complete preliminary tasks. The data you wish to access must be saved in a word processing file before you attempt the import operation.

You will need a word processing program to try this exercise. You will also want to check your word processor's documentation to ensure that you use the correct option for creating an ASCII text file without all the edit characters. Some word processors create the document and require you to strip off special characters to create an ASCII file; others have an option for creating it directly.

Do not be concerned if you do not have a word processor to try this exercise with. You can still practice this command by entering the data shown in Figure 11.5 into the worksheet and printing this worksheet to a file, using the command /Print File. Specify the range just as if you were printing it to your printer. In fact, the only differences are that you must specify a file name for saving the data and you should choose Options Other Unformatted from the print menu before printing to the disk. This process will create a text file for you and will automatically have the file name extension of .PRN that you need to import the data.

Figure 11.5 shows some data that was entered with WordStar.

You can duplicate these entries with your word processor, then import that data into 1-2-3. Follow these steps:

1. Enter **/Quit Yes** to exit 1-2-3. Load your word processor, enter the data shown in Figure 11.5 into your word processor, and save the file as a text file with a filename extension of .PRN and the name TEXT (making it TEXT.PRN). If your word processor assigns its own filenames, you will have to rename the file in step 3. If you print a 1-2-3 file to disk rather than the printer, 1-2-3 creates an ASCII text file on the disk with a filename extension of .PRN. It is unlikely that your word processor follows the same nam-

FIGURE 11.5   Text data entered with Wordstar

ing convention; it is very likely that you will have to rename the text file to change the extension name.

2. Exit your word processor.

3. Use the DOS RENAME command if you do not have a filename extension of .PRN.

Using the /File Import command is the next step. This command can bring up to 2048 lines of text data into the worksheet under release 1A. Under Release 2, the limit on the size of the imported file is 8192. Each line of the files can have a maximum of 240 characters.

You have two basic options for importing text data into your worksheet. After entering /File Import, you can choose either Text or Numbers. Your selection will affect the manner in which the data is placed on the worksheet. Use the Text option when you want to import the entire file, including all the label entries. Use Numbers when you want to strip away everything but the numbers.

If you import the data in Figure 11.5 as Text, each line of the word processing document will become one long, left-aligned label. You will have an entire column of left-aligned labels. If you have Release 2, the /Data Parse command provides a supplemental method of dealing with these long, left-aligned labels.

If you select the Numbers option, only characters enclosed in double quotes and numbers will be imported. Characters not in quotation marks as well as blanks will be eliminated in the import process. Each number in a line of the text file will generate a numeric cell entry, and each quote-enclosed label will create a left-justified label cell. Entries from the same line of a text file will produce entries in the same row of the worksheet, proceeding from the left to the right of the row with each new entry.

You will want to try both File Import options with the data you entered a few minutes ago. Continue with these steps:

1. Reload 1-2-3 or enter **/Worksheet Erase Yes** to ensure that memory is clear.

2. Enter **/File Import Numbers** to produce these results:

3. As 1-2-3 searches the disk for all the files with the filename extension .PRN, select a text file from the list presented to produce this display:

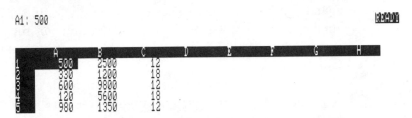

Notice how the quantity figures are in column A and the prices are stored in column B.

4. Clear memory by entering /**Worksheet Erase Yes**.

5. Enter /**File Import Text** and select TEXT.PRN to produce these results:

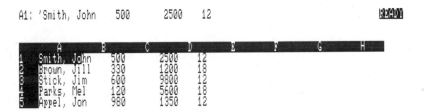

Notice the difference between this example and the earlier one. All these entries are stored in column A as long labels. There is no automatic way to work with the quantity in the first row because it is not easily accessible. It is buried in the middle of a long label entry. (Note that if you used tabs to separate the columns in your word processing document, Release 2 and above will expand these tabs correctly while Release 1A will not.)

Separating the Text Into Fields With Data Parse

It is great to display data from your word processor in the work-sheet environment, but the data imported with the Text option is not especially useful in its current format. Importing the data as numbers does not solve the problem, since only numeric entries and quote enclosed labels are brought over to the spreadsheet application.

You cannot use the data imported as Text in calculations reference any of the individual pieces of information separately. The Release 2 / Data Parse command offers a solution to this problem. Parse is a fancy word that has been used by programmers for a long time. In 1-2-3, it means splitting the long label entries into smaller pieces. You can use it to split the long labels created by / File Import into separate cell values. Using / Data Parse to accomplish this task is a multi-step process. You must create a pattern that will be used for the parsing operation, define the labels to be parsed, define the area where the newly generated cell values should be stored, and tell 1-2-3 to begin the parse operation. The menu that provides these options is accessed by entering / Data Parse, and is shown below:

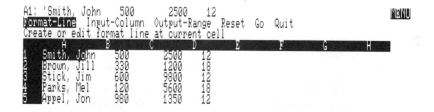

CREATING A FORMAT LINE The format line is an edit pattern that will be used against each long label to determine how it should be split into its component parts and what each component should look like. Each cell in the column of long labels will have this format line applied to it unless another format line is encountered within the column. At that point, the new format line will be used

Character	Meaning
D	Marks the first character of a date block
L	Marks the first character of a label block
S	Indicates that the character below should be skipped during the parse operation. This character is never generated by 1-2-3 but you can enter it when you are editing a format line.
T	Marks the first character of a time block
V	Marks the first character of a value block
>	Indicates that the block started by the letter that precedes it is continued. The entry that began with a letter will be placed in one worksheet cell until a skip or another letter is encountered.
*	Represents a blank space immediately below the character. This position can become part of the block that precedes it if additional space is required.

TABLE 11.1   Format line characters for data parse

until the end of the labels or until another format line is encountered.

1-2-3 makes its best guess at the format that should be used for each component, using the symbols shown in Table 11.1 to present each of the options. It makes its determination from the entries in the line where you place your cursor, and it positions the format line immediately above this. When it encounters a space in the label it assumes that a field has ended.

If you want, you can create many format lines for one column of labels; however, each of them must be generated separately. Despite the fact that you can create multiple format lines, some consistency in the organization is required. You would not want to create a format line for each line that is parsed.

Try this by moving the cell pointer to the column of long labels you imported. Follow these steps:

1. Move the cell pointer to A1.

    This is the top entry in the column of long labels generated with File Import.

2. Enter /**Data Parse**.

3. Enter **Format-Line**.

    This produces the following menu of Format-Line options:

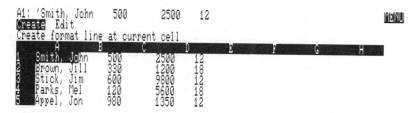

4. Enter **Create**.

    1-2-3 will insert a blank line above the cell pointer's location and generate a format line at this location. The line generated for your data should look like this:

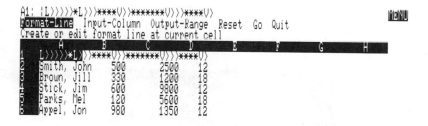

If you were to continue with Data Parse and use this format line, five fields would be generated. A separate field would be generated for both the first and last name. If you want both the first and last name within the same cell, you will need to modify the format line. The CALC indicator will be turned on at the bottom of the screen, but there is no cause for concern.

MODIFYING THE FORMAT LINE   You can modify the format line that was generated by selecting Format-Line again, since the /Data Parse menu remains on the screen for further selections. This time you will choose Edit to make your changes. Try this technique to alter the two name fields to make them one field. Follow these instructions to make the change:

1. Enter **Format-Line**.

2. Enter **Edit** to produce this display:

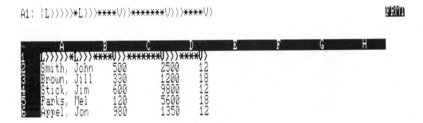

The OVR indicator is turned on to indicate that you are in overstrike mode. Any character you type will replace a character in the existing format line.

3. Move the cell pointer to the * that precedes the second L, and type >> to change the display to look like this:

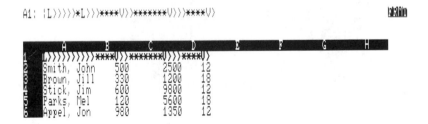

This will cause the two name fields to be combined into one field.

4. Press RETURN to finalize.

PRODUCING THE FINAL PRODUCT   There are still a few more steps. You have to tell 1-2-3 where the input is located and where you would like to store the output of the parse operation. Your last step is to select Go from the menu so that 1-2-3 will apply the information entered in the preliminary steps to your column of long labels, producing individual entries.

Follow these steps to define the input and output areas and create the finished product:

1. Enter **Input-Column**, then highlight A1..A6 with the cell pointer like this:

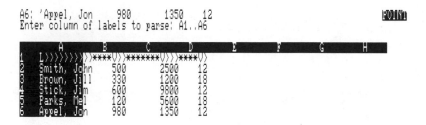

2. Press RETURN.

3. Enter **Output-Range** and move the cell pointer to A10 like this:

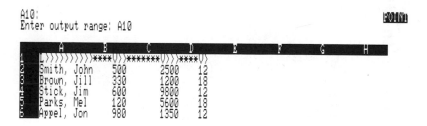

You can position the cell pointer in the upper left corner of the range rather than calculating the exact space require-ments and making a mistake.

4. Press RETURN and enter **Go** to produce these results in Figure 11.6.

5. Enter **/Worksheet Column Set-Width**, type **11**, and press RETURN to expand the column width, as shown in Figure 11.7.

This conversion required a number of steps and would not be a worthwhile investment of time for so little data. With volumes of data, this command can provide a real productivity enhancement that can save hours of time.

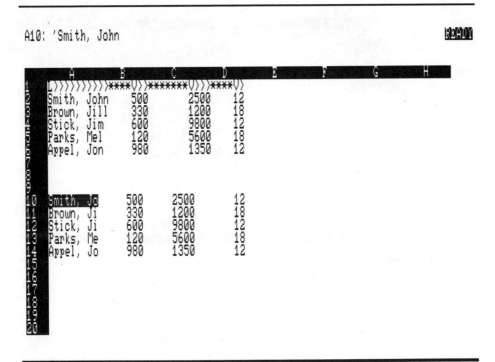

FIGURE 11.6   Imported data which has been parsed

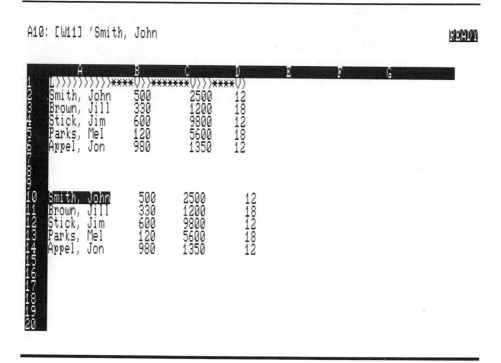

FIGURE 11.7   Widening column A for readibility

SUMMARY

You have added to your knowledge of 1-2-3's file commands in this chapter. Features such as File Xtract and File Import let you use the data you already entered for existing applications more effectively by making it the basis for new worksheets. You have also been introduced to the File Combine command, which is actually three commands in one. First, it performs a replace function for data in the current worksheet. Second, it adds data in a worksheet file to the current worksheet. Third, if you wish, you can use the

Subtract feature of File Combine to reduce the figures in the current worksheet by the amount stored in corresponding cells in the worksheet stored on disk. Finally, you have learned how to import both text and numbers and parse the text into individual cell entries. All together, these commands provide a powerful set of tools that extend the use of worksheet files well beyond the simplistic concepts of File Save and File Retrieve.

12

CREATING
1-2-3
MACROS

Many 1-2-3 users are intimidated by macros. They have heard about the failures that others have experienced when attempting to use them. But this failure is not inevitable; in fact, if you use the step-by-step approach presented in this chapter, you will have no need for concern. There is no reason why you cannot be just as successful with macros as you are with 1-2-3's Format and File Save commands.

In their simplest form, macros are nothing more than a way to automate the selections you have been making from 1-2-3's menus. These macros are referred to as *keyboard alternative macros*. In their most complex form, macros provide an entire programming language with the special 1-2-3 command language instructions. Attempting to use the most sophisticated form of macros without mastering the keyboard variety is a little like practicing diving before you have learned to swim. If you jump in at the deep end of the pool without knowing how to swim to the edge, you will be well over your head and doomed to failure. Clearly, using the command language macros before mastering the keyboard alternative variety is asking for problems; why, then, do so many new users use this approach? This chapter introduces the material in a logical sequence to help you avoid this problem.

This chapter gives you a step-by-step approach to the creation of keyboard alternative macros that can ensure your success. You will learn how to record menu selections and special keyboard entries for later execution. You will also learn 1-2-3's rules for naming macros and how you can execute the macro instructions you have stored. You will create several ready-to-use macros, which will be your foundation for creating macros that fit your particular needs. Since macros are based on a series of building blocks, you will need to learn something about each of them before creating a macro. In this chapter you will be introduced to the building blocks and then combine them in your first macro example, before making your entries.

WHAT ARE KEYBOARD ALTERNATIVE MACROS?

Keyboard alternative macros are nothing more than a column of label entries that have a special name assigned to them. The contents of the label entries are the sequence of 1-2-3 keystrokes that you want 1-2-3 to execute for you. Once the keystrokes are entered in the column of worksheet cells, you will use the / Range Name Create command to assign a special name to the top cell in the macro. Once the cell is named, you can execute the macro by holding down the ALT key and the letter used in the macro name. When you save the worksheet on which you entered the macro, you save the macro for later use with the worksheet on which it was entered. If you were to use the macro on another worksheet, you would have to reenter it or use the /File Combine command covered in Chapter 11.

Keyboard alternative macros provide a wealth of time-saving features. You can use them to automate printing, formatting, or any other 1-2-3 task that can be handled with menu selections. After you have learned the basics, you will want to examine the tasks you execute repeatedly. The more frequently a task is performed, the greater the potential payback of automating it with macro instructions. Some users find that data-management tasks such as sorting and extracting are most important to automate; other users feel that printing or formatting have the highest priority because they use these commands most frequently. Although the macros in the remainder of the chapter have widespread application, only you can decide which tasks offer you the greatest payback when automated.

MACRO BUILDING BLOCKS

The secret to creating macros that run correctly the first time you try them is having a structured approach that you use consistently for each new macro you create. At first glance the steps recommended here might seem unnecessarily time consuming; however, you will find that they guarantee immediate success and thereby save debugging time.

The first step to successful macros is to lay out a road map of where you want to go with the macro, and to test the instructions that you hope will get you there. Next, store all the pretested macro instructions, then name them. Documenting the workings of the macro is an often overlooked step, but it can guarantee continued trouble-free execution. Complete this step for every macro. Only then will you be ready to try your new macro.

You can examine each of these steps more closely in the sections that follow.

Knowing Where You are Going Before Beginning

The only way to guarantee first-try success for every macro is to try the 1-2-3 instructions that you want to store in a macro and to monitor their effect on the worksheet. As you enter each instruction, write it on a piece of paper. If the results meet your needs, you can enter the keystrokes you have written on your sheet of paper as a series of label entries on the worksheet. If the commands do not perform the required tasks, you can alter them and try again. Once you discover the correct combination of menu requests, you have a guarantee (if you enter them carefully) that they will function. You have already tried these commands and ensured their correct operation before recording them. The other objective of this planning phase for the macro is to ensure that you have not forgotten any of the requirements.

Recording Menu Selections

You will want to select an out-of-the-way location on the worksheet for recording your macro's commands. With Release 2, put these instructions at the far right side of the worksheet. With Release 1A, you need to moderate how far to the right you store the macro; Release 1A uses memory less efficiently when information is scattered on the worksheet.

To prevent 1-2-3 from executing the menu commands you want to record, begin the macro sequence with a single quotation mark so that it is treated as a label. Indicate each request for the menu with a slash, and record each menu selection as the first letter of the selection. To record the keystrokes necessary to obtain a worksheet status report, type '/**ws** or /**WS** in the cell. Case is never important when you are entering menu selections.

In addition to entering the menu selections, you sometimes have to indicate that the ENTER key would be pressed if you were entering the command sequence from the keyboard. In a macro, this key is represented by the tilde mark (˜). When you are entering data other than menu selections, such as a file name or a range name, enter the names in full. For example, to record the keystrokes necessary to retrieve a file named Sales, you would enter **'/frSales˜** in the macro cell.

Menu selections should always be recorded with the first letter of the selection. Typing the full name of the command is not a substitute for the first letter and will cause errors in the macro. While it is possible to select commands by pointing to the menu selections through the successive use of the RIGHT ARROW key, followed by the use of the RETURN key, this should be avoided in macros. In subsequent releases of the product, Lotus might alter the sequence of the menu selections, causing the cursor-movement method to fail. However, you can be assured that the first letters of the selections are not likely to change. This guarantees that your macros will be compatible with future releases of the 1-2-3 product.

Recording Special Keys

There are a number of special keyboard keys, such as the function and cursor movement keys, that you will want to include in your macros. These keys and the macro keywords that stand for them are shown in Table 12.1. Notice that all the special keywords are enclosed in curly brackets or braces ({}). You will find it easy to remember most of these words; they are the same words you probably connect with the special keys — for example, EDIT represents F2. The only thing you will need to remember is to use the braces like this, {EDIT}. Without the braces, 1-2-3 will not recognize the entry as a special key.

There are several special keys that cannot be represented in a macro. The NUM LOCK key has no representation and must be turned on by the operator if a macro requires it. The use of the SCROLL LOCK key follows the same procedure, since it too cannot be represented. CAPS LOCK also has no representation, although this is less important than the other two keys; you will be able to control capitalization if you are requested to input directly during a macro. If macro instructions include cell entries for other parts of the worksheet, you will get to choose whether to make

Cursor Movement Keys	Keywords
UP ARROW	{UP}
DOWN ARROW	{DOWN}
RIGHT ARROW	{RIGHT}
LEFT ARROW	{LEFT}
HOME	{HOME}
END	{END}
PGUP	{PGUP}
PGDN	{PGDN}
CTRL-RIGHT	{BIGRIGHT}
CTRL-LEFT	{BIGLEFT}

Editing Keys	Keywords
DEL	{DEL}
INS	{INS}
ESC	{ESC}
BACKSPACE	{BACKSPACE} or {BS}

Function Keys	Keywords
F2 (EDIT)	{EDIT}
F3 (NAME)	{NAME}
F4 (ABS)	{ABS}
F5 (GOTO)	{GOTO}
F6 (WINDOW)	{WINDOW}
F7 (QUERY)	{QUERY}
F8 (TABLE)	{TABLE}
F9 (CALC)	{CALC}
F10 (GRAPH)	{GRAPH}

TABLE 12.1   Special keys in macro commands

these entries in upper or lower case when building the macro. The case you choose will be maintained when the macro is executed.

CURSOR MOVEMENT KEYS   When you are creating a macro, movement of the cell pointer to the right will be represented by {RIGHT} or {right}. Case is never important for the special macro words, although upper case will be used throughout this chapter. Movement to the left is {LEFT}, movement down is {DOWN}, and movement up is {UP}.

In Release 1A, moving the cursor up three cells is represented by {UP}{UP}{UP}. If you have a long distance to move, you will want to explore the GOTO option listed with the function keys to avoid all the entries required by Release 1A. In Release 2, there is a short-cut approach that lets you enter this same instruction as {UP 3}.

When you are working from the keyboard, the effect of the HOME key depends on whether you are in READY mode or EDIT mode. This is also true in the macro environment. If you record {HOME} in a macro, its effect will depend on what you are having the macro do for you. If you have placed 1-2-3 in EDIT mode, the instruction will take you to the left side of the entry in the current cell; otherwise, it will place you in A1.

The END and ARROW key combinations are supported in macros. You can enter END{RIGHT} to have the cell pointer moved to the last occupied cell entry on the right side of the worksheet. To specify paging up and down you can use {PGUP} and {PGDN}.

FUNCTION KEYS   With the exception of the F1 (HELP) key, all function keys can be represented by special macro keywords. To use F2 (EDIT), you would enter {EDIT}. The F5 (GOTO) key is another key that is used frequently. To record the fact that you wanted the cell pointer moved to D10, you would make this entry in a macro:

{GOTO}D10~

Notice that the cell address you want the cell pointer moved to is placed outside the braces and is followed by a tilde (~). Remember that the tilde represents the RETURN key and is required to finalize the request, just as you would press RETURN to finalize if you were executing the command directly.

Other keys required frequently are the representation for F6 (WINDOW) and F9 (CALC). As you might expect, {WINDOW} is the macro representation for F6 and {CALC} is thr representation for F9. The remaining function keys are shown in Table 12.1.

THE EDIT KEYS   In addition to F2 (EDIT), which places you in the EDIT mode, there are several keys that are used frequently when you are correcting cell entries. The ESC key can remove an entry from a cell and can delete a menu default, such as a previous setup string. This option allows you to cancel the default and make a new entry. When ESC is used in a macro, everything works the same except that braces are required. Therefore, the entry would be {ESC}.

To delete a character to the left of the cursor while in EDIT mode, or to delete the last character entered, use either {BS} or {BACKSPACE} in your macro. To delete the character above the cursor from EDIT mode, use {DEL} or {DELETE}. For example, you could create a macro that requests a change in the label prefix to center justification. The sequence of entries in a macro would be:

{EDIT}{HOME}{DEL}^~

This is the exact same sequence of keys that you would press if you were typing the request to be executed directly, rather than storing the keystrokes in a macro.

In Release 2, repeat factors can also be used with these keys. {DELETE 4} is equivalent to pressing the DELETE key four times. {BACKSPACE 7} will delete seven characters to the left of the cursor on the edit line.

Creating the Macro

As you may recall, we promised you not the fastest path to macro entry but the fastest path to a macro that would run correctly the first time you tried. Your first step in creating a macro will be to make a plan and to try your plan before recording your first keystroke. This step is the critical one if you want to ensure success.

PLANNING THE MACRO If you are thinking of creating a macro, you must have a task that you want to automate. For your first example, you will automate a request for formatting, based on the assumption that you need to format data as currency frequently and would like to create a macro that will save you a few keystrokes. Your first step is to ask yourself which 1-2-3 commands you normally use to handle this task. The answer should be the / Range Format Currency command sequence. Also ask yourself if you want the macro to specify the number of decimal places and the range for formatting or whether you want the operator to complete the instruction from the keyboard. For your example, the number of decimal places will be supplied but the range will be controlled by the operator at execution.

Once your decisions are made you will want to test the series of instructions you plan to use before recording them. You will need some test data on the worksheet before beginning. Follow these directions for creating some test data to see if the formatting commands and subsequent macro function correctly.

1. Make the following worksheet entries:

A1:	2
A2:	5
A3:	4
A4:	9
A5:	7
C6:	8
C7:	9
C8:	3

There is nothing special about these entries. They are just a few numbers that will be stored in the default format of

General and that will provide practice entries for formatting. Copy them across the worksheet to create additional entries.

2. Move the cell pointer to A1 and enter **/Copy**, press the END key, followed by the DOWN ARROW key. Press RETURN, move the cell pointer to B1, type a **.**, move the cell pointer to F1, and press RETURN.

3. Move the cell pointer to C6, enter **/Copy**, move the cell pointer to C8, and press RETURN. Move the cell pointer to E6, type a **.**, move the cell pointer to F6, and press RETURN to create this display:

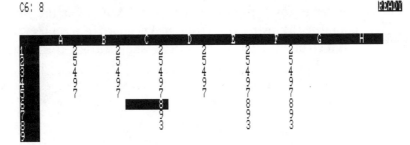

This provides a little variety in the length of the column of numbers you will be formatting with your macro once it is created. Now you are ready for a trial run of the instructions you plan to record.

4. Move the cell pointer to A1.
   This is the first cell you will format. The movement of the cell pointer could be incorporated in the macro but it would eliminate some of the macro's flexibility and is probably not desireable.

5. Enter **/** and record a slash on the piece of paper where you are recording the keystrokes from the trial.

6. Enter **Range** and record an R on the piece of paper.

7. Enter **Format** and record an F on the piece of paper.

8. Enter **Currency** and record a C on the piece of paper.

9. Type a **0** and record a 0 on the piece of paper.

10. Press RETURN and record the tilde (˜) on the piece of paper. Press ESC to return to READY mode.
    Notice how every keystroke that you enter, whether it is from the menu or just a keyboard entry, should be written on the piece of paper. Most beginners would skip steps five through ten. This is the very cause of failure in their macros. Once you become a 1-2-3 expert and have all the menu selections committed to memory, there is no problem with skipping these steps. But until you reach that point, the importance of these steps cannot be overemphasized.

11. Press RETURN again to record the range selection. However, do not record this; you are leaving the range selection up to the user when the macro is executed.

12. Enter **/File Save**, type **NUMBERS,** and press RETURN. This will save a copy of the numeric entries under the file NUMBERS. You can retrieve it at a later time to practice with this or other macros.

MAKING THE MACRO ENTRIES   The macro entries you need to make are recorded on your sheet of paper. All you need to do now is record these entries on the worksheet. You can record them all in one cell or you can split them into more than one cell — just as long as the cells are in a consecutive column on the worksheet. With such a short macro it will not make much difference but as your macros become longer, you may want to split them well before you reach the 240-character limit for a cell entry. Keeping the length of an individual cell entry to a minimum will allow you to document each step in the macro.

Normally you would place your macro to the right side of the worksheet. However, since this is your first macro, you will want to keep it in view as it executes, so place it at the lower portion of column B. Follow these steps to record the macro keystrokes you have recorded on your sheet of paper:

1. Move the cell pointer to B15.

2. Type '/r, then move the cell pointer to B16.
   The single quotation mark is used to prevent immediate execution of your entries. The slash represents the request for the menu and the r is used to invoke the Range commands (the r can be either upper or lower case).

3. Press the DOWN ARROW key, type **fc0˜**, then press RETURN.
   These entries tell 1-2-3 that you want to use the Format option and have selected Currency with 0 decimal places as the format you want to use.

This is all that is required for entering any macro. The only mandatory step that remains is naming the macro.

Naming the Macro

Now that you have recorded all the keystrokes, you are ready to name the macro. Before doing this you will want to position the cell pointer on the top cell in the macro, as this is the only cell that you will name. You will use the /Range Name Create command that you were introduced to in earlier chapters to apply the name to this cell. You must assign a special name, consisting of a backslash and a single letter, to the cell. The backslash identifies your entry as a macro name, which will allow you to execute the macro. This naming convention lets you create 26 unique macros on one worksheet, since 1-2-3 does not distinguish between upper- and lower-case letters in a macro name.

If you follow the recommendation of positioning the cell pointer before you begin, the process is really quite simple. You will only need to press RETURN to have the name applied to the macro.

Saving a macro after you name it will save both the macro entries and the name, so they will be available when you use the worksheet.

Follow these steps to name the formatting macro you just entered:

1. Move the cell pointer to B15.

2. Enter **/Range Name Create**.

3. Type **\c** and press RETURN twice.
   This will apply the name to the current cell.

Theoretically you can now execute the macro; however, it is best to document it first. If you do not take the time to document your work now you will never do it; later, it will be difficult to remember what name you chose for the macro and what each step accomplishes unless you document it.

Documenting the Macro

You will want to develop a few easy documentation rules for yourself so that your documentation is always stored in the same place. A good strategy to use for documentation is to place the macro name in the cell immediately to the left of the top cell in the macro. If the macro is named \a, you would enter '\a in this cell. The single quotation mark is required to prevent the backslash from being interpreted as a repeating label indicator and filling your cell with the letter a.

A good area to use for documenting the macro is the column of cells to the right of the actual macro instructions. Depending on the length of the macro instructions, this documentation may extend one or more cells to the right of the macro column. Entering a brief description of every command can make the purpose of the macro much clearer when you go back to examine it at a later time.

Follow these steps to document the formatting macro.

1. Move the cell pointer to A15, type **\c**, and press RETURN.

2. Move the cell pointer to C15, type **request Range command**, and press RETURN.

3. Move the cell pointer to C16, type **select Currency format with 0 decimal places**, and press RETURN.
   The macro is now ready to execute with the instructions in the next section.

Executing the Macro

Once you have entered and named a macro, you can use it whenever you wish. Whenever you have a macro that requires the cell pointer to be positioned in a certain cell, you will need to put the cell pointer there before you execute the macro. The cell pointer does not need to be on the macro itself in order to execute it. After you have positioned your cell pointer, you can execute the macro by holding down the ALT key and, while the key is pressed, touching the letter key you used in your macro name. The macro will begin executing immediately. Follow these instructions to try your new formatting macro:

1. Move the cell pointer to B1.

2. Press the ALT key and, while holding the key down, type **c**, and release the ALT key.
   This causes the macro to execute. This particular macro requests formatting and ends in time for you to complete the range that should be formatted.

3. Move the cell pointer to B5 and press RETURN.
   The entries in B1..B5 should now be formatted as currency with 0 decimal places. You will want to try this again to see how flexible the macro is.

4. Move the cell pointer to C1, and press the ALT key and the c. Move the cell pointer to C8 and press RETURN to create this display:

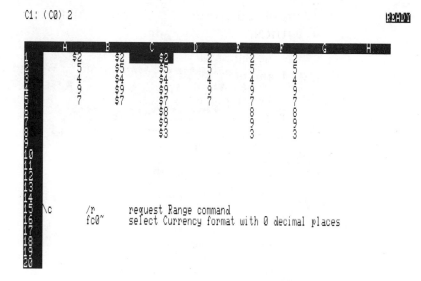

C1: (C0) 2

READY

```
\c        /r        request Range command
          fc0~      select Currency format with 0 decimal places
```

This time the entries in C1..C8 are formatted. This same macro can format one cell or a large range of cells. You can try the macro several more times with the remaining numeric entries on the worksheet.

5. Enter /**File Save,** press ESC, type **FORMAT**, and press RETURN to save this example.

CREATING A FEW MORE MACROS

Now you have created your first macro, but you haven't begun to experience the variety that macros can offer. You can follow the instructions in this section to create two more macros. This practice should help you improve your skill level with macro instructions.

Creating a Print Macro

Print macros are useful because print must be created from most worksheets periodically. In addition, by adding instructions in a print macro you can add any special form feeding, range printing, headers, footers, borders, or extra copies. Make these entries to provide a few lines of data to print:

1. Enter **/Worksheet Erase Yes**, then enter **/Worksheet Column Set-Width**, type **15**, and press RETURN.

2. Place these entries on the worksheet:

A1:	**Name**
A2:	**John Smith**
A3:	**Bill Brown**
A4:	**Karen Hall**
A5:	**Janice Gold**
B1:	**Salary**
B2:	**25600**
B3:	**45300**
B4:	**18900**
B5:	**42500**
C1:	**Location**
C2:	**Dallas**
C3:	**Chicago**
C4:	**Dallas**
C5:	**Chicago**

Your worksheet should look like this:

Now you are ready to create a print macro. It will print two copies of the data you just entered on the worksheet.

3. Make these entries to create the macro:

F2:	**^\p**
G2:	**'/pp**
H2:	**Invoke print printer command**
G3:	**rA1.C5~**
H3:	**Specify range**
G4:	**g**
H4:	**Begin printing**
G5:	**pa**
H5:	**Page and align**
G6:	**g**
H6:	**Print a second copy**
G7:	**pa**
H7:	**Page and align**
G8:	**q**
H8:	**Quit the print menu**

4. Move the cell pointer to G2, enter /**Range Name Create**, type \p, and press RETURN twice.
    Make sure your printer is on and online before following the directions in the next instruction.

5. Press ALT and p to execute the macro and print the worksheet.

Creating a Macro to Insert Rows

You can create a macro to insert one or more blank rows in a worksheet, and use it with the print data you entered for the last example. A macro like this will be useful if you work frequently in the data-management environment and want to have some blank rows between the field names. Since blank rows can cause problems for the Query commands, you can have one macro to add them when you need them and another macro to remove them again. In this section, you will create a general-purpose macro: It will insert blank rows anywhere. If you wish, you can add a {GOTO} instruction to position the cell pointer right below the field names, so that the blanks are automatically inserted at the correct location for a database. To create a macro to insert blank rows, follow these instructions:

1. Place the following entries in the cells listed, using a single quotation mark in front of the entry for S2 and T2:

S2:	**\i**
T2:	**/wi**
U2:	**Request worksheet insert**
T3:	**r**
U3:	**Specify rows**
T4:	**{DOWN}**
U4:	**Move down to insert 2 rows**

2. Move the cell pointer to S2 and enter **/Range Name Label Right**, then press RETURN to name the top cell in the macro.

3. Move the cell pointer to A2.

4. Press ALT and i to execute the macro.
   The macro will insert blank rows in the worksheet, and it will look like this:

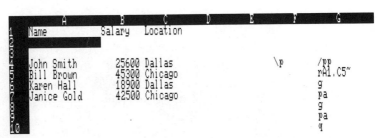

5. Enter /**Worksheet Erase Yes**.

SPECIAL MACRO TOPICS

There are many macro options — so many, in fact, that complete books are written on the subject. We cannot cover all possible options in this chapter, but we can show you a few of particular interest that go beyond the simpler keyboard alternatives to add command-language ability, minus all the complexity. In this section, you will take a look at a few of the special options as well as several command-language instructions.

Creating Automatic Macros

1-2-3 has a unique feature that lets you create an automatic macro. Every time a worksheet containing an automatic macro is retrieved, 1-2-3 immediately executes this macro without requiring you to press any keys. There are numerous applications for this feature, once you begin to use the advanced command language features, but there are still a few applications for the keyboard macros. For example, you might want to create a worksheet in which the input area is immediately erased. This means that even if the file is saved with previous data, the slate will be wiped clean with each new retrieval and you will be ready for data input.

The only difference between an automatic macro and one that you must execute is the name that you assign to the macro. An automatic macro must have a name of \0 (zero).

You can put the automatic macro to use with a model that calculates the monthly payments on a loan. The model is designed to function regardless of the principal, interest, or time. So that you can easily tell what data elements have been entered for each use of the model, the old data fields will be erased and new entries will be made. Follow these directions to set up the basic model before setting up the automatic macro:

1. Enter /**Worksheet Erase Yes**, move the cell pointer to column E, enter /**Worksheet Column Set-Width**, type **1**, and press RETURN.

2. Move the cell pointer to column G, enter /**Worksheet Column Set-Width**, type **1**, and press RETURN.

3. Move the cell pointer to B3, type **Enter desired borrowings:**, and move the cell pointer to E2.

4. Type **************.

5. Enter /**Copy**, press RETURN, move the cell pointer to E4, and press RETURN. Move the cell pointer to E3 and type *****.

6. Move the cell pointer to B6, type **Enter interest rate:**, and move the cell pointer to B10.

7. Type **Enter term in years:** and move the cell pointer to B13.

8. Type **** Your Payments Will Be **** and move the cell pointer to F13.

9. Type @**PMT(F3,F6/12,F10*12)** and press RETURN. Everything is now entered for this model, except for a few more asterisks to form boxes on the data entry form and except for the data itself.

10. Move the cell pointer to E2, enter /**Copy**, move the DOWN ARROW key to E4, and press RETURN. Move the cell pointer to E5 and press RETURN.

11. Keeping the cell pointer in E2, enter /**Copy**, move the DOWN ARROW key to E4, and press RETURN. Move the cell pointer to E9 and press RETURN.

12. Add the remaining three asterisks to complete the boxes by placing an asterisk in G3, G6, and G10.

13. Move the cell pointer to F13, enter /**Range Format Currency**, and press RETURN twice.
    You have already completed quite a bit of work but you

have yet to enter the automatic macro. Follow these instructions to create the macro:

14. Move the cell pointer to B21, type **'/reF3˜**, and move the cell pointer to B22.

15. Type **'/reF6˜** and move the cell pointer to B23.

16. Type **'/reF10˜** and move the cell pointer to B24.

17. Type **{GOTO}F3˜** and move the cell pointer to B21. The tilde mark (˜) is a very important part of the last three steps. It is easy to forget, but make the effort to remember; problems will occur if you leave it off.

18. Enter **/Range Name Create**, type **\0**, and press RETURN twice.

19. Move the cell pointer to A21, type **'\0**, and press RETURN.

20. Make the following documentation entries:

> **C21:**   **Erases previous borrowing entry**
>
> **C22:**   **Erases previous interest rate**
>
> **C23:**   **Erases previous term**
>
> **C24:**   **Positions the cell pointer for the first entry**

21. Make these entries to perform the first payment calculation:

> **F3:**   **65000**
>
> **F6:**   **.1025**
>
> **F10:**   **30**

Your display should now match Figure 12.1.

22. Enter **/File Save**, type **PAYMNT**, and press RETURN.

23. Enter **/File Retrieve**, point to PAYMNT in the list of file names, and press RETURN.

24. Complete entries in F3, F6, and F10 to calculate a new payment with different numbers.

Adding Sophistication With a Few Command-Language Instructions

You have already explored the workings of the keyboard alternative macros. The command-language instructions make up a complete programming language for 1-2-3 instructions. However, you can look at just a few that can add power to your macros. The macro instructions in the section are the Release 2 versions of the instructions. Some of the features covered in this section are also available in Release 1A but the commands are different. Release

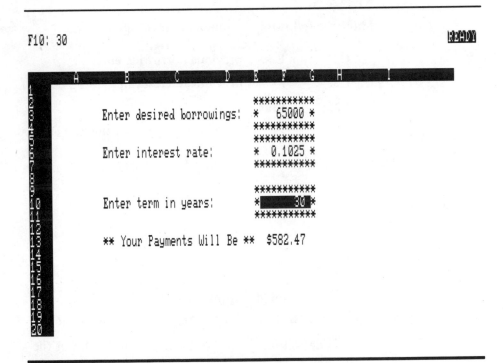

FIGURE 12.1   Calculating a payment amount

1A commands, which are quite different from the Release 2 versions, will not be covered. If you plan to seriously use the command-language instructions, you will want to acquire an upgraded version anyway to have access to a full set of commands.

Each of the special command-language commands uses braces around keyword entry for the command, as in the {QUIT} command that ends a macro. Some of the command-language commands also use arguments similar to the built-in function's use of arguments. These arguments refine the use of the command to a specific situation. They look something like this:

{BRANCH End}

This command will cause the macro to begin executing the instructions stored at the range named End. Notice that the command-language argument is also enclosed within the braces.

BRANCHING WITHIN A MACRO   The {*BRANCH*} command allows you to change the flow of execution within a macro to another location on the worksheet. This location can be specified as a cell address or a range name. The format of the command is {BRANCH location}. This command is seldom used alone; normally, it is combined with a condition test that will cause the macro to branch only if a certain condition is true.

This command does not alter the location of the cell pointer. It is not related to the {GOTO} command, which is designed to position the cell pointer rather than to alter the execution flow of a macro.

ADDING A COUNTER   A *counter* will permit you to count the number of times that you have executed a group of instructions. This is the typical use for a counter; to use it in that way, however, you must combine it with other instructions in this section. For now, you will find out how counters are established; then, later in this section, you will see how it is combined with other instructions to create a macro that executes certain instructions repetitively. As you learn more about the macro, you will find that 1-2-3 has a

{FOR} instruction that automatically initializes a counter and increments it for you. You may want to use this option later; in beginning with macros, however, you will find it more beneficial to establish your own counter so you can understand exactly what is happening.

A counter can be a cell address or a range name that you have assigned to a cell address. Once you decide on a location to use for a counter, you should reserve the location's use for this counter.

The {*LET*} command is used to set the value for a counter. When used in a macro with repetitive processing, {LET} must be used in two different ways: first, to initialize the value of the variable at the start of the macro, and second, to increment the variable each time you process the repetitive instructions within the macro. To use A1 as a counter and initialize it to zero, you could use this instruction at the beginning of the macro:

    {LET A1,0}

To increment this counter within a macro after completing an iteration of the processing, you could use this instruction:

    {LET A1,A1+1}

This instruction is written to work regardless of the current value of A1, as long as it contains a value entry.

The two instructions affecting the value of the counter might be incorporated in macro that performed repetitive processing something like this:

```
\m        {Let A1,0}
          . . .
          . . .
Top       . . .
          . . .
          {LET A1,A1+1}
          . . .
End       {QUIT}
```

You would enter the instructions to be executed repetitively in the section between Top and End. Top represents the beginning of the repetitive section. End marks the first instructions following the section that would be executed repetitively. Naturally, other instructions must be added to control the execution flow.

ADDING A CONDITION CHECK   Just as the @IF function is one of the most powerful built-in function tools, the {*IF*} macro instruction is one of the most powerful command-language instructions. It serves a similar purpose because it also allows you to deal with logical conditions. Its power is far more extensive because it lets you perform any other macro instruction, depending on the result of the condition test. It is not limited to controlling the value of a single cell the way that @IF is. In fact, the {IF} command is normally combined with {BRANCH} to completely change the execution flow within a macro.

Any condition can be tested. In macros where you have established a counter to control processing, the condition that is normally checked is the value of the counter. If the condition tested is true, the command on the same line as the {IF} will be executed. You might find a line like this within a macro:

{IF A1>10}{BRANCH End}

This line checks the value of A1. If A1 is greater than 10, the macro will branch to the range named End and execute the macro instructions it finds at that location.

ACCEPTING INPUT FROM THE KEYBOARD   There are several commands that let you accept data from the keyboard while a macro is executing. This simplest of these is {?}. When a macro encounters this special entry, it suspends execution and waits for input from the keyboard. When the operator presses RETURN, the macro continues where it left off.

You can use this feature to create a macro that removes the repetition involved in entering a series of built-in functions. You can supply the variable portion of the function and have the macro automate the entry of the portion that is the same.

A macro like this enters the date for you; all you need to supply is the year, month, and day:

	X	Y	Z
1	\d	@DATE(	Start date function
2		{?}	Wait for year to be input
3		,	Add comma after year
4		{?}	Wait for month to be input
5		,	Add comma after month
6		{?}	Wait for day to be input
7		)~	End function and finalize with RETURN
8		/rfd1~	Formats entry as a date

Make sure that you place a single quotation mark in front of the entries in X1, Y1, Y3, Y5, Y7, and Y8 to ensure that the contents of these cells are interpreted as labels.

If you like, you can enter this macro and give it a name. The following section provides a version of this same macro that is a bit more sophisticated. It incorporates several advanced macro features into the one macro and creates a macro that will enter 10 dates. You will take a little different strategy with this macro and document each instruction immediately after entering it. This will help you understand what each step is doing.

BUILDING A DATE-ENTRY MACRO This section combines the advanced features just discussed into a working macro example. It uses the concept of a counter, branching, and keyboard input all in one macro, since it is common to include multiple advanced instructions in a macro. Follow these directions to enter the macro:

1. Enter /**Worksheet Erase Yes**, move the cell pointer to J1, enter /**Worksheet Column Set-Width**, type 23, and press RETURN. Type {**LET A1,0**} and move the cell pointer to K1.

2. Type **Initialize A1 to 0 as a counter** and move the cell pointer to J2.

3. Type **{IF A1=10}{BRANCH End}** and move the cell pointer to K2.

4. Type **Check for max value in the counter** and move the cell pointer to J3.

5. Type **{LET A1,A1+1}** and move the cell pointer to K3.

6. Type **Increment counter** and move the cell pointer to J4.

7. Type **'@DATE(**, then move the cell pointer to K4.
   The single quotation mark is required to prevent 1-2-3 from interpreting the @ as a value entry in the cell.

8. Type **Enter first part of function** and move the cell pointer to J5.

9. Complete the remaining entries like this:

J5:	**{?}**
K5:	**Pause for the entry of the year**
J6:	**,**
K6:	**Enter the comma separator**
J7:	**{?}**
K7:	**Pause for the entry of the month**
J8:	**,**
K8:	**Enter comma separator**
J9:	**{?}**
K9:	**Pause for the entry of the day**
J10:	**)~**
K10:	**Generate function close and finalize entry**
J11:	**{DOWN}**
K11:	**Move the cell pointer down one cell**
J12:	**{BRANCH Top}**
K12:	**Begin Loop again**

I1: '\z   READY

```
         I        J                 K           L        M        N
1    \z        {LET A1,0}                Initialize A1 to 0 as a counter
2    Top       {IF A1=10}{Branch End}   Check for max value in the counter
3              {LET A1,A1+1}            Increment counter
4              @DATE(                   Enter first part of the function
5              {?}                      Pause for the entry of the year
6                                       Enter comma separator
7              {?}                      Pause for entry of the month
8                                       Enter comma separator
9              {?}                      Pause for the entry of the day
10             )~                       Generate close and finalize
11             {DOWN}                   Move the cell pointer down one cell
12             {BRANCH Top}             Begin loop again
13   End       {UP}{END}{UP}            Move to the top of the date column
14             /rfd1                    Invoke date format
15             {END}{DOWN}~             Expand format range
16             /wcs12~                  Widen column
17             {QUIT}                   End macro after 10 entries and format
18
19
20
```

FIGURE 12.2   A macro to enter dates

J13:	**{UP}{END}{UP}**
K13:	**Move to the top of the date column**
J14:	**'/rfd1**
K14:	**Invoke date format**
J15:	**{END}{DOWN}~**
K15:	**Expand format range**
J16:	**'/wcs12~**
K16:	**Expand width**
J17:	**{QUIT}**
K17:	**End macro after 10 entries and format**

The {QUIT} command is the only one that has not been discussed. It is used to end the execution of a macro just as a blank cell will do. Using {QUIT} rather than a blank cell makes it clearer that you intended the macro to end at that point.

10. Enter these labels in the cells specified:

> **I1:**   \z
>
> **I2:**   **Top**
>
> **I17:**   **End**

The macro should now match Figure 12.2.

11. Move the cell pointer to I1, enter /**Range Name Label Right**, expand the range to I13, and press RETURN.

The Range Name Label Right command saves you from having to use the /Range Name Create command three times. It assigns the labels in the range you specify to the entries in the cells immediately to the right of the cell containing the label.

12. Move the cell pointer to D1, press the ALT and z keys, then release to execute the macro.
You can enter anything you want for the year, month, and day for each date as long as the entries are valid and you press RETURN after each entry. Figure 12.3 shows one set of date entries that were completed with the macro.

Debugging Macros

The debugging process involves testing and correcting macros to ensure that you are obtaining the desired results. One of the most common mistakes users make in creating keyboard macros is forgetting to enter the tilde mark to represent each time the RETURN key is pressed. When you add command-language commands to a macro, you do not have the ability to test it completely before entering it.

1-2-3 has a step mode that executes a macro one keystroke at a time. This allows you to follow its progress and spot the area of difficulty if problems are encountered. In Release 2, pressing the SHIFT and F2 keys simultaneously will turn on the STEP mode. In Release 1A, pressing the SHIFT key plus the F1 key activates the STEP mode. Since this process is a toggle process, holding the keys down too long will toggle the STEP mode into the off position again. When this mode is operational, you will see the word STEP at the bottom of your screen, as shown in Figure 12.4.

When the step mode is on, any macro you invoke will be executed one step at a time. You will press the SPACE BAR each time you are ready for the next keystroke. The menu selections

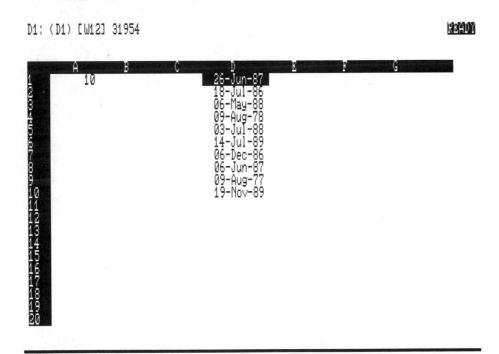

FIGURE 12.3   Dates entered with the macro

I1: '\z   READY

```
     I          J                    K        L        M        N
 1  \z      {LET A1,0}              Initialize A1 to 0 as a counter
 2  Top     {IF A1=10}{Branch End}  Check for max value in the counter
 3          {LET A1,A1+1}           Increment counter
 4          @DATE(                  Enter first part of the function
 5          {?}                     Pause for the entry of the year
 6          ,                       Enter comma separator
 7          {?}                     Pause for entry of the month
 8          ,                       Enter comma separator
 9          {?}                     Pause for the entry of the day
10          )~                      Generate close and finalize
11          {DOWN}                  Move the cell pointer down one cell
12          {BRANCH Top}            Begin loop again
13  End     {UP}{END}{UP}           Move to the top of the date column
14          /rfd1                   Invoke date format
15          {END}{DOWN}~            Expand format range
16          /wcs12~                 Widen column
17          {QUIT}                  End macro after 10 entries and format
18
19
20
```

STEP

FIGURE 12.4   Placing the macro in step mode

invoked will display in the control panel to provide information on the operation of the macro. You will not be able to input direct commands while the macro is executing. SST will appear at the bottom of the screen while the macro is executing.

To stop a malfunctioning macro, press the CTRL and BREAK keys simultaneously. This cancels the macro operation immediately and presents an error indicator at the upper right corner of the screen. Pressing ESC will return you to READY mode so you can make the necessary corrections to your macro.

Follow these instructions to try a macro in STEP mode:

1. Enter **/File Retrieve**, type **FORMAT**, and press RETURN.

2. If you are using Release 2, press the SHIFT and F2 keys. If you are using Release 1A, press SHIFT and F1.

3. Move the cell pointer to F1, and press the ALT and c keys.

4. Press the SPACE BAR to execute a keystroke.

5. Continue pressing the SPACE BAR until you are asked to supply the range to format.

6. Press the END key followed by the DOWN ARROW key, then press the RETURN key.

7. Execute step 2 again to toggle the STEP mode into the off position.

8. Enter **/Worksheet Erase Yes**.

SUMMARY

In this chapter you have had the opportunity to explore the world of keyboard alternative macros. The possibilities are limited only by the 1-2-3 menu command set and your imagination as you combine a series of menu selections into a set of stored instructions that you can use over and over again. Once you have mastered the keyboard alternative macros, you are well on your way to becoming an advanced 1-2-3 user. Your next step will be to explore the remaining command-language instructions in your 1-2-3 manual.

13

USING HAL TO MAKE YOUR 1-2-3 TASKS EASIER

Hal is an exciting new product introduced by Lotus to add features and functionality to the 1-2-3 package. Hal allows you to complete 1-2-3 tasks by entering English-like requests rather than having to use the sequence of menu commands required when you interface with 1-2-3 directly. Hal is truly a revolutionary way to make your interface with 1-2-3 match your way of thinking about tasks to be performed.

In this chapter you will have an opportunity to explore how the Hal product can increase your productivity with the 1-2-3 product. If you already have the Hal product, you can read through the chapter and enter the exercises. If you do not have Hal, you can still read through the chapter and follow the screen examples that show the product in action. Screen examples of each type of Hal request are provided.

WHAT IS HAL?

Hal is a separate program that you must place in memory along with 1-2-3. Once both programs are loaded into memory, the features of both will be available throughout the session. When you want to use 1-2-3's menus, all the features will still be available. Simply enter a slash (/), just as you have always done, to activate 1-2-3's menu system. When you want to interface with Hal, enter a backslash (\) to activate a Hal *request box* — the way to make your needs known to Hal. Both options are always available during the existing 1-2-3 session. When you end the session, whether through a Hal request or a 1-2-3 menu option, you will be exiting both programs.

WORKING WITH HAL REQUESTS

Hal requests are your way of interfacing with the program. There are Hal requests to duplicate many 1-2-3 menu selections as well as additional features that are beyond the scope of 1-2-3 menu options. These requests are entered with English-like commands that resemble how most users actually think about tasks more than the hierarchy of menu selections do. For example, when you want to format the Sales data as currency you can just tell Hal, **format Sales as curr**.

Benefits

Hal provides benefits to both new 1-2-3 users and experienced users. New users will find that the Hal request needed to perform a task is easier to remember than the sequence of menu commands.

Hal's ease of use stems partly from its many synonyms. Since there are two or more ways of expressing each task to be completed, you can substitute words within the request and still get the same results. The menu structure, on the other hand, is rigid; there is only one possible set of menu selections that will work properly. Hal requests simplify complicated tasks such as sorting or extracting data from a database, because they can be expressed in a simple phrase such as "sort by LastName" or "give me ones with Salary greater than 25000". Also, Hal has more defaults than 1-2-3; it makes decisions for you, unless you decide to override them.

Advanced 1-2-3 users often use Hal requests to replace 1-2-3 menu selections. However, they are also attracted to the package for features like the *linking option*, in which Hal lets you create permanent links between worksheets that will be updated each time a file is retrieved. This means that you do not have to remember to combine updated data into the current worksheet. It is handled for you automatically.

Advanced users will want to take advantage of the *macro learn* feature. Once this feature is activated, Hal begins to store every Hal request and 1-2-3 command onto this file. At any time, you can bring the data on this file into the worksheet with the File Import option. After that, all you need do is name the top cell as a macro. These intructions can then be executed repeatedly whenever you need them.

Advanced users will also want to customize Hal. It is easy to add synonyms to the product. You can also create customized help screens and synonyms for 1-2-3 commands, in addition to the synonyms for words in Hal requests.

Both new and advanced users will appreciate Hal's *undo* feature. This command gives you the option of undoing the last Hal request executed or the last 1-2-3 command entered. This option can undo a sort, a formula change, an alteration of a format, or the column width. All you have to do is press the backspace key with the Hal request box on the screen.

Syntax of Hal Requests

Although Hal does not have the rigid structure of 1-2-3 commands, there are still some rules you need to follow when specifying a 1-2-3 request. These rules relate to the structure of your Hal request and are referred to as *syntax rules*. Syntax rules also apply to the construction of English sentences, in terms of the parts of speech that you use in the sentence and the order you use for combining the various words in the sentence into one intelligible whole.

VERBS WITHIN THE HAL REQUEST   The *verb* in a Hal request expresses the action in the request. Almost all Hal requests contain a verb. Some verbs you might encounter in a request are **save, graph, retrieve, sort,** and **print.** Most Hal verbs have one or more synonyms that have the same meaning. For example, **sort** can be used to start a request when you want to change the sequence of some of the data on the worksheet; however, **arrange**, **group**, and **organize** also have the same meaning and can be used instead. Since you are giving Hal a command, the subject is implied, just as it would be in an imperative English sentence. What you are really saying is: "Hal, you sort," or "Hal, you print"; therefore, no subject is required.

So far, nothing is really very different from an English sentence. The next few optional components of requests also are similar to sentence components, although unlike the verbs used in Hal requests they are not parts of speech.

USING A LOCATION IN A HAL REQUEST   A *location* is an optional part of a Hal request that is used to specify where the action of the verb is to be applied. In the request **sort a1..d25 by LastName**, A1..D25 is the location to which the action of the sort verb will be applied. It may seem as though a location would be required for every Hal request, but some requests do not require a location; Hal uses a default in many other requests when a location is not specified. You can ask Hal to **format as currency** and it will use the current cell as the default location for this request. The request **widen by 5** will increase the width of the current column unless a column is specified.

Two special words can be used as the location in a Hal request. The first is **this**, which refers to the current table — the group of cells on the current worksheet that contain data and your cell pointer. This area ends when it is bordered by two or more blank columns or rows, or by the worksheet row or column names. There can be more than one table of entries on the worksheet, but only the table that contains the cell pointer is considered to be the current table. If you tell Hal to **format this**, it will format all the cells in the range, which includes every entry in the current table. This option can be a real time-saver; it frequently frees you from having to enter a range in the request. Right now, this special option may seem a little confusing, but when you try it in a few Hal requests you will appreciate its convenience.

It is another special location within a Hal request. This word refers to the same location referenced in the previous request. If the last request was **format a1..d10 as currency**, then **erase it** will erase A1..D10.

USING QUALIFYING WORDS IN A REQUEST Qualifying words can be used in a Hal request to override some of the defaults in the request. If you asked Hal to **graph a1..b10**, Hal would use the default-graph type of bar. If you prefer a line graph, you can add the qualifier **line** to the request, like this: **graph A1.B10 as line**.

SPECIFYING A DESTINATION IN A REQUEST A *destination* is also an optional component of a Hal request. It tells Hal where to store the results of the request's action. You can ask Hal to extract records that match your criteria and it will use a default location that is five rows below the top of the criteria area (which it also establishes). You can also specify a location of Z10 for these results in a request like this: **extract records where Salary greater than 35000 in Z10**.

OTHER OPTIONS Hal has many other special options to make your work easier. By now you probably noticed that Hal is not fussy about case; either upper or lower case is fine for everything except most label entries, in which case you must use exactly what you wish to see on the worksheet. The exception to this is special labels. such as the months of the year.

You can create multiple requests, and you can usually abbreviate words within Hal requests to their first three letters. Since this chapter is only meant to give you a quick glimpse into Hal's features, take a look at some of the things that Hal requests can do, and reserve all the details of the package for the time when you decide to use it in your 1-2-3 sessions.

PUTTING HAL TO WORK FOR YOU

The manual accompanying the Hal package provides a comprehensive list of all the 1-2-3 commands that can be completed with Hal requests. You will have an opportunity to look at a small subset of these options as you explore some of the tasks that Hal can handle in the worksheet, data-management, and graphics environments of 1-2-3.

Making Hal Active in Your System

If you have the Hal product, you will want to make Hal active along with 1-2-3. Since the two are always used in tandem, you will need to follow a special procedure for loading both packages into memory at once. Assuming that you have the product, follow the steps that correspond to your type of hardware. Once Hal is loaded, your screen should have the word HAL on the bottom line, as shown in Figure 13.1. Naturally, if you do not have a copy of Hal skip this section and begin reading about worksheet tasks.

TWO FLOPPY DRIVES   If you have a system with two floppy drives, follow these steps:

1. Boot your system with DOS, then type **B:** to make the B drive active.

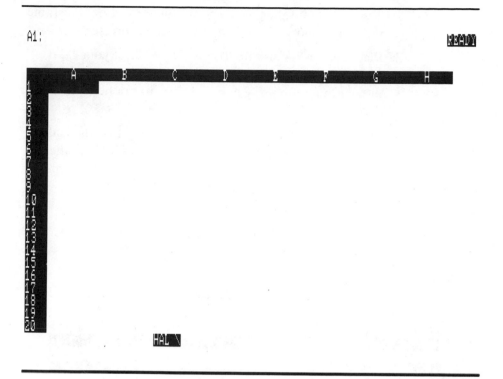

FIGURE 13.1   Initial Hal screen

2. Place the 1-2-3 System Disk in drive A and the Hal disk in drive B.

3. Type **HAL** @A:
   Hal will prompt you to insert the Hal resource disk you have created from the instructions in your Hal manual. You will want to leave this resource disk in drive A and store your data in drive B.

A HARD DISK SYSTEM   With a hard disk the process is easier, assuming that you followed the directions in your Hal manual for storing your files on the hard disk. First you need to activate the directory containing your Hal files.

1. Type **cd \123** if the files are in the directory 123. Substitute the correct name if they are in a different directory.

2. Place your 1-2-3 disk in drive A. However, if your 1-2-3 files are permanently stored on the hard disk with the installation option or Copyhard, you do not need the key disk.

3. Type **HAL** and press RETURN, assuming that the Hal and 1-2-3 files are in the directory 123. If 1-2-3 is in the directory Lotus and Hal is in the current directory, type **HAL @\LOTUS** and press RETURN.

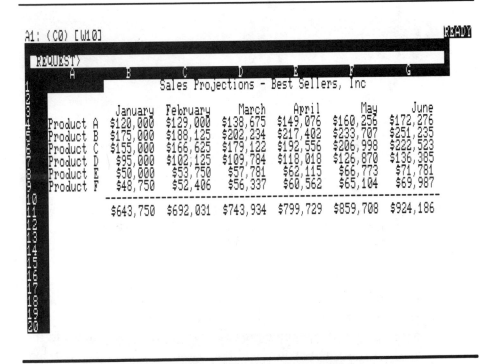

FIGURE 13.2   Sales-projection model before totals are added

Using Hal in the Worksheet

Hal can handle many worksheet tasks, including entering numbers, labels, and formulas. It even has some special options for entering formulas quickly. Look at the Hal instructions that were used to build the basic Sales projection model shown in Figure 13.2, then look at a quick way Hal offers for adding all the columns.

MAKING ENTRIES FOR THE SALES-PROJECTION MODEL

All the work for this model was created with Hal requests. Even if you do not have Hal, follow these steps to see how it works:

1. Type a \.

   This activates the Hal request box, as the following illustration shows:

   You can choose to precede each command with this entry, or you can ask Hal to keep the request box on the screen.

2. Type **stay** and press RETURN.

   This request tells Hal to stay around and keep its request box available. This is convenient if you have a number of requests to enter; you will not have to enter the backslash (\) before each request. When you decide you do not want it around anymore, just enter **go away**.

3. Type **enter "Sales Projections-Best Sellers, Inc" in c1** into the request box and press RETURN to produce this result:

Notice that lower-case letters were used for the verb **enter** and for the cell address, since Hal does not differentiate case on words in the request. Also notice that upper-case letters were used in the entry you want Hal to make for you. In this case, they are needed because you decided to use upper case for some of the letters in the entry. Also notice that the entire entry you are asking Hal to make is enclosed in quotation marks, due to the comma within the entry. Without the quotation marks, the comma would be regarded as a separator and the entry would be split into two cells. Also notice that you do not have to move your cell pointer to C1 to have Hal place the entry there. You can leave the cell pointer in one place while Hal is making all your entries.

4. Type **enter jan thru june across in b3** and press RETURN.

   This invokes one of Hal's powerful features that automatically generates a row of label entries, which consist of the month names, and produces the following results:

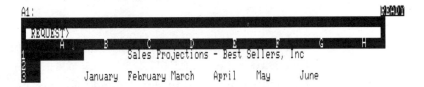

   Later, when this model is graphed, you will see a command that allows you to abbreviate these names. But for now, it is more important to widen the columns and right-align the labels.

5. Type **widen all to 10** and press RETURN.

   This command widens all the columns in the current table. Actually, however, the command is much more flexible than this. In this instance the width for the current table is determined by the 10 in the request. The location, **all**, tells Hal that you want every column in the current table changed. The change is made to each column

individually and is not done on a global basis. You can
verify this by moving your cell pointer to other columns
in the current table and noting the [W10] (if you are using
Release 2 and above) in the control panel, which indicates
that the column was individually widened.

Hal allows you to state the final width by using **to** and
the width you want. It also allows you to use **by** in the
request and specify the increment amount. Lastly, you can
just tell it to widen, and it will increase the column width
by 50 percent.

6. Type **right align b3.g3** and press RETURN.

This request will align all of the month labels at the right
side of the cells so they will be directly above the numbers
you are about to enter. The result will look like this:

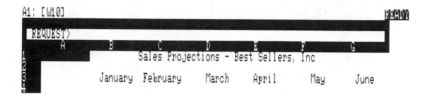

7. Type **type Product A,Product B, Product C,Product D,
Product E,Product F in A4** and press RETURN to produce this display:

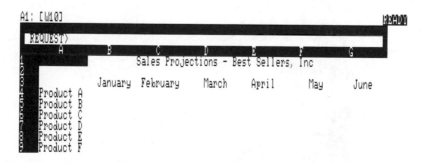

This places the labels for the various products in A4..A9,
since the default for a group of entries in one request is to
place them down the column. This can be overridden, as it

was with the month names, by including the word **across** in the request. No quotation marks are required; the commas in the request will function as separators.

8. Type **enter 120000,175000,155000,95000,50000,48750 in b4**, then press RETURN.

    This places the first numbers in the worksheet in the January column, like this:

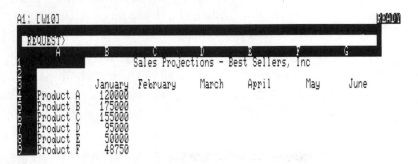

If you want commas in these numbers, you must get them by using the formatting options. If you placed commas in the Hal request, they would be interpreted as separators.

9. Type **format all as curr with 0 places** and press RETURN.

    This command applies the currency format to the entire current table like this:

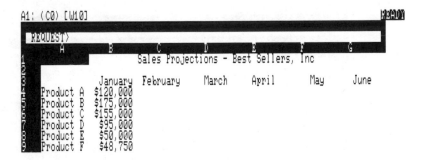

When the remaining numbers are entered within the table, they will also be formatted. In the request, currency is abbreviated as **curr** as an example of Hal's ability to interpret abbreviations of the request entries. With only a few exceptions, the special Hal words can be abbreviated as three characters.

10. Type **project Jan across at 7.5%** and press RETURN. Almost as if by magic, all the January figures are projected across the worksheet for all the products, creating this display:

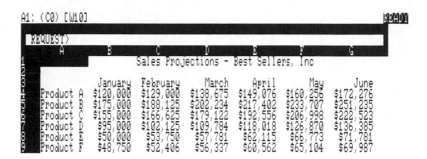

Hal automatically created formulas for all of February and, in the same step, copied these formulas across to the other steps. If you wanted to create the same result with 1-2-3, you would have to carry out three steps: (1) enter the February formula for Product A, (2) copy the formula down the February column, and (3) copy the February column to March through June. Hal also accomplishes this task with an English-like request that fits the thought processes of most business users.

11. Type **total all cols** and press RETURN. This command draws a series of -'s across at the bottom of the columns and places the @SUM formula beneath each column to produce the totals shown in Figure 13.3. Again, there is no need to remember the syntax for the built-in function; all you need is a simple English request, just like one you might give to a staff member whom you wanted to do some computations. Computing the average, minimum, and maximum are just as easy. Also if you want to control the location of these results, all you need to do is specify a destination in your request.

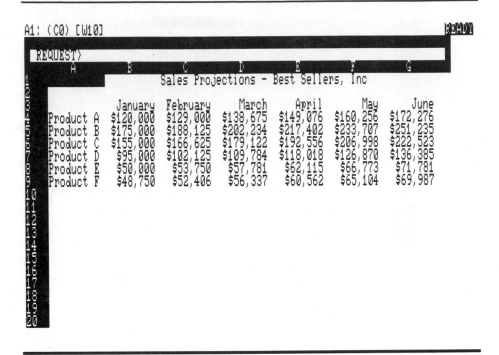

FIGURE 13.3   Having Hal total your columns

MAKING CHANGES TO THE MODEL   All the methods that worked under 1-2-3 are still viable options for updating entries in the model. You can edit or retype entries as often as you wish and the model will be updated for your new entries. Since this model is based upon the January numbers, you can choose to change a single value or the entire column this way. Alternately, you can use the Hal verb **alter** or **fix** to begin your request and Hal will place the data from the location that you specify into the edit line for your changes. You could write the request as **alter b5** if you wanted to edit the contents of B5, in which case Hal would produce this display:

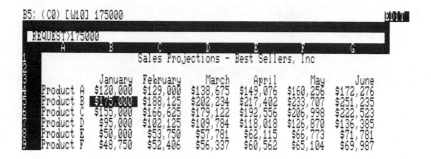

Notice that Hal moves the cell pointer to the entry being edited and displays its contents within the request box for editing. Press RETURN to keep the current entry in B5.

PRINTING THE MODEL   Basic printing features with Hal are a real snap. Simple print requests will print the current table or the entire worksheet. Although you can always specify a specific range or range name, you will find that the option to print the current table is a real convenience: All you need to enter is **print this**. Likewise, if you want to print the entire worksheet, all you need to enter is **print all**. Other simple requests can advance the paper, change the margin settings, or send setup strings to the printer. Some special options, such as print headers and footers, do not have requests that correspond to the menu options. You will still need to resort to the 1-2-3 menu structure for these entries.

If you have the Hal product, turn your printer on now and make sure that it is online. Then you can follow these steps to see how easy it is to create print output:

1. Type **print this** and press RETURN.
   Hal will print everything in the current table. For the current worksheet, there is no difference between the current table and the complete worksheet, although many models will contain multiple table areas.

2. Type **advance paper** and press RETURN.
   Since the default for advance is one page, Hal will advance the printer to the top of the next page.

3. Type **print a2.c9** and press RETURN.
   This will print the data from the first quarter that is contained in A2..C9 of your worksheet model.

SAVING THE DATA AND ERASING THE WORKSHEET   You are finished with the Sales projection model temporarily. Hal can save this model and clear memory with these requests:

1. Type **save as SLSPRJ** and press RETURN.
   Hal immediately saves the file, since it has not been saved before. If it finds a file by the name you specified on the disk, it gives you the same prompt message as 1-2-3 to see if you want to replace the file or cancel the request.

2. Type **erase everything** and press RETURN. Confirm with Y to clear the worksheet.

3. Type **go away** and press RETURN to remove the request box from the screen.

Using Hal in the Database Environment

Hal offers just as many exciting features to the database environment as it does to the worksheet environment. You can complete all of your data entry without moving the cell pointer around the worksheet. You can also use the same time-saving techniques for formatting, aligning, and correcting data that you used in the worksheet. In addition, the options for sorting your data and extracting data from the database are so easy that even if you are a new user you can succeed with tasks that once were relegated to the 1-2-3 expert. And if you are a power user, you will also appreciate these functions because they eliminate the multiple menu selections required for sorting or querying a database. Now everything can be handled with one simple request.

You will use Hal's data-entry features to create a small database. Then you will try several sorts and queries to see just how easy the process is.

ENTERING THE DATA   You will need to use **across** in each of your requests, since normally database data is entered by row. Every record and field will be input with the cell pointer in one stationary location. Follow these steps to complete your entries:

1. Type **stay** and press RETURN to bring the request box back to the screen.
   This will keep you from having to precede each request with a backslash (\\).

2. Type **put Inv_No,Dept,Equipment,Cost,Pur_Yr across**.
   The verb "put" is synonymous with "enter" and "type". Put has the same function in this request as one of the other words, and it enters the field names across the top of the worksheet like this:

3. Type **widen col c to 15**.
   You are already familiar with this request from the worksheet exercise. It changes column C to a width of 15.

4. Type **right align a1.c1** and press RETURN.

5. Type **enter 97154,"ACCT,Jetson Printer,3400,1987 across in A2** and press RETURN.
   The double quotation mark in front of ACCT causes the label to be right-aligned when it is placed in B2, producing these results:

6. Type **enter 78654,"PAY,Zip Plotter,1775,1986 across in a3** and press RETURN.

The second database record is entered with this command.

7. Type **enter 45235,"ACCT,EGA Monitor,1500,1987 across in a4** and press RETURN.

8. Type **enter 69875,"MKTG,King Computer,2500,1986 across in a5** and press RETURN.

9. Type **enter 11225,"PAY,EGA Monitor,1800,1986 across in A6** and press RETURN.

10. Type **enter 99880,"MKTG,Portable Printer,450,1987 across in a7** and press RETURN.

This completes the entry of six records for the database. Your screen should look like this:

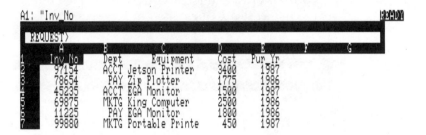

Additional records can be added with the same process, or you can enter some of the information by column if it is available in that format. Although you do save a little time in not having to move the cell pointer each time, the real payback from the use of Hal in the database environment will be realized when you use the sort or query features.

SORTING THE DATA   If you have worked through the exercises in the database chapter, you already know that sorting a database requires a series of menu selections. You have to tell 1-2-3 where your data is located, what field you want to control the sort, and what secondary field to use if the first field contains duplicates. Finally, you must select a menu option to have the data sorted.

With Hal, the process is much easier. You can use the verbs **sort**,

arrange, **organize**, or **group** to begin your request when you want Hal to change the sequence of your database information. It is convenient that Hal assumes that the location you wish to sort is the current table, since this usually means that you do not need to specify the data range for the sort within your request. Hal is also smart enough to know to exclude the first row in the current table; it assumes that the field names are stored in that location.

If you want the database sorted by the data in the first column you do not even need to qualify the request to tell Hal what to sort. In the database you just created, telling Hal to **sort** would cause Hal to reorganize the data in Inv_No sequence. You also have the flexibility to say **sort by col c** if you want the data in sequence by the entries in the Equipment column. Another way of making this same request is to use the request **sort by Equipment**.

Adding a second-level sort key to cope with duplicates in the primary key means adding another phrase to qualify the request. You would add **then by** to the request and follow it with the second key, as in **sort by column c then by column a**. In this request the data will be sorted according to the values in column C. Where duplicate values exist in column C, the values in column A will determine which record is listed first.

Hal always assumes that the sort sequence is ascending unless you tell it otherwise. The request **sort by column c** will arrange the data in the current table by the values in column C, with the record having the lowest value in this field listed first and the record with the highest value listed last. To use descending sequence, you can add a minus sign (–) or the word **descending** to the request. For example, **sort by InvNo descending** or **sort by InvNo -** are equivalent instructions that arrange the data in the database according to the InvNo but list the highest InvNo first.

If you have Hal, you will want to try a few sort requests with the current data, using these steps:

1. Type **sort** and press RETURN.
   This request resequences the database into ascending sequence by Inv_No to produce these results:

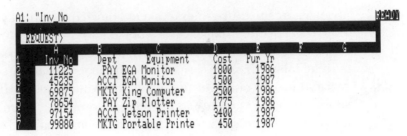

2. Type **sort -** and press RETURN.

   You can see the effect of the minus sign immediately; it should reverse the sequence of the records to look like this:

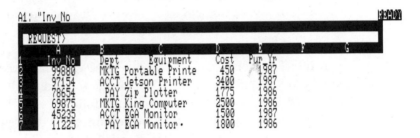

3. Press the BACKSPACE key.

   This is Hal's undo feature. It undoes the last Hal request, which in this case was the descending sequence sort. The screen should look like this:

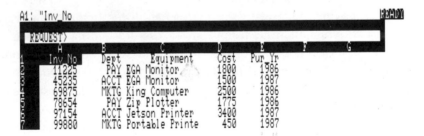

4. Type **sort by Dept then by Cost** and press RETURN.

   Hal will only look at the Cost field when the entries in the Dept field are identical. When they are, the Cost entry will determine which database record will appear first in the list. The final result looks like this:

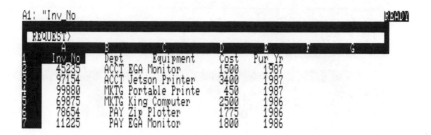

It is so easy to sort records with Hal that you can create a variety of sort sequences in just a few minutes. If you add a request to print after each sort sequence, your report will be easy to prepare.

EXTRACTING DATA FROM THE DATABASE   If you think it is somewhat complicated to sort data under 1-2-3, you may have found the Query options to require even more concentration. In order to accomplish anything, not only do you need to make a number of selections from the menu but you also must also remember to enter special information on the worksheet from the READY mode. For example, you cannot select the menu option for Criteria to define its location unless you have already selected an area on the worksheet and stored your criteria or record selection specifications on the worksheet. The same is true for the definition of the Output area for the extract report.

Hal makes the Query operations much easier to work with. To extract data from an existing database you can start a Hal request with **which ones have**, **give me**, **match**, or **extract**. Then all you need to tell Hal is which criteria to use. The criteria are specified as a field name, a logical operator using either symbols or words, and a value or label. For example, you might write an extract request as **which ones have Dept equal to ACCT, which ones have Dept = ACCT**, or **give me Dept equal to ACCT**. All three of these requests tell Hal to extract records with the Dept equal to ACCT.

You do not have to worry about an output area. Hal will automatically choose an area and create an output area. This output area will be below the area Hal sets up in the worksheet

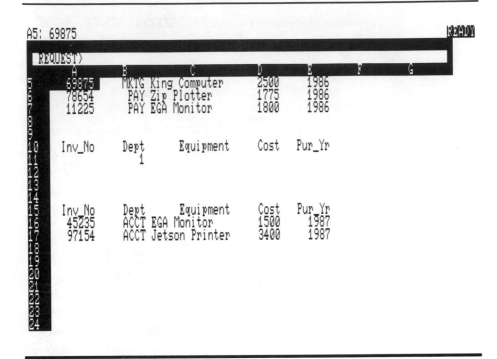

FIGURE 13.4   Extract Dept equal to ACCT

for the criteria you enter in your request. Let's take a look at what happens when these requests are entered:

1. Type **give me ones with Dept = ACCT** and press RETURN.

   Hal does several things for you. First, it creates a criteria area, as shown in A10..E11 of Figure 13.4, and stores your criteria in this location. Next, it creates an output area and executes your request, writing matching records to this output area. The output area is also shown in Figure 13.4 in A15..E17 and contains the two records that meet your criteria. Lastly, it also automatically shifts the data displayed on the screen to ensure that the output area is visible.

2. Type **extract Cost > 2000** and press RETURN.
   Hal first asks you if it is OK to write in the area used by
   the last request, using the prompt screen shown in Figure
   13.5.

3. Press RETURN to continue and produce the results
   shown in Figure 13.6.
   Data-management tasks are easy to master with Hal as a
   helper, since even more complex options can be created
   with simple requests like these.

4. Type **save as INV** and press RETURN.

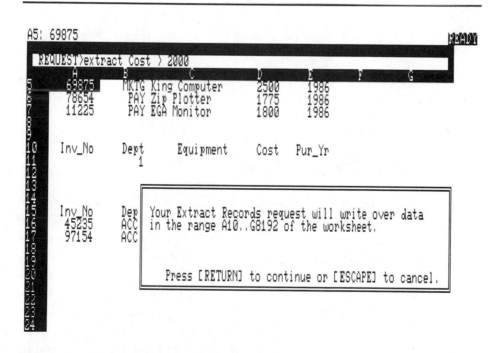

FIGURE 13.5 Confirming a request to overwrite

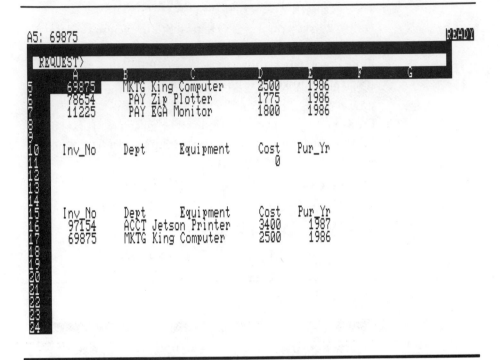

A5: 69875   READY

```
REQUEST>
        A           B       C            D        E         F        G
5       69875       MKTG King Computer   2500     1986
6       78654       PAY  Zip Plotter     1775     1986
7       11225       PAY  EGA Monitor     1800     1986

10      Inv_No      Dept    Equipment    Cost     Pur_Yr
11                                          0

15      Inv_No      Dept    Equipment    Cost     Pur_Yr
16      97154       ACCT Jetson Printer  3400     1987
17      69875       MKTG King Computer   2500     1986
```

FIGURE 13.6   Cost greater than 2000

Using Hal to Create Graphs

Hal has built-in assumptions for the graphics environment that can eliminate much of the tedium in the multiple selections 1-2-3 requires for a graph. You can create a basic graph with just a simple request. You can use additional requests to add titles if you wish. There are other graph options that cannot be handled with Hal. One of these is the addition of a legend to your graph. If you elect to use this graphic option, you will need to make the proper selections from 1-2-3's menus for this option.

Look at a few examples of simple graphs created with Hal by following these steps:

1. Type **get SLS_PRJ** and press RETURN.
   This will retrieve the sales-projection worksheet that was
   created earlier in the chapter.

2. Type **graph rows 4 thru 9** and press RETURN to create
   the graph shown in Figure 13.7.
   The graph has a problem with the overlapping labels at the
   bottom of the X axis, but this can be fixed.

3. Press ESC, then type **abbreviate b3.g3** and press
   RETURN.
   The labels on the worksheet are abbreviated to three char-
   acters, which is the default.

4. Press the F3 key twice.
   This moves back through the previous requests and should
   now display **graph rows 4 thru 9**.

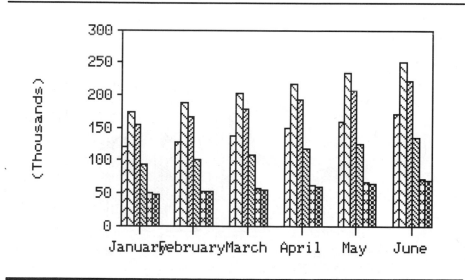

FIGURE 13.7   Bar graph with overlapping labels

5. Press RETURN to reexecute this request, producing the results in Figure 13.8, in which the overlapping label problem is solved.

6. Press ESC, then type **graph row 4 as pie** to produce the results in Figure 13.9.
   The graph type was specified to override the default-graph type of bar.
   Hal uses the PrintGraph program to print its graph, just as 1-2-3 does. First save the graph with a request that starts like **save graph as**, then end your 1-2-3 session.

7. Press ESC, then type **save graph as pie** and press RETURN.

8. Type **Quit** and press RETURN. Confirm with a Y and press RETURN to end the combined Hal/1-2-3 session.

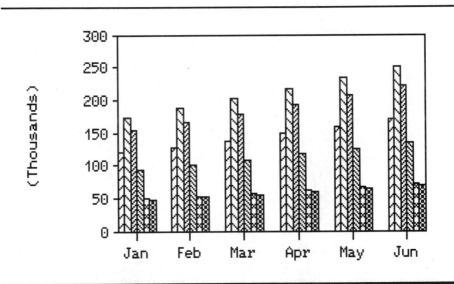

FIGURE 13.8   Abbreviating labels to correct the problem

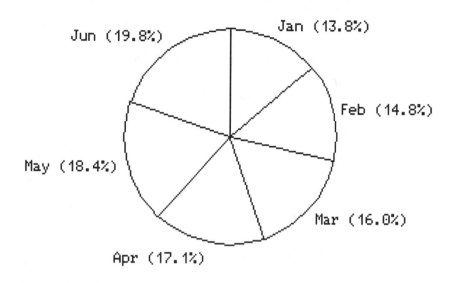

FIGURE 13.9   Pie chart of Product A sales

SUMMARY

Although you explored only a subset of Hal's features in this chapter, you saw the time savings they can offer. You reviewed some of Hal's features for entering labels, totaling columns, and projecting numbers in the worksheet environment. In the data-management environment, you saw the ease with which data can be sorted or extracted. You learned how one command can create a graph with Hal. Hal has many other features for linking worksheets, creating a learn mode that automates macro creation in 1-2-3, and customization options that let you tailor the use of 1-2-3 applications to your specific needs. Even if you do not currently have a copy of Hal, you will want to add this software option to your wish list of packages, since you can more than recover its cost in time savings over a short period of time.

INSTALLING
1-2-3

This appendix is designed to serve as an introduction to installing Lotus 1-2-3 for your system. It will cover 1-2-3 installation on various types of equipment. Whether you use a hard disk or a floppy disk, you will find detailed instructions to ensure that the installation process proceeds smoothly.

If your copy of 1-2-3 has already been installed by your computer dealer or someone else in your organization, you do not need to read this appendix. If your copy of 1-2-3 is still covered in shrink wrap, you will need to install the package. In that case you will find this appendix to be a valuable reference for the steps that you must take. It will also provide some information on various equipment options to help you make intelligent selections during the installation process.

Before beginning with 1-2-3 specifics, this appendix will introduce the hardware options for 1-2-3 and the various system components. You cannot install 1-2-3 if you do not have at least some general knowledge about the system you will be using. In order for the Install program to configure your copy of 1-2-3 to run with your specific hardware components, you must be able to tell the program what those components are.

YOUR EQUIPMENT

1-2-3 is designed to run on a personal computer from AT&T, Compaq, or IBM. A number of certified IBM PC compatibles are also able to run 1-2-3 successfully. The Zenith Z-100 and 248, the TI Professional, and the Wang Professional are just a few of the many systems with which the package will work. Since the compatible market is constantly changing, you will need to check with your dealer for the most up-to-date list of certified compatibles. In case of doubt, have the dealer demonstrate 1-2-3 on the machine you are considering.

Throughout this appendix we will assume that you have an IBM PC or XT. If you have an IBM AT or an AT&T, refer to your keyboard to determine the location of the special keys. If you have a certified compatible, look at the keyboard of your machine and the peripheral devices, such as disk drives, to determine which of the listed machines most closely matches your configuration.

Minimum Configuration

The minimum system configuration required for 1-2-3 is listed in Figure A.1. An optimal configuration for your application may require more equipment. Notice the differences in memory and disk drive support between version 1A and version 2. The minimum memory under Release 2 and 2.01 has been increased to 256K from 192K for Release 1A and 128K for Release 1. Also,

Release 1A	Release 2
IBM PC, XT, AT, or Compaq	IBM PC, XT, AT, Portable, or PCjr Compaq Portable, Plus, or Deskpro AT&T 63000
Keyboard	Keyboard
192K	256K
2 double-sided/double-density diskettes or 1 hard disk and 1 double-sided/double-density diskette	1 double-sided/double-density diskette
Monochrome or color monitor	Monochrome or color monitor

FIGURE A.1   Minimum configuration

Release 2 can be used with one double-sided diskette, whereas Release 1A requires either two diskettes or a hard disk and one double-sided diskette.

KEYBOARD   You will begin using the keyboard in this appendix as you work with the Install program. Any directions given will refer to key names on the keyboard for the IBM PC. The same keyboard configuration is used for the IBM PC/XT, the IBM Portable, and the Compaq. There are some differences between this configuration and the keyboards of other popular systems that work with 1-2-3.

MONITOR   Monitors come in two basic varieties, color and monochrome. Monochrome implies one color. This may be white, green, or amber on black. Normally a monochrome monitor will display only text, although you can add cards such as an Enhanced Graphics Adapter or a Hercules card. Even with the graphics adapter, a monochrome monitor will display one-color graphs. A color monitor can display graphs in color as well as utilize color for highlighting some of the 1-2-3 screens; for example, it can use red for the error indicator and blue to highlight menu choices.

Expansion

With the minimum configuration you will be able to load the 1-2-3 package and use most of its features. However, you may find that you want to expand beyond the minimum configuration for convenience and to obtain maximum benefit from the package features.

ADDING MEMORY   The models you create will be limited by the amount of memory on your system. Operating 1-2-3 at the lowest level possible, you will be able to use all the package features but will be restricted in the size of your data files and spreadsheet applications. If you plan to build large models, consider expanding the memory of your machine. The standard memory expansion can take your PC up to 640K. A variety of multifunction boards can be added in an empty slot of your PC to achieve this memory expansion. Frequently these cards will offer other functions, such as a battery-operated clock to keep track of the time, a print buffer, or additional printer or communications ports.

With Release 2, you also have the option of expanding memory beyond the standard 640K. To do this you will need to select a card that conforms to the Lotus/Intel Expanded Memory Specification, such as the Above Board card. With these cards, 1-2-3 can use up to 4 MB of memory (approximately 4,000,000 characters) above the 640 KB memory limit. This expanded memory will allow you to build large data files and spreadsheets with the 1-2-3 program. You will need to run the expanded-memory management software that comes with your card before 1-2-3 can access this additional memory.

Release 2 also supports the addition of a math coprocessor.

Both the 8087 and the 80287 coprocessor chips are supported and will be automatically recognized once they are installed. Spreadsheet models with a significant number of calculations will be calculated much faster with one of these chips added to the motherboard of your machine.

ADDING DISK DRIVES   Although Release 2 can be used with one disk drive, if you are a frequent user you will find that the required disk swapping is quite cumbersome. Data cannot be stored on the System Disk containing the program and help files, so you will find yourself changing disks frequently.

If you have two drives, one drive can be used for the program and the other can be used for data. This will work whether both drives are floppy drives or one is a hard disk and one is a floppy. The best configuration for using 1-2-3 is to have a hard drive along with a floppy so that you can load all the 1-2-3 programs on the hard drive and have the flexibility of storing data files on either the hard disk or a floppy. You will then be able to switch from 1-2-3 to Translate or PrintGraph without having to search for the proper diskette, since all three programs will be on your hard drive. Also, with a hard drive you will be able to store files that exceed a floppy diskette's 360K capacity. Hard drives are available with capacities from 10MB to 40MB or more. At present, the most popular size is a 20MB drive.

ADDING A PRINTER   1-2-3 will support a wide variety of printers. In the installation program you will be able to select from a menu listing an assortment of makes and models. 1-2-3 will even support separate printers for text and graphics if you desire, but it is important that the printer type chosen for either graphs or text be on the installation list. Although a different brand may in fact emulate one of the listed models, you will want to verify the support at the time you purchase the printer rather than after you have taken it to your office, if the printer type does not appear on the list.

1-2-3 supports both a text and a graphics printer because some text printers will not print graphs. A letter-quality daisy wheel printer may be used to print your text, for example, but this printer could not support printing graphs. A dot matrix printer can print both text and graphs in either draft or near-letter-quality mode in most cases. Laser and ink jet printers are also gaining in popularity and are supported by Release 2 of 1-2-3.

If you have both a dot matrix and a letter-quality printer, you may want to use the letter-quality device for text and the dot matrix for printing graphics. To connect either of these printers to your system, you will also need a cable and an available port. It is possible to connect printers to both parallel and serial ports as long as they are compatible, but there are some special settings if you use a serial connection. First, you must set the printer's baud rate to control the speed of data transfer. At any baud rate except 110 you should also set 1 stop bit, 8 data bits, and no parity. With a speed of 110 there should be 2 stop bits. Once the program is loaded, use the Worksheet Global Default Printer Interface command and select the baud rate that matches your printer's rate. Do this by typing **/WGDPI**, pointing to the baud rate you need, and pressing ENTER. Save this change with the Worksheet Global Default Update command (/WGDU). With PrintGraph, you need to make a similar change by using Settings Hardware Interface. If you are purchasing your system at the same time as 1-2-3, your dealer will normally assist you with this installation.

Adding a Plotter

A plotter provides another option for producing graphs. With most devices you can use either paper or transparencies in your plotter, with the appropriate pens, to create the display medium of your choice. Since 1-2-3 supports only a limited number of plotters, make sure that the one you are considering purchasing is on the acceptable list; otherwise it may not function with 1-2-3.

The Operating System

The operating system is the control program that resides in the memory of your computer regardless of the software you are working with. It controls the interface between the various devices and establishes the format for data storage on disk. The different releases of 1-2-3 are compatible with different versions of the DOS operating system. Since DOS is absolutely essential to utilizing your computer and its software, make sure you have a version of DOS that is compatible with your release of 1-2-3.

Release 1A of 1-2-3 was designed to run under DOS 1.1 or higher. With Release 2.0 and Release 2.01, the version number depends on the type of system you have. For the IBM PC, PC/XT, Portable, P, and 3270-PC, use DOS 2.0 or higher. For the IBM PC/AT, use DOS 3.0 or higher. Using the IBM PCjr with the Utility program requires DOS 2.1. With the Compaq machines, use 2.02 or higher; and with the AT&T, use 2.11 or higher. All this may seem a bit confusing, but your dealer can advise you based upon your configuration. The dealer can also give you information about new versions of DOS and the OS/2 operating system.

Noting Your Equipment

You are now ready to proceed with the steps needed to install your 1-2-3 disks. First, however, make a note of your hardware configuration. Figure A.2 provides a convenient form for doing this. You will want this information available when you use the Install program.

INSTALLING 1-2-3

The purpose of installation is to tailor your 1-2-3 disks to run with your specific hardware configuration. If 1-2-3 only ran with one type of hardware, this step would not be necessary. But since it is,

Hardware

Computer manufacturer   _____

Computer model   _____

Graphics card   _____

Monitor   _____

RAM   _____

Printer manufacturer/model   _____

Printer interface
(serial or parallel)   _____

Plotter model   _____

Plotter interface
(serial or parallel)   _____

Disk drives — number and type _____
(Hard vs. Floppy)

Software

DOS version number   _____

Lotus 1-2-3 version   _____

FIGURE A.2   Configuration worksheet

remember that it offers you an advantage: You can continue to use the package even if you change your hardware configuration to include a plotter, a new printer, or a color monitor.

Preliminary Steps

When you purchase 1-2-3, the package you receive contains an envelope with several diskettes. With release 2.0 and 2.01 you receive the System Disk, the Backup System Disk, the Utility Disk, the PrintGraph Disk, the Install Library Disk, and A View of

1-2-3. With release 1A you receive only five disks; there is no Install Library Disk in the earlier release. Release 1A has a Tutorial Disk in place of Release 2's A View of 1-2-3. The following description of the various disks refers to the set of disks that make up the Release 2 package.

The disk you will use most often is the *System Disk*, since it contains the 1-2-3 program and the Lotus Access System. The Backup System Disk is an exact duplicate of this disk. The second disk is needed because the System Disk cannot be copied. (Although you might be successful in copying each of the files, your new disk would not run because of a special protection scheme.) Lotus would not want you to be unable to use your 1-2-3 system because of a damaged System Disk.

The *Utility Disk* contains two important routines. The first is the Install program, which copies drivers from the library disk to your other disks so they will work with your individual equipment configuration. Drivers are files that contain information concerning the interface requirements for your specific equipment. For example, 1-2-3 will interface differently with a laser printer than with a dot matrix model. Once these driver sets are installed, you will not have to be concerned further with equipment needs unless you change your system. Placing these driver files on your diskettes or hard drive is a critical step if you plan to use the printer or other output device for worksheets and graphs.

The second application on your Utility Disk is the Translate program. This program allows you to maximize the benefit from data recorded in another program such as dBASE III or VisiCalc by translating the data to a format that 1-2-3 can use.

The *Install Library Disk* contains the driver files for all the equipment Lotus supports, including printer drivers, plotter drivers, and display drivers. When you run the Install program and indicate your equipment selection, the drivers will be copied from the library disk to your other disks.

A *View of 1-2-3* is new with Release 2. It replaces the Tutorial Disk provided with Release 1A. You will find that this provides an excellent overview whether you are a new user wanting to get a feel for the package or an experienced user wanting a quick look at some of Release 2's new features. It is organized into lessons to allow you to spend a few minutes or a few hours with the program. Release 2.0 and 2.01 also include a comprehensive tutorial manual to introduce you to a variety of 1-2-3 commands and techniques.

The *PrintGraph Disk* is essential for printing copies of graphs created with the package. It interfaces with a wide variety of graphics printers and plotters. It also allows you to access a variety of fonts for titles on your graphs.

You will want to complete several preliminary steps with this set of disks before running Install. First, locate your DOS disk, the keyboard guide, all six 1-2-3 disks, and five blank formatted diskettes (unless you have a hard disk). Since the steps required for installation with a hard disk are different from those required with diskettes, the procedures will be covered separately.

Installing With Diskettes

Use the instructions in this section if you have a system with one or two diskette drives but no hard drive (see Figure A.3). The basic steps in installation, in this case, are making backup copies of four of the Lotus disks, copying critical DOS files to the disks, and running the Lotus installation program. Note that for Release 2, these preliminary steps will not allow you to make the System Disk a bootable disk, as was true with earlier releases. Since Release 1A is no longer being marketed, the installation instructions given here are for Release 2.0 and 2.01. If you have an uninstalled copy of 1A, read the instructions at the front of your Lotus manual, as there are a few differences in the installation process between Release 1A and Release 2.

MAKING BACKUP DISKETTES You already have a backup copy of the System Disk, and the hidden protection scheme will not allow you to make additional backup copies. The disks you will be backing up, therefore, are the Utility Disk, the PrintGraph Disk,

One floppy disk drive

Two floppy disk drives

One floppy and one hard disk

FIGURE A.3   System configurations

the Install Library Disk, and A View of 1-2-3. It is worthwhile to back up all the diskettes, even if you think you will not use some of them. After completing the backup, store the original disks in a safe place and use the backups.

The procedure for backing up the disks is as follows:

1. Format six diskettes by placing your DOS disk in drive A and a blank diskette in drive B and typing **FORMAT B: /S**. The /S will put part of DOS on the disk. When the format operation is complete, DOS will prompt you to create another disk. Respond by entering a Y and press RETURN until all six disks are formatted. If you only have one disk drive you will need to wait until DOS prompts you to insert the disk to be formatted and then place it in drive A.

2. Create an appropriate label for each of the disks: Backup PrintGraph, Backup Utility Disk, and so on.

3. With DOS loaded in your system, place the PrintGraph Disk in drive A and a formatted blank diskette in drive B.

4. Type **COPY A:*.* B: /V** and press the ENTER key. Lotus recommends the use of the Copy command rather than Diskcopy because the /V parameter for Copy causes DOS to verify each file after it is copied to ensure that it matches the original exactly.
With a one-drive system, DOS will prompt you to take the disks in and out several times, since DOS can copy only a limited amount of data at one time.

5. Once the first disk has been copied, remove both the original and the copy from the drives and apply the label to the newly copied disk. Then proceed to copy the other three disks.
If you use the copies and store the originals, you can remedy a failure in one of the copies by making another copy from the original disk. If the System Disk should fail, use the Backup System Disk and refer to the instructions in the Lotus Customer Assurance Plan for obtaining a replacement.

COPYING COMMAND.COM TO YOUR DISKETTES   Although
it is not possible to place all of the DOS files on your Lotus disks
because of space limitations, you may want to place the DOS
COMMAND.COM file on the disks. This will prevent an error
message from appearing every time you exit 1-2-3 or one of the
other programs. If you choose to omit this step, you will see the
error message "Insert disk with /COMMAND.COM in drive A
and strike any key when ready" every time you exit 1-2-3 or an
auxiliary program.

You will probably want to add COMMAND.COM to the
System Disk, the Backup System Disk, A View of 1-2-3, Print-
Graph, and the Utility Disk. Placing COMMAND.COM on the
disks will not make the disks bootable, however, so you will have to
load DOS into your system before beginning to work with any of
these programs. The following directions for copying COM-
MAND.COM are for a two-drive system, but you can easily adapt
them to a one-drive system by using the instructions in the preceding section.

1. Insert your DOS disk in drive A and boot your system if
   the DOS A> prompt is not on your screen.

2. Place your System Disk in drive B without a write protect
   tab.

3. Type **COPY A:COMMAND.COM B:** /V and press
   ENTER.
   This will copy COMMAND.COM to drive B and verify
   the copy to ensure that it is correct.

4. Remove the System Disk. Repeat the procedure for the
   Backup System Disk, A View of 1-2-3, the Utility Disk,
   and PrintGraph.

You are now ready to install 1-2-3 for your equipment.
Make sure that you have your completed equipment configuration worksheet (Figure A.2) handy.

RUNNING INSTALL WITH A FLOPPY DISK SYSTEM   It is possible to use your 1-2-3 package without running the Install pro-

```
┌─────────────────────────────────────────────────────────────┐
│                    M A I N   M E N U                          │
├─────────────────────────────────────────────────────────────┤
│                                                               │
│                                      ┌────────────────────────┤
│                                      │Select First-Time Installation │
│  Use ↓ or ↑ to move menu pointer.    │for a guided path through the  │
│                                      │installation procedure.  This  │
│                                      │path lets you select drivers   │
│  ▓First-Time Installation▓           │for screen display and for     │
│   Change Selected Equipment          │printers.                      │
│   Advanced Options                   │                               │
│   Exit Install Program               │                               │
│                                      │                               │
│                                      │                               │
│                                      │                               │
│                                      └────────────────────────┐     │
│                                                               │
├───────────────────────────────────┬───────────────────────────┤
│ ↓ and ↑ move menu pointer.         │ [F1] displays a Help screen.  │
│ [RETURN] selects highlighted choice.│ [F9] takes you to main menu.  │
│ [ESCAPE] takes you to previous screen.│ [F10] shows current selections.│
└───────────────────────────────────┴───────────────────────────┘
```

FIGURE A.4

gram, but without it you will not be able to use a printer or display a graph. Since you probably will want to do at least one of these things eventually, you might as well get the installation completed now. You will want to start the Install program directly from DOS, so make sure the DOS disk is in drive A. Then boot your system.

1. Check for the A> prompt on your screen and reboot if it is not there. Next, place the Utility Disk in drive A. Type **Install** and press ENTER.

2. Follow the directions on your screen for inserting the Utility, Install, and System disks. Install will repeat its message if you should accidentally place the wrong disk in the drive.

3. Since this is a first-time installation, select that option from the menu screen presented to you (see Figure A.4). 1-2-3

will then take you on a guided tour through the entire installation process. Since keyboards vary slightly between systems, you will want to refer to the manual that came with your computer system if you wish to make selections described at the bottom of the screen and are uncertain of the location of keys on your keyboard.

4. You will be asked to select the monitor and the text and graphics printers in your configuration. Figures A.5, A.6, and A.7 show several of the selection screens that will be presented to you during installation. Refer to the equipment configuration you listed on your worksheet to supply the correct selections.

5. If you are creating only one set of installation parameters, you will want to save your selections as 123.SET. If you

```
                 S I N G L E   M O N I T O R
┌──────────────────────────────────────────────────────────────────┐
│ Hercules card (80 x 25)                                            │
│ Hercules card (90 x 38)                                            │
│ IBM color card, single-color monitor    ┌──────────────────────┐  │
│ IBM color card                          │ Select this for an IBM│  │
│ Plantronics ColorPlus card              │ monochrome monitor with a│
│ Enhanced Graphics Adapter               │ Hercules graphics card if│
│ AT&T 6300, single-color monitor         │ you want a standard 80 x 25│
│ AT&T 6300, color monitor                │ screen display.        │  │
│ AT&T 6300 (80 x 50)                     │                        │  │
│ IBM 3270-PC, color monitor              │                        │  │
│ IBM 3270-PC, monochrome monitor         │                        │  │
│ IBM 3270-PC/GX                          │                        │  │
│ COMPAQ, single-color monitor            │                        │  │
│ COMPAQ, color monitor                   │                        │  │
│ IBM Portable Computer                   └──────────────────────┘  │
│ Use ↓ to see more selections below.                                │
├──────────────────────────────────────────────────────────────────┤
│ ↓ and ↑  move menu pointer.       [F1] displays a Help screen.     │
│ [RETURN] selects highlighted choice.  [F9] takes you to main menu. │
│ [ESCAPE] takes you to previous screen.  [F10] shows current selections.│
└──────────────────────────────────────────────────────────────────┘
```

FIGURE A.5

plan to create two or more sets, you can start over with the first-time installation option for each driver. It is important that you use a different name for each driver. After proceeding to the end of the installation process and saving your choices on the System Disk, the PrintGraph Disk, and A View of 1-2-3, you will be back at the main installation menu (Figure A.4).

At this time you may want to press F10 to view your current selections (you will see something like Figure A.8), or you may want to alter some of the advanced options such as sort sequences that will control the order that 1-2-3 uses for resequencing information in its data management environment. The only way to access the advanced options is to select Modify Current Driver Set from

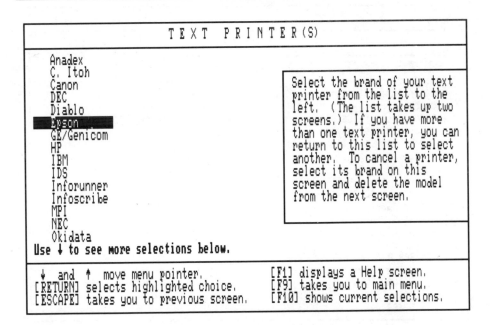

FIGURE A.6

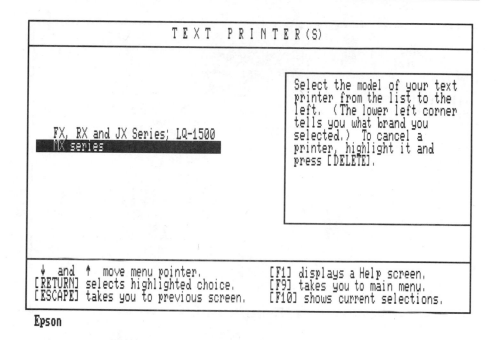

TEXT PRINTER(S)

FX, RX and JX Series; LQ-1500
MX series

Select the model of your text
printer from the list to the
left. (The lower left corner
tells you what brand you
selected.) To cancel a
printer, highlight it and
press [DELETE].

↓ and ↑ move menu pointer.   [F1] displays a Help screen.
[RETURN] selects highlighted choice. [F9] takes you to main menu.
[ESCAPE] takes you to previous screen. [F10] shows current selections.

Epson

FIGURE A.7

the Advanced Options menu. This will be covered in the "Modifying the Current Driver" section later in the chapter. You have the option of placing numbers first or last in the sort sequence with one of the advanced installation options.

INSTALLING WITH A HARD DISK   Installing with a hard disk is actually a little easier than installing with a floppy disk system. You will not have to make separate backup copies of the Lotus disks because you will be copying them to your hard disk and can therefore use your original diskettes as backups. This eliminates the formatting step to prepare the diskettes and expedites the installation program, since you will not have to interchange disks in your drives. Everything that Install needs will already be on your hard drive.

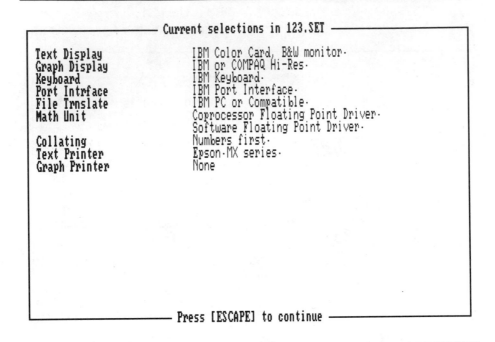

┌──────────── Current selections in 123.SET ────────────┐

Text Display   IBM Color Card, B&W monitor.
Graph Display   IBM or COMPAQ Hi-Res.
Keyboard   IBM Keyboard.
Port Intrface   IBM Port Interface.
File Trnslate   IBM PC or Compatible.
Math Unit   Coprocessor Floating Point Driver.
                        Software Floating Point Driver.
Collating   Numbers first.
Text Printer   Epson-MX series.
Graph Printer   None

└──────────── Press [ESCAPE] to continue ────────────┘

FIGURE A.8

You will have one additional step, establishing a subdirectory for your 1-2-3 files, with this approach. Subdirectories provide a method for establishing different categories of information on your disk. They can save a significant amount of time, since 1-2-3 will have to search through only a section of the entries on the disk rather than through a directory with an entry for every file.

Our instructions for this section assume that DOS is on your hard drive and that you are using Release 2.0 or 2.01 of 1-2-3. This section also contains information on the optional removal of the System Disk from the startup procedure for 1-2-3. This disk must normally be inserted in drive A even though you have copied the data to your hard disk. 1-2-3 checks the authorization code from the diskette before proceeding unless you take a special step to prevent this from happening.

ESTABLISHING A SUBDIRECTORY   The preliminary steps for a hard disk installation will proceed quickly. You need only set up your 1-2-3 subdirectory and copy the files to the hard disk.

1. Start DOS in your system by booting with the door to drive A open. This will force your system to boot from the copy of DOS stored on your hard disk, drive C.

2. Enter the date if you do not have a clock card. The format you should use is 12-15-87 for a date of December 15, 1987. Press ENTER after supplying the date.

3. Enter the time in the form HH:MM. If the time is 1:30 P.M., for example, type **13:30** and press ENTER. If there is a clock card in your system, you do not have to enter the time.

Now establish the subdirectory that will contain all your 1-2-3 files. For our example we will use a subdirectory name of 123, but the choice of a name is up to you.

1. At C>, the DOS prompt, type **MD \123** to make a subdirectory called 123. This directory will be immediately below the root directory for your disk.

2. Make 123 the current directory by typing **CD \123**.

You now have a directory to which you can copy all your 1-2-3 files. This is a real convenience, since it will save you from having to swap disks as you transfer from 1-2-3 to PrintGraph to Translate.

1. Place your 1-2-3 System Disk in drive A and close the door.

2. Type **COPY A:*.* C:**. This will copy every file except the hidden protection to the hard disk. Remove the System Disk from drive A.

3. Repeat this with every disk except the Backup System Disk. When you have completed the process, every file from every disk will reside in the 123 directory.

RUNNING INSTALL WITH A HARD-DISK SYSTEM   With the DOS C> prompt on your screen, type **Install** and press ENTER. The rest is easy, since all of the installation files you will need are now on your hard disk. With the information from Figure A.2 handy, type in the information that Install needs. One of your options with Release 2.01 will be to make one copy of 1-2-3 on the hard disk that will not require the use of the key disk. With Release A, this permanent copy was not an option. It was available in Release 2 but required the Copyhard program provided on the Lotus disk. If you have Release 2.01, you can still use Copyhard if you encounter difficulty with the automated process or change your mind after installation. Specifics on how to use it are included in this appendix.

1. Since this is a first-time installation, select that option from the menu screen presented to you (see Figure A.4). 1-2-3 will then take you on a guided tour through the entire installation process. Since each computer has slight variations in the arrangement of its keyboard, you will want to refer to the manual that came with your computer if you wish to make selections described at the bottom of the screen and are uncertain of the location of keys on your keyboard.

2. With a first time installation under Release 2.01, 1-2-3 will ask you if you wish to make a single-use copy of 1-2-3 on the hard disk that does not require the key disk. You can enter Yes to make this copy, or you can continue to input the key disk in drive A whenever you use the program.

3. You will be asked to select the monitor, text, and graphics printers in your configuration. Figures A.5 through A.7 show several of the selection screens that will be presented to you during installation. Refer to the equipment configuration you listed on your worksheet to supply the correct selections.

4. If you are creating only one set of installation parameters, save your selections as 123.SET. If you are creating two or

more sets, each set must have a different name. After proceeding to the end of installation and saving your choices on the Systems Disk, the PrintGraph Disk, and A View of 1-2-3, you will be back at the main installation menu (Figure A.4).

At this time you may want to press F10 to view your current selections (you will see something like Figure A.8), or you may want to alter some of the advanced options such as sort sequences. The only way to access the advanced options is to select Modify Current Driver Set from the Advanced Options menu. This will be covered in the "Modifying the Current Driver" section later in the chapter. You have the option of placing numbers first or last in the sort sequence with one of the advanced installation options.

With Install completed, you are now ready to use 1-2-3. You can display graphs and interface with your printer or plotter. Changing between 1-2-3 programs will be easy; all the Lotus files are stored on your disk. Since the System Disk contains a key to unlock 1-2-3's features, however, you will still need to insert that disk in drive A every time you load 1-2-3 into your system. Once 1-2-3 is started, you can remove this key disk and use the files on your hard disk. There are two separate processes for doing this, depending on whether you are using the AT or another system. The next section will provide instructions for completing this task for an IBM PC or compatible while the section after that will provide instructions for an IBM AT.

COPYON AND COPYOFF   Copyon and Copyoff are optional programs for adding the key information to your hard disk and taking it off again when working with Release 2.0. With Release 2.01, this process is automated directly from the Install program, or you can use Copy hard to place it on the disk yourself. This information allows you to start 1-2-3 from your hard disk without having to place the System Disk in drive A. These two programs are not designed to work with the IBM AT. To transfer the key information on that system, use the two programs described in the next section.

The Copyon program takes the key information recorded on the System Disk and places it on your hard drive. Copyon can be used with only one hard-disk system at a time. If you wish to use it with another system, you must first use Copyoff to remove the information from the first hard disk. After this process is complete, you can use Copyon with the second system.

Take precautions to ensure that the key information is not damaged once it is placed on your hard disk. Use the DOS command RESTORE /P for file restoration. The /P option causes DOS to prompt you before restoring files that were changed since the last backup and to wait for your confirmation before restoring a file. When you restore files from a backup, you must tell DOS that you do not wish to restore read-only files. Since this key information is in a read-only file, it will remain unaffected. Also, if you ever need to reformat your hard disk, first remove the key information with either Copyoff or Copyhard /U. Note that Copyon and Copyhard cannot be used if your device is a server in a local area network.

Copyon and Copyoff expect your hard disk to be drive C. Start with the C> prompt on your screen.

1. Make 123 the current directory by typing **CD \123** and pressing ENTER. Of course, if you used a different directory name for your 1-2-3 files, you will want to make that directory current instead.

2. Remove the write protect tabs from the PrintGraph Disk and the System Disk.

3. Place PrintGraph in drive A.

4. Type **A:** and press ENTER. Drive A will now be the current drive.

5. Type **Copyon** and press ENTER. Review the screen message as a reminder that your disk should be drive C.

6. You can press any key to continue or CTRL-C to stop.

7. Remove PrintGraph from drive A at the prompt.

8. Place the System Disk in drive A, close the drive door, and press ENTER. A message will ask you if you wish to copy the protected information to the hard disk, and you can respond with **Y** for yes. Messages will appear, indicating that both the key information and the serial number have been copied to your hard disk. If you had typed **N**, Copyon would have stopped and a DOS prompt would have appeared on your screen.

Copyoff allows you to remove the key information from your hard disk temporarily or permanently. The procedure for removing this key information is as follows:

1. Start with the C> prompt on your screen.

2. Make 123 your current directory with CD \123. If you used a diffcrent directory for 123, use the name of the other directory.

3. Remove the write protect tabs from the System Disk and the PrintGraph Disk.

4. Place the PrintGraph Disk in drive A.

5. Make drive A the current drive by typing **A:** and pressing ENTER.

6. Type **Copyoff** and press ENTER.

7. Press any key to continue or CTRL-C to stop.

8. If you chose to continue, remove PrintGraph when prompted. Insert the System Disk in drive A and press ENTER.

9. Type **Y** and press ENTER to continue or **N** and ENTER to stop.

When Copyoff finishes, a message on your screen will inform you that the key information has been removed from your hard disk. You can now use Copyon to place the information on a new hard disk.

COPYHARD AND COPYHARD /U   Copyhard is used for systems where the hard drive has a designation other than drive C. If you use Copyhard on your IBM AT, you will want to run it from your low-capacity disk drive (360K). If you remove the key information with Copyhard /U using the 1.2MB high-density drive, you will not be able to access that information later from a low-capacity drive.

The steps required for adding the key information to a hard disk with Copyhard are as follows:

1. Make sure your hard-disk prompt (D>, for example) is on the screen.

2. Make your 1-2-3 directory the current directory; that is, type **CD \ 123** and press ENTER if your directory name is 123.

3. Remove the write protect tabs from PrintGraph and the System Disk and place the PrintGraph Disk in drive A.

4. Type **A:** as the current drive unless you are using an AT and B is your low-capacity drive. In the latter case, type **B:**. Press ENTER after your entry.

5. Type **Copyhard** and press ENTER to access the program.

6. Type the same disk drive letter that you used in step 4.

7. Type the letter for your hard-disk drive, for example, **D:**.

8. Remove the PrintGraph Disk from the drive specified in step 6, insert the System Disk, and press ENTER.

9. Type **Y** and press ENTER to proceed. If you want to stop, type **N** and ENTER.

The Copyhard program will now have copied the key code to your hard disk. You will not need to insert the diskette when starting 1-2-3 as long as the code remains on your hard disk.

Before you can use Copyhard on a second hard disk, you must remove the key code from the first hard disk with the Copyhard / U option. In addition to removing the code from the hard disk, this program flags your disks so they can be used to place the key code on another hard disk. Here are the steps required for this program:

1. Ensure that your hard disk prompt (D>, for example) is on the screen.

2. Type **CD \123** and press ENTER to change the current directory.

3. Remove the write protect tabs from your System Disk and PrintGraph Disk, then insert PrintGraph in drive A (or drive B, the low-density drive, on an AT).

4. Type the drive letter and a colon, then press ENTER. Use the same drive as in step 3.

5. Type **Copyhard /U** and press ENTER.

6. Enter the drive letter used in step 4 and press ENTER.

7. Type the drive letter for your hard disk (for example, D) and press ENTER.

8. Remove PrintGraph at the prompt and insert the System Disk in the same drive, then press ENTER.

9. Type **Y** and press ENTER to continue. To abort the process, leaving the key information intact, type **N** and press ENTER.

When this step completes, the key information will be removed from your hard disk. This will allow you to use Copyhard to place it on a new hard disk if you wish.

Creating More Than One Driver Set

If you are using your Lotus software on more than one computer, or if you frequently alter the configuration of your system, you will want more than one driver set. This will allow you to use 1-2-3 with both your home system and the one at the office, for example, without having to change the installation parameters each time.

If you use more than one driver set, pick a meaningful driver name for each, such as 2MONITOR.SET, PLOTTER.SET, or HOME.SET. You can use up to eight characters for the first part of the name. You must avoid the following symbols: , . ; : / ? * ^ + = < > [ ] / '. You also must use SET as the extension for the file name after the dot (.), for example, COLOR.SET.

Use the first-time installation option to create each driver set. Save each driver set under a different name. You may want to store these multiple drivers on a separate disk, as there will not be room on your Lotus disks for more than one or two driver sets. In this case, when you are prompted to insert your System Disk to save the newly created driver set, insert a blank disk instead. Then return to the installation menu rather than inserting PrintGraph and the other disks.

To use one of your other driver sets, copy it to the 1-2-3 disk before starting the program. Another option is to specify the path-name of the driver set when you start 1-2-3, for example, 123 B:\HOME.SET. The pathname is the drive designation followed by the directory and file name. On a floppy disk without subdirectories, simply give the drive designation and the file name, separated by a backslash (\).

Modifying the Current Driver

Install has two kinds of options for modifying the 1-2-3 driver files: the Modify option and the Advanced options. Modify allows you to change the hardware configuration for your existing driver set. It is the option to use if you have upgraded your hardware with a new printer or a plotter, for example, and wish to make a permanent change in your driver set.

The Advanced options allow you to change the collating sequence for the existing driver set. With earlier releases you had no choice about the collating sequence, since standard ASCII sequence was used for sorting. However, Release 2 provides three options: Numbers First, Numbers Last, and the standard ASCII sequence. If you are not familiar with sorting sequences, look at the 1-2-3 help screen shown in Figure A.9 for a sample of the three options. The Advanced options also offer choices such as making another driver set current and adding new drivers. To make a

```
┌──────────────── Help Screen ────────────────┐
│                                              │
│ The collating sequence determines the order in which 1-2-3 sorts entries
│ that include both numbers and letters.  Here are the results of a sort in
│ ascending order, depending on which collating sequence you choose:
│
│   Numbers first         Numbers last          ASCII
│   -------------         -------------         -----
│   22 Rye Road           One emerald city      22 Rye Road
│   23 Chestnut Avenue    One Emerson Place     23 Chestnut Avenue
│   39 Columbus Street    Parkway Towers        39 Columbus Street
│   One emerald city      Three Center Plaza    One Emerson Place
│   One Emerson Place     22 Rye Road           One emerald city
│   Parkway Towers        23 Chestnut Avenue    Parkway Towers
│   Three Center Plaza    39 Columbus Street    Three Center Plaza
│
│ Note that ASCII is identical to Numbers first, except that uppercase letters
│ come before lowercase.  Earlier releases of 1-2-3 use the ASCII collating
│ sequence.
│
└──────────────── Press [ESCAPE] to leave Help ────────────────┘
```

FIGURE A.9

change to a feature like the collating sequence, select Advanced
Options from the menu and then select Modify Current Set from
the second-level menu.

Changing Other Configuration Parameters

Most of the hardware configuration options are specified in the
installation process. However, two additional options that could
require frequent change can be changed directly from 1-2-3. One is
the disk-drive assignment for data files, and the other is the printer
settings. The disk-drive assignment can be changed from the

default drive of B to A or C. The command to do this within 1-2-3 is /Worksheet Global Default Disk. Printer options can be changed with /Worksheet Global Default Printer.

Preparing Data Disks

Whether you have Lotus on a hard or a floppy disk system, you can use diskettes for data storage. They will need to be prepared before you can store data on them. Use the formatting process described in your DOS manual under FORMAT before storing data on new diskettes. Since you already have an extra diskette prepared, you can wait to prepare additional data diskettes if you choose.

B

GLOSSARY

@Function A prerecorded formula that is already stored internally in 1-2-3. You can access these functions by following a set of rules stating that built-in functions are accessed with the @ followed by a keyword and, in most cases, a set of parentheses encasing arguments that state the specific use functions with relation options, including statistical, mathematical, and financial. For example, @SUM(A1..B10) will total all the values in the cells within the range A1..B10.

Absolute A type of reference used in a worksheet formula. An absolute cell reference always refers to the original cell regardless of where the formula is copied. An absolute reference is distinguished from other types of references by the $ in front of both the row and the column portion of the address. For example, $A$2, $D$50, $Z$3.

Alignment   The placement of a label entry within a cell. 1-2-3 allows left, right, or center alignment of label entries within a cell. Special label indicators are used to control the alignment. The caret (^) is used for center alignment, a single quotation mark (') represents left alignment, and the double quotation mark (") represents right alignment.

Arguments   Individual values, quote-enclosed labels, range references, or range names that define how you wish to use a built-in function or a command language instruction. The number and type of arguments supplied will depend on the function or command language instruction selected. When cell references are included in your arguments, you have the option of typing the reference or pointing to the cell or range you wish to select.

Arithmetic Operators   Symbols used within 1-2-3 formulas to define the type of mathematical operation to be performed. When more than one arithmetic operator is included in a formula, they are evaluated from left to right, using a priority order for the operators. The valid arithmetic operators and their order of precedence is:

^	exponentiation
+, -	positive, negative number
*, /	multiplication, division
+, -	addition, subtraction

Parentheses can be used to override the order of precedence.

ASCII   A format for file storage where text and special characters are assigned code numbers. This standard coding system facilitates the exchange of information between programs, since standard codes represent each character. 1-2-3 is able to bring ASCII data into the worksheet with the / File Import command. The characters in the acronym ASCII represent American Standard Code for Information Interchange.

Axis   The horizontal (X axis) or vertical (Y axis) line, which provide the framework for the construction of most types of graphs. The Y axis functions as a scale for a quantitative measurement of the data shown on the graph. The X axis is used to represent the categories in the data series that are being plotted.

Built-in Function   See @ *Function*.

Cell   A single location on the worksheet. You have the option of storing a number, label, or formula in a worksheet cell. Other characteristics, such as label alignment and formatting, can also be specified for one or more worksheet cells.

Cell Pointer   The highlighted bar that marks the current cell on the worksheet. The cell pointer can be moved with the arrow keys, and with other special keys such as HOME, PGUP, and PGDN, and the F5 (GOTO) key.

Cell Reference   A reference to a worksheet cell in a formula. There are three types of cell references that you can use: a relative reference (A1), an absolute reference ($A$3), and a mixed reference (A$4 or $A4).

Circular Reference   A reference that depends on itself to calculate a result. For example, if a formula were stored in A1 as +A3/A1*2, this would be a circular reference. This particular example is a direct use of a reference to the cell itself. In many cases, the dependence on itself is indirect. 1-2-3 will place a CIRC indicator at the bottom of the screen when a worksheet contains a circular reference. In Release 2, you can use the / Worksheet Status command to identify the cell causing the circular reference.

Column   The vertical division of the worksheet, consisting of one cell from each row of the worksheet in a vertical column. A column of cells on the worksheet can be widened or narrowed as well as hidden with Release 2.

Column Width   The number of characters that can be stored in a column. You can change this number globally or for an individual column. The default column width is 9 characters. In Release 2, you can widen a column to 240 characters; in Release 1A, you can widen it to 72. The narrowest width permissible for both releases is 1 character.

Command Language   The advanced macro commands that make up the 1-2-3 macro command language. These commands provide a full programming language to 1-2-3 users that can extend the usefulness of the macro features beyond a duplication of 1-2-3 menu commands. The command-language instructions are all encased in braces ({}) and many use one or more arguments to refine their task. For example, {LET A1,0} is a command-language instruction.

Configuration File   The file that contains the default parameters for 1-2-3. Some of the options can be set with the /Worksheet Global Default command. Choosing the Update option from this same menu can save this file so that your changes are present in subsequent 1-2-3 sessions.

Control Panel   The area at the top of the 1-2-3 screen, consisting of three lines. The top line displays the current cell address, cell contents, and cell characteristics. The top line also displays a mode indicator in the right corner, which informs you that 1-2-3 is ready to process a new task or shows 1-2-3's current task. The second line serves a dual purpose. In EDIT mode, it functions as the edit line for altering your data. In MENU mode, the current menu is displayed in this line. The third line provides a description of the current menu selection in MENU mode.

Criterion   Specifications for searching the database. These criteria are entered on the worksheet and the /Data commands are invoked to either copy, highlight, or delete records that match the criterion you have entered.

Database   A collection of individual pieces of data about a group of objects. In 1-2-3, a database is an organized structure for storing items of information (fields) about objects on the worksheet. Taken together, all the data about one object in the set are considered to be a record, which is stored across a row of the worksheet. Fields are stored vertically in columns of the worksheet, with a record having one value in each field. There are numerous 1-2-3 commands to select records from the database, as well as those that sort it into a new sequence.

Debugging   The process of removing errors from a computer program. Since macros can be used to write a program within 1-2-3, it is appropriate to refer to the process of testing and eliminating errors from a macro as debugging.

Destination   An optional component of a Hal request, which is used to specify where the result of a Hal request is stored. A destination is used in a Hal request when you want to override the default destination.

Directory   The current location serving as the default for 1-2-3's disk files. Within the worksheet environment, the command /File Directory allows you to change the disk drive and subdirectory that are currently serving as the default. The PrintGraph program also has menu options for changing the default directory for both graph and font files.

Edit   The process of making corrections to an entry without needing to completely reenter the data.

Edit Line   The second line of the control panel. This is the line where 1-2-3 displays your data as you enter it. It also uses this line to display data that is being edited.

End   In READY mode, this indicates that you want to move your cursor to the last entry in a specific direction. After pressing

END, you will always press a direction arrow to indicate the direction you want to move. In EDIT mode, END takes you to the last character in a cell.

Erase   To remove from the worksheet or disk file. There are Worksheet Erase and Range Erase options in 1-2-3's menus. The Range Erase command removes the entries from the cells you specify. The Worksheet Erase option removes the current worksheet from memory completely. It requires a confirmation before proceeding with this option. The File Erase command makes the space a file is using available for the storage of new files and alters the entry within the file directory.

Error Message   A message that appears at the lower-left corner of the screen when an error condition is encountered. This message will appear when the printer is not ready or when the disk is full.

Expanded Memory   Memory above the 640K that can be added to the motherboard of a standard PC. This memory is added on an expansion card.

Extract   The process of pulling selected information from a database. Before you can use the /Data Extract command to accomplish this, you will need to set up an Output area and Criterion on the worksheet.

Field Names   The names that are used for the types of data stored in a database. In an employee database, some of the field names you might have are Last Name, Job Code, and Salary. In 1-2-3 they are always stored at the top of a column, with the values for each record placed beneath them.

File   An organized collection of data on the disk. 1-2-3 uses filename extensions to distinguish between the various types of files it stores on disk. Print files have a filename extension of .PRN, worksheet files an extension of .WK1, and graph files have an extension of .PIC.

Filename   The name that is used to access data stored on a diskette. This name must follow standard DOS rules and consist of from 1 to 8 characters in the name portion of the entry. It may also include an optional 1- to 3-character filename extension. If this extension is used, a period will separate it from the filename.

Fonts   A set of characters in a specific format. 1-2-3's graphic features support various fonts for use in graph titles, legends, and labels.

Format   The type of display used to present values. The format displayed may portray less internal accuracy than the package can support. Some of the permissible formats are currency, percent, scientific notation, and date.

Formula   A value entry in a worksheet cell that performs a calculation. A formula in 1-2-3 can be up to 240 characters long.

Function Keys   Special keys at the left or top of the keyboard that give you quick access to some of 1-2-3's features. 1-2-3 may use these keys differently from how other packages use the same keys, as each software vendor may use them in any way it chooses.

Graph   A representation of numeric worksheet data in a graphic format, which permits easy interpretation of results. 1-2-3 supports five graph formats: pie charts, line graphs, XY graphs, bar charts, and stacked bar charts.

Gridlines   Horizontal and vertical lines that can be added to a graph to aid interpretation of the data points. These lines extend from the points on one or both axes.

Header   A line that can be printed at the top of every page. This line can include a report name, the preparer's name, the date, the page number, or any other information you would like to include at the top of each page of a report.

Home   The A1 location on the worksheet screen. In EDIT mode, the HOME position is the first character in the entry being edited.

Import   The process of bringing text into the worksheet. Text can be imported with the /File Import command as numbers or text. The text option brings in the complete line in the text file as a long label. The numbers option only brings in the numeric values from a line of text but stores each one as a separate cell entry across a row of the worksheet.

Label   A series of characters you want treated as text. Label entries cannot be used in arithmetic formulas. Release 2 allows you to use labels in special string formulas and functions.

Label Indicator   The special character at the beginning of a cell entry that identifies the entry as a label. If you enter a non-numeric character in a cell, 1-2-3 will generate this indicator for you. If you enter a numeric character as the first character in a cell, you will have to enter the label indicator unless you want 1-2-3 to treat the entry as a label. The default label indicator is a single quotation mark, indicating that the entry should be left-aligned within the cell. A double quotation mark can be used for right alignment, and a caret symbol can be used for center alignment.

Legend   A description, added to the bottom of a graph, that distinguishes one set of data on the graph from other data series that may also be shown. If a hatch-mark pattern is used to shade bars, the legend identifies which data sets each pattern represents. If symbols are used to mark the various points on a line graph, the hatch-mark pattern identifies the data represented by each.

Location   An optional component in a Hal request that specifies where an action is to be performed. In the request **format row 10 as currency**, row 10 is the location.

Logical Operator   Used when you want 1-2-3 to evaluate an expression to determine whether the expression is true or false. The simple logical operators and their meanings are:

=	equal to
>	greater than
>=	greater than or equal to
<	less than
<=	less than or equal to
<>	not equal

In addition, three compound logical operators are used to join logical expressions: #AND#, #OR#, and #NOT#. For example, @IF(A1>7 #AND# B3=6,0,12).

Macro   A form of shorthand that allows you to record 1-2-3 formulas in worksheet cells easily and to execute these same entries as commands at a later time with equal ease. Macros also extend beyond this and allow you to create complete applications with your own menus and other features, using the extensions that the command-language instructions provide.

Macro Keyword   An instruction from 1-2-3's macro command language. This word is encased in braces and used with arguments to make your specific needs known to 1-2-3. A macro keyword might look something like this within a macro:

{LET A1,1}

Margin   The amount of white space that you wish to leave around a printed document. 1-2-3 has default settings for a top, bottom, right, and left margin but allows you to change any of them.

Math Co-processor   A special chip that can be added to your computer to enhance the processing speed.

Menu   A selection of features presented in a horizontal line at the top of the screen. You can activate each menu option by pointing to it and pressing RETURN or by typing the single letter beginning the selection.

Mode Indicator   The indicator in the upper right corner of the 1-2-3 display screen that lets you know what 1-2-3 is doing at any point in time. 1-2-3 will be waiting to process your next request only when this indicator reads READY.

Operator Precedence   The order in which the operators are processed. A list from the highest to the lowest priority follows, and you will find that formulas containing multiple operators with the same priority level will have these operators evaluated from left to right.

(	parentheses for grouping
^	exponentiation
+–	positive and negative indicators
/*	division and multiplication
+–	addition and subtraction
=<	
><=	logical operators
<=<>	
#NOT#	complex Not indicator
#AND#	complex And
#OR#	complex Or
&	string operator

Pointing   A method for building worksheet formulas. With the pointing method, you type the special characters and arithmetic operators but you point to the cell addresses of interest.

PrintGraph   A program that prints your 1-2-3 graphs. This program is included in your 1-2-3 package and supports interface with a variety of printers and plotters. It provides a variety of options, including different characters, sets (fonts), colors, sizes, and rotation.

Qualifier   An optional component in a Hal request that lets you override some of HAL's default settings. The request **\graph this** would creat a bar graph since that is the default. If the qualifier **as pie** is added, a pie chart will be produced instead.

RAM   Random Access Memory. The location where your 1-2-3 program and worksheet are stored.

Range   A group of cells on the worksheet. There are many commands in 1-2-3's menus that will operate on ranges, including /Range Erase, /Range Format, and /Range Name.

Range Name   A name that you assigned to a group of cells on the worksheet. This name can be from 1 to 14 characters in length. It can be used anywhere you would have used a range address to refer to the same cells. If you assign names to all ranges used in formula calculations, your formulas will be self-documenting.

Range Reference   A reference to one or more cells on the worksheet. To specify a range reference, use two cells at opposite corners of the range. For example, A1..A10, A2..B4, B4..A2, A1..A1 are all valid ranges. Just as a cell reference can be relative, absolute, or mixed, so a range reference has the same options.

Recalculation   The process of reevaluating all the formulas on the worksheet. The default for 1-2-3 is to use automatic recalculation, which means that every time you make a change to a cell entry, every formula on the worksheet will be reevaluated. If you disable the automatic recalculation, you will need to press F9 (CALC) when you want to recalculate the worksheet.

Relative   A type of cell reference used in formulas. A relative reference is entered as a reference to a specific cell in the original formula, but when this formula is copied the reference is updated based on the new location. It will still represent a cell with the same relative direction and distance as the original cell reference, but the reference will not be to the exact same cell as the original. A relative reference to a cell might look like A1, M2, or B5. It is the default reference type that is placed into a formula that you build with the pointing method, unless you take a special action to override this default.

Request   A phrase entered in a HAL request box to replace selections from a 1-2-3 menu. It can be as long as 240 characters.

Request Box   The box that appears in the panel for the entry of a Hal request when you enter a backslash (\).

Rounding   The process of effecting the internal precision of a number in memory. You can use 1-2-3's @ROUND function to reduce this internal precision. A number stored as 123.567 will be stored as 123.57 after being rounded to two decimal places. If this same number is rounded to a whole number, it will be 124. You can control which numbers are rounded and the place at which you would like rounding to occur.

Row   A horizontal line of consecutive cells on the worksheet. With Release 1A, there are 2048 rows on the worksheet; with Release 2 there are 8192 rows.

Setup String   A series of characters transmitted to the printer to activate certain printer features. Each printer has its own set of characters for its features. On an Epson MX 100 printer, compressed print is activated with a setup string of \015.

String   Series of characters. Release 2 of 1-2-3 has added features that work with strings. You can use the concatenation character & to join two strings. There are also a number of built-in functions that focus on string manipulation.

Titles   The text characters that are used to provide description on a graph. They can be placed at the top of the graph or along the X axis or Y axis. In the worksheet environment, titles can also refer to the data that you want to freeze on the top or left side of the screen as you scroll the cell pointer down or to the right.

Value   A number or formula entry on the worksheet.

Verb   A word in a Hal request that conveys the basic task to be accomplished. Almost all Hal requests begin with a verb.

Worksheet   The entire electronic sheet of paper that 1-2-3 creates in the memory of your computer system. This worksheet is composed of many cells organized into rows and columns.

X Axis   The horizontal axis on a graph. This is the axis on which the categories of a data series are shown.

Xtract   A file menu selection that creates a worksheet file containing a subset of the current worksheet. Only the range you specify will be saved to the worksheet file with this operation. You will have the option of saving formulas, labels, and values to this file. If you choose, you can create this file as a snapshot of the current worksheet with only labels and values stored in the new file. Xtract should be distinguished from Extract, which is used in the data-management environment to copy information from the database to another area of your worksheet.

Y Axis   The vertical axis on a bar, line, or XY graph that measures quantitative units such as dollars, units sold, or number of employees.

1-2-3's
BUILT-IN
FUNCTIONS

Function	Type	Available only in Release 2
@@(cell)	Special	•
@ABS(number)	Math	
@ACOS(number)	Math	
@ASIN(number)	Math	
@ATAN(number)	Math	
@ATAN2(number)	Math	
@AVG(list)	Statistical	
@CELL(attribute string, range)	Special	•
@CELLPOINTER(attribute string)	Special	•
@CHAR(code)	String	•

Function	Type	Available only in Release 2
@CHOOSE(number,list)	Special	
@CLEAN(string)	String	•
@CODE(string)	String	•
@COLS(range)	Special	•
@COS(number)	Math	
@COUNT(list)	Statistical	
@CTERM(interest,future value,present value)	Financial	•
@DATE(year,month,day)	Date & Time	
@DATEVALUE(date string)	Date & Time	•
@DAVG(input range,offset column,criteria range)	Database	
@DAY(serial date number)	Date & Time	
@DCOUNT(input range,offset column,criteria range)	Database	
@DDB(cost,salvage,life,period)	Financial	•
@DMAX(input range,offset column, criteria range)	Database	
@DMIN(input range,offset column,criteria range)	Database	
@DSTD(input range,offset column,criteria range)	Database	
@DSUM(input range, offset column,criteria range)	Database	
@DVAR(input range,offset column,criteria range)	Database	
@ERR	Special	
@EXACT(string1,string2)	String	•
@EXP(number)	Math	
@FALSE	Logical	
@FIND(search string,entire string,starting location)	String	•
@FV(payment,interest,term)	Financial	
@HLOOKUP(code to be looked up,table location,offset)	Special	
@HOUR(serial time number)	Date & Time	
@IF(condition to be tested,value if true,value if false)	Logical	

Function	Type	Available only in Release 2
@INDEX(table location,column number,row number)	Special	
@INT(number)	Math	
@IRR(guess,range)	Financial	
@ISERR(value)	Logical	
@ISNA(value)	Logical	
@ISNUMBER(value)	Logical	
@ISSTRING(number)	Logical	•
@LEFT(string,number of characters to be extracted)	String	•
@LENGTH(string)	String	•
@LN(number)	Math	
@LOG(number)	Math	
@LOWER(string)	String	•
@MAX(list)	Statistical	
@MID(string,start number,number of characters)	String	•
@MIN(list)	Statistical	
@MINUTE(serial time number)	Date & Time	•
@MOD(number,divisor)	Math	
@MONTH(serial date number)	Date & Time	
@N(range)	String	•
@NA	Special	
@NOW	Date & Time	•
@NPV(discount rate,range)	Financial	
@PI	Math	
@PMT(principal,interest,term of loan)	Financial	
@PROPER(string)	String	•
@PV(payment,periodic interest rate,number of periods)	Financial	
@RAND	Math	
@RATE(future value,present value,number of periods)	Financial	•

Function	Type	Available only in Release 2
@REPEAT(string,number of times)	String	•
@REPLACE(original string,start location, # characters, new string)	String	•
@RIGHT(string,number of characters to be extracted)	String	•
@ROUND(number to be rounded,place of rounding)	Math	
@ROWS(range)	Special	•
@S(range)	String	•
@SECOND(serial time number)	Date & Time	•
@SIN(number)	Math	
@SLN(cost,salvage value,life of the asset)	Financial	•
@SQRT(number)	Math	
@STD(list)	Statistical	
@STRING(number,number of decimal places)	String	•
@SUM(list)	Statistical	
@SYD(cost,salvage value,life,period)	Financial	•
@TAN(number)	Math	
@TERM(payment,interest,future value)	Financial	•
@TIME(hour,minute,second)	Date & Time	•
@TIMEVALUE(time string)	Date & Time	•
@TRIM(string)	String	•
@TRUE	Logical	
@UPPER(string)	String	•
@VALUE(string)	String	•
@VAR(list)	Statistical	
@VLOOKUP(code to be looked up,table location,offset)	Special	
@YEAR(serial date number)	Date & Time	

Trademarks

IBM is a registered trademark of International Business Machines Corp.

1-2-3 is a registered trademark of Lotus Development Corporation.

HAL is a trademark of Lotus Development Corporation.

MS-DOS is a registered trademark of Microsoft Corporation.

OS/2 is a trademark of International Business Machines Corporation.

Lotus is a registered trademark of MicroPro International.

Microsoft is a registered trademark of Microsoft Corporation.

Intel is a registered trademark of Intel Corporation.

COMPAQ is a registered trademark of COMPAQ Corporation.

Zenith is a trademark of Zenith Data Systems.

IMB PC AT is a registered trademark of International Business Machines Corp.

IMB PC XT is a registered trademark of International Business Machines Corp.

INDEX

The manuscript for this book was prepared and submitted to Osborne/McGraw-Hill in electronic form. The acquisition editor for this project was Jeffrey Pepper, the associate editor was Liz Fisher, the technical reviewer was Martin Matthews, the copyeditor was Naomi Steinfeld, and the project coordinator was Irene Imfeld.

Text body is set in Times Roman and display type in Eras. Typesetting by Judy Perry, Dakota Press. Cover art is by Bay Graphics Design Associates. Cover supplier is Phoenix Color Corp. Text designed by Irene Imfeld Graphic Design, Berkeley. Index by Robyn Brode. Book printed and bound by R.R. Donnelley & Sons Company, Crawfordsville, Indiana.

Other related Osborne/McGraw-Hill titles include:

dBASE III PLUS™ Made Easy
by Miriam Liskin

Liskin's *Advanced dBASE III PLUS™* and Jones' *Using dBASE III PLUS™* have been so successful that we're filling in the gap for beginners with *dBASE III PLUS™ Made Easy*. Learning dBASE III PLUS™ couldn't be simpler. You'll install and run the program, enter and edit data. Discover all the features of using dBASE III PLUS at the dot prompt. Each concept is clearly explained and followed by examples and exercises that you can complete at your own speed. Liskin discusses sorting and indexing, performing calculations, and printing reports and labels. Multiple databases are emphasized, and Liskin presents strategies for working with them. You'll also find chapters on customizing the working environment and exchanging data with other software. If you're curious about higher-level use, Liskin's final chapter shows how to combine the commands you've learned into batch programs so you can begin to automate your applications. (Includes two command cards for quick reference.)

$18.95 p
0-07-881294-1, 350 pp., 7³/₈ x 9¹/₄

DOS Made Easy
by Herbert Schildt

If you're at a loss when it comes to DOS, Herb Schildt has written just the book you need, *DOS Made Easy*. Previous computer experience is not necessary to understand this concise, well-organized introduction that's filled with short applications and exercises. Schildt walks you through all the basics, beginning with an overview of a computer system's components and a step-by-step account of how to run DOS for the first time. Once you've been through the initial setup, you'll edit text files, use the DOS directory structure, and create batch files. As you feel more comfortable with DOS, Schildt shows you how to configure a system, handle floppy disks and fixed disks, and make use of helpful troubleshooting methods. By the time you've gone this far, you'll be ready for total system management—using the printer, video modes, the serial and parallel ports, and more. *DOS Made Easy* takes the mystery out of the disk operating system and puts you in charge of your PC.

$18.95 p
0-07-881295-X, 385 pp., 7³/₈ x 9¹/₄

WordStar® 4.0 Made Easy
by Walter A. Ettlin

WordStar® Made Easy, the original "Made Easy" guide with 350,000 copies sold worldwide, has been so successful that Osborne has published a companion volume on the new WordStar® version 4.0. All 4.0 commands and features are thoroughly described and illustrated in practical exercises so you can put WordStar to immediate use, even if you've never used a computer before. Walter Ettlin, who has written four books and taught high school for 23 years, guides you from the fundamentals of creating a memo or report to using WordStar's calculator mode, macro commands, and Word Finder™. You'll also learn to use WordStar's latest spelling checker. *WordStar® 4.0 Made Easy* puts you in control of your software with the acclaimed "Made Easy" format now found in 11 Osborne titles. (Includes a handy pull-out command card.)

$16.95 p
0-07-881011-6, 300 pp., 7³/₈ x 9¹/₄

DisplayWrite 4™ Made Easy
by Gail Todd

Upgrading from DisplayWrite 3™ to DisplayWrite 4™? Here's the book that provides a thorough introduction to IBM's word processing software. Handle new menus, screens, and options with ease as Todd leads you from basic steps to more sophisticated procedures. The famous "Made Easy" format offers hands-on exercises and plenty of examples so you can quickly learn to produce letters and reports. All of DisplayWrite 4's new features are covered, including printing interfaces; the voice add-on; Paper Clip, the cursor control that lets you take up where you left off; and Notepad, a convenience that enables you to insert notes into documents. Todd, the author of numerous user guides and manuals, has the know-how to get you up and running fast.

$19.95 p
0-07-881270-4, 420 pp., 7³/₈ x 9¹/₄

WordPerfect® Made Easy
by Mella Mincberg

Here's the book that makes learning WordPerfect® quick, easy . . . even enjoyable. With Mincberg's follow-along lessons, this IBM® PC compatible word processing software will be at your command in just a couple of hours. Edit text, save and print a document, set tabs, format pages. You'll become a skillful Word-Perfect user as you work through practical applications. When you're ready to explore more sophisticated WordPerfect features, Mincberg is there with detailed instructions to help you run WordPerfect's spell checker and mail merge, manage files, create macros, and use special enhancements like windows and line numbering. Mincberg, author of the ever-so-useful *WordPerfect®: Secrets, Solutions, Shortcuts*, draws on her years of computer training experience to help you become an assured, savvy WordPerfect user. (Includes quick-reference command card.)

$18.95 p
0-07-881297-6, 400 pp., 7⅜ x 9¼

Microsoft® Word Made Easy, Second Edition
by Paul Hoffman

Hoffman's top-selling *Microsoft® Word Made Easy* has been revised to cover Microsoft's latest version of this widely used word processing software. Both beginning and experienced users will find a clear presentation of Word's new features, "made easy" for immediate application. Hoffman covers text outlining, spelling correction, hyphenation, creating indexes and tables of contents, and laser printers. Word's new functions, style sheets, windows, and glossaries are described in depth, and you'll find extra tips for using the mail-merge function. In the tradition of Osborne's "Made Easy" series, all techniques are explained with practical hands-on examples and are illustrated with helpful screen displays.

$16.95 p
0-07-881248-8, 300 pp., 7⅜ x 9¼

Your IBM® PC Made Easy
(Includes IBM PC (DOS 2.0) And PC-XT)
by Jonathan Sachs

"In one word, OUTSTANDING! Perfect for beginning and advanced users, an excellent tutorial/reference. A very thorough guide to most facets of your IBM PC, from PC-DOS, hardware, software, resources supplies, batch files, etc. Rating: A"
(Computer Book Review)

$14.95 p
0-07-881112-0, 250 pp., 7½ x 9¼

C Made Easy
by Herbert Schildt

With Osborne/McGraw-Hill's popular "Made Easy" format, you can learn C programming in no time. Start with the fundamentals and work through the text at your own speed. Schildt begins with general concepts, then introduces functions, libraries, and disk input/output, and finally advanced concepts affecting the C programming environment and UNIX™ operating system. Each chapter covers commands that you can learn to use immediately in the hands-on exercises that follow. If you already know BASIC, you'll find that Schildt's C equivalents will shorten your learning time. *C Made Easy* is a step-by-step tutorial for all beginning C programmers.

$18.95 p
0-07-881178-3, 350 pp., 7⅜ x 9¼

The Osborne/McGraw-Hill Guide to Using Lotus™ 1-2-3,™ Second Edition, Covers Release 2
by Edward M. Baras

Your investment in Lotus™ 1-2-3™ can yield the most productive returns possible with the tips and practical information in *The Osborne/McGraw-Hill Guide to Using Lotus™ 1-2-3.™* Now the second edition of this acclaimed bestseller helps you take full advantage of Lotus' new 1-2-3 upgrade, Release 2. This comprehensive guide offers a thorough presentation of the worksheet, database, and graphics functions. In addition, the revised text shows you how to create and use macros, string functions, and many other sophisticated 1-2-3 features. Step by step, you'll learn to implement 1-2-3 techniques as you follow application models for financial forecasting, stock portfolio tracking, and forms-oriented database management. For both beginners and experienced users, this tutorial quickly progresses from fundamental procedures to advanced applications.

$18.95 p
0-07-881230-5, 432 pp., 7⅜ x 9¼

The Advanced Guide to Lotus™ 1-2-3™
by Edward M. Baras

Edward Baras, Lotus expert and author of *The Symphony™ Book, Symphony™ Master,* and *The Jazz™ Book,* now has a sequel to his best-selling *Osborne/McGraw-Hill Guide to Using Lotus™ 1-2-3.™* For experienced users, *The Advanced Guide to Lotus 1-2-3* delves into more powerful and complex techniques using the newest software upgrade, Release 2. Added enhancements to 1-2-3's macro language, as well as many new functions and commands, are described and thoroughly illustrated in business applications. Baras shows you how to take advantage of Release 2's macro capabilities by programming 1-2-3 to simulate Symphony's keystroke-recording features and by processing ASCII files automatically. You'll also learn to set up your own command menus; use depreciation functions, matric manipulation, and regression analysis; and convert text files to the 1-2-3 worksheet format.

$18.95 p
0-07-881237-2, 325 pp., 7³/₈ x 9¹/₄

Financial Modeling Using Lotus™ 1-2-3,™ Covers Release 2
by Charles W. Kyd

Readers of Kyd's monthly "Accounting" column in *Lotus™* magazine already know how helpful his 1-2-3™ tips can be. Now his *Financial Modeling Using Lotus™ 1-2-3™* shows experienced users how to set up a data bank that can be used by everyone in the office to make more effective use of numerous financial applications. Kyd provides models for managing the balance sheet, controlling growth, handling income statements and management accounting, using Z scores for business forecasts, and more. Each model features a summary of 1-2-3 techniques, including helpful information for using the new Release 2, and explains the financial theories behind the application. You'll also find out how data for many of these financial models can be shared in the office data bank, creating an even greater resource for business productivity.

$16.95 p
0-07-881213-5, 225 pp., 7³/₈ x 9¹/₄

Using HAL™
by Andrew Postman

Using HAL™ helps you tap into the full capabilities of Lotus® 1-2-3®. Whether you're a beginning 1-2-3 user or an experienced one who demands top software performance, you'll be amazed at the increased productivity that HAL adds to 1-2-3. Postman shows you how to use HAL to execute 1-2-3 commands and functions through English phrases that you select. You'll find out about graphing with HAL and how to use the undo command, which lets you experiment with "what-if" questions without losing data. You'll also master cell relations for greater analytical abilities, linking worksheets for data consolidation, macros, and table manipulation. *Using HAL™* gets you past the introduction so you can become thoroughly acquainted with Lotus' new 1-2-3 companion.

$19.95 p
0-07-881268-2, 380 pp., 7³/₈ x 9¹/₄

Running 4Word™
by Kay Nelson

If you've been running behind in word processing with 1-2-3® lately, now is the time to start *Running 4Word™*. Find out how to use Turner Hall's newly released 4Word™, the Add-In Word Processor™ for 1-2-3®, that lets you integrate word processing functions with Lotus' spreadsheet by pressing a computer key. You'll start with the basics of installing the program and formatting text, then work up to advanced procedures including macros and importing/exporting text and data. Practical business examples are cited so you can clearly understand how to create memos, reports, and financial documents using 4Word.

$19.95 p
0-07-881258-5, 350 pp., 7³/₈ x 9¹/₄

1-2-3®: The Complete Reference
by Mary Campbell

1-2-3®: The Complete Reference is the authoritative desktop companion for every Lotus® 1-2-3® user. All commands, functions, and procedures are explained in detail and are demonstrated in practical "real-world" business applications. Conventionally organized according to task, this essential reference makes it easy to locate information on topics such as printing, macros, graphics production, and data management. Each chapter thoroughly describes a 1-2-3 task and all the procedures it requires, followed by an alphabetical listing of every command or function applied. Special emphasis is placed on compatible software packages, including Report Writer™, Reflex™ and others, that you can use to extend 1-2-3's capabilities. Campbell, a consultant and writer whose magazine columns appear monthly in *IBM PC UPDATE*, *Absolute Reference*, and *CPA Journal*, draws on her years of 1-2-3 expertise to provide you with this outstanding, comprehensive resource.

$25.95 p, Hardcover Edition
0-07-881288-7, 928 pp., 7⅜ x 9¼

$22.95 p, Paperback Edition
0-07-881005-1, 928 pp., 7⅜ x 9¼

DOS: The Complete Reference
by Kris Jamsa

Why waste computing time over a baffling PC-DOS™ command or an elusive MS-DOS® function? *DOS: The Complete Reference* has the answers to all of your questions on DOS through version 3.X. This essential resource is for every PC- and MS-DOS user, whether you need an overview of the disk operating system or a reference for advanced programming and disk management techniques. Each chapter begins with a discussion of specific applications followed by a list of commands used in each. All commands are presented in the same clear, concise format: description, syntax, discussion of arguments or options, and examples. For comprehensive coverage, *DOS: The Complete Reference* discusses Microsoft® Windows and EDLIN, and provides two special appendixes covering the ASCII chart and DOS error messages. A ready resource, *DOS: The Complete Reference* is the only DOS consultant you'll need.

$27.95 p, Hardcover Edition
0-07-881314-x, 840 pp., 7⅜ x 9¼

$24.95 p, Paperback Edition
0-07-881259-3, 840 pp., 7⅜ x 9¼

dBASE III PLUS™: The Complete Reference
by Joseph-David Carrabis

This indispensable dBASE III PLUS™ reference will undoubtedly be the most frequently used book in your dBASE III® library. *dBASE III PLUS™: The Complete Reference* is a comprehensive resource to every dBASE III and dBASE III PLUS command, function, and feature. Each chapter covers a specific task so you can quickly pinpoint information on installing the program, designing databases, creating files, manipulating data, and many other subjects. Chapters also contain an alphabetical reference section that describes all the commands and functions you need to know and provides clear examples of each. Carrabis, author of several acclaimed dBASE books, discusses the lastest features of dBASE III PLUS, including networking capabilities; the Assistant, a menu-driven interface; and the Applications Generator, a short-cut feature for creating database files and applications without programming. *dBASE III PLUS™: The Complete Reference* also includes a glossary and handy appendixes that cover error messages, converting from dBASE II to dBASE III PLUS, and add-on utilities.

$25.95 p, Hardcover Edition
0-07-881315-x, 600 pp., 7⅜ x 9¼

$22.95 p, Paperback Edition
0-07-881012-4, 600 pp., 7⅜ x 9¼

C: The Complete Reference
by Herbert Schildt

Once again Osborne's master C programmer and author Herb Schildt, shares his insight and expertise with all C programmers in his latest book, *C: The Complete Reference*. Designed for both beginning and advanced C programmers, this is an encyclopedia for C terms, functions, codes, applications, and more. *C: The Complete Reference* is divided into five parts, each covering an important aspect of C. Part one covers review material and discusses key words in C. Part two presents an extensive summary of C libraries by category. Part three concentrates on various algorithms and C applications and includes information on random number generators as well as artificial intelligence and graphics. Part four addresses interfacing efficiency, porting, and debugging. Finally, part five is for serious programmers who are interested in C++, C's latest direction. The book also includes complete information on the proposed ANSI standard.

$27.95 p, Hardcover Edition
0-07-881313-1, 740 pp., 7⅜ x 9¼

$24.95 p, Paperback Edition
0-07-881263-1, 740 pp., 7⅜ x 9¼

WordPerfect®: The Complete Reference

by Karen L. Acerson

Osborne's highly successful Complete Reference series has a new addition, *WordPerfect®: The Complete Reference*. Every WordPerfect feature, key, menu, prompt, and error message is explained in simple terms for new users, and with sophisticated technical information supplied for those with experience. Acerson, an early member of WordPerfect Corporation who has been helping WordPerfect users get the most from their software since 1983, discusses the techniques for integrating WordPerfect with Lotus® 1-2-3®, dBASE® III, and other widely used software. Here's another ideal desktop companion to add to your collection.

$27.95 p, Hardcover Edition
0-07-881312-3, 675 pp., 7³/₈ x 9¹/₄
$24.95 p, Paperback Edition
0-07-881266-6, 675 pp., 7³/₈ x 9¹/₄

Available at fine bookstores and computer stores everywhere.

For a complimentary catalog of all our current publications contact:
Osborne/McGraw-Hill, 2600 Tenth Street, Berkeley, CA 94710

Phone inquiries may be made using our toll-free number.
Call 800-227-0900 or 800-772-2531 (in California). TWX 910-366-7277.

Prices subject to change without notice.

MAXIT™ increases your DOS addressable conventional memory beyond 640K for only $195.

- Add up to 256K above 640K for programs like FOXBASE+ and PC/FOCUS.

- Short card works in the IBM PC, XT, AT, and compatibles.

- Top off a 512 IBM AT's memory to 640K and add another 128K beyond that.

- Run resident programs like Sidekick above 640K.

- Add up to 96K above 640K to all programs, including PARADOX and 1-2-3.

- Compatible with EGA, Network, and other memory cards.

Break through the 640 barrier.
MAXIT increases your PC's available memory by making use of the vacant unused address space between 640K and 1 megabyte. (See illustrations)

Big gain—no pain.
Extend the productive life of your, IBM PC, XT, AT or compatible. Build more complex spreadsheets and databases without upgrading your present software.

Installation is a snap.
The MAXIT 256K memory card and software works automatically. You don't have to learn a single new command.

If you have questions, our customer support people will answer them, fast. MAXIT is backed by a one-year warranty and a 30-day money-back guarantee.

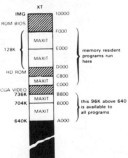

XT class machine (8088, 8086) w/640K and a CGA Color Monitor or a Compaq Type Dual Mode Display

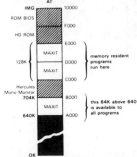

AT class machine (80286) w/640K and a Mono HERC Monitor

Order toll free 1-800-227-0900. MAXIT is just $195 plus $4 shipping, and applicable state sales tax. Buy MAXIT today and solve your PC's memory crisis. Call Toll free 1-800-227-0900 (In California 800-772-2531). Outside the U.S.A. call 1-415-548-2805. We accept VISA, MC.

MAXIT is a trademark of Osborne **McGraw-Hill**. IBM is a registered trademark of International Business Machines Corporation; 1-2-3 and Symphony are registered trademarks of Lotus Development Corporation; Sidekick is a registered trademark of Borland International, Inc; PARADOX is a trademark of ANSA Software; FOXBASE+ is a trademark of Fox Software; Hercules is a trademark of Hercules Computer Technology, Inc; XT and AT are registered trademarks of International Business Machines Corporation; Compaq is a registered trademark of Compaq Computer Corporation.

COMMAND CARD: 1-2-3®Made Easy

WORKSHEET COMMANDS

/ Worksheet Global
  Format
   Fixed
   Scientific
   Currency
   ,
   General
   +/−
   Percent
   Date
    Time •
   Text
   Hidden •
  Label-Prefix
   Left
   Right
   Center
  Column-Width
  Recalculation
   Natural
   Columnwise
   Rowwise
   Automatic
   Manual
   Iteration
  Protection
   Enable
   Disable
  Default
   Printer
    Interface
     Auto-LF
     Left
     Right
     Top
     Bottom
     Pg-Length
     Wait
     Setup
     Name

WORKSHEET COMMANDS

  Quit
  Directory
  Status
  Update
  Other
   International •
    Punctuation •
    Currency •
    Date •
    Time •
    Quit •
   Help •
   Clock •
  Quit
  Zero
/ Worksheet Insert
  Column
  Row
/ Worksheet Delete
  Column
  Row
/ Worksheet Column
  Set-Width
  Reset-Width
  Hide
  Display
/ Worksheet Erase
/ Worksheet Titles
  Both
  Horizontal
  Vertical
  Clear
/ Worksheet Window
  Horizontal
  Vertical
  Sync
  Unsync
  Clear
/ Worksheet Status
/ Worksheet Page

RANGE COMMANDS

/ Range Format
  Fixed
  Scientific
  Currency
  ,
  General
  +/−
  Percent
  Date
   Time •
  Text
  Hidden
  Reset
/ Range Label
  Left
  Right
  Center
/ Range Erase
/ Range Name
  Create
  Delete
  Labels
  Reset
  Table •
/ Range Justify
/ Range Protect
/ Range Unprotect
/ Range Input
/ Range Value •
/ Range Transpose •

COPY COMMAND
/ Copy

MOVE COMMAND
/ Move

PRINT COMMANDS (Printer or File)

/ Print Printer Range
/ Print Printer Line
/ Print Printer Page
/ Print Printer Options
  Header
  Footer
  Margins
   Left
   Right
   Top
   Bottom
  Borders
   Columns
   Rows
  Setup
  Pg-Length
  Other
   As-Displayed
   Cell-Formulas
   Formatted
   Unformatted
  Quit
/ Print Printer Clear
  All
  Range
  Borders
  Format
/ Print Printer Align
/ Print Printer Go
/ Printer Printer Quit

• Release 2 commands

COMMAND CARD: 1-2-3®Made Easy

FILE COMMANDS
/ File Retrieve
/ File Save
  Cancel
  Replace
/ File Combine
  Copy
   Entire-File
   Named-Range
  Add
   Entire-File
   Named-Range
  Subtract
   Entire-File
   Named-Range
/ File Xtract
  Formulas
  Values
/ File Erase
  Worksheet
  Print
  Graph
  Other•
/ File List
  Worksheet
  Print
  Graph
  Other•
/ File Import
  Text
  Numbers
/ File Directory

GRAPH COMMANDS
/ Graph Type
  Line
  Bar
  XY
  Stacked Bar
  Pie
/ Graph X
/ Graph A
/ Graph B
/ Graph C
/ Graph D
/ Graph E
/ Graph F
/ Graph Reset
  Graph
  X
  A
  B
  C
  D
  E
  F
/ Graph View
/ Graph Save
/ Graph Options
  Legend
   A through F
  Format
   Graph
   A through F
   Quit
  Titles
   First
   Second
   X-Axis
   Y-Axis
  Grid
   Horizontal
   Vertical
   Both

GRAPH COMMANDS
  Clear
  Scale
   Y Scale
    Automatic
    Manual
    Lower
    Upper
    Format
    Indicator•
    Quit
   X Scale
    Same options
     as Y Scale
   Skip
   Color
   B&W
   Data-Labels
    A through F
    Quit
/ Graph Name
  Use
  Create
  Delete
  Reset
/ Graph Quit

DATA COMMANDS
/ Data Fill
/ Data Table
  1
  2
  Reset
/ Data Sort
  Data-Range
  Primary-Key
  Secondary-Key
  Reset
  Go
  Quit

DATA COMMANDS
/ Data Query
  Input
  Criterion
  Output
  Find
  Extract
  Unique
  Delete
   Cancel
   Delete
  Reset
  Quit
/ Data Distribution
/ Data Matrix•
  Invert•
  Multiply•
/ Data Regression•
  X-Range•
  Y-Range•
  Output-Range•
  Intercept•
   Compute•
   Zero•
  Reset•
  Go•
  Quit•
/ Data Parse•
  Format-Line•
   Create•
   Edit•
  Input-Column•
  Output-Range•
  Reset•
  Go•
  Quit•

OTHER COMMANDS
/ System
/ Quit

•Release 2 commands

©1988 Osborne/McGraw-Hill. *1-2-3 Made Easy*